MALAYSIAN "BAIL OUTS"?

MALAYSIAN "BAIL OUTS"?
Capital Controls, Restructuring and Recovery

WONG SOOK CHING
JOMO K.S.
CHIN KOK FAY

SINGAPORE

© Singapore University Press
an imprint of NUS Publishing
AS3-01-02, 3 Arts Link
Singapore 117569

Fax: (65) 6774-0652
E-mail: nusbooks@nus.edu.sg
Website: http://www.nus.edu.sg/npu

First Edition 2005
Reprint 2006

ISBN 9971-69-319-4 (Paper)

Typeset by: Scientifik Graphics (Singapore) Pte Ltd
Printed by: Photoplates Pte Ltd

Contents

About the Authors

Wong Sook Ching is an Executive in the Knowledge Resources Department of the Institute of Bankers Malaysia. She has taught and has also been a researcher at another research institute in Kuala Lumpur.

Jomo K.S. was Professor, Faculty of Economics and Administration, University of Malaya, and then Visiting Senior Research Fellow, Asia Research Institute, National University of Singapore.

Chin Kok Fay is Lecturer in the Strategic Studies & International Relations Program, Faculty of Social Sciences & Humanities, National University of Malaysia (UKM), Bangi, Selangor, Malaysia.

Tables

Figures

Boxes

Note on Currency

Before September 1998, the Malaysian ringgit (RM: ringgit Malaysia) was ostensibly floated in relation to a basket of the major currencies of its major trading partners. In effect, however, it had been mainly pegged to the US dollar after the system of fixed exchange rates gave way to flexible exchange rates in 1973. Under the Bretton Woods system, which lasted until 1971, the Malaysian ringgit was pegged at RM3 to the US dollar. From the mid-1970s until July 1997, it moved in the range of RM2.4–2.8 to the US dollar, depreciating from around RM2.4 in 1984 to RM2.7 in 1987. However, it began to slide after the central bank gave up the defence of the RM in mid-July 1997 following the float of the Thai baht on 2 July 1997. In January 1998, it fell to RM4.88, its lowest ever level, following pro-cyclical measures introduced in early December 1997. Since 2 September 1998, it has been pegged again at RM3.8 to the US dollar.

Acknowledgements

To all the people, especially my family, who have been instrumental in shaping my outlook towards life and enriched my life experience, I convey my deepest and most heartfelt thanks. I reserve my greatest indebtedness to my parents for their years of unconditional love, patience, dedication, support and sacrifice. To my beloved Thomas, my utmost thanks for his unconditional love, care, strength, encouragement and understanding. The journey to complete this book was filled with numerous challenges and turning points in my life. I thank God for blessing me and surrounding me with people of unparalleled character and spirit as well as for the various trials and tribulations in my life. This book is dedicated to my loved ones, who have principally shaped what I am today and will be in the future.

This book has grown from my Master of Economics research paper for the University of Malaya. Many thanks go to Mr Foo Ah Hiang for his help in preparing the manuscript.

Wong Sook Ching

Many thanks go to Professor Jomo for his assistance in securing funding for my research from which I have been able to contribute a chapter to this book. I am also appreciative of his confidence in entrusting me with helping him edit several chapters of this book.

To my mother, who is never out of my thoughts, I owe my greatest debt for her years of unconditional love, care and patience. Her perseverance in fighting cancer for twelve years has taught me the meaning of life and has always been an inspiration for me to carry on. To my dearest Meng Wai, my greatest gratitude for her unconditional love, support, and understanding.

Chin Kok Fay

I am grateful to Wong Sook Ching for continuing to work on this manuscript after securing her degree despite being weighed down by job demands and health problems. Chin Kok Fay also came through with his chapter despite his difficult personal circumstances, especially his visual handicap, his mother's protracted illness and untimely death, and the demands of getting married.

The Centre for Regulation and Competition based at the University of Manchester provided helpful financial support for this work. As usual, Foo Ah Hiang has helped prepare this manuscript, while Muthalahee and Kalai Selvi helped prepare the References. A number of other friends have also been helpful, but would prefer to remain anonymous.

Most of the work was undertaken while I was at the University of Malaya in Kuala Lumpur, while final preparation of this book took place in the second half of 2004 while I was at the Asia Research Institute (ARI) at the National University of Singapore.

As usual, my family has taken the brunt of my efforts to finish this book. I thank them for their tolerance and unconditional love.

Jomo K.S.

Abbreviations

ABMB	Aircraft Business Malaysia Bhd
ADB	Asian Development Bank
ACF	average cost of funds
AFSCAs	Asian Freight and Supply Chain Awards
ALR	average lending rate
AMC	asset management company
AMF	Asian monetary facility/fund
ASEAN	Association of Southeast Asian Nations
ATM	automatic teller machine
BAFIA	Banking and Financial Institutions Act, 1989
BBMB	Bank Bumiputra Malaysia Bhd
BIBF	Bangkok International Banking Facility
BIMP–EAGA	Brunei Indonesia Malaysia Philippines-East ASEAN Growth Area
BIS	Bank for International Settlements
BLR	base lending rate
BNM	Bank Negara Malaysia
BRA	bank recapitalisation approach
CAHB	Commerce Asset-Holdings Bhd
CAMEL	capital, assets, management, earnings, liquidity
CBBs	Coupon-Bearing Bonds
CDRC	Corporate Debt Restructuring Committee
CEO	chief executive officer
CFO	chief financial officer
CIMA	Cement Industries of Malaysia Bhd
CIMB	Commerce International Merchant Bankers
CLOB	Central Limit Order Book
CLSA	CLSA Asia-Pacific Markets
CMS	Cahya Mata Sarawak Bhd
CPI	corruption perception index
COMMEX Malaysia	Commodity and Monetary Exchange of Malaysia

Crest	Crest Petroleum Bhd
CSFB	Credit Suisse First Boston
CULS	convertible unsecured loan stocks
CVO	conditional voluntary offer
Danaharta	Pengurusan Danaharta Nasional Bhd
Danamodal	Danamodal Nasional Bhd
Danasaham	Syarikat Danasaham Nasional Bhd
ELITE	Expressway Lingkaran Tengah Sdn Bhd
EMAS Index	KLSE All Shares Index
EPE	EPE Power Corp Bhd
EPF	Employees Provident Fund
EPS	earnings per share
EPU	Economic Planning Unit
Faber	Faber Group Bhd
Fahim	Fahim Capital Sdn Bhd
FAPL	FA Premier League
FDI	foreign direct investment
FSC	Financial Supervisory Commission
FSMP	Financial Sector Masterplan
FY	financial year
G-5	Group of Five, the consultative group of the world's five richest Western economies — comprising Britain, France, Germany, Japan and the United States.
G-7	Group of Seven, the consultative group of the world's seven richest Western economies — comprising Britain, Canada, France, Germany, Italy, Japan and the United States
GATT	General Agreement on Tariffs and Trade
GLC	government-linked company
GDP	gross domestic product
GNP	gross national product
GO	general offer
HK	Hong Kong
Ho Hup	Ho Hup Construction Company Bhd
HPAEs	high-performing Asian economies

HSBC	Hongkong and Shanghai Banking Corporation
ICOR	incremental capital-output ratio
IDC	Infrastructure Development Corporation
IMF	International Monetary Fund
Intria	Intria Bhd
IPO	initial public offering
IPP	independent power producer
IRI	Instituto per la Riconstruzione Industriale or Institute for Industrial Reconstruction (Italy)
IT	information technology
IWK	Indah Water Konsortium
JKR	Public Works Department (Jabatan Kerja Raya)
Khazanah	Khazanah Nasional Bhd
Kinta Kellas	Kinta Kellas Public Limited Company
KKMB	Kumpulan Kenderaan Malaysia Bhd
KLCE	Kuala Lumpur Commodity Exchange
KLCI	Kuala Lumpur Stock Exchange Composite Index
KLIA	Kuala Lumpur International Airport
KLIBOR	Kuala Lumpur Inter-bank Offered Rates
KLOFFE	Kuala Lumpur Options and Financial Futures Exchange Bhd
KLSE	Kuala Lumpur Stock Exchange
KLSEB	Kuala Lumpur Stock Exchange Bhd
KPIs	key performance indices/indicators
KPUN	Kementerian Pembangunan Usahawan or Ministry of Entrepreneur Development
KTM	Keretapi Tanah Melayu
KUB	Kooperasi Usaha Bersatu Bhd
KWAP	Kumpulan Wang Amanah Pencen
LA	Latin America
Linkedua	Linkedua (Malaysia) Bhd
LIOFC	Labuan International Offshore Financial Centre
LLM	Lembaga Lebuhraya Malaysia
LRA	loan rights acquired
LRT	light rail transit

LSG	Lufthansa Services Holding AG
LTAT	Lembaga Tabung Amanah Tentera or Armed Forces Trust Fund Board
LTCM	Long-Term Capital Management
MaCTRAN	Malaysian Centre for Transportation Studies
MAHB	Malaysia Airports Holdings Bhd
MAS	Malaysian Airline System Bhd
MASkargo	Malaysia Airlines Cargo Sdn Bhd
MCD	Malaysian Central Depository
MD	managing director
MDCH	Malaysian Derivatives Clearing House Bhd
MDEX	Malaysia Derivatives Exchange
MESDAQ	Malaysian Exchange of Securities Dealing and Automated Quotation
MFCC	Malaysian Futures Clearing Corporation Bhd
MME	Malaysia Monetary Exchange
MoF Inc.	Ministry of Finance, Incorporated
MOT	Ministry of Transport
MOU	memorandum of understanding
MRCB	Malaysian Resources Corporation Berhad
MSCI	Morgan Stanley Capital International Inc.
MSEB	Malaysia Securities Exchange Bhd
MSWG	Minority Shareholder Watchdog Group
NAFTA	North American Free Trade Area
NEAC	National Economic Action Council
NEP	New Economic Policy
NERP	National Economic Recovery Plan
Newco	newly incorporated company
NIC	newly industrializing country
NPL	non-performing loan
NSC	National Steel Corporation (Philippines)
NTA	net tangible assets
OECD	Organisation for Economic Cooperation and Development
PATI	Pati Sdn Bhd
PET	Penjanaan EPE-Time Sdn Bhd
Pharmaniaga	Pharmaniaga Bhd

PIBF	Provincial International Banking Facility
PLUS	Projek Lebuhraya Utara-Selatan Bhd
PMB	Penerbangan Malaysia Bhd
PN4	Practice Note No 4/2001: Criteria and Obligations Pursuant to Paragraph 8.14 of the Listing Requirements of the KLSE (now Bursa Malaysia)
Prolink	Prolink Development Sdn Bhd
PROPEL	Projek Penyelenggaraan Lebuhraya Bhd
PROTON	Perusahan Otomobil Nasional Bhd
PRSB	Powertron Resources Sdn Bhd
PUTRA	Projek Usahasama Transit Ringan Automatik Sdn Bhd
R&D	research and development
RCPS	redeemable convertible preference share
Renong	Renong Bhd
RHBRI	RHB Research Institute
RM	ringgit Malaysia (Malaysian currency)
RMS	revenue management system
Rp.	rupiah (Indonesian currency)
RWCR	risk-weighted capital ratio
S&P	sale and purchase
Sapura	Sapura Telecommunications Bhd
SAR	Special Administrative Region
SARS	severe acute respiratory syndrome
SC	Securities Commission
SCANS	Securities Clearing Automated Network Services Sdn Bhd
SE Asia	South East Asia
SEMS	Stock Exchange of Malaysia and Singapore
SES	Stock Exchange of Singapore
S. Korea	South Korea
SMEs	small and medium (sized) enterprises
SOE	state owned enterprise
SPNB	Syarikat Prasarana Negara Bhd
SPV	special purpose vehicle
STAR	Sistem Aliran Ringan Sdn Bhd

Telekom	Telekom Malaysia Bhd
Time dotCom	Time dotCom Bhd
Time Engineering	Time Engineering Bhd
TNB	Tenaga Nasional Bhd
TNC	transnational corporation
TTRS	two-tier regulatory system
UBG	Utama Banking Group Bhd
UEC	UE Construction Sdn Bhd
UEM	United Engineers (M) Bhd
UEM World	UEM World Bhd
UK	United Kingdom
UMNO	United Malays National Organisation
US	United States (of America)
VSS	voluntary separation scheme
WAU	widespread asset unbundling
Wall St.	Wall Street
WB	World Bank

Preface

This book is primarily concerned with critically understanding the Malaysian economic crisis of 1997–98 as well as the efficacy of the unique policy measures introduced by the Malaysian authorities to deal with the crisis. Contemporary media coverage, political rhetoric as well as more recent academic literature (e.g. Johnson and Mitton 2003) suggest that the Malaysian government's policy responses were principally intended to "bail out" the politically influential business interests closely connected to the executive body of the government. On the other hand, the Malaysian authorities claim that their policy responses, especially those not associated with then Finance Minister Anwar Ibrahim, were responsible for Malaysia's strong economic recovery in 1999 and 2000. This book seeks to set the record straight by refuting both types of claims.

This study is organised as follows. Chapter 1 argues for a heterodox explanation of the 1997–98 East Asian financial crises in light of the failure of existing currency crises theories as well as corporate governance claims to persuasively account for what happened in 1997–98. To be sure, the crises differed in nature from previous financial crises including the 1994 tequila crisis in Mexico. In particular, we reject the claim that the crises represented the failure of the so-called Asian models of economic development and corporate governance. Those taking such views insist that the crisis was rooted in the flawed East Asian economic development model with its institutions, industrial policies and corporate governance practices. Instead, we argue that financial liberalisation and inadequate financial controls and supervision created the conditions culminating in the crisis. In addition, the socio-economic repercussions experienced in Thailand, Indonesia, South Korea and Malaysia are briefly discussed.

Chapter 2 critically discusses the Malaysian government's responses to the outbreak of the regional currency and financial crises. It distinguishes between four phases. The first five months from July to November 1997 when the Mahathir government's various flawed attempts to check the spread of the crisis and its consequences inadvertently served to exacerbate the decline. This was followed by a period from December 1997 until May 1998 — associated with Anwar Ibrahim — when the government adopted more pro-cyclical measures, which further worsened the situation. From around May 1998, Anwar turned to more counter-cyclical fiscal measures and also put in place various key institutions for bank restructuring and recapitalisation as well as corporate debt restructuring. During the fourth period from September 1998, capital controls and other monetary measures sought to reflate the economy. However, the changed world and regional situation from September 1998 due to a change of US Fed policy helped stabilise the situation and facilitate strong recoveries throughout the region (except for Indonesia), which makes fair evaluation of the success of the September 1998 Malaysian measures especially difficult.

Following that, Chapter 3 defines certain key concepts — such as corporate governance, bail outs and rents — and reviews the various forms that bail outs can take. This is followed by a review of the debate between those favouring government intervention and "no bail out" advocates. The former maintain that governments have a crucial and necessary role to play in saving financially distressed firms, which might otherwise drag down the entire economy and lead to more adverse consequences if left unattended. Opponents of bail outs, on the other hand, believe that government intervention is necessarily wasteful, unfair and counter-productive, inevitably worsening situations. For them, it is always best to allow market forces and processes to sort things out and to allocate resources efficiently to ensure economic recovery and sustained growth. There may be instances when government assistance to corporations in distress may be desirable, especially when the social costs of bail outs are much lower than the costs of allowing such firms to collapse.

Chapter 4 then critically reviews various possible corporate restructuring policies, especially their respective advantages and disadvantages. In the face of the sudden downturn of the East Asian economies in 1997–98, it was imperative for the governments to lead economic recovery with appropriate counter-cyclical initiatives, rather than allow pro-cyclical market forces and processes to wreak further havoc. In fact, the crises emphasised the need for well-conceived, well-implemented and appropriate policies and initiatives. As such, the debate should not really be over whether the government should intervene in such circumstances, but rather over how.

The next three chapters focus on Malaysia's bank and corporate restructuring proper. Chapter 5 outlines and evaluates Malaysia's bank restructuring programme. Malaysia was fortunate not to have been allowed to incur so much foreign debt so as to have no choice but to accept IMF policy conditionalities for its emergency credit facilities. It thus averted the ill-conceived and poorly timed bank closures, pro-cyclical macroeconomic policy responses and other measures demanded by the IMF. While the Malaysian bank debt restructuring agency, Danaharta, and its bank recapitalisation agency, Danamodal, strengthened the banking sector, there have also been abuses as well as other weaknesses in doing so. Powerful interest groups have been able to compromise and "capture" otherwise desirable policies, especially their implementation. It also remains doubtful whether domestic Malaysian banks are significantly better prepared now to face imminent foreign competition with greater international financial liberalisation after the government directed consolidation of the financial sector which seems to have favoured certain politically influential interests.

Chapter 6 assesses the role and progress of Malaysia's special purpose vehicles (SPVs) established by the government in mid-1998. The creation of these new institutions by the Malaysian government served to insulate distressed institutions from market forces and processes and provide them with precious "windows of opportunity" for recovery. However, restructuring, re-nationalisation and other related programmes have been fraught with abuses and weaknesses. Such apparent government failure is due to abuse by the politically influential rather than an unavoidable consequence of government intervention *per se*. In other words, such "failure" does not suggest that government intervention was wrong or inferior in principle since government intervention *per se* does not necessarily lead to such abuses and weaknesses, as can be seen in other instances of government intervention in Malaysia and elsewhere.

The seventh chapter examines and evaluates four cases of direct and indirect government bail outs; outlines the strategies and measures employed in financial (debt) and operational restructuring and their progress — some six years after the crisis first broke out in Thailand in mid-1997. The government's efforts to resolve the NPL problem and to restructure the corporate landscape may improve corporate governance and performance. In fact, the four corporations considered have seen improvements in financial performance, also attributable to government assistance, greater external discipline imposed by the authorities and improving economic conditions.

The concluding chapter begins with a summary of the main arguments in the book. Various policy lessons are then drawn from the Malaysian experience of capital controls from September 1998. Various priorities for reform of the international financial system are then considered from the perspective of developing countries. These include the need to improve efforts to avert currency and financial crises as well as to manage them when they occur. Reforms should also address the need for development finance, counter deflationary macroeconomic tendencies favoured by the ascendance of international finance and ensure that international financial institutions, including new regional arrangements, better serve developing countries. The closing remarks note that the last IMF Managing Director has conceded the possible need for capital controls on outflows, especially in the face of crisis, while recent IMF research undermines the ostensible case for financial liberalisation.

Chronology: East Asian Crises and Recovery Timeline

Apr. 1970	Indonesia removes foreign capital and exchange controls introducing open account for financial inflows and outflows.
1971	US President Richard Nixon devalues US$, destroying post-war Bretton Woods system, which had set price of gold at US$35/oz. After a couple of years of international monetary instability, world switched from fixed to flexible exchange rates in 1973.
June 1983	Indonesian financial liberalisation begins with removal of controls on interest rates and abolition of credit ceilings.
Sep. 1985	Plaza Accord among G5 countries (France, West Germany, UK, US and Japan) to allow US$ to devalue, especially against Japanese yen.
June 1987	First "Sumarlin Shock" in Indonesia as finance minister institutes tight money policy.
19/10/87	Wall Street stock market crash.
Oct. 1988	PAKTO (October Package) of banking deregulation in Indonesia.
1989	Malaysian Banking and Financial Institutions Act (BAFIA) promulgated after banking crisis with non-performing loan level reaching 30%. Malaysian central bank (BNM) becomes directly responsible for all foreign exchange control matters.
1/1/90	Singapore-incorporated companies delisted from Kuala Lumpur Stock Exchange (KLSE) and Malaysian-incorporated companies de-listed from Stock Exchange of Singapore (SES).
1/10/90	Establishment of Labuan International Offshore Financial Centre (IOFC) by Malaysia.

Dec. 1990	Korea's foreign reserves reach US$48.5 billion, highest level so far.
1/2/91	Base lending rate of Malaysian banking institutions freed.
27/2/91	Second "Sumarlin Shock" in Indonesia.
1992	Capital account liberalisation measures instituted in Philippines by newly elected President Fidel Ramos.
1993	Bangkok International Banking Facility (BIBF) introduced, followed by Provincial International Banking Facility (PIBF) in 1994.
1/3/93	Establishment of Malaysian Securities Commission (SC); Futures Industry Act promulgated.
24/1/94	Imposition of capital controls on inflows by BNM after late 1993 capital flight following massive capital inflows since 1992. Capital controls gradually dismantled from August until December 1994.
22/6/95	Further liberalisation measures to help promote Kuala Lumpur as a regional financial centre.
26/9/95	International stock exchange and monetary exchange set up in Labuan.
Dec. 1995	Development of financial derivatives markets in Malaysia.
Jan. 1997	Surprise collapse of Korean *chaebol*, Hanbo Steel.
Mar. 1997	Sammi Steel, a Korean conglomerate, fails, provoking fears of a looming corporate debt crisis.
14–15/5/97	Thai baht hit by massive speculative attack. Thailand and Singapore jointly intervene to defend baht. Philippines affected, with central bank raising overnight rate.
23/5/97	Thailand's largest finance company, Finance One, collapses.
19/6/97	Amnuay Viravan, staunchly against devaluing baht, resigns as Thailand's finance minister. Philippines' overnight rate rises again.

27/6/97	Bank of Thailand suspends operations of 16 cash-trapped finance companies and orders them to submit restructuring plans.
30/6/97	Thai Prime Minister Chavalit Yonchaiyudh promises no baht devaluation.
Jul. 1997	Second largest Korean carmaker, Kia Motors, technically bankrupt.
2/7/97	Thailand floats baht. Heavy intervention by Bangko Sentral ng Filipinas to defend peso. Money injection by BNM to ease interbank rates.
3/7/97	Philippine central bank raises overnight lending rate from 15% to 24%.
8/7/97	BNM intervenes to defend ringgit.
11/7/97	Philippine peso is devalued. Indonesia widens its trading band for rupiah (Rp.) in a move to discourage speculators.
14/7/97	BNM abandons defence of ringgit. IMF offers Philippines almost US$1.1billion in financial support under fast-track regulations drawn up after 1995 Mexican crisis.
15/7/97	South Korean won's prolonged decline accelerates when eighth largest conglomerate, Kia Group, asks for emergency loans. Several more large Korean conglomerates face financial turmoil.
18/7/97	IMF announces more than US$1billion available to Philippines to relieve pressure on peso. First uses of its post-Tequila crisis "emergency funding mechanism".
24/7/97	Singapore $ starts gradual decline. Mahathir accuses "rogue speculators" of causing Southeast Asia's economic upheaval, later singling out billionaire financier George Soros. HK$ remains steady, but US$1 billion was spent on intervention during two-hour period on unspecified day in July.
26/7/97	Mahathir calls George Soros "moron" responsible for attack on ringgit.

28/7/97	Thailand calls in IMF.
5/8/97	Thai government accepts tough IMF economic measures in return for a US$17 billion loan, closing 42 ailing finance companies and raising tax.
11/8/97	IMF unveils rescue package for Thailand including loans totalling US$16 billion from IMF and Asian nations.
13/8/97	Rp. begins to come under severe pressure. Central bank actively intervenes in its defence.
14/8/97	Indonesia floats Rp. which plunges. Bank Indonesia abandons exchange rate band policy.
15/8/97	Speculative attack against HK$.
16/8/97	Unnamed Beijing source tells a local Hong Kong (HK) newspaper that China is prepared to use US$50 billion to defend HK$.
20/8/97	Thailand receives IMF standby facility.
Sep. 1997	Failure of Malaysian Security Commission's designation measure to thwart short-selling in KLSE.
3/9/97	Malaysian cabinet approves RM60 billion facility to buy shares of "selected shareholders".
4/9/97	Philippine peso continues decline despite central bank intervention. Ringgit breaks through 3.0000/US$ barrier. Mahathir delays several multi-billion ringgit construction projects.
10/9/97	Japanese proposal to establish US$100-billion Asian monetary facility (AMF), soon opposed by West and IMF.
16/9/97	Indonesia says it will postpone projects worth 39 trillion Rp. in attempt to slash budget shortfall.
20/9/97	Mahathir tells delegates to IMF/WB annual conference in HK that currency trading is immoral and should be stopped.
21/9/97	Soros says "Dr Mahathir is a menace to his own country."
	IMF Interim Committee confirms April decision to amend Articles of Agreement to include capital

account. Sakakibara proposal to establish US$100 billion.

Asian monetary facility opposed by West.

1/10/97	Mahathir repeats his call for tighter regulation, or total ban, on forex trading. Ringgit falls 4% in less than two hours.
6/10/97	Rp. hits low of 3,845.
8/10/97	Indonesia says it will ask IMF and WB for financial assistance.
14/10/97	Devaluation of new Taiwan $.

HK$ attacked again.

Vietnam, after months of pressure on its dong, doubles permitted trading range to 10% on either side of official daily rate.

17/10/97	Malaysia presents a belt-tightening budget in attempt to stop sliding into recession.
20–23/10/97	HK stock market sheds nearly a quarter of its value in four days on fears over interest rates and pressures on HK$. More severe than 1987 crash.

South Korean won weakens.

27/10/97	On Wall Street, Dow Jones industrial average, Nasdaq and S&P 500 index tumbles. Decline prompts stock exchange officials to suspend trading. Latin American (LA) stock markets suffer record losses.
30/10/97	Speculators cause heavy losses in Brazil, Argentina, Mexico.
31/10/97	IMF financial package for Indonesia to stabilise financial system.

IMF announces delay of US$700 million quarterly disbursement to Russia due to lax tax collection.

Mid-Nov. 1997	Anwar suspends KLSE requirement to allow UEM-Renong reverse takeover without making mandatory general offer. KLSE loses RM70 billion (20%) in three days.

3/11/97	Chavalit resigns as Thai Prime Minister.

Financial aid package for Indonesia helps restore calm to region.

Sanyo Securities, one of Japan's top 10 brokerage firms, goes bankrupt, with liabilities of more than US$3 billion — first Japanese securities house to go bust since World War II.

5/11/97   IMF approves loan to Indonesia as part of bail out package.

6/11/97   South Korean government's sweeping financial measures to stem deepening financial crisis. Trading halted for third consecutive day, minutes after market opens when won falls. Central Bank of Korea defends won.

Camdessus confident that IMF multi-billion US$ financial support package for Indonesia should stop economic destabilisation in Asia, and that Korean government measures adequate.

7/11/97   Asian stocks nosedive with currency jitters in South Korea and high interest rates and falling property prices in HK. Heavy losses in Asia and US extend to LA markets.

8/11/97   Market prices fall sharply as foreign investors pull out, fearing South Korean economic crisis on scale of Southeast Asia's. Continuing worries over falling value of South Korean won. South Korea's foreign reserves dwindling (South Korean economy larger than Thailand, Indonesia and Malaysia put together).

13/11/97   IMF Managing Director Camdessus visits Kuala Lumpur, meets Anwar.

14/11/97   Faced with potential financial crisis, South Korea's ruling party vows to pass reform package to clean up debt-ridden banks and to encourage foreign investors to return to South Korea.

17/11/97   Hokkaido Takushoku Bank, one of Japan's top 10 banks, collapses under pile of bad debt.

South Korea abandons defence of won. Sudden weakening of won sends stocks plunging and puts renewed pressure on currency.

18/11/97   Financial reform bills fail to pass Korean National Assembly, putting pressure on all regional currencies.

19/11/97   Deputy finance ministers meeting in Manila propose formation of new mechanism to enhance IMF's role in identifying and addressing possible financial crises in Asia. IMF asked to come up with short-term facility, which US Deputy Treasury Secretary Summers says is needed because crises in Asia was not due to balance of payments problems, but confidence issues that cannot be addressed by traditional IMF packages.

To avoid having to turn to the IMF, the South Korean government announces sweeping financial support measures to stem the country's deepening financial crisis — measures too little too late, as IMF support becomes only way to restore foreign and domestic confidence.

20/11/97   Mahathir announces setting up National Economic Action Council (NEAC).

South Korea's currency falls after country unveils emergency bail out package.

Most regional currencies fall sharply with won. South Korea asks Japan to persuade banks to roll over maturing short-term loans to South Korea.

21/11/97   South Korea requests IMF aid.

22/11/97   South Korean nationalists criticise IMF loan request. President Kim Young Sam apologises for country's economic malaise.

23/11/97   President Clinton describes SE Asian economies as temporarily experiencing a "few glitches in the road".

25/11/97   Yen tumbles to lowest level against US$ in more than five years.

Standard & Poor's ratings agency lowers South Korea's currency ratings.

Dec. 1997   President Kim Dae Jung's government wins election in South Korea.

1/12/97   South Korea main trouble spot in Asia. IMF resumes talks on Korean package after initial deal flounders. Several Korean commercial and merchant banks on brink of collapse.

3/12/97   Cabinet meeting in Langkawi unanimously endorses new Anwar market-friendly measures in Mahathir's absence.

IMF insists all South Korean presidential candidates agree not to interfere in IMF negotiations. IMF approves a US$57-billion bail out package to South Korea, the largest in history, after Clinton urges "tough medicine".

4/12/97   South Korean IMF programme begins.

Mahathir announces land bridge project with Thailand.

Record loan package led by IMF calms jitters in most regional markets.

Seoul desperate for assistance. US and Japan use South Korea's financial crisis as leverage to force Seoul to further open markets. Seoul raises foreign stock ownership ceiling on a combined or individual basis to 50%, effective 15 December, from 26% and 7% respectively. South Korea allows Japanese products greater access to Korean market. Most Asian stock markets join Korean rally to varying degrees, with Japan an exception due to its own fragile financial system.

5/12/97   New measures announced by Anwar; growth projection for 1998 revised down to 4–5% from 7.5%.

South Korea agrees to lower its economic growth target for 1998 under terms of IMF rescue package, seek budget surplus through spending cuts and tax hikes, limit its current account deficit to less than 1% of GDP and close insolvent financial institutions.

Monetary stability in Southeast Asia short-lived with renewed currency volatility due to regional concerns.

8/12/97   Anwar announces new fiscal package.

Thai government announces it will close 56 insolvent finance companies as part of IMF economic restructuring plan. 30,000 white-collar workers lose jobs. Camdessus, IMF managing director, praises Thailand for "solid progress".

Stocks in Seoul and Tokyo dragged lower by concerns over local financial problems, while other regional markets react positively to IMF bail out of South Korean economy.

9/12/97   Rumours that Soeharto is gravely ill sending rupiah into tailspin.

10/12/97   Despite repeated denials by South Korea's Minister of Finance and Economy that closure of commercial banks was not discussed with IMF, internal IMF document shows that unviable local commercial banks will be closed.

12/12/97   IMF restarts loan disbursement to Russia, and urges Russia to boost revenues and cut spending.

18/12/97   Kim Dae Jung confirmed as South Korea's first president elected from country's opposition party. Within days, South Korean won hits new lows.

23/12/97   WB releases emergency loan of US$3 billion, part of US$10-billion support package to help South Korea.

24/12/97   Seoul wins early payment of US$10 billion in loans from IMF and G-7 to forestall default on short-term debt. In return, South Korea agrees to expedite financial reforms and open domestic financial markets.

Jan. 1998   Foreign creditors agree to roll over South Korea's US$23-billion short-term debts.

1/1/98   New Malaysian guidelines for classification of non-performing loans (NPLs) increases grace period from 3 to 6 months.

7/1/98	Approval of NEAC and its composition by Malaysian cabinet. Ringgit falls to RM4.88 against greenback following near collapse of Indonesian Rp.
	WB chief economist, Joseph Stiglitz, publicly questions assumptions and effects of "Washington Consensus".
8/1/98	International creditors agree to 90-day rollover of South Korea's short-term debt.
	Indonesian Rp. falls to all-time low after Soeharto unveils state budget plan, which does not comply with IMF reform programme.
8-9/1/98	Indonesians hoard food and staple goods fearing further currency collapses will lead to shortages.
10/1/98	Pressured by IMF, Soeharto postpones 15 major government projects to cut expenditure and foreign debt.
12/1/98	HK-based Peregrine Investments, Asia's largest private investment bank, files for liquidation owing to Indonesian loan exposure.
13/1/98	Students in Jakarta rally to protest against IMF-imposed policies.
14/1/98	South Korean labour unions agree to discuss layoffs with businesses and government leaders. Layoffs are key condition insisted upon by IMF in exchange for record US$57-billion aid package. IMF chief Camdessus defends IMF demand for mass layoffs as only way for Seoul to restore financial credibility and attract foreign investment.
15/1/98	Soeharto signs new loan deal with IMF agreeing to eliminate country's monopolies and state subsidies. Prices for basic food staples increase by as much as 80%. IMF signing follows a week of Rp. free-fall, which prompts waves of panic buying in Indonesia.
16/1/98	Summers asks South Korean leaders for more reforms and receives assurances from outgoing President Kim Young Sam that South Korea will abide by terms of IMF bail out.

18/1/98   President-elect Kim Dae-jung says worst yet to come in South Korea's struggle to overcome economic problems under IMF. While promising to strengthen skimpy social safety nets, he urges workers to accept layoffs to lure back foreign investors and to get foreign lenders to roll over South Korea's short-term debt of US$92 billion due within the year.

22/1/98   Officials from South Korea meet with international bankers in New York in effort to restructure country's short-term debt.
               One week after package of stiff new IMF-led reforms show no signs of alleviating country's debt and confidence crisis, Indonesia's currency plunges to new all-time low.

28/1/98   International banks and South Korea agree on plan to exchange US$24 billion of short-term debt for longer-term loans.

29/1/98   South Korean government agrees to exchange about US$24 billion of private short-term debt for government-guaranteed medium-term loans in deal expected to end Korea's liquidity crisis.

30/1/98   South Korea closes a third of its 30 merchant banks to restructure its ailing financial industry.

Feb. 1998   Objections by IMF and US President Clinton to Jakarta plan to peg Rp. to greenback through currency board system.

6/2/98   South Korean unions, government and businesses reach landmark agreement to legalise layoffs.

10/2/98   Won drops sharply against US currency on fears that union opposition to job losses and possible strikes would undermine country's restructuring programme.

11/2/98   Stocks in Indonesia and South Korea fall sharply amid fears countries will be hit by mounting social backlashes against economic crises.

19/2/98   Camdessus announces IMF will extend its loan programme to Russia by one year, says IMF will

	relax stringent tax-revenue targets used as criteria for awarding loans to Russia.
9/3/98	IMF delays US$3-billion instalment of US$40-billion loan package to Indonesia, citing Soeharto unwillingness to implement reforms. Soeharto replies that IMF reforms "unconstitutional".
10/2/98	Re-election of Indonesian President Soeharto for 7th 5-year term.
23/2/98	Yeltsin abruptly dismisses entire cabinet, including Prime Minister Chernomyeardin, appoints Energy Minister Kirienko as acting premier.
24/2/98	US announces it will send US$70 million in food and medical emergency aid to Indonesia, although IMF has suspended its loan package. US emergency aid to quell food riots.
8/4/98	Indonesia and IMF reach third pact in six months for bail out. Both sides make concessions: IMF withdraws requirement that government dismantle food and fuel subsidies, Soeharto agrees to close more insolvent banks. IMF Deputy MD Fischer declares "worst of the crisis is over".
May 1998	Anwar announces new reflationary measures. IMF U-turn, allows South Korean government to lower interest rates and increase budget deficits.
4/5/98	IMF resumes stalled lending programme to Indonesia, approving payment of US$1 billion.
5/5/98	Students in Indonesia demonstrate across country, protesting steep fuel and energy price hikes. Students denounce Soeharto administration for failed economic policies and demand extensive political reforms.
12/5/98	Indonesian troops fire into peaceful protest at a Jakarta university, killing six students and sparking a week of riots.
19/5/98	Soeharto promises early elections, but key parliamentary allies call for his resignation.
20/5/98	Malaysian government announces setting up Danaharta as national asset management company (AMC).

21/5/98	Soeharto resigns after 32 years in power. Vice President Habibie becomes president.
22/5/98	IMF indefinitely postpones US$1 billion aid disbursement to Indonesia. US Treasury Secretary Rubin says aid should be delayed until political situation stabilises.
27/5/98	Russian financial market turmoil begins.
27–28/5/98	Two-day nation-wide strike in South Korea by union workers to protest growing unemployment.
June 1998	Market interest rates in South Korea drop below pre-crisis level.
	Closure of five commercial banks in South Korea.
1/6/98	Russia's stock market crashes. Clinton pledges support for Yeltsin.
12/6/98	Japan announces economy in recession for first time in 23 years.
17/6/98	Yen falls to nearly 144/US$1, prompting US Treasury and Federal Reserve to intervene to prop up yen. Japan and US spend US$6 billion to strengthen yen.
20/6/98	Legal incorporation of Danaharta under Malaysian Companies Act, 1965.
24/6/98	Russian Prime Minister Kirienko submits budget austerity plan to IMF, which releases previously held loan instalment.
25/6/98	Indonesia and IMF announce fourth agreement to rescue economy. IMF agrees to restore food and fuel subsidies.
Jul. 1998	Creation of Danamodal to recapitalise Malaysian banks announced.
1/7/98	Russia's Duma postpones action on spending and tax reforms needed to close budget deficit and qualify for IMF loans.
6/7/98	Moscow markets fall as government fails to raise cash by selling shares in a state-owned oil company. Moscow hints IMF loan agreement near.
10/7/98	Clinton calls on IMF to quickly provide emergency loans for Russia after getting call from Boris Yeltsin, sparking rally in Moscow markets.

13/7/98	RM7-billion Malaysian fiscal stimulus package and additional measures to boost economic growth. IMF announces US$23-billion package for Russia. Russian stocks and bonds soar.
16/7/98	Russia's Duma approves some of Yeltsin's proposed tax reforms needed to meet IMF loan conditions, but rejects higher sales and land taxes.
19/7/98	Yeltsin vetoes tax cuts approved by parliament and decrees 3% tax on imports and quadrupling land taxes to close budget deficit to secure IMF loans.
20/7/98	IMF approves US$22.6 billion loan package to Russia. However, Duma fails to enact some austerity measures required by loan agreement; first two planned instalments are reduced.
23/7/98	Malaysian National Economic Recovery Plan unveiled.
28/7/98	IMF announces eased conditions on US$57-billion aid package to South Korea blamed for rising unemployment and overburdened welfare programmes.
3/8/98	Dow plunges as Wall Street reacts to deepening crisis.
4/8/98	Amid speculation that China will be forced to devalue, HK$ and stock market attacked.
6/8/98	WB approves US$1.5 billion loan for Russia as Moscow puts pressure on striking miners and taxpayers. Asian markets plummet as HK and China defend currencies against attack.
11/8/98	Russian market collapses. Stock market trading suspended. World markets rocked by fears of financial meltdown in Asia and Russia.
13/8/98	Russia's markets collapse on fears that Moscow will run out of money and default.
14/8/98	Yeltsin calls for emergency parliament session and declares "no devaluation" of ruble. In HK, authorities spark stock rally by moving to foil speculators with surprise purchases of stocks and US$.

17/8/98	Establishment of Corporate Debt Restructuring Committee (CDRC) in Malaysia.
	Russia announces devaluation of ruble and 90-day moratorium on foreign debt repayment, triggering panic in Moscow as Russians buy US$. Western leaders denounce Russian default.
	LA stock and bond markets plunge on fears of default and devaluation.
19/8/98	Russia officially defaults. IMF and G-7 refuse additional loans until Russia meets conditions.
21/8/98	Russia's economic crisis shakes world markets. Russia's Duma calls for Yeltsin's resignation. Investors buy US Treasury bonds as safe option.
24/8/98	Yeltsin replaces Kirienko as prime minister with Chernomyrdin.
31/8/98	After weeks of decline, Wall Street overwhelmed by turmoil in Russia and world markets. Dow Industrial average plunges 512 points, second-worst point loss in Dow's history.
Aug. 1998	Russian crisis leads to collapse of Long-Term Capital Management (LTCM) hedge fund.
Sep. 1998	South Korean government injects public funds into financial sector.
1/9/98	Implementation of selective capital controls in Malaysia.
2/9/98	RM exchange rate fixed at RM3.80/US$1.
	KLSE index closes at lowest level in 11 years at 263 points.
	Anwar sacked as Deputy Prime Minister and Finance Minister.
4/9/98	Prime Minister Mahathir becomes Acting Minister of Finance.
	Greenspan says US ready to cut interest rates to keep crisis from snuffing out US growth.
	LA stocks and bonds plummet.
7–8/9/98	Russia's political and economic turmoil deepens.
10/9/98	Yeltsin nominates Primakov as prime minister.

11/9/98	IMF announces debacle in LA markets is "over-reaction to Russian events" and that it is ready to lend LA countries by providing emergency lines of credit. Investors flee Brazil.
16/9/98	Central Limit Order Book (CLOB) International in Singapore to trade in Malaysian shares closed.
17/9/98	Tokyo's Nikkei index hits 12-year low amid steep declines in HK, France, Britain and US. US Congress blocks Clinton request for US$18 billion in funding for IMF.
23/9/98	Federal Reserve Bank of New York organises LTCM bail out.
24/9/98	Stocks on Wall Street and in Europe fall amid fears that losses suffered by world's largest banks in LTCM debacle could put entire banking system at risk.
29/9/98	US Fed cuts interest rates.
30/9/98	Worries that US Fed isn't doing enough causes sharp drop in Dow. Investors around world flock to US Treasury bonds for safety.
Oct. 1998	"Big Deals" — business swaps among *chaebols* — in Korea.
3/10/98	Japan announces US$30-billion aid package for Southeast Asia to help region recover. G-7 ministers rescue plan for Brazil.
15/10/98	Fed cuts interest rates for second time. World markets rally.
22/10/98	Amid warnings of winter food shortages in Russia, Moscow creates emergency food reserve and approves emergency spending plan that requires central bank to print money to pay back wages, rescue banks and bring food to desperate regions.
27/10/98	Brazil President Cardoso announces austerity plan of US$80-billion in tax increases and spending cuts over three years to secure IMF assistance package.
31/10/98	IMF refuses to disburse US$4.3-billion instalment of US$22.6-billion aid package Russia agrees to in

	July, and says it will not resume negotiations about disbursement until Russia produces realistic budget for 1999.
5/11/98	Russia reschedules foreign debt and gets US$800-million loan from Japan.
6/11/98	US agrees to provide food to Russia to help offset worst grain harvest in 45 years and declining food imports because of ruble fall.
13/11/98	IMF, WB and leading industrial nations announce US$41.5-billion rescue package for Brazil.
17/11/98	US Fed cuts interest rates for third time in seven weeks.
2/12/98	WB estimates crisis has cut world growth in half and possible recession in 1999. Official studies report 80 million Indonesians — 40% of population — have fallen below poverty line since crisis.
3/12/98	Brazil congress rejects social security tax increase sought by IMF, prompting stock sell-offs throughout LA and on Wall Street.
15/1/99	Brazil government allows currency to float freely by lifting exchange controls, leading to market surge as investors buy Brazil stocks at cut prices.
27/1/99	Brazil Central Bank raises interest rates to stabilise market and stem capital flight, which has reached US$200–500 million a day.
Feb. 1999	Unemployment rate in South Korea rises from 2.6% in 1997 to 8.6% in February 1999.
2/2/99	Arminio Fraga, former Soros portfolio manager, named president of Brazil's Central Bank.
15/2/99	Malaysia offers option of replacing twelve-month holding period from September 1998 for repatriation of portfolio capital with exit levy of 10–30%.
25/3/99	IMF approves US$1-billion increase in emergency loan package for Indonesia and release of US$460-million instalment held back due to delay in closing down insolvent banks.

29/3/99	Dow Jones Industrial Average closes above 10,000 for first time.
12/5/99	Dow Jones Industrial tops 11,000.
7/6/99	Indonesia holds its first free elections since 1955.
Aug. 1999	Daewoo Group technically bankrupt.
1/9/99	End of one-year capital controls in Malaysia.
Aug. 2001	South Korean government fully repays its US$19.5 billion IMF loan, three years ahead of schedule.
24/7/02	South Korea's ratings by 3 major credit rating agencies (Moody's, Fitch, Standard & Poor) return to pre-crisis 'A' level.
31/12/02	South Korea's foreign currency reserves of US$121.4 billion fourth largest in world, following Japan, China and Taiwan.

Chronology: Malaysian Economic Crisis and Corporate Restructuring

31/8/57	Federation of Malaya gains independence from Britain.
10/3/58	Malaya joins International Monetary Fund (IMF) and World Bank (WB).
26/1/59	Bank Negara Malaya (BNM) set up under Central Bank of Malaya Ordinance, 1958.
9/5/60	Malayan Stock Exchange is formed.
Sep. 1963	Malaysia formed by Federation of Malaya, Singapore, Sabah and Sarawak.
1964	Stock Exchange of Malaysia formed.
9/8/65	Singapore secedes from Federation of Malaysia to become independent republic, but common Stock Exchange of Malaysia and Singapore (SEMS) continues.
Oct. 1967	*Hartal* (general strike) following devaluation of sterling and Board of Currency Commissioners currency shared with Singapore and Brunei; BNM issued currency unaffected.
1971	US President Richard Nixon devalues US dollar, destroying post-war Bretton Woods system, which had set price of gold at US$35/oz. After couple of years of international monetary instability, most of the world switches from fixed to flexible exchange rates in 1973.
2/7/73	Termination of currency arrangements between Malaysia and Singapore. SEMS is divided into Kuala Lumpur Stock Exchange Bhd (KLSEB) and Stock Exchange of Singapore (SES).

27/12/76	Establishment of Kuala Lumpur Stock Exchange (KLSE) following Securities Industry Act 1973.
Jul. 1980	The futures and options industry commences with establishment of Kuala Lumpur Commodity Exchange (KLCE).
12/11/83	Securities Clearing Automated Network Services Sdn Bhd (SCANS) began providing clearing and settlement facilities for contracts done between clearing participants.
Sep. 1985	Malaysian economy experiences mild recession. Plaza Accord between G5 countries (France, West Germany, UK, US and Japan) to allow US$ to devalue, especially against Japanese yen. RM depreciates again US$, and therefore even more against other major currencies.
19/10/87	Wall Street stock market crash.
1987–88	Non-performing loans (NPLs) reach almost 30% of all commercial bank loans.
1989	Banking and Financial Institutions Act (BAFIA) promulgated. BNM becomes directly responsible for all foreign exchange control matters.
1/1/90	Singapore-incorporated companies are delisted from KLSE and Malaysian-incorporated companies are delisted from Stock Exchange of Singapore (SES).
2/1/90	Launch of Central Limit Order Book (CLOB) in Singapore to trade in KLSE counters.
14/4/90	The Malaysian Central Depository (MCD), subsidiary of Bursa Malaysia, established to provide efficient central clearing and settlement of securities. The Securities Industry (Central Depositories) Act 1991 later authorises establishment of Central Depository and provided legal safeguards for users and participants.
1/10/90	Establishment of Labuan International Offshore Financial Centre (LIOFC).
Nov. 1990	BNM sets up Rating Agency Malaysia Bhd (RAM).
Jan. 1991	Launch of KLSE Second Board Index.

1/2/91	Base lending rate of banking institutions freed.
17/10/91	Launch of KLSE Main All Shares (EMAS) Index, to track all shares on Main Board compared to KLSE Composite Index (KLCI) focus on top hundred counters.
1993	Bangkok International Banking Facility (BIBF) introduced, followed by Provincial International Banking Facility (PIBF).
1/3/93	Establishment of Malaysian Securities Commission (SC); Futures Industry Act 1993 promulgated.
24/1/94	Imposition of capital controls on inflows by BNM after late 1993 capital flight following massive capital inflows since 1992. Capital controls gradually dismantled from August until December 1994.
1/1/95	Malaysia joins World Trade Organisation (WTO), which replaces General Agreement on Tariffs and Trade (GATT), but has much broader scope than reducing trade barriers to manufacturers.
22/6/95	Further liberalisation measures to help promote Kuala Lumpur as regional financial centre.
26/9/95	International stock exchange and monetary exchange set up in Labuan.
Dec. 1995	Development of financial derivatives markets with establishment of Malaysian Derivatives Clearing House Bhd. MDCH formed to clear stock index futures, and in May 1996, begins clearing interest rate futures. On 29 November 1997, it merges with clearing house for commodities futures, Malaysian Futures Clearing Corporation Bhd (MFCC). MDCH then clears various futures and options traded on Malaysia Derivatives Exchange Bhd (MDEX).
15/12/95	Kuala Lumpur Options and Financial Futures Exchange Bhd (KLOFFE) launches its stock index futures contract.
28/5/96	The Malaysia Monetary Exchange (MME, later

	renamed Commodity and Monetary Exchange of Malaysia, COMMEX Malaysia) starts operations, offering futures contracts on three-month Kuala Lumpur Interbank Offered Rates (KLIBOR).
2/7/97	Bank of Thailand floats baht.
	Money injection by BNM to ease interbank rates.
8/7/97	BNM intervenes to defend its currency, ringgit (RM).
14/7/97	BNM abandons defence of RM.
24/7/97	Mahathir accuses "rogue speculators" of causing Southeast Asia's economic upheaval; later singles out George Soros.
	The HK$ remains steady, but US$1 billion spent on intervention during period of two hours on unspecified day in July.
26/7/97	Mahathir names hedge fund manager George Soros as man responsible for attack on RM. He later brands Soros "moron".
Late Aug. 1997	Securities Commission "designates" KLCI top 100 counters to thwart short-selling in KLSE; measure tightens liquidity, but backfires.
3/9/97	Malaysian cabinet approves RM60-billion facility to buy shares of "selected shareholders" seen as bail out facility to save cronies.
10/9/97	New measures to boost confidence announced by Finance Minister Anwar Ibrahim.
20/9/97	Mahathir tells delegates to IMF/WB annual conference in HK that currency trading is immoral and should be stopped.
21/9/97	Soros says Mahathir "menace to his own country".
1/10/97	Mahathir repeats his call for tighter regulation, or total ban, on forex trading. The currency falls 4% in less than two hours.
6/10/97	Malaysian Exchange of Securities Dealing and Automated Quotation (MESDAQ) launched.
17/10/97	Malaysia presents budget to try to stop economy sliding into recession, denounced for being "in denial".

13/11/97	IMF Managing Director Michel Camdessus visits Kuala Lumpur, meets with Anwar.
Mid-Nov. 1997	Anwar suspends KLSE requirement to allow UEM-Renong reverse takeover without making mandatory general offer; KLSE loses RM70 billion (20%) in three days.
20/11/97	Mahathir announces setting up National Economic Action Council (NEAC) after special UMNO Supreme Council meeting.
3/12/97	Cabinet meeting in Langkawi unanimously endorses new Anwar measures in Mahathir's absence.
4/12/97	Mahathir announces land bridge project with Thailand.
5/12/97	New measures announced by Anwar; growth projection for 1998 revised down to 4–5% from 7.5%.
8/12/97	Anwar announces new fiscal package.
1/1/98	New guidelines for classification of non-performing loans (NPLs) reduce grace period from 6 to 3 months. Launch of "Buy Malaysian Products" campaign by Mahathir.
7/1/98	Approval of NEAC and its composition by cabinet.
14/2/98	UEM shareholders approve UEM purchase of a 32.6% stake in Renong for RM2.34 billion and put option offer by UEM-Renong boss Halim Saad.
May 1998	Anwar announces new fiscal reflationary measures.
20/5/98	Government announces setting up Pengurusan Danaharta Nasional Berhad (Danaharta) as national asset management company (AMC).
21/5/98	Soeharto resigns after 32 years in power.
June 1998	Daim Zainuddin appointed Minister with Special Functions.
19/6/98	Anwar announces fiscal reflationary measures for agriculture, small business, poor.
20/6/98	Legal incorporation of Danaharta under Companies Act, 1965.

20–21/6/98	UMNO General Assembly: Mahathir releases selected lists of those awarded privatised contracts and special share allocations to embarrass Anwar.
Jul. 1998	Creation of Danamodal Nasional Berhad (Danamodal) announced. New BNM Liquidity Framework (Guidelines for Issuance of Private Debt Securities).
13/7/98	RM7-billion fiscal stimulus package and additional measures to boost economic growth.
23/7/98	National Economic Recovery Plan (NERP) unveiled.
4/8/98	Official establishment of Danamodal.
5/8/98	Danaharta Bill passed by Parliament.
6/8/98	Mahathir informs NEAC Exco of his decision to implement capital controls.
17/8/98	Establishment of Corporate Debt Restructuring Committee (CDRC).
26/8/98	Resignation of BNM Governor Ahmad Don and Deputy Fong Weng Phak.
28/8/98	Appointment of Zeti Akhtar Aziz as BNM Acting Governor.
1/9/98	Implementation of selective capital controls.
2/9/98	RM exchange rate fixed at RM3.80/US$1. KLSE index closes at lowest level in 11 years at 263 points. Anwar sacked as Deputy Prime Minister and Finance Minister.
4/9/98	Prime Minister Mahathir becomes Acting Minister of Finance.
7/9/98	Ali Abul Hassan becomes BNM Governor. Zeti appointed Deputy Governor.
10/9/98	Appointment of Salomon Smith Barney as financial advisor to government and Danamodal.
16/9/98	CLOB International terminated.
20/9/98	Anwar arrested under Internal Security Act (ISA).
25/9/98	NPL grace period lengthened from 3 to 6 months.
1/10/98	Ringgit no longer tradeable overseas.

23/10/98	Reflationary 1999 Budget from First Finance Minister Mahathir.
Oct. 1998	Renong proposes government guarantee RM10.5 billion bond issue to refinance overdue loans. Proposal later rejected.
1/11/98	New KLSE guidelines for share buybacks take effect.
30/11/98	Malaysia removed from Morgan Stanley Capital International Inc. (MSCI) Indices.
7/12/98	Commodity and Monetary Exchange of Malaysia (COMMEX Malaysia) established following merger of KLCE and wholly owned subsidiary, MME, for commodity futures market and to facilitate effective hedging of RM-denominated money market instruments.
29/12/98	Malaysian government borrows from consortium of foreign banks.
Jan. 1999	New Code on Takeovers and Mergers.
1/1/99	Appointment of Daim Zainuddin as Finance Minister.
15/2/99	Option offered of replacing twelve-month holding period from September 1998 for repatriation of portfolio capital with exit levy of between 10–30%.
2/3/99	Japanese financial aid to Malaysia under Miyazawa Initiative amounting to RM4.8 billion, of which government only draws down RM 610 million, with remainder to be drawn down over next 3–5 years. Yen credit lines offered at concessionary interest rates with maturities of up to 40 years.
8/3/99	Proposal for PLUS to issue RM8.4 billion of zero-coupon bonds (present day value), yielding 10% per annum, maturing in 7 years. PLUS would then lend RM5.4 billion to Renong and RM3.0 billion to UEM to settle creditors' claims.
7/4/99	Elimination of Two-Tier Regulatory System (TTRS) bank classification.
29/5/99	Merger programme for domestic banking institutions announced by BNM.

1/9/99	End of one-year capital controls.
15/9/99	Renong and UEM complete Malaysia's largest ever corporate bond exercise issuing PLUS bonds of RM4.3 billion.
21/9/99	Graduated exit levy on portfolio investment simplified and replaced by flat 10% levy on profit repatriation.
30/12/99	CDRC assists Park May Bhd with debt restructuring of RM146 million.
11/2/00	UEM acquires 45% of Intria from Mekar Idaman Sdn Bhd to become largest shareholder in Intria which holds 25-year concession to collect Penang Bridge tolls.
13/3/00	Renong announces PLUS bonds will only have annual yield of 9.4% instead of 10% announced in March 1999.
1/5/00	Appointment of Zeti Akhtar Aziz as BNM Governor.
31/5/00	Malaysia reintroduced in MSCI indices.
10/7/00	Time Engineering announces sale of 30% of interest in Time dotCom to Khazanah for RM2.12 billion.
28/8/00	Renong announce group net profit of RM246 million and turnover of RM456 million for year ended 30 June 2000.
23/11/00	Labuan International Financial Exchange (LFX) launched on 23 November 2000.
20/12/00	KLSE introduces shorter (T+3) delivery and settlement period.
20/12/00	MoF Inc. becomes largest MAS shareholder after buying 29.09% stake in MAS from Naluri Bhd (controlled by Tajudin Ramli) at original purchase price of RM8, more than double current market price.
22/12/00	Government proposes to issue RM6 billion in bonds to buy PUTRA and STAR. Proposal later put on hold in May 2001.
18/1/01	Renong enters sale & purchase agreement for disposal of certain assets to UEM for RM5.3 billion.

1/02/01	New guidelines repatriated profits levy.
14/02/01	Naluri, Tajuddin Ramli's listed holding company, announces sale of controlling 29% stake in MAS back to MoF.
22/02/01	Launch of *Capital Market Masterplan* by Securities Commission.
Mar. 2001	Launch of *Financial Sector Masterplan* by BNM.
27/03/01	RM3-billion stimulus package announced.
1/5/01	Exit levy system dropped.
29/5/01	MAS announces largest ever RM1.3-billion net loss for FY ended 31 March 2001. MAS unveils first turnaround plan.
31/5/01	Finance Minister Daim resigns from all government posts and as UMNO Treasurer (since 1984).
11/6/01	Malaysia Derivatives Exchange (MDEX) launched. MDEX offers wide range of derivatives products and services including KLSE Composite Index Futures and Options, Crude Palm Oil Futures and Kuala Lumpur Interbank Offered Rate (KLIBOR) Futures.
20/6/01	Inaugural listing on Labuan International Financial Exchange (LFX) takes place.
27/6/01	KLSE and MESDAQ agree to detailed negotiations to facilitate consolidation exercise.
Jul. 2001	Malaysian government offers to "nationalise" UEM.
23/7/01	Danasaham, wholly owned subsidiary of Khazanah, makes Conditional Voluntary Offer (CVO) to buy all UEM shares and warrants, including Renong's 37.9% interest in UEM at RM4.50/share and warrants at RM0.40 each.
29/8/01	CDRC announces government plan to acquire 80% of KL LRTs from STAR and PUTRA, leaving Renong, Taylor Woodrow, state-run pension funds and other shareholders with 20%.
1/9/01	PNB takes over PUTRA operations and assets.
25/9/01	Second stimulus package of RM4.3 billion announced.

1/10/01   UEM appoints former Telekom Malaysia CEO, Wahid Omar, Managing Director and CEO.

4/10/01   MAS announces new international network, withdrawing from unprofitable non-core destinations to cut losses and focus on profitable, high growth routes as part of turnaround plan.

21/11/01   UEM terminates Halim Saad "put option" to buy back shares he sold to UEM in late 1997, due in February 2001, for RM3.2 billion.

30/11/01   PUTRA 1st company to be divested from UEM-Renong stable after 1997–98 crisis; taken over by SPNB as part of govt plan to rationalise Kelang Valley transportation system. CDRC announces SPNB purchase of outstanding debts of STAR and PUTRA of RM5.7 billion via issue of RM5.468 billion of fixed rate serial guaranteed bonds to creditors.

Dec. 2001   UEM announces major corporate and debt restructuring plan operations into six units and divesting stakes in six companies to trim group debt of RM30.3 billion to RM14 billion by mid-2002.

7/12/01   CDRC completes first phase of PUTRA/STAR debt restructuring.

22/1/02   CIMB announces proposed reorganisation of MAS group operations.

Feb. 2002   MAS debt approximately RM9.2 billion.

21/2/02   CIMB files winding-up petition to close down STAR for not repaying RM1 billion; claiming that, together with interest, STAR owes it RM1,051,509,127.16 as of 26 December 2001 under loan agreement dated 13 August 1993.

18/3/02   MESDAQ market at KLSE launched.

20/3/02   PUTRA served two winding-up petitions by CIMB after failing to pay RM2-billion loan obligations.

26/4/02   High Court winds up PUTRA with appointment of liquidators.

7/5/02	As part of PLUS debt restructuring scheme to enhance value upon listing, Renong transfers RM8.2-billion zero coupon bonds from PLUS to UEM after SC agrees on 3 May to transfer guarantee for Renong bonds to UEM.
29/5/02	MAS announces group net loss after tax of RM835.6 million for FY ended 31 March 2003 following post 9/11 aviation disruption.
20–22/6/02	UMNO General Assembly. Mahathir announces resignation from all UMNO and Barisan Nasional posts, but withdraws resignations after appeals from UMNO cabinet members.
29/7/02	UEM Land announces change of FY end from 30 June to 31 December.
30/7/02	MAS unveils details of Widespread Asset Unbundling (WAU), transferring 73 MAS aircraft valued at RM5.109 billion with associated liabilities of RM6.966 billion to Penerbangan Malaysia Berhad (PMB).
31/7/02	CDRC concludes debt-restructuring efforts.
15/8/02	CDRC closes, marking conclusion of government debt-restructuring efforts.
1/9/02	SPNB, wholly-owned subsidiary of Ministry of Finance, takes over assets of PUTRA, wholly-owned subsidiary of Renong Berhad.
11/11/02	SCANS completes acquisition of MDCH, thus making MDCH wholly owned subsidiary.
30/1/03	MAS unveils expansion plans, with particular focus on regional and domestic routes after improved performance & increased yields following restructuring exercise and turnaround plan.
11/3/03	UEM World first incorporated as Global Converge Sdn Bhd.
27/3/03	UEM-Renong group announces five-step restructuring plan which will include taking Renong private with listed status transferred to UEM World, with operations streamlined.

20/5/03	MAS announces group net profit after tax of RM339.1 million for FY ended 31 March 2003 partly due to effectiveness of operating model and strategies employed.
8/9/03	Global Converge Sdn Bhd changes name to UEM World Sdn Bhd.
12/9/03	UEM World converts into public limited company UEM World Bhd.
17/10/03	Trading of UEM Land shares suspended.
27/10/03	Completion of UEM Land privatisation.
31/10/03	Mahathir retires and replaced by Abdullah Ahmad Badawi, who takes over as Finance Minister.
14/11/03	UEM World becomes owner of entire shareholding in UEM Land through exchange of shares and assumes UEM Land's listing status on Main Board of Malaysia Securities Exchange Bhd (MSEB) or Bursa Malaysia Bhd.
31/12/03	Danamodal ends operations.
5/1/04	Following demutualisation of KLSE, stock exchange to be known as Malaysia Securities Exchange Berhad (MSEB). KLSE now referred to as MSEB.
16/1/04	Federal Court rules that Section 72 of Danaharta Act, which prohibits granting of any injunction against Danaharta, is valid and constitutional.
22/3/04	Abdullah Badawi wins general elections handsomely after changes in political style.
14/5/04	Abdullah announces that government wants Khazanah to become biggest and most dynamic investment house in region, remaking "Malaysia Incorporated". Azman Mokhtar appointed CEO from 1 June 2004.
24/5/04	MAS announces fourth quarter ended 31 March 2004 profit of RM294.506 million and net profit of RM261.143 million for financial year ended 31 December 2003.

CHAPTER 1

The 1997–98 East Asian Crises

Jomo K.S.

The East Asian crises of 1997–98 gave rise to two major responses from mainstream or orthodox economists. The first was an attempt to explain the unexpected events from mid-1997 in terms of several aspects of the orthodoxy, especially theories of currency crisis. Proponents of this explanation made much of current account or fiscal deficits, real as well as imagined. When this line of reasoning clearly proved to be wrong, inadequate, or unpersuasive, the second line of defence was to turn the preceding celebration of the East Asian miracle on its head by suggesting that key elements of East Asian exceptionalism, e.g. government intervention and social capital, were responsible for the crises. Those promoting this explanation emphasised cronyism (government favouritism for particular business interests) and poor corporate governance — both genuine problems, but irrelevant in this context — with some grudging acknowledgment of the poor or wrong sequencing of financial liberalisation, rather than the implications of liberalisation itself with its open capital accounts.

Two consequences of this failure to deal with the full implications of the East Asian debacle require revisiting the crises to try to ensure that their most important lessons are not lost. Subsequent currency and financial crises elsewhere suggest that many important lessons have not been appreciated nor translated into appropriate policy. First, erroneous lessons drawn by orthodox economists, financial analysts, and the media have obscured the important policy-relevant analysis that has emerged. Second, the policies and policymakers responsible for creating the conditions that culminated in the crises need to be identified. Perhaps more importantly, the wrong lessons

1

have diverted attention away from the intellectual and ideological bases of the erroneous thinking, analyses, and policies responsible for the crises. Suggesting that such ideas are associated with the so-called Washington consensus's advocacy of economic liberalisation at both the national and global levels would not be an exaggeration. Needless to say, drawing the right lessons would likely undermine the intellectual, analytical, and policy authority of the interests and institutions upholding this consensus.

Even though considerable work was critical of East Asia's record and potential, none actually anticipated the East Asian debacle of 1997–98 (Krugman 1994). While certain aspects of the crises were common to all four East Asian economies most adversely affected — Indonesia, South Korea, Malaysia, and Thailand — others were unique to a particular country or common only to the more open economies of Southeast Asia, namely, Indonesia, Malaysia, and Thailand. Of course, some of the weaknesses identified in the literature did imply that the region was economically vulnerable. The dominance of manufacturing activities, especially the most technologically sophisticated and dynamic ones, by foreign transnationals subordinated domestic industrial capital in the region, allowing finance capital, both domestic and foreign, to become more influential (Jomo 1998). None of the critical writing seriously addressed the crucial implications of the greater role and fluidity of foreign capital in Southeast Asia, particularly with regard to international financial liberalisation, which had become more pronounced in the 1990s.

Indeed, financial capital developed a complex symbiotic relationship with politically influential *rentiers*, now dubbed cronies, in the aftermath of 1997–98. Although threatened by the full implications of international financial liberalisation, Southeast Asian financial interests were quick to identify and secure new possibilities for capturing rents from arbitrage, as well as other opportunities offered by gradual international financial integration. In these and other ways (Gomez and Jomo 1999; Khan and Jomo 2000), transnational dominance of Southeast Asian industrialisation facilitated the ascendance and consolidation of financial interests and politically influential *rentiers*. This increasingly powerful alliance was primarily responsible for promoting financial liberalisation in the region, both externally and internally. However, insofar as the interests of domestic financial capital did not entirely coincide with those of international finance capital, the processes of international financial liberalisation were partial and uneven. The varying policy influence of domestic financial interests in different parts of the region also played a part.

This chapter considers various views of the origins of the crisis and its development and spread through the region (referred to as contagion). This is then set against the larger drama of the transformation of the East Asian miracle into a debacle. All this is placed against the larger context of policy advocacy for financial liberalisation, especially since the late 1980s. It also argues that the crises were of a new type and were somewhat different from earlier currency and financial crises. In particular, it emphasises the implications of easily reversible capital flows made possible by international financial liberalisation. While much of the literature emphasises the problems associated with foreign bank borrowing, this chapter also draws attention to the dangers of portfolio capital flows and looks at the role of the International Monetary Fund (IMF) in exacerbating the crises.

From Miracle to Debacle

Rapid economic growth and structural change, mainly associated with export-led industrialisation in the region, can generally be traced back to the mid-1980s. Then devaluation of the currencies of Indonesia, Malaysia, and Thailand, as well as selective deregulation of onerous rules, helped to create attractive conditions for the relocation of production facilities in these countries and elsewhere in Southeast Asia and in China. This was especially attractive for Japan, and the first-tier or first-generation newly-industrialising economies, that is, Hong Kong (China), South Korea, Singapore, and Taiwan (China), most of which experienced currency appreciation, tight labour markets, and higher production costs. This sustained export-oriented indus-trialisation well into the 1990s and was accompanied by the growth of other manufacturing, services, and construction activities.

High growth was sustained for about a decade, during much of which fiscal surpluses were maintained, monetary expansion was not excessive, and inflation was generally under control. Table 1.1 shows various summary macroeconomic indicators for the 1990s,

Table 1.1 East Asian Four: Macroeconomic Indicators, 1990–99

Country	90–95	1996	Savings/GDP 1997	1998	1999
Indonesia	31.0	26.2	26.4	26.1	23.7
South Korea	35.6	33.7	33.3	33.8	33.5
Malaysia	36.6	37.1	37.3	39.6	38.0
Thailand	34.4	33.0	32.5	34.9	31.0

	90–95	1996	(Savings-Investment)/GDP 1997	1998	1999
Indonesia	−0.3	−3.4	−2.3	4.0	4.4
South Korea	−1.2	−3.1	−1.8	4.1	5.5
Malaysia	−0.9	−5.4	−5.8	12.8	15.7
Thailand	−5.6	−8.1	−0.9	12.8	10.0

	90–95	1996	Investment/GDP 1997	1998	1999
Indonesia	31.3	29.6	28.7	22.1	19.3
South Korea	36.8	36.8	35.1	29.8	28.0
Malaysia	37.5	42.5	43.1	26.8	22.3
Thailand	41.0	41.1	33.3	22.2	21.0

	87–89	90–92	Incremental Capital-Output Ratios 93–95	1997	1998
Indonesia	4.0	3.9	4.4	1.7	0.4
South Korea	3.5	5.1	5.1	4.2	−15.1
Malaysia	3.6	4.4	5.0	3.9	28.2
Thailand	2.9	4.6	5.2	12.9	−11.5

	90–95	1996	Fiscal Balance/GDP 1997	1998	1999
Indonesia	0.2	1.4	1.3	−2.6	−3.4
South Korea	0.2	0.5	−1.4	−4.2	−2.9
Malaysia	−0.4	0.7	2.4	−1.8	−3.2
Thailand	3.2	2.4	−0.9	−3.4	−3.0

Country	1990	1996	Unemployment Rate 1997	1998	1999
Indonesia	–	4.1	4.6	5.5	6.3
South Korea	2.4	3.0	2.6	6.8	6.3
Malaysia	6.0	2.5	2.4	3.2	3.0
Thailand	4.9	1.1	0.9	3.5	4.1

Note: – Not available.
Sources: ADB (1999); Radelet and Sachs (1998a; Table 11); Bank of Thailand, Bank Indonesia, Bank of Korea, and Bank Negara Malaysia data.

highlighting particularly the period from 1996. Prior to 1997, savings and investment rates were high and rising in all three Southeast Asian economies. Foreign savings supplemented high domestic savings in all four East Asian crisis economies, especially in Malaysia and Thailand. Unemployment was low, while fiscal balances generally remained positive until 1997–98.

This is not to suggest, however, that fundamentals in East Asia were not experiencing any problems (Rasiah 2001). As Table 1.1 shows, the incremental capital-output ratio rose in all three Southeast Asian economies during the 1990s before 1997, with the increase being the largest in Thailand and the smallest in Indonesia. The rising incremental capital-output ratios suggest declining returns to new investments before the crises. Export-led growth had been followed by a construction and property boom, fuelled by financial systems favouring such "short-termist" investments — which involved loans with collateral, that is, the kind that bankers like — over more productive, but also seemingly more risky, investments in manufacturing and agriculture. The exaggerated expansion of investment in such non-tradeables exacerbated the economies' current account deficits. Although widespread in East Asia, the property-finance nexus was particularly strong in Thailand, which made it especially vulnerable to the inevitable bursting of the bubble (Jomo 1998; Pasuk and Baker 2000).

Financial liberalisation from the 1980s had major ramifications in the region, as foreign savings supplemented the already high domestic savings rates to further accelerate the rate of capital accumulation, albeit in increasingly unproductive activities, because of the foreign domination of most internationally competitive industries. The rapid growth of the previous decade gave rise to several related macroeconomic concerns that had emerged by the mid-1990s.

First, the savings-investment gap had historically been financed by heavy reliance on foreign direct investment (FDI), as well as by public sector foreign borrowing, with the latter declining rapidly from the mid-1980s. Both FDI and foreign debt, in turn, caused investment income outflows abroad.[1] In the 1990s, the current account deficit was being financed increasingly by short-term capital inflows, as in 1993 and 1995–96, with disastrous consequences later when such flows reversed.[2] Many recent confidence restoration measures seek to induce such short-term inflows once again, but they cannot be relied upon to address the underlying problem in the medium to long term. Although always in the minority, foreign portfolio investments increasingly influenced stock markets in the region in the 1990s. With incomplete information exacerbated by limited transparency, the presence of foreign portfolio investment, the biased nature of fund managers' incentives and remuneration, and the short-termism of fund managers' investment horizons, foreign financial institutions were much more prone to herd behaviour than they might otherwise have been, and thus contributed decisively to regional contagion.

Second, private sector debt exploded in the 1990s, especially from abroad, not least because of the efforts of debt-pushers keen to secure higher returns from the fast-growing region.[3] Commercial banks' foreign liabilities also increased quickly, as the ratio of loans to gross national product rose rapidly during the period. Over-investment of investible funds, especially from abroad, in non-tradeables only made things worse, especially in relation to the current account. Only a small proportion of commercial banks and other lending agencies were involved with manufacturing and other pro-ductive activities. This share is likely to have been even smaller with foreign borrowing, most of which was collateralised with such assets as real property and stock.[4]

Thus much of the inflow of foreign savings actually contributed to asset price inflation, mainly involving real estate and share prices. Insofar as such investments did not increase the production of tradeables, they actually exacerbated the current account deficit rather than alleviated it as they were thought to be doing. This, in turn, worsened the problem of currency mismatch, with borrowing in US dollars invested in activities that did not generate foreign exchange. As a high proportion of this foreign borrowing was short-term in nature and deployed to finance medium- to long-term projects, a term mismatch problem also arose. According to the Bank for International Settlements (BIS) (*Asian Wall Street Journal*, 6 January 1998), well over half of the foreign borrowing by commercial banks was short-term in nature: 56 per cent in Malaysia, 59 per cent in Indonesia, 66 per cent in Thailand, and 68 per cent in South Korea.

More generally, the foreign exchange risks of investment rose, increasing the vulnerability of these economies to the maintenance of currency pegs to the US dollar.[5] The pegs encouraged a great deal of unhedged borrowing by an influential constituency with a strong stake in defending the pegs regardless of their adverse consequences for the economy. Because of the foreign domination of export-oriented industries in Southeast Asia, unlike in Northeast Asia, no politically influential industrial community that was oriented toward national exports was available to lobby for floating or depreciating the Southeast Asian currencies, despite the obvious adverse consequences of the pegs for international cost competitiveness. Instead, after pegging their currencies to the US dollar from the early 1990s, and especially from the mid-1990s, most Southeast Asian central banks resisted downward adjustments to their exchange rates, which would have reduced, if not averted, some of the more disruptive consequences of the 1997–98 currency collapses.[6] Yet economists now generally agree that the 1997–98 East Asian crises saw tremendous "overshooting" in exchange rate adjustments well in excess of expected corrections.

The economic literature before the crises tended to characterise the affected Southeast Asian economies in terms of the following key fundamentals:

*   Viability of domestic financial systems[7]
*   Responsiveness of domestic output and exports to nominal devaluations[8]
*   Sustainability of current account deficits[9]
*   Prevalence of high savings rates and robust public finances.

Crises of a New Type

Many economists were obliged to reconsider their earlier assessments of the causes of the Asian crises, most notably Krugman. In the immediate aftermath of its outbreak, some saw the crises as vindication of Krugman's earlier popularisation of a critique of the East Asian miracle as primarily due to massive factor inputs subject to diminishing returns (Krugman 1994). In March 1998, Krugman dissented from the view — associated with Radelet and Sachs (1998b) — of the East Asian crises as being due to a "good old-fashioned financial panic ... a panic need not be a punishment for your sins ... an economy can be 'fundamentally sound' ... and yet be subjected to a devastating run started by nothing more than a self-fulfilling rumor".

Clearly no one fully anticipated the crises in East Asia mainly because they were crises of a new type. Some observers argue that the crises had important parallels with the Mexican tequila crisis of 1995, while others emphasise the differences (Kregel 1998). There were, of course, sceptics who regarded the claims of an East Asian economic miracle as somewhat exaggerated in the first place (e.g. Krugman 1994). However, these were different criticisms of the East Asian miracle and certainly did not anticipate, let alone predict, the East Asian debacle of 1997–98.

The East Asian crises differed from conventional currency crisis scenarios in at least several important ways[10] (Krugman 1998a), namely:

- The absence of the usual sources of currency stress, whether fiscal deficits or macroeconomic indiscipline.[11]
- The governments' lack of any incentive to abandon their pegged exchange rates, for instance, to reduce unemployment.
- The pronounced boom and bust cycles in asset prices (real estate and stock markets) preceded the currency crises, especially in Thailand, where the crises began.
- The fact that financial intermediaries were key players in all the economies involved.
- The severity of the crises in the absence of strong, adverse shocks.
- The rapid spread of the initial crisis from Thailand even to economies with few links or similarities to the first victims.

Thus, the traditional indexes of vulnerability did not signal crises because the source of the problem was not to be found in government fiscal balances, or even in national income accounts. The liabilities of the mainly private financial intermediaries were not part of the governments' liabilities until after the crises, after foreign lenders and the international financial institutions "persuaded" them to nationalise much of the private foreign debt. Other issues also need to be taken into account for an adequate analysis of the East Asian crises, namely:

- The crises had severe adverse effects on growth by disrupting the productive contribution of financial intermediation.

- The crises involved not only excessive investment, but also unwise investment.
- The huge real currency depreciations caused large output declines and seemed to do little to promote exports.

Other kinds of market failure also need to be taken into account.

Furman and Stiglitz (1998) emphasise that economic downturns caused by financial crises are far more severe and have longer-lasting effects than those caused by inventory cycles. High leveraging by companies and high lending for asset price (stock or property market) booms enhance financial fragility and increased insolvencies disrupt the credit mechanism. Large unanticipated interest rate increases may not only precipitate financial crises, but are also likely to cause economic downturns as the value of bank assets and highly indebted firms collapse. Such adverse effects are likely to persist well after the interest rate has returned to more normal levels. In addition to asset price bubbles, excessive investments, and other problems caused by moral hazard resulting from implicit government guarantees for weakly regulated financial intermediaries, as well as the exchange rate peg, a more comprehensive analysis must also consider the following phenomena:

- The implications of the growth in currency trading and speculation for the post-Bretton Woods international monetary system.
- The reasons why the Southeast Asian monetary authorities defended their quasi pegs against the strengthening US dollar, despite the obvious adverse consequences for export competitiveness, and hence for growth.
- The consequences of financial liberalisation, including the creation of conditions that contributed to the magnitude of the crises.
- The role of herd behaviour in exacerbating the crises.
- The factors accounting for the contagion effects.

Dangers of International Financial Liberalisation

Analysts have increasingly acknowledged the role of easily reversible capital flows into the East Asian region as the principal cause of the

1997–98 crises. They now generally accept that the national financial systems in the region did not adapt well to international financial liberalisation (Jomo 1998). The bank-based financial systems of most of the East Asian economies affected by the crises were especially vulnerable to the sudden drop in the availability of short-term loans as international confidence in the region dropped suddenly during 1997. Available foreign exchange reserves were exposed as inadequate to meet financial obligations abroad, requiring governments to seek temporary credit facilities to meet such obligations that had been incurred mainly by their private sectors.

Data from the BIS show that the banks were responsible for much of this short-term debt, though some of it did consist of trade credit and other short-term debt deemed essential for ensuring liquidity in an economy. However, the rapid growth of short-term bank debt during stock market and property boom periods suggests that much short-term debt is due to factors other than trade credit expansion. In Malaysia, the temporary capital controls the central bank introduced in early 1994 momentarily dampened the growth of such debt, but by 1996 and early 1997, a new short-term borrowing frenzy was evident that involved not only the banks, but also other large, private companies with enough political influence to circumvent the central bank's guidelines.

As Table 1.2 shows, in Indonesia, Malaysia, and Thailand, the non-bank private sector was the major recipient of international bank loans, accounting for more than half of total foreign borrowing by the end of June 1997, that is, well above the developing country average of slightly under half. In contrast, 65 per cent of borrowing in South Korea was by banks, with only 31 per cent by the non-bank private sector. Government borrowing was low, and was lowest in South Korea and Malaysia, although the data do not permit differentiating between state-owned public companies or partially private, but corporatised previously fully state-owned enterprises.

Jomo ([ed.] 2001: Appendix Tables 2a–2d) shows the remarkable growth of mainly private foreign debt in the early and mid-1990s, especially in the three most externally indebted economies of Indonesia, South Korea, and Thailand. While FDI grew in all four economies in the 1990s, it grew the least in South Korea. Profit remittances on FDI were least from South Korea and Thailand and highest from

Table 1.2 Lending by Banks Reporting to BIS by Sector, East Asian Four and Developing Countries, End June 1997 (US$ bn)

Sector	Indonesia	S. Korea	Malaysia	Thailand	Developing Countries
Total borrowing, of which:	58.6	103.4	28.9	79.4	743.8
Bank	12.4	67.3	10.5	26.1	275.3
	(21.1)	(65.1)	(36.3)	(32.9)	(37.0)
Private non-bank	39.7	31.7	16.5	41.3	352.9
	(67.7)	(30.6)	(57.1)	(52.0)	(47.4)
Government	6.5	4.4	1.9	12.0	115.6
	(11.1)	(4.3)	(6.6)	(15.1)	(15.5)

Note: Figures in parentheses are percentages.
Source: BIS data.

Malaysia, reflecting its historically greater role, although FDI in Indonesia was actually higher in 1995–96. Portfolio equity flows into all four economies grew strongly in the mid-1990s.

External debt as a share of export earnings rose from 112 per cent in 1995 to 120 per cent in 1996 in Thailand and from 57 to 74 per cent over the same period in South Korea, but declined in Indonesia and grew more modestly in Malaysia. By 1996, foreign exchange reserves as a share of external debt were 15 per cent in Indonesia, 30 per cent in South Korea, 43 per cent in Thailand, and 70 per cent in Malaysia. By 1997, this ratio had dropped further to 15 per cent in South Korea, 29 per cent in Thailand, and 46 per cent in Malaysia, reflecting the reserves lost in futile currency defence efforts. Despite recessions in 1998, reserves picked up in all four economies, mainly because of the effects of currency devaluations on exports and imports. The short-term debt share of total external debt in 1996 stood at 58 per cent in South Korea, 41 per cent in Thailand, 28 per cent in Malaysia, and 25 per cent in Indonesia.

Table 1.3 shows that French, German, Japanese, UK, and US banks that reported to the BIS accounted for much of the lending to developing countries, with the share of UK and US banks being far less significant than lending to other emerging markets. This pattern was quite different from that of lending before the 1980s debt crises,

Table 1.3   Exposure of Banks Reporting to BIS and Non-BIS Borrowers, End June 1997 (US$ bn)

Banks' National Location	Amount
Total	1,054.9
Germany	178.2
Japan	172.7
United States	131.0
France	100.2
United Kingdom	77.8
Percentage of private non-bank borrowers	45

Source: BIS data.

and suggests that Anglo-American banks were generally far more reluctant to lend in the 1990s following their experiences in the 1980s. Little evidence suggests that such banks were more averse to lending either to governments or to developing economies. Indeed, the pattern of lending in the late 1970s and early 1980s suggests the contrary.

From the beginning of the 1990s, Malaysia sustained a current account deficit. Over-investment of investible funds in non-tradeables only made things worse. Insofar as such investments did not contribute to export earnings, e.g. in power generation and telecommunications, they aggravated the problem of currency mismatch, with foreign borrowing invested in activities that did not generate foreign exchange. An additional problem of term mismatch also arose, as a high proportion of the foreign borrowing was short-term in nature (Table 1.4), but was deployed to finance medium- to long-term projects.

Foreign capital inflows into East Asia augmented the high domestic savings rate to boost the domestic investment rate and East Asian investments abroad in the 1990s. Thus, even though some evidence suggests that foreign capital inflows may have had an indirect adverse effect on the domestic savings rate, they generally supplemented, rather than substituted for, domestic savings (Wong and Jomo 2001). Being conclusive on this point is difficult, because the nature of foreign capital inflows has changed significantly over time. Hence even if earlier foreign capital inflows may have adversely affected

Table 1.4   Maturity Distribution of Lending to the East Asian Four by Banks Reporting to the BIS, 1996–97 (US$ m)

Country	All Loans			Under 1 Year			1–2 Years		
	June 1996	*Dec. 1996*	*June 1997*	*June 1996*	*Dec. 1996*	*June 1997*	*June 1996*	*Dec. 1996*	*June 1997*
Indonesia	49,306	55,523	58,726	29,587	34,248	34,661	3,473	3,589	3,541
S. Korea	88,027	99,953	103,432	62,332	67,506	70,182	3,438	4,107	4,139
Malaysia	20,100	22,234	28,820	9,991	11,178	16,268	834	721	615
Thailand	69,409	70,147	69,382	47,834	45,702	45,567	4,083	4,829	4,592

Source: BIS data.

domestic savings, one possibility is that the changed composition of foreign capital inflows just before the crises no longer adversely affected domestic savings.

International financial liberalisation undoubtedly succeeded in temporarily generating massive net capital inflows into East Asia, unlike into many other developing and transition economies, some of which experienced net outflows. However, it also exacerbated systemic instability and reduced the scope for the government interventions responsible for the region's economic miracle. Increased foreign capital inflows reduced foreign exchange constraints, allowing the financing of additional imports, but thereby also inadvertently encouraging current account deficits. Finally, foreign capital inflows adversely affected factor payment outflows, export and import propensities, terms of trade, and capital flight, and thus the balance of payments. These consequences suggest that governments should be cautious when determining the extent to which they should encourage foreign capital inflows. Furthermore, the Southeast Asian trio's heavy dependence on FDI in relation to gross domestic capital formation, especially for manufacturing investments, probably also limited the development of domestic entrepreneurship, as well as many other indigenous economic capabilities, by the increased reliance on foreign capabilities usually associated with some types of FDI (Jomo *et al.* 1997).

As noted earlier, starting in the mid-1990s, three major indicators began to cause concern. The current account of the balance of payments

Table 1.5   Debt Service and Short-term Debt, East Asian Four, Selected Years

Country	Debt Service as a Percentage of Exports			Short-term Debt (US$ billions)[a]				Current Account Deficit Plus Short-term Debt as a Percentage of International Reserves			
	1980	1992	1995	1992	1994	1995	1996	1992	1994	1995	1996
Indonesia	13.9	32.1	30.9	18.2	14.0	16.2	17.9	191	139	169	138
S. Korea	14.5	6.9	5.8	11.9	31.6	46.6	66.6	133	125	131	127
Malaysia	6.3	6.6	7.8	3.6	7.6	7.5	8.5	29	46	60	55
Thailand	18.9	14.1	10.2	14.7	29.2	41.1	44.0	101	127	152	153

Note: ᵃ Year end figures.
Source: UNCTAD (1997: Table 14); World Bank (1994: Tables 20, 23; 1997: Table 17).

and the savings-investment gap were recording large imbalances in the Southeast Asian economies, especially Malaysia and Thailand. However, as Table 1.5 shows, the short-term foreign debt and current account deficits as proportions of international reserves were better in Malaysia than in Indonesia, South Korea, and Thailand, thereby averting the need for IMF emergency credit. Domestic credit expansion had also soared in all four countries by the mid-1990s. Prior to the crises, since the mid-1980s, East Asia had moved steadily toward financial liberation, including bank liberalisation, promotion of the region's newly emerging stock markets, and greater capital account convertibility. Thus East Asia succeeded in attracting a great deal of capital inflow.

Where the other three crisis-affected East Asian economies succeeded in attracting considerable, mainly short-term, US dollar bank loans into their more bank-based financed systems, Malaysia's vulnerability was mainly due to the volatility of international portfolio capital flows into its stock market. As a consequence, the nature of Malaysia's external liabilities at the beginning of the crisis was quite different from that of the other crisis-stricken East Asian economies. A greater proportion of Malaysia's external liabilities consisted of equity rather than debt. Compared with Malaysia's exposure in the mid-1980s, many of the liabilities, including the debt, were private rather than public. In addition, much of Malaysia's debt in the late 1990s was long-term rather than short-term in nature, again in contrast to the other crisis-affected economies.

Monetary policy and banking supervision had generally been much more prudent in Malaysia than in the other crises victims, e.g. Malaysian banks had not been allowed to borrow heavily from abroad to lend on the domestic market. Such practices involved currency and term mismatches, which increased the vulnerability of countries' financial systems to foreign bankers' confidence and exerted pressure on the exchange rate pegs. These differences have lent support to the claim that Malaysia was an innocent bystander that fell victim to regional contagion by being in the wrong part of the world at the wrong time. Such a view takes a benign perspective of portfolio investment inflows and does not recognise that such inflows are even more easily reversible and volatile than bank loan inflows (Jomo 2001). Contrary to the innocent bystander hypothesis, Malaysia's experience actually suggests greater vulnerability because of its greater reliance on the capital market. As a consequence, the Malaysian economy became hostage to international portfolio investors' confidence. Hence when government leaders engaged in rhetoric and policy initiatives that upset such investors' confidence, Malaysia paid a heavy price when portfolio divestment accelerated.

Some dangers associated with financial liberalisation have now become evident (see Eatwell 1997), but most have not been sufficiently recognised, let alone debated and addressed. Most initiatives in this regard cannot be undertaken unilaterally without great cost, as market reactions to then Malaysian Prime Minister Mahathir's critical remarks in the second half of 1997 showed (see Jomo [ed.] 2001). The few options available for unilateral initiatives need to be carefully considered and only implemented if deemed desirable. Selectively invoking instances of bad or incompetent policymaking or implementation does not justify leaving matters to liberalised markets that render systematic policymaking impossible. Instead, the experience of financial crisis emphasises the importance of creating an environment and developing the capability such that good and competent policy is effective.

Many policies need to be actively pursued through multilateral initiatives, for which governments need the support of neighbouring countries and others. Given the power of the dominant ideology that infuses the prevailing international system, asserting control over the financial system is virtually impossible without a fundamental change in priorities and thinking by the governments of the major economic powers. The currencies of a small number of countries — Germany, Japan, the United Kingdom, and the United States — were involved in more than three-quarters of currency transactions in 1995. Thus such countries have the capacity and capability to monitor and control transborder capital flows by acting in concert.

The Role of the IMF

Critical consideration of the causes and consequences of the East Asian crisis requires paying close and careful attention to the nature and implications of IMF rescue programmes and conditionalities, as well as policies favoured by international, as distinct from domestic, financial communities. IMF prescriptions and conventional policy-making wisdom urged bank closures, government spending cuts, and higher interest rates in the wake of the crises. Such contractionary measures transformed what had started as currency crises, and then become full-blown financial crises, into crises of the real economy. Thus Indonesia, South Korea, and Malaysia, which had previously enjoyed massive capital inflows in the form of short-term bank loans or portfolio investments, went into recession during 1998, following Thailand, which went into recession in 1997.

Not only did the IMF underestimate the severity of the collapse in all the East Asian economies, it also underestimated the speed and strength of recovery (IMF 1997, 1998; Lane *et al.* 1999). This suggests that the IMF not only did not understand the causes of the crises, but was also incapable of designing optimal policies in response to it. Critics still doubt whether the IMF recognised the novel elements of the crises and their implications, especially at the outset. The IMF's apparent failure to anticipate the crises in its generally glowing reports on the region prior to the crises and role in exacerbating the downturns in Indonesia, South Korea, and Thailand certainly did not inspire much confidence. In addition, even though the Philippines had long been involved in IMF programmes and supervision, it was not spared the contagion.[12] International scepticism about the IMF's role in and prescriptions for the East Asian crises is considerable.

Most economists now agree that the early IMF programmes for Indonesia, South Korea, and Thailand were ill-conceived, although they do not seem able to agree on why the IMF made such mistakes. Perhaps partly out of force of habit from dealing with situations in Africa, Eastern Europe, Latin America, and elsewhere where fiscal deficits had been part of the problem, the IMF insisted on the same prescription of deflationary policies in its early policy responses to the East Asian crises. Thus many of its programmes were effectively contractionary, though this was sometimes disguised by poorly conceived measures to provide social safety nets for the poor. Hence what started off as currency and financial crises led — partly because of policy responses recommended or imposed by the IMF — to economic recessions in much of the region in 1998. The accounts vary with the different countries involved [see Jomo 1998; *Cambridge Journal of Economics*, November 1998; Jomo (2001: Chapter 1) for an account of the Malaysian experience].

The early IMF policy prescription to raise domestic interest rates not only failed to stem capital flight, but instead exacerbated the impact of the crises, causing financial pain through currency depreciation, stock market collapses, and rising interest rates. Even if higher interest rates had succeeded in preventing capital flight, it can only be halted temporarily, and even then at great and permanent costs to productive investments in the real economy. When inflows are eventually reversed in the precipitous manner East Asia experienced from the second half of 1997, a large amount of collateral damage is inevitable.

Furman and Stiglitz (1998) provide a critical review of the literature and argue against raising interest rates to protect the exchange rate. In particular, where leveraging is high, as in East Asia, high interest rates will take a huge toll by weakening aggregate demand and increasing the likelihood and frequency of insolvencies. Unexpected interest rate hikes tend to weaken financial institutions, lower investment, and thereby reduce output. Furman and Stiglitz (1998) offer the following three main reasons why keeping interest rates low while letting the exchange rate depreciate may be a preferable option in light of the trade-off involved:

- To avoid crisis, policymakers should be more concerned about interest rate increases than about exchange rate declines (Demirguc-Kunt and Detragiache 1998; Furman and Stiglitz 1998).

- Any government intervention to stabilise the exchange rate is likely to encourage economic agents to take positions they would otherwise not take, later compelling the government to support the exchange rate to avoid the now larger adverse effects. This point is based on a moral hazard argument.

- When a government defends its currency, it is often making a one-way bet, where the expected loss is speculators' expected gain. In contrast, if the government does not wager any reserves, the gains of some speculators are simply the losses of others. Thus invoking an equity argument, they ask why borrowers, workers, firms, and others adversely affected by higher interest rates should be compelled to pay for speculators' profits.

Despite their sound fiscal balances before the crises, the IMF also asked the East Asian economies to cut government spending to restore confidence in their currencies, despite the ominous implications for economic recovery. Even though all the affected East Asian economies had been running fiscal surpluses in the years preceding the crises (except Indonesia, which had a small deficit in 1996), the IMF expected the governments to slash public expenditure. With the possible exception of Indonesia, which could not raise the financing required, the other crises-affected economies eventually ignored this advice and began to undertake Keynesian-style reflationary, counter-cyclical measures starting in the second half of 1998, which have been primarily responsible for their economic recovery.

Incredibly, the IMF did not seem to be cognisant of the subjective elements that had contributed to the crises and seemed to approach it as if it was solely due to weaknesses in the countries' macroeconomic or financial systems. Examining the changing risk premiums on Eurobonds issued by East Asia, Woo (2000) finds evidence of "irrational exuberance", implying that the potential for investor panic also existed. Moreover, even though the risk premiums on Thai Eurobonds increased by 10 basis points following the July 1997 devaluation, they jumped by four times as much with the acceptance of the IMF programme for Thailand in August 1997. This suggests that the latter's deflationary macroeconomic policies and abrupt closure of financial institutions had undermined, rather than restored, investor confidence.

Insolvent financial institutions should have been restructured so as to avoid the possibility of triggering bank runs and consequent social instability. By insisting on closing down banks and other financial institutions in Indonesia, South Korea, and Thailand, the IMF undermined much of the remaining confidence, inducing further panic in the process. Nasution (2000) points out that the IMF's way of taking insolvent banks out of Indonesia's financial system in late 1997 exacerbated the country's economic crisis. He argues that the Indonesian government should have temporarily taken over the insolvent banks rather than closing them down suddenly to sustain credit to solvent borrowers and to retain depositors' confidence. Also, even though the IMF insisted that the crises-affected governments and those subject to IMF conditionalities be more transparent, it continued to operate under considerable secrecy.

Such double standards on the part of the IMF, reflected by the priority it gave to protecting the interests of foreign banks and governments, also compromised its ostensible role as an impartial agent working in the interests of affected economies. The burden of IMF programmes invariably fell on the respective countries' domestic financial sectors and, eventually, on the public at large, who bear most of the costs of adjustment and reform. The social costs of the public policy responses have been considerable, usually involving bail outs of much of the financial sector and of the corporate sector more generally.

Unhappiness in East Asia about how the IMF responded to the East Asian crises compared with the earlier Mexican one is widespread. People generally believe that the IMF was far more generous in helping Mexico because of the interest of the US in ensuring that the tequila crisis was not seen as an adverse consequence of Mexico joining the North American Free Trade Agreement. In contrast, East Asians saw the IMF as far less generous and more demanding with all three countries, which had long seen themselves as allies of the US and of the West in general.

The IMF has invariably given priority to liabilities and other commitments to foreign banks, even though both foreign and domestic banks may have been equally irresponsible or imprudent in their lending practices. As the BIS noted: "In spite of growing strains in Southeast Asia, overall bank lending to Asian developing countries showed no evidence of abating in the first half of 1997" (Raghavan 1998). From mid-1996 to mid-1997, South Korea received US$15 billion in new loans while Indonesia received US$9 billion from the banks. Short-term lending continued to dominate, with 70 per cent due within one year, while the share of lending to private non-bank borrowers rose to 45 per cent by the end of June 1997. The banks were also actively acquiring non-traditional assets in the region, for instance, in higher-yielding local money markets and other debt securities. Most of this lending was by Japanese and European banks.

Thus Japanese and Western banks have emerged from the crises relatively unscathed and stronger than the domestic financial sectors of the crises-affected economies, which have taken the brunt of the cost of adjustment. Some merchant banks and other financial institutions were also able to make lucrative commissions from marketing sovereign debt, as the short-term private borrowing that precipitated the crises is converted into longer-term, government-guaranteed bonds under the terms of IMF programmes.

Conclusion

The central thesis of this volume then is that government intervention may be necessary during "systemic crises" when bank or corporate collapses are less likely to be resolved if simply left to market-based solutions. Our critical evaluation of Malaysia's unorthodox crisis management measures should not obscure their potential and desirability especially when such problems can be avoided or overcome by other means. Instead, we argue that better performance standards, monitoring mechanisms and institutional arrangements for financial crisis management are needed to minimise moral hazard and abuse, as well as to ensure positive outcomes.

After reviewing the 1997–98 East Asian crises above in order to draw important analytical and policy lessons, which will be elaborated later in the concluding chapter, the second chapter critically considers the influential recent literature on corporate governance because corporate governance failures have been invoked, especially in the business and finance media, to explain these crises. The third chapter turns to the Malaysian experience to show why the Malaysian economy was less vulnerable to crisis in some crucial respects, but was nonetheless a victim. It goes on to consider Malaysia's controversial policy responses, especially the capital controls of September 1998. Taken together, these three introductory chapters serve to set the context for the remainder of the volume, which considers Malaysia's experience with corporate and bank restructuring in the wake of the crisis.

Notes

1. Of course, the availability of cheap foreign funds, for example, because of a low real interest rate, can help to temporarily close both domestic savings-investments and foreign exchange gaps, especially if the funds have been well invested or deployed.
2. Financial analysts had become fixated with the current account deficit, especially since the Mexican meltdown of early 1995. In earlier times, some economies sustained similar deficits for much longer without comparable consequences. In the immediate aftermath of the Mexican crisis, several Southeast Asian economies already had comparable current account deficits, despite, or rather because of, rapid economic growth.
3. In some countries, government-owned, non-financial, public enterprises were very much part of the growth of supposedly private sector debt.
4. There is also no evidence that the stock market boom of the mid-1990s raised funds for productive investment more effectively. Indeed, the converse was true, with financial dis-intermediation from commercial banks to the stock market.
5. Even though the US economy was strengthening, the Southeast Asian economies were growing even faster.
6. In the mid-1990s, as the US dollar strengthened with the US economy, both the Germans and the Japanese allowed their currencies to depreciate against the US dollar, with relatively little disruption, in efforts to regain international competitiveness.
7. Sentiments can influence fundamentals and the health of financial systems either favourably or unfavourably (Montes 1998). In particular, the collapse of the Southeast Asian currencies because of sentiments adversely affected the viability of investments made at different exchange rates, which in turn exacerbated the domestic banking crises.

8. Montes (1998) argues that the more rural-based Southeast Asian economies were better able to carry out real devaluations from nominal changes in currency value, because their export sectors were not too tied down by supply-side inflexibilities to respond to real devaluations. After asserting that stock markets served to share risks among asset owners rather than to raise financing, he notes that, except for financial system weaknesses, Southeast Asian real sectors were relatively immune from the 1997–98 asset market frenzy.

9. Equity and portfolio investments had overtaken direct investment, loans, and trade credit in providing external financing by the 1990s. Montes (1998: 34) cites Reisen's warning that offers of foreign financing should be resisted if they "cause unsustainable currency appreciation, excessive risk-taking in the banking system, and a sharp drop in private savings". Hence, in a sentiment-driven market, currencies become too strong with the prospect of strong external financing and too weak when capital withdraws or threatens to.

10. Krugman's (1998c) attempt at theoretical catching-up is particularly worthy of consideration in light of his own previous attempts to understand related international economic phenomena as well as East Asian economic growth. As the crises were still unfolding, such an attempt was hardly definitive, especially without the benefit of hindsight. Yet, as policy was very much being made on the hoof, his attempt to highlight certain relationships were illuminating. Hence Krugman (1998c) argues that:

> It is necessary to adopt an approach quite different from that of traditional currency crisis theory. Of course Asian economies did experience currency crises, and the usual channels of speculation were operative here as always. However, the currency crises were only part of a broader financial crisis, which had very little to do with currencies or even monetary issues per se. Nor did the crisis have much to do with traditional fiscal issues. Instead, to make sense of what went wrong, we need to focus on two issues normally neglected in currency crisis analysis. These are the role of financial intermediaries (and of the moral hazard associated with such intermediaries when they are poorly regulated), and the prices of real assets such as capital and land.

11. None of the fundamentals usually emphasised seemed to have been important in the affected economies: all the governments had fiscal surpluses and none were involved in excessive monetary expansion, while inflation rates were generally low.

12. Arguably, the Philippine currency did not take quite as hard a hit as those of the other crises-affected economies, in part because its banking and accounting standards were relatively better, but also because its short-term capital inflows before the crises were relatively low.

CHAPTER 2

Crisis and Crisis Management in Malaysia, 1997–98

JOMO K.S.

F ourteen months after the East Asian currency and financial crises began with the floating of the Thai baht on 2 July 1997, then Malaysian Prime Minister Mahathir Mohamad introduced several controversial currency and capital control measures. In the last quarter of 1998, the regional turmoil came to an end as East Asian currencies strengthened and stabilised after the US Federal Reserve Bank lowered interest rates enough to reverse capital flight to the US. In the first quarter of 1999, Thailand, Indonesia and South Korea posted positive growth rates, while Malaysia's recession went into its fifth quarter. However, by the end of 1999, of the four, Malaysia's recovery was second only to South Korea's, with their stronger recoveries continuing into 2000.

This chapter considers the evolution of the Malaysian financial system and its regulation in the decade preceding the outbreak of the crisis in mid-1997. Early Malaysian policy responses from July 1997 until September 1998 are then considered. The 1–2 September policy package including capital controls are then discussed in some detail in order to distinguish the measures as well as to assess their efficacy. Thus, this chapter seeks to explain the circumstances in which the September 1998 controls were introduced as well as their likely effects.

Capital Flows and Crisis

For several decades, foreign capital inflows into Malaysia have augmented the high domestic savings rate to raise the domestic investment rate as well as Malaysian investments abroad in the 1990s. Compared to most of its neighbours in the East Asian region, the Malaysian central bank authorities were generally more cautious and prudent about financial liberalisation, both domestically and internationally. Malaysia experienced a severe banking crisis in the late 1980s, following the mid-1980s' recession and stock market collapse, when "non-performing loans" (NPLs, then defined on a six-month basis) reached 30 per cent of the total commercial banks' lending portfolios. In 1989, the authorities legislated the Banking and Financial Institutions Act (BAFIA) that sought to improve banking supervision and regulation.

Comparatively speaking, Malaysian debt was predominantly long-term rather than short-term in nature. Monetary policy as well as banking supervision in Malaysia had generally been much more prudent compared to the other crisis victims. Banks in Malaysia had not been allowed to borrow heavily from abroad to lend in the domestic market, as in the other economies. Such practices involved currency and term mismatches, which increased financial system vulnerability to foreign bankers' confidence as well as pressure on the exchange rate pegs. Thus, the Malaysian central bank regulation and earlier consolidation of the banking sector helped ensure its greater robustness compared to its neighbours.

Malaysia accumulated relatively less foreign borrowings than most other crisis-hit countries with a smaller proportion of debt of short-term maturity. For instance, in June 1997, short-term debt as a share of total reserves for Malaysia was approximately 60 per cent, significantly lower than South Korea (more than 200 per cent), Indonesia (about 170 per cent) and Thailand (just under 150 per cent). The costs of hedging foreign loans in Malaysia were relatively lower compared to its neighbours besides Singapore, though there are anecdotal claims that the central bank actually discouraged Malaysian external borrowers from hedging their debt.

Malaysia's total external debt to foreign exchange reserves ratio was becoming dangerously high before the crisis, reaching 139.6 per cent in 1996 before jumping to 298.2 per cent in 1997 (Jomo [ed.] 2001: Table 5.13). As the economic recession deepened in 1998, foreign borrowings decreased to 1996 levels, after peaking at RM29.2 billion in 1997. With a lower proportion of short-term loans compared to the other East Asian economies hit by the crisis, fluctuations in foreign bank borrowings in Malaysia have been less severe.

In the early and mid-1980s, FDI inflows were significantly augmented by increased inflows of portfolio capital, mainly to invest in the booming stock market accompanying the decade long boom from the late 1980s. Such inflows were encouraged by the promotion of "emerging market economies" by the international financial institutions from the late 1980s after the international sovereign debt crisis of the early and mid-1980s following the Volcker/US Fed-induced world recession. Thus, there was considerable, but partial and uneven financial liberalisation dating back to the 1980s, which was slowed by the mid-1980s' stock market scandals and recession as well as the subsequent banking crisis. While exercising caution and prudence with regards to private sector foreign bank borrowings, the authorities actively encouraged development of the capital market in Malaysia.

Official efforts included considerable promotion of the Kuala Lumpur's "newly emerging" stock market, growing central bank speculative activity abroad (until it lost at least RM16 billion after the sterling collapse of September 1992) and greater capital account convertibility. By splitting from the Stock Exchange of Singapore (SES), the Malaysian authorities ensured that such flows directly entered the Kuala Lumpur Stock Exchange (KLSE). Malaysia was far more successful in attracting considerable portfolio capital flows, which proved to be even more volatile than bank borrowings, whereas foreign bank borrowings figured more significantly in Korea, Thailand and Indonesia during the early and mid-1990s.

International financial liberalisation succeeded in generating net capital inflows into Malaysia, and much of East Asia during the early and mid-1990s, unlike many other developing and transitional economies that experienced net outflows. Increased foreign capital inflows reduced foreign exchange constraints, allowing the financing of additional imports, and thus, inadvertently encouraging current account deficits. Such foreign capital inflows into Malaysia also adversely affected factor payment outflows, export and import propensities, the terms of trade and capital flight, and thus, the balance of payments. But financial liberalisation also exacerbated systemic instability and reduced the scope for the developmental government interventions responsible for the region's economic miracle.

In contrast to limited influence of Malaysian industrial capital, finance capital was clearly far more influential in Malaysia, enhanced by the country's British colonial inheritance and more recent American cultural influences favouring finance over industry. The influence of financial interests was enhanced by the many and extensive investments of the Malaysian authorities in the financial sector, more than any other sector of the Malaysian economy, partly due to previous interventions to bail out banks after earlier financial crises. The stock market and other property asset price bubbles due to capital inflows induced "wealth effects" which benefited much of the middle class as well. However, there is no evidence that these portfolio capital inflows actually contributed to domestic capital formation and thus growth rates, rather than asset price bubbles and consumer binges.

After mid-1995, the Southeast Asian currency pegs to the US dollar — which had enhanced the region's competitiveness as the dollar declined for a decade after the 1985 Plaza accord — became a growing liability as the yen began to depreciate once again. The overvalued currencies became attractive targets for speculative attacks, resulting in futile, but costly defences of the Thai baht and Malaysian ringgit, and the rapid regional spread of herd panic called contagion. After the Thai baht was floated on 2 July 1997, like other currencies in the region, the ringgit came under strong pressure to depreciate, especially because — like Thailand — Malaysia had maintained large current account deficits during the early and mid-1990s. The monetary authorities' efforts to defend the ringgit actually strengthened the national currency against the greenback for a few days before the futile ringgit defence effort was given up by mid-July. The failed ringgit defence effort is widely believed to have cost over RM9 billion.

The ringgit fluctuated wildly until mid-1998, weeks before the ringgit was fixed at RM3.8 against the US dollar on 2 September 1998. While much of the downward pressure on the ringgit was external, inappropriate political rhetoric and policy measures exacerbated the situation. Malaysia's foreign exchange reserves depleted rapidly from July until November 1997, before improving in December, especially after the imposition of capital controls in September 1998.

Massive portfolio capital inflows during the early and mid-1990s had fundamentally transformed the nature of Malaysia's capital market. While holding an estimated third of the stock of the hundred largest companies comprising the Kuala Lumpur Stock Exchange (KLSE) Composite Index (KLCI), foreign institutional investors "made" or "moved" the Malaysian market. Malaysian institutions were generally too small in comparison, while the larger Malaysian institutions generally took longer-term stock positions and were less inclined to be involved in short-termism and speculation, reflected in much more active day-trading, for example. Needless to say, "retail" investors had little real influence on the market, but generally exacerbated market volatility by more speculative behaviour and greater tendencies of following — and thus increasing — the market's irrational exuberance or pessimism.

Much more global in outlook, foreign fund managers were generally more inclined to consider investing in Malaysia against alternative options elsewhere in the world. Thus, they were probably key to the phenomenon referred to as "contagion" involving cross-border investment trends. As outsiders operating with apparently limited information and incentive packages encouraging conformism and "followership", especially in the face of uncertainty and market downturns, they were also more likely to contribute to "herd" behaviour. Hence, the Malaysian stock market was the most vulnerable to both irrational exuberance and pessimism among the four most crisis-affected economies. Not surprisingly, the KLCI fell most during the East Asian crisis despite government interventions and the greater role of government controlled investors in the stock market who sought to limit and offset the downward slide.

The magnitude of gross inflows and outflows reflect the much greater volatility of these flows, often obscured by focussing on net flows. But even the net flow data indicates the relative size of these flows. A net sum of over RM30 billion of portfolio investments flowed out in the last three quarters of 1997, much more than the total net inflows from 1995, an equivalent to almost a fifth of the annual GNP. This exodus included RM21.6 billion of shares and corporate securities, and RM8.8 billion of money market instruments. In just one quarter, from July to September 1997, a net RM16 billion of portfolio investments left the country.

These differences have lent support to the claim that Malaysia was an "innocent bystander" which fell victim to regional contagion for being in the wrong part of the world at the wrong time. Such a view takes a benign perspective on portfolio investment inflows, and does not recognise that such inflows are even more easily reversible and volatile than bank loan inflows. Contrary to the "innocent bystander" hypothesis, Malaysia's experience actually suggests the greater vulnerability of its heavier reliance on the capital market. As a consequence, the Malaysian economy became hostage to international portfolio investor confidence. Hence, when the government leadership engaged in rhetoric and policy initiatives that upset such investor confidence, Malaysia paid a heavy price as portfolio divestment accelerated. The Malaysian stock market dropped dramatically from almost 1,300 in February 1997 to a low of 262 in early September 1998, 18 months later.

Policy Responses and Deepening the Crises

The resulting precipitous asset price collapses — as the share and property market bubbles burst — undermined Malaysia's heavily exposed banking system for the second time in little over a decade, causing economic recession. IMF prescriptions and conventional policy-making wisdom urged government spending cuts in the wake of the crisis. Conventional policy-making wisdom — including IMF prescriptions — raised interest rates and otherwise tightened monetary and fiscal policies (e.g. by cutting government spending) in the wake of the meltdown. Such policy responses further transformed what had started as a currency crisis into a full-blown financial crisis, and then into a crisis of the real economy as the Southeast Asian region sharply went into recession in 1998.

The ringgit's collapse was initially portrayed by then Malaysian Prime Minister Mahathir as being exclusively due to speculative attacks on Southeast Asian currencies. In a study published in mid-April 1998, the IMF acknowledged that currency speculation precipitated the collapse of the baht, but denied the role of currency speculation in the collapse of the other East Asian currencies. While currency speculation *per se* may not have brought down the other currencies, contagion undoubtedly contributed to the collapse of the other currencies in the region not protected by the large reserves held by Japan, China, Taiwan, Hong Kong and Singapore. Contagion — exacerbated by the herd-like panicky investment decisions of foreign portfolio investors who perceived the region as much more similar and integrated than it actually is (e.g. in terms of trade or investment links, or even structural characteristics) — quickly snowballed to cause massive capital flight.

As acknowledged by Mahathir, the ringgit probably fell much further than might otherwise have been the case due to international market reactions to his various contrarian statements, including his tough speech in Hong Kong on 20 September 1997, at a seminar before the Joint World Bank-IMF annual meeting. Arguing that "currency trading is unnecessary, unproductive and immoral", Mahathir argued that it should be "stopped" and "made illegal". Most damagingly, he seemed to threaten a unilateral ban on foreign exchange purchases unrelated to imports by the Malaysian authorities (which never materialised). Even before his Hong Kong speech, Mahathir had railed against George Soros (calling him a "moron") and inter-national speculators for weeks, even suggesting that dark Western conspiracies were attempting to undermine the East Asian achieve-ment. Thus, Mahathir's remarks continued to undermine confidence and to aggravate the situation until he was finally reined in by other government leaders in the region, and perhaps, some of his cabinet colleagues and kitchen cabinet advisers.

Mahathir's partly — but not entirely — ill-founded attacks reinforced the impression of official denial, by blaming the crisis entirely on foreign manipulation. The fact that there was some basis for his rantings was hardly enough to salvage his reputation in the face of an increasingly hostile Western media. Thus, until Soeharto's illness (in December 1997) and subsequent recalcitrant behaviour (in the eyes of the IMF and the international financial community) in 1998, Mahathir was demonised as the regional "bad boy". Meanwhile, some other governments in the region had little choice but to go "cap in hand" to the IMF and the US and Japanese governments, in desperate efforts to restore confidence and secure funds for the governments to settle the fast-growing non-performing privately held foreign debt liabilities.

Other official Malaysian policy responses did not help. In late August 1997, the authorities *designated* the top 100 indexed KLCI share counters. Designation required actual presentation of scrip at the moment of transaction (rather than later, as had been the practice), ostensibly to check "short-selling", which was exacerbating the stock market collapse. This ill-conceived measure adversely affected liquidity, causing the stock market to fall further. The government's threat to use repressive measures against commentators making unfavourable reports about the Malaysian economy strengthened the impression that the government had a lot to hide from public scrutiny. Anwar's mid-October 1997 announcement of the 1998 Malaysian Budget was seen by the market, i.e. mainly foreign financial interests, as only the latest in a series of Malaysian government policy measures tantamount to denial of the gravity of the crisis and its possible causes.

A post-Cabinet meeting announcement, on 3 September 1997, of the creation of a special RM60 billion fund for selected Malaysians was understandably seen as a bail out facility designed to save "cronies" from disaster. Although the fund was never properly institutionalised as announced, and government officials later denied its existence, government-controlled public funds have been deployed to bail out some of the most politically well-connected and influential business interests. These public funds comprised pension funds, the Employees Provident Fund (EPF), Petronas and Khazanah. The recipients of this assistance included Mahathir's eldest son, the publicly-listed corporation set up by the ruling party's co-operative (KUB) and the country's largest conglomerate (Renong), previously controlled by his party and believed to be ultimately controlled by Mahathir and then government Economic Adviser, Mahathir confidante, and later, second-time Finance Minister Daim. The protracted UEM-Renong saga which began in mid-November 1997 was probably most damaging. The nature of this bail out — to the tune of RM2.34 billion — gravely undermined public confidence in the Malaysian investment environment as stock market rules were suspended at the expense of minority shareholders' interests, with the KLSE losing RM70 billion in market capitalisation over the next three days.

The situation was initially worsened by the perception that Mahathir and Daim had taken over economic policy-making from Anwar, who had endeared himself over the years to the international financial community. Daim's return to the frontline of policy-making caused ambiguity as to who was really in charge from early to mid-1998, and about what to expect. Some measures introduced by the Finance Ministry and the central bank from early December 1997 and in late March 1998 were also perceived as pre-empting the likely role and impact of Mahathir's National Economic Action Council (NEAC). The establishment of the NEAC had been announced in late 1997 to be chaired by then Prime Minister, with Daim clearly in charge as executive director. Daim was later appointed Minister with Special Functions, operating from the Prime Minister's Department, in late June 1998 — right after the annual UMNO general assembly. He was subsequently made First Finance Minister in late 1998, with his protégé Mustapa Mohamed serving as Second Finance Minister while retaining the Ministry of Entrepreneurial Development portfolio.

The issue of IMF intervention in Malaysia has become the subject of some exaggeration, as various groups have rather different perceptions of the IMF's actual record and motives. For many of those critical of Malaysian government policy (not just in response to the crisis), IMF intervention was expected to put an end to all, or at least much, which they considered wrong or wished to be rid off. In the wake of the protracted wrangling between the IMF and Soeharto's government in Indonesia, this pro-IMF lobby in Malaysia saw the IMF as the only force capable of bringing about desired reforms which domestic forces could not bring about on their own. Ironically, some of them failed to recognise that the measures introduced from December 1997 were akin to what the IMF would have liked to see. These measures (*White Paper*, Box 1, pp. 25–6) included:

- Bank Negara raising its three-month intervention rate from 8.7 per cent at the end of 1997 to 11.0 per cent in early February 1998;
- drastic reductions in government expenditure; and
- redefining non-performing loans as loans in arrears for three months, not six months as before.

Such contractionary measures helped transform the financial crisis into a more general economic crisis for the country.

Tighter monetary policy from late 1997 exacerbated deflationary pressures due to government spending cuts from around the same time. Thus, contractionary macroeconomic policy responses also worsened the situation. Given the massive currency devaluation in Malaysia's very open economy, the rise of inflation at this time was virtually unavoidable, with little to be achieved by such tight macroeconomic policy. Of course, such policies were also intended to stem capital flight, which was facilitated by the long-standing official commitment to capital account convertibility. But there is little evidence of any success for such measures in the conditions of contagion as well as speculative and herd behaviour.

The Malaysian Government's *White Paper on the Status of the Malaysian Economy*, issued on 6 April 1999, sums up many factors contributing to the ongoing economic crisis as well as most policy responses. However, it did so by whitewashing Mahathir's and Daim's roles in worsening the crisis, and instead implied that Anwar Ibrahim was solely responsible for all domestic policy errors. Conversely, Anwar was not credited with the second U-turn where he attempted to reflate the economy by fiscal means from May 1998 and established the key institutions for financial restructuring and recovery, such as Danaharta, Danamodal and the Corporate Debt Restructuring Committee (CDRC). However, the White Paper did show how foreign investments were selectively encouraged to protect and save interests the regime favoured, including those who had contributed to causing the crisis. In any case, its tendentious account of recent developments then still fresh in the minds of most readers not only contradicted some facts, but was also unlikely to inspire investor confidence so badly needed to ensure economic recovery. Subsequent abuses of the debt workout process further undermined its integrity and the overall credibility of the recovery strategy.

At the time, most observers still remembered that Mahathir's KLCI "designation" ruling had drastically reduced liquidity in the stock market, precipitating a sharp collapse in late August 1997 and necessitating its cancellation a week later. Similarly, the United Engineers Malaysia Bhd (UEM) reverse takeover to bail out Renong in mid-November 1997, apparently supported by Mahathir and Daim, had resulted in a 20 per cent stock market contraction of RM70 billion in three days! Mahathir's rhetoric about various Western conspiracies against Malaysia and the region further undermined international confidence and the value of the Malaysian ringgit.

The gravity of the crisis and the difficulties of recovery were clearly exacerbated by injudicious policy responses, compromised by nepotism and other types of cronyism. However, there is little persuasive evidence that cronyism, in itself, led to or precipitated the crisis — as alleged by US Fed Chairman Alan Greenspan, then US Deputy Treasury Secretary Larry Summers and IMF Managing Director Michel Camdessus — in early 1998. All this transformed the inevitable correction of the overvalued ringgit into a collapse of both the ringgit and the Kuala Lumpur stock market as panic set in, amplified by herd behaviour and contagion. Government efforts to bail out politically influential business interests and to otherwise protect or advance such interests — usually at the expense of the public (the public purse, workers' forced savings, taxpayers or minority shareholders) — exacerbated the crisis by undermining public and foreign confidence.

Mahathir's September 1998 Recovery Package

On 1 September 1998, then Prime Minister Mahathir Mohamad announced new capital and other currency controls. This was clearly an important challenge to the prevailing orthodoxy, especially as promoted by the Fund. While it is moot how crucial the controls were for the subsequent V-shaped recovery, it is nevertheless clear that they do not seem to have caused any significant permanent damage, as predicted by some critics. Different parties in the debate now invoke the 1998 Malaysian controls for all kinds of purposes, often contributing more heat than light.

The September 1998 Package

The measures introduced on 1 September 1998 were designed to (Rajaraman 2003):

- *kill the offshore ringgit market,* by prohibiting the transfer of funds into the country from externally held ringgit accounts except for investment in Malaysia (excluding credit to residents), or for purchase of goods in Malaysia. The offshore ringgit market could only function with externally held ringgit accounts in correspondent banks in Malaysia. Thus, offshore ringgit deposits could no longer be used for this purpose. Offshore banks required freely usable access to onshore ringgit bank accounts to match their ringgit liabilities, which the new ruling prohibited. Holders of offshore deposits were given the month of September 1998 to repatriate their deposits to Malaysia. This eliminated the major source of ringgit for speculative buying of US dollars in anticipation of a ringgit crash. Large-denomination ringgit notes were later demonetised to make the circulation of the ringgit currency outside Malaysia more difficult.

- *close off access by non-residents to domestic ringgit sources* by prohibiting ringgit credit facilities to them. All trade transactions now had to be settled in foreign currencies, and only authorised depository institutions were allowed to handle transactions in ringgit financial assets.

- *shut down the offshore market in Malaysian shares* conducted through the Central Limit Order Book (CLOB) in Singapore.

- *obstruct speculative outward capital flows* by requiring prior approval for Malaysian residents to invest abroad in any form, and limiting exports of foreign currency by residents for other than valid current account purposes.

- *protect the ringgit's value and raise foreign exchange reserves* by requiring repatriation of export proceeds within six months from the time of export.

- *further insulate monetary policy from the foreign exchange market* by imposing a 12-month ban on outflow of external portfolio capital (only on the principal; interest and dividend payments could be freely repatriated).

Malaysia had so free a capital account regime leading up to the 1997 crisis, that there was even an offshore market in ringgit, perhaps the only case of an offshore market in an emerging market currency (Rajaraman 2003). Rajaraman (2003) argues that the offshore ringgit market developed, mainly in Singapore, because of the absence of a domestic market for hedging instruments. The offshore ringgit market developed in response to non-residents' demand for hedging instruments when import and export settlements were still ringgit-denominated to exempt Malaysian based importers and exporters from the need to hedge. With imports and exports now dollar-denominated as part of the package of exchange control measures of September 1998, developing such a domestic market for hedging instruments has been postponed indefinitely. However, Rajaraman insists that such markets will have to be developed over the long term as there will eventually be a need for hedging instruments once the peg is abandoned.

This offshore ringgit market then facilitated exchange rate turbulence in 1997–98. Recognising this, the September 1998 measures sought to eliminate the offshore market to insulate domestic monetary policy from the foreign exchange market during the crisis, in order to lower interest rates. Although several factors contributed to the rise in ringgit interest rates from the second half of 1997, the offshore ringgit market facilitated speculative offshore borrowing of ringgit to finance dollar purchases in anticipation of a crash in the ringgit's value. High interest rates had devastating consequences for the real economy and its banking institutions, already overexposed to share and property lending.

The policy package is generally recognised as comprehensive and cleverly designed to limit foreign exchange outflows and ringgit speculation by non-residents as well as residents, while not adversely affecting foreign direct investors.[1] The measures were also effectively enforced by the central bank. In so far as the package was successful, this has often been attributed to Malaysian conditions, particularly the adequacy of its foreign exchange reserves, its lower exposure to foreign debt and strong economic fundamentals.

However, the impact of the package can only be assessed with respect to a Malaysian counterfactual, since the various countries differed in terms of their vulnerability to the crisis. The Malaysian recovery in 1999 was weaker than South Korea's but stronger than those of Thailand and, of course, Indonesia. The speed of turnaround in the Malaysian economy — from –10.6 per cent in the second half of 1998 to –1.5 per cent in the first quarter of 1999, and positive growth in all the following quarters — was undoubtedly impressive, but not really better than the other East Asian crisis economies, all of which registered positive growth from the first quarter of 1999.

However, it is likely that the reduction in interest rates helped contain the increase in NPLs (non-performing loans) in the banking system. Standard and Poor estimated that NPLs would have risen to 30 per cent if interest rates had not fallen as sharply as they did. Also, the Federation of Malaysian Manufacturers (FMM) noted that the exchange rate peg and reduced interest rates lowered corporate uncertainty and made business planning easier (Rajaraman 2003), but again, the comparison is with the previous period, rather than trends in the other crisis economies, where exchange rate volatility and interest rates also eased from the last quarter of 1998.

The benchmark for setting the ceiling on the base lending rate (BLR) of banks — previously the three-month interbank rate[2] — was changed to the Bank Negara Malaysia (BNM) intervention rate (with the same formula as before), to enhance BNM leverage over lending rates, with the permissible margin above the benchmark reduced (by 10 per cent) from 2.5 to 2.25 percentage points. The cap on the maximum lending rate was also reduced for the first time since financial deregulation began from a spread of 4 per cent above the BLR, to 2.5 per cent (Rajaraman 2003: Table III.4). The average lending rate fell from 11.5 per cent at the end of 1997 to 9.7 per cent at the end of 1998, while the one-year real deposit rate fell from 6.6 per cent to 0.4 per cent over the same year. As inflation subsequently declined from the 1998 peak of 5.3 per cent, real interest rates rose, though nominal rates remained low.

The September 1998 measures imposed a 12-month waiting period for repatriation of investment proceeds from the liquidation of external portfolio investments. To pre-empt a large-scale outflow at the end of the 12-month period in September 1999 and to try to attract new portfolio investments from abroad, a system of graduated exit levies was introduced from 15 February 1999, with different rules for capital already in the country and for capital brought in after that date. For capital already in the country, there was an exit tax inversely proportional to the duration of stay within the earlier stipulated period of 12 months. Capital that had entered the country before 15 February 1998 was free to leave without paying any exit tax. For new capital yet to come in, the levy would only be imposed on profits, defined to exclude dividends and interest, also graduated by length of stay. In effect, profits were being defined by the new rules as realised capital gains.

As a levy applicable only at the time of conversion of ringgit proceeds into foreign exchange, and hence not a capital gains tax, it could not be offset through double taxation agreements. The 10 per cent levy on profits, even on funds invested for over 12 months, was seen as generally discouraging portfolio inflows, and even equity investments in particular, since interest and dividends were exempted. The higher levy of 30 per cent on gains from investments of less than a year, attracted especially heavy criticism on the grounds that potential investors would apply the higher levy rate of 30 per cent to all investments regardless of actual maturity periods because of the "last in, first out" rule (IMF 1999). On 21 September 1999, the higher levy was eliminated, leaving only a single rate of 10 per cent on capital gains regardless of duration of investment, which eliminated the incentive to invest longer in Malaysia. The 10 per cent levy on capital gains repatriated after investing in Malaysia for more than one year was removed from 1 January 2001.

Rajaraman (2003) has argued that "The very criticism directed at the new package helped identify what was good about it, and more importantly, underlined why it could prove of enduring worth in reducing volatility in capital flows. It is true that the levy reduced the expected rate of return on equity to foreign investors, and thus raised the required pre-levy rate of return needed relative to other markets. This was an intended effort to reduce casual entry into Malaysia, and to ensure that capital would enter only when the fundamentals justified the expectation of a higher pre-levy rate of return." However, her argument does not seem to recognise that the new arrangements would not serve as an effective deterrent to capital flight in the event of panic. With the levy only imposed on profits, investors will not be disinclined to withdraw their funds from Malaysia in the event of a stock market downturn or anticipation of one, which would then become a self-fulfilling prophecy.

Credit facilities for share as well as property purchases were actually increased as part of the package. The government has even encouraged its employees to take second mortgages for additional property purchases at its heavily discounted interest rate. Although otherwise appreciative of Malaysian measures, including the role of the central bank, Rajaraman (2003) notes that the property sector "continues to account for 40 per cent of NPLs", and that the controls introduced "in 1999 to prohibit lending for construction of high-end properties came five years too late to avert the financial sector softening that was a contributory, if not the precipitating, factor in the 1997 crisis. Controls on connected lending, now in place, again came five years too late". Ringgit credit facilities by residents to non-residents are also allowed for up to RM200,000, well below the earlier pre-1998 limit of RM5 million, though not to purchase immovable property in Malaysia.

The offshore ringgit market was wiped out by the September 1998 measures. The exchange controls, still in place, limit access to ringgit for non-residents, preventing the re-emergence of an offshore ringgit market. Free movement from ringgit to dollars for residents is possible, but dollars must be held in foreign exchange accounts in Malaysia, e.g. at the officially approved foreign currency offshore banking centre on Labuan.

For effective control of the capital account, Rajaraman (2003) maintains that it is sufficient that the foreign exchange accounts are held by banking institutions under the central bank's regulatory authority since the export of currency outside the country is not otherwise allowed. Outward portfolio flows — whether from corporates or resident individuals — require approval, which is rarely granted, though portfolio inflows are still being encouraged by the Malaysian authorities. By late 1999, international rating agencies had begun restoring Malaysia's credit rating, e.g. the Malaysian market was re-inserted on the Morgan Stanley Capital International Indices in May 2000. But as in Chile, the barriers can be lowered over time without a formal change of regime.

Did Malaysia's 1998 Controls Succeed?

Malaysia's bold measures of 1–2 September 1998 received very mixed receptions. There has been a tendency since for both sides in the debate over Malaysia's capital control measures to exaggerate their own cases, with little regard for what actually happened. Initially, market fundamentalists loudly prophesied doom for Malaysia, and after Malaysia recovered more strongly than Thailand and Indonesia, only second to South Korea, the criticisms have shifted ground, always predicting that the economic chickens must inevitably come home to roost. Besides the chequered record of Malaysian recovery, there are clearly also complications of attributing causation. Both sides often forget that capital controls are often a necessary means to other policy objectives, rather than ends in and of themselves.

Proponents of capital account liberalisation generally opposed them as a setback to the growing capital account liberalisation of the previous two decades. For them, the measures undermined freer capital movements and capital market efficiency — including net flows from the capital rich to the capital poor, cheaper funds, reduced volatility, lower inflation and higher growth — besides encouraging reversal of the larger trends towards greater economic liberalisation and globalisation. Doctrinaire neo-liberals also disagree with the IMF's interventionism, albeit minimalist, while counter-cyclical interventionists condemned the IMF's early pro-cyclicality. The Fund's own policy stance has also changed over time, and has often been shown to be doctrinaire, poorly informed, and heavily politically influenced, especially by Western interests, led by the US.

Most, though not all, heterodox economists have endorsed the Malaysian challenge to contemporary orthodoxy for the converse reasons, emphasising that financial — including capital account — liberalisation has exacerbated financial system vulnerability and macroeconomic volatility. More importantly, they emphasise that such measures create the conditions for restoring the monetary policy autonomy, considered necessary for engendering economic recovery. Many intermediate positions have also emerged, e.g. the IMF's then Deputy Managing Director Stanley Fischer endorsed Chilean-style controls on capital inflows, implying that the September 1998 Malaysian controls on outflows were far less acceptable, ostensibly because of their greater adverse consequences.

The Malaysian experience suggests that the orthodoxy's predictions of disaster (e.g. by the late Nobel Laureate Merton Miller, among others) were simply not borne out by events. However, it is much more difficult to prove that the Malaysian controls were the resounding success claimed by its proponents. After all, the regional currency turmoil came to an end throughout the region by the last quarter of 1998, probably due mainly to the US Fed's lowering of interest rates (strengthening East Asian currencies) after the regional crisis seemed to be spreading dangerously westward, with the August 1998 Russian crisis and its subsequent reverberations on Wall Street, including the collapse — and Fed-orchestrated bail out — of Long-Term Capital Management (LTCM). However, proponents of reflationary measures generally agree that fiscal measures tend to be far more effective than monetary policies in this regard.

The actual efficacy of the Malaysian measures is difficult to assess. Supporters of the Malaysian measures emphasise that Malaysia recovered more strongly in 1999 (and 2000) than neighbouring Thailand and Indonesia, both of which were subjected to onerous IMF programmes. However, Malaysia's 6.3 per cent recovery in 1999 was more modest than the 10.7 per cent achieved in South Korea. It seems likely that the stronger recoveries in Malaysia and South Korea can be attributed to stronger fiscal reflationary efforts as well as increased electronics demand (probably in anticipation of the Y2K problem in the year 2000).

Since South Korea was also subjected to an IMF programme, one cannot attribute the different rates of recovery in 1999 to different monetary policy measures or IMF conditionalities at this stage. Before that, Thai interest rates — long well above Malaysian levels — fell below Malaysian rates after September 1998, after being well above the Malaysian rates for years (Jomo [ed.] 2001: 206, Figure 7.1). This suggests that the US Fed's lowering of interest rates did more to reduce interest rates in the East Asian region than the September 1998 Malaysian initiatives did. However, this is also consistent with the general observation that monetary policy is far less effective than fiscal measures in reflating the economy.

Malaysian Prime Minister Mahathir's September 1998 capital controls were correctly seen as a bold rejection of both market orthodoxy as well as IMF market-friendly neo-liberalism. Where Thailand, South Korea and Indonesia had gone cap in hand — humiliatingly accepting IMF imposed conditions — to secure desperately needed credit, the Malaysian initiative reminded the world that there are alternatives to capital account liberalisation. For many, enthusiastic support for the Malaysian controls and claims of its success are crucial in the opposition to market fundamentalism as well as Fund neo-liberalism.

The capital control measures were significantly revised in February 1999. The modifications recognised some problematic consequences of the capital controls regime, and represented attempts to mitigate them. As of 1 September 1999, the September 1998 regime was fundamentally transformed with the end of the original curbs on capital outflows. There have since been no new curbs on inflows, but rather, strenuous efforts to encourage the return of capital inflows, including short-term capital.

Neo-liberal critics have claimed that the reduced inflows of foreign direct investment since 1996 have been due to the reduced credibility of the Malaysian authorities after its imposition of the September 1998 controls. However, there is considerable evidence of a decline of FDI throughout Southeast Asia, including those countries that did not close their capital accounts. The more plausible argument would be that the 1997–98 crises drew dramatic attention to Southeast Asia's declining competitiveness and attractiveness, compared to, say, China.

Meanwhile, many opponents of capital account liberalisation have gone to the other extreme, with some wishful exaggeration about what the Malaysian measures actually implied and achieved. For example, one supporter has extolled the controls' ostensibly virtuous consequences for labour with scant regard for the Malaysian authorities' self-confessed motive of saving big business interests, ostensibly in order to protect jobs for workers. The desirability of some measures is also in doubt as evidence mounts of favouritism or cronyism in their implementation (Johnson and Mitton 2001) and the dubious contribution of rescued interests to national economic recovery efforts (Tan 2002; Wong 2002).

So, did Malaysia's September 1998 selective capital control measures succeed? The merits and demerits of the Malaysian government's regime of capital controls in dealing with the regional currency and financial crises will continue to be debated for a long time to come as the data does not lend itself to clearly supporting any particular position. Proponents can claim that the economic decline came to a stop soon after, and the stock market slide turned around, while opponents can say that such reversals have been more pronounced in the rest of the region.

Industrial output, especially for manufacturing, declined even faster after the introduction of capital controls in Malaysia until November 1998, and continued downward in January 1999 before turning around. Except for a few sectors (notably electronics), industrial output recovery has not been spectacular since then, except in comparison with the deep recession the year before. Meanwhile, unemployment has risen, especially affecting those employed in construction and financial services. Domestic investment proposals were almost halved, while "green field" FDI seems to have declined by much less, though cynics claim actual trends were obscured by faster processing of applications as well as subsequent reconsideration and approval of previously rejected applications (see Jomo [ed.] 2001: Figure 7.2).

As is generally recognised, the one-year lock-in of foreign funds in the country was too late to avert the crisis, or to lock in the bulk of foreign funds that had already fled the country. Instead, the funds "trapped" were those that had not already left in the preceding 14 months, ironically and inadvertently "punishing" those investors who had not already taken their funds out of Malaysia.

It appears that, at best, the capital controls' actual contribution to the strong recovery in 1999–2000 was ambiguous. At worst, it may have slowed down the recovery led by fiscal counter-cyclical measures and the extraordinary demand for electronics, thus explaining the weaker recovery in Malaysia compared to South Korea. In the longer term, some critics claim that it diminished the likely recovery of foreign direct investment — which compelled the authorities to seek more domestic sources of economic growth — though the evidence for this is ambiguous as the entire region has experienced diminished post-crisis FDI. More importantly, the regime remains untested in checking international currency volatility, as such instability abated throughout the region at around the same time, due to the US Fed's lowering of interest rates. Although recovery of the Malaysian share market, which had declined much more than other stock markets during the crisis, lagged behind the other (relatively smaller) markets in the region, not too much should be made of this.

Malaysia was fortunate in the timing of the imposition of capital controls if, indeed, as stated by Mahathir in his speech to the symposium on the first anniversary of the controls, it came about almost in desperation. At the time it was introduced, the external environment was about to change significantly, while the economy had seen the outflow of the bulk of short-term capital, so that in a very real sense, the regime was never tested. If the turmoil of the preceding months had continued until the end of 1998, or beyond, continued shifts and re-pegging would have been necessary, with consequent deleterious effects.

Clearly, the ringgit peg brought a welcome respite to business-men after over a year of currency volatility. But, as noted earlier, exchange rate volatility across the region also effectively abated shortly thereafter, with the later Brazilian and other crises not renewing such volatility in the region. Moreover, it is ironic that an ostensibly nationalistic attempt to defend monetary independence against currency speculators should, in effect, hand over determination of the ringgit's value to the US Federal Reserve with the dollar peg.

If the US dollar had strengthened significantly against other currencies, Malaysia may have had to re-peg against the US dollar to retain export competitiveness. In the event, the greenback initially weakened due to the lowered US interest rates. After strengthening from 1999, it has weakened again since 2001, which has put much less pressure for re-pegging or de-pegging. For reasons which are not entirely clear, there does not seem to be any inclination for the Mahathir government to get off the peg, though it is unclear how long the peg will last after his retirement in October 2003.

While interest rates were undoubtedly thus brought down by government decree in Malaysia, the desired effects were limited. Interest rates came down dramatically across the region, in some cases, even more than in Malaysia, without others having to resort to capital controls. For example, while interest rates in Thailand were much higher than in Malaysia for over a year after the crisis began, they declined below Malaysian levels during September 1998 (see Jomo [ed.] 2001: Figure 7.1).

Perhaps more importantly, loan and money supply growth rates actually declined in the first few months after the new measures were introduced despite central bank threats to sack bank managers who failed to achieve the 8 per cent loan growth target rate for 1998. It has become clear that credit expansion has been a consequence of factors other than capital controls or even low interest rates. Across the region, especially in South Korea and Thailand, counter-cyclical spending also grew, again without resorting to capital controls.

The Malaysian authorities' mid-February 1999 measures effectively abandoned the main capital control measure introduced in September 1998, i.e. the one-year lock-in. While foreign investors were initially prohibited from withdrawing funds from Malaysia before September 1999, this was revised in February 1999 to allow earlier withdrawals after paying a scaled exit tax (pay less for keeping funds for a longer period in Malaysia), in the hope that this would reduce the rush for the gates come September 1999. Meanwhile, in an attempt to attract new capital inflows, new investors would only be liable for a less onerous tax on capital gains.

As noted earlier, it is unlikely that the capital gains tax effective from February 1999 will actually deter exit in the event of panic as investors rush to get out cutting their losses. At best, however, it served to discourage some kinds of short-selling from abroad owing to the much higher capital gains tax rate on withdrawals within less than a year of 30 per cent, as opposed to 10 per cent. The differential capital gains exit tax rate may have discouraged some short-selling from abroad, but did little to address other possible sources of vulnerability and, as emphasised above, would not have deterred capital flight in the event of financial panic. In September 1999, the capital gains exit tax rate was set at a uniform 10 per cent, thus eliminating the only feature of the February 1999 revised controls that might have deterred short-selling from abroad.

Effectively, Malaysia remains virtually defenceless in terms of new control measures in the event of a sudden exodus of portfolio capital in future. Admittedly, however, this is not the most urgent problem for the time being, in light of the limited international interest in Malaysia's capital market. In mid-1994, as the rising stock market renewed foreign portfolio investors' interest in the Malaysian market, those who stood to gain from a stock market bubble success-fully lobbied for the early 1994 controls on portfolio capital inflows to be abandoned. This reversal later rendered Malaysia vulnerable to the flight of portfolio capital of 1997–98, reflected in the collapse of about four-fifths of the stock market.

By setting the peg at RM3.8 to the US dollar on 2 September 1998, after it had been trading in the range of RM4–4.2 per US dollar, the Malaysian authorities were then seeking to raise the value of the ringgit. In mid-September 1998, however, the other currencies in the region strengthened after the US Federal Reserve Bank lowered interest rates in the aftermath of the Russian and LTCM crises, strengthening the yen and other regional currencies. Thus, the ringgit became undervalued for about a year thereafter, which — by chance rather than by design — boosted Malaysian foreign exchange reserves from the trade surplus, largely due to import compression, as well as some exchange rate-sensitive exports. Malaysia's foreign exchange reserves depleted rapidly from July until November 1997, before improving in December, and then, especially after the imposition of capital controls in September 1998 (Jomo [ed.] 2001: Figure 5.10). Thus, the ringgit undervaluation may have helped Malaysian economic recovery, but certainly not in the way the authorities intended when pegging the ringgit in September 1998.

While the undervalued ringgit may have favoured an export-led recovery strategy in 1998–99 and since 2001, this certainly was not the intent. (Then, as now, government efforts have been focussed on a domestic-led recovery strategy.) The undervalued ringgit is said to have had a (unintended) "beggar-thy-neighbour" effect. Due to trade competition, the undervalued ringgit is said to have discouraged other regional currencies from strengthening earlier for fear of becoming relatively uncompetitive with regards to Malaysian production costs and exports, though the evidence for this claim remains unclear. There were also fears that the weak Southeast Asian currencies might cause China's authorities to devalue the renminbi, which could have had the undesirable effect of triggering off another round of "competitive devaluations", with concomitant dangers for all.

The low volume of actual capital outflows since the end of the lock-in on 1 September 1999 has been interpreted in different ways. One view was that since the stock market had recovered and could be expected to continue to rise, there was little reason to flee. A second view emphasised the role of the nominal exchange rate, which has been fixed against the US dollar at RM3.8. With the greenback perceived to be still strengthening then, there was little exchange rate risk to discourage investors from holding ringgit. A third perspective suggested that the capital controls were probably unnecessary, having been introduced 14 months after the crisis began, i.e. after most of the capital flight had already taken place.

Taking the Rajaraman (2003) argument further, Kaplan and Rodrik (2001) have argued that the controls averted another crisis that had yet to hit Malaysia. They note that the offshore overnight ringgit market (principally in Singapore) interest rates had remained at high levels (around 40 per cent) for some months, putting tremendous upward pressure on domestic interest rates. A leading Malaysian neo-liberal economist, Thillainathan has disputed this assertion, claiming a very thin, and mainly speculative offshore market despite the huge amount of ringgit held abroad (reputedly RM25–30 billion). The significance of these conflicting claims can ultimately only be settled empirically.

Notes

1.   The Statutory Reserve Ratio (SRR) was brought down abruptly from 13.5 per cent — to which it had been raised in 1996–97 to contain liquidity as part of an initially orthodox response to downward pressure on the ringgit — to 4 per cent from 1998 (Rajaraman 2003: Table III.6). As banks were not keen to lend to private sector customers after the crisis began, they bought the government bonds used to finance the Danaharta asset management agency (to restore bank liquidity by taking over NPLs) and the Danamodal bank recapitalisation agency.

2.   The benchmark was 0.8 (three-month inter bank rate)/(1-SRR) (BNM 1999).

CHAPTER 3

Corporate "Bail Outs"

WONG SOOK CHING

The contemporary discussion of corporate "bail outs" has largely emerged from the literature dealing with crisis management or policy responses. However, the recent growth in influence of Anglo-American paradigms for corporate finance and corporate governance has greatly redefined the terms of this discourse in recent years. Hence, it is necessary to introduce the new terms of this discourse, particularly since some terms are used differently in different discourses.

Concepts and Parameters

At this juncture, different terms employed here need to be clarified. Corporate governance has been defined as "the legal and institutional arrangements governing the behaviour of an economic entity, by which owners, creditors, markets and the government compel or induce agents to behave according to the interests of the principals, or those of the broader society" (Lanyi and Lee 1999: 19).[1] The discourse on corporate governance is very much based on the distinction between principals and agents, and involves two key elements.

First, the structure of incentives and rules facing agents with respect to issues such as lending, borrowing, bankruptcy, the rights of directors, compensation, and employment. Second, the structure of information flows from agents to principals, i.e. the rules and incentives affecting accountability, transparency and information disclosure. Corporate and financial governance operates through five channels: owners, creditors, government regulation, market competition and internal organisation.[2]

The government plays an important role in setting the rules by which private actors operate (i.e. influencing actions as they respond to incentives and disincentives). "Good" governance is generally characterised by effectiveness, transparency,[3] accountability, predictability, integrity, equity and participation. Improvements to corporate governance, e.g. by modifying the broad regulatory framework, involve medium and/or long-term commitments. (The role of government will be discussed in more detail below.)

For the OECD, "insolvency" is defined as "[T]he fact of being unable to pay one's debts or discharge one's liabilities". However, as suggested by Armour (2001), it is essential to distinguish between (i) "balance sheet insolvency"; (ii) cash flow insolvency (or "financial distress"); (iii) economic failure (or "economic distress"); (iv) liquidation; (v) reorganisation; and (vi) insolvency proceedings or "bankruptcy" (e.g. Wruck 1990: 421–2; Belcher 1997: 39–55), in order to assess the right measures to undertake.

Balance sheet insolvency is an accounting concept (Belcher 1997: 46–8). It indicates that the book value of a firm's assets is less than that of its liabilities. This differs from "cash flow" insolvency,[4] where a firm is unable to repay its *debt when it falls due* (see also The Insolvency Services website <http://www.insolvency.gov.uk>). In English law, such inability may be inferred from a company's failure to pay, on demand, a debt which is due.[5] "Financial distress", on the other hand, refers to the condition experienced by a firm having difficulty paying its creditors. Although there are some terminological differences among authors,[6] the phrase is often used to refer to the condition of a firm in substantial default on its debt obligations (e.g. Gilson *et al.* 1990: 325; Wruck 1990: 422). Following this definition, "financial distress" is similar to "cash flow" insolvency.

Since Armour (2001) defines these terms simply and understandably, most of his definitions will be employed here. For Armour (2001), financial distress depends on the structure of repayments of outstanding debt obligations, and the nature of the assets available to satisfy them, to a far greater extent than the balance sheet test of insolvency. Illiquid assets and large repayment obligations may mean that a firm, which is solvent in a balance-sheet sense, cannot meet its debt obligations as they fall due. Conversely, a firm, which has significant growth opportunities and debt repayments spread over a number of years, may be insolvent in a balance sheet sense, but may nonetheless be able to pay its debts as they fall due.

Solvency should be distinguished from economic viability (White 1989). Insolvency is concerned with the relationship between a firm's assets or cash flows, and the amount of debt in its financial structure. Viability is a function of the net present value of its business as a going concern. A corporation is economically-viable if and only if the business has a going concern value greater than the value of its assets sold on a break-up basis, and also greater than zero.[7] To put it differently, its assets are being put to higher value use.[8] "Economic distress" refers to lack of economic viability, while all economically distressed firms *will* also become financially distressed.[9] The opposite, however, does not necessarily hold. A firm with an economically viable business *may* become financially distressed, simply because it has taken on more debt than it can service.

The terms "liquidation" and "reorganisation" refer to consequences or *outcomes* of financial distress. According to Bebchuk (1998), when a corporation becomes insolvent and bankruptcy proceedings commence, the corporation will be either liquidated or reorganised. In this context, liquidation simply implies the conversion of a firm's assets into cash by sale. This should be distinguished from its usual usage as a synonym for winding-up proceedings. Although liquidation is a necessary aspect of winding-up proceedings, it can also occur in other procedures, such as administrative receivership (see Keen Phillips' website <http://www.keen-phillips.co.uk/>).[10] The sale of assets can take two forms — either on a "going concern" basis, which involves sale of the entire business, including goodwill and other intangibles, or on a "break-up" basis, where assets are sold piecemeal.

Reorganisation here refers to the financial restructuring of a financially distressed firm. Claimants exchange their old claims against the firm for new ones, which will necessarily be less than the face value of their old claims because the firm has been unable to pay its debt. A reorganisation is functionally equivalent to a going-concern liquidation, in which existing claimants are the purchasers (Baird 1986). There are differences between these and various other types of legal (corporate) insolvency procedures (known as "bankruptcy" in the US) related to them.[11]

According to Claessens (1998), "restructuring" refers to several related processes — recognising financial losses, restructuring claims and reorganising the operations of corporations and banks. In cases of "systemic" restructuring, the institutional framework for the financial and corporate sector undergoes major changes in tandem with these restructuring processes. Recognition involves allocation of existing losses. Losses can be allocated to: shareholders by dilution;[12] depositors and external creditors,[13] by reduction of (the present value of) their claims; or the government and hence, the public at large, through increased taxes and expenditure cuts. Restructuring financial claims can take many forms — rescheduling (extension of maturities), lower interest rates, debt-for-equity swaps, debt forgiveness, indexing interest payments to earnings, and so on. Operational restructuring, an ongoing process, includes improvements in efficiency and management, reductions in staff and wages, asset sales, enhancing marketing efforts, and so on, with the expectation of increased profitability and cash flow.

Restructuring will have to be assessed on a case-by-case basis. Claessens (1998) provides the following classification of corporations — those that are profitable in the medium-term, those that cannot cover their financial costs [financially, but not economically distressed], and those that cannot cover their financial, labour and material costs [financially and economically distressed]. For him, the first probably do not require any financial assistance, the second have potential for financial relief, while the third are candidates for liquidation.[14] Obviously, projected medium-term profitability is contingent on the intensity of operational restructuring and overall economic conditions.

It should now be easier to understand the definition of a bail out and associated difficulties. Bail outs involve assistance to corporations that would have "exited" from the marketplace — due to market forces — if not for such assistance (Financial Supervisory Commission, South Korea, 1999). Hence, bail outs involve government financial assistance to *apparently* non-viable corporations.[15]

According to Bansfield (1995), clear-cut forms of bail out include the government providing a "failed entity" with grants or cheap loans, or allowing it to write off creditors without liability, so that it can resume business operations despite past failure. Unlike a bail out, a "workout", as defined by the Financial Supervisory Commission (FSC) of South Korea, involves creditor financial institutions working closely with and providing support for an *economically viable* corporation. Hence, workouts require objective assessment of viability, involving transparent and fair procedures. This is synonymous with the government "bailing in" corporations, rather than bailing them out by providing temporary financing where needed (to catalyse or complement private funds), *conditional* on corporate reforms.

Bail outs are often associated with "cronyism" since it is the common assumption that government officials will try to aid corporations that have influence over them. Bail outs can take numerous forms. According to Adam and Cavendish (1995: 15), "cronyism is the distribution of rentier opportunities to companies controlled by politicians, retired bureaucrats, parties in the ruling coalition and politically well-connected businessmen, which in turn 'raised concerns about the transparency of government policymaking and implementation'". Yoshihara, on the other hand, views crony capitalists as "rent-seeking 'private-sector businessmen who benefit enormously from close relations' with government leaders by obtaining 'not only protection from foreign competition, but also concessions, licenses, monopoly rights, and government subsidies (usually in the form of soft loans)', resulting in 'all sort of irregularities' in the economy" (Yoshihara 1988: 3–4, 71).

However, a "rent", like a bail out, is in itself neither good nor evil since rents and even rent-seeking *may or may not be output-enhancing*, depending on how and why they are obtained and deployed. Financial assistance given to firms would involve the transfer of rents. Put differently, bail outs can be seen as state-provided rents in the form of financial assistance or other "protection" against market discipline. Such rent allocations can be socially undesirable as they involve allocating resources to aid failed firms, but may also be justified as desirable to conserve existing economic capacities and capabilities. In the latter circumstance then, the crucial question may well be the terms and conditions of providing such bail outs, rather than the provision of the bail out in itself. This chapter considers the debate between those favouring such government interventions and those opposed to all such bail outs.

Are Corporate Bail Outs Desirable?

The interconnected relations between banks and corporations have created connections that can be extreme in their effects — exceptional and impressive growth when the environment proves favourable for a virtuous cycle, or severe contraction of output when the reverse happens, resulting in a vicious cycle. In other words, there are positive externalities or synergies in the former case, and negative externalities and synergies in the latter.

A "systemic crisis"[16] is especially paralysing since it involves the contraction of both financial as well as corporate sectors. Such a crisis could prove catastrophic, imposing high costs in terms of foregone economic output and employment, slowing investments leading to a credit crunch and other developments that could well lead to permanent repercussions for the country's future economic prospects. The desire to ameliorate such crises and their consequences could thus well justify appropriate government interventions.

Neo-liberals perceive bail outs by governments as preventing markets and market signals from efficiently allocating scarce resources. Bail outs may also result in public and private funds (if banks are required to roll over and write off bad debts) being allocated to more deserving corporations that should remain in the market.[17] Hence, governments are seen as obstructing the "natural selection" of firms and preventing "survival of the fittest" from taking place in line with the "social Darwinist" view that weak or uneconomic corporations should be weeded out, so that successful and solvent companies can take their place, with funds flowing to these companies instead (Ohanga 1999). Firms that are economically and therefore financially distressed should be liquidated for capital markets to function well, with positive externalities for other markets as well.

Those advocating bail outs are aware that their arguments contradict the orthodox "free market" view that presumes that the demise of "weak" and "nonviable" corporations will naturally lead to greater efficiency in the marketplace.[18] However, corporate liquidity problems may be due to various factors other than those reflecting the viability and feasibility of business investments or operations.

"Too Big to Fail"

And even if the corporation is not viable because of permanent (rather than temporary) decline in demand, orderly — as opposed to sudden — exit of the corporation may be desirable or preferable to contain adverse side effects. Furthermore, Enoch *et al.* (1999) point out that allowing firms to collapse, solely on the basis of financial and operational criteria, will not provide a desirable solution for banks and corporations that are weak, but deemed strategically essential, or of systemic importance to the economy. It may not be feasible to close a very *large* bank or corporation in an orderly fashion, or even one that dominates or is strategic in a country, region or sector (Enoch *et al.* 1999). The fate of other linked firms and industries as well as their financiers may be at stake when a crucial or strategic industry or firm is allowed to collapse. Likewise, a corporation that has huge borrowings from banks or has a special niche in the credit market may cause the banks to become insolvent by defaulting, thereby aggravating or exacerbating the banking crisis.[19]

Bailing out corporations that are considered "too big to fail", i.e. as being of systemic or strategic importance, may thus become unavoidable or the "lesser evil" because doing otherwise could lead to greater negative externalities (through domino or ripple effects, for example) adversely affecting the real economy, especially production, investment and unemployment.[20] According to Wijnbergen (1997: 55), loss-making corporations kept *temporarily afloat* will allow workers to, at least, be productively engaged. If workers create enough value added to pay the excess of their own wages over what it would cost the government in terms of unemployment expenses [including the administrative and other transaction costs of "social security", unemployment insurance, dole, social safety net and other provisions (if any)], the government would actually be better off from a fiscal point of view. There are also some circumstances when insolvent [and nonviable] companies may need to be rescued in order to rescue (at least in the short term) viable *businesses* belonging to strategic groups (Ohanga 1999).[21] Allowing corporations to "exit" with adverse consequences for otherwise viable linked companies can hardly be deemed desirable, e.g. in terms of "creative destruction".[22]

However, all these counter-arguments must be weighed against the fact that bail outs entail high fiscal costs, often borne by the public through higher taxes and lower public expenditure for other purposes. Unlimited deposit guarantees, open-ended liquidity support, repeated recapitalisations, debtor bail outs and regulatory forbearance add significantly and sizably to fiscal costs.[23] Furthermore, liquidity support may prolong crises, as crisis recovery takes longer and output loss is bigger. For Honohan and Klingebiel (2000: 3), "the assumption by government of large and unforeseen bail out costs can destabilise the fiscal accounts, triggering high inflation and currency collapse — costly in themselves — as well as adding to the deadweight cost of taxation".

With respect to the argument that bail outs are needed to check unemployment, bailing out corporations may not be the only or best way to contain the unemployment problem during a crisis. The government can opt for direct (re)nationalisation instead, preferably involving a change of management. As long as earlier problems are not addressed, they will continue to hamper turning around and revitalising the corporation, or worse, provide new opportunities to the managers, owners and their political as well as business associates to abuse the bail out facilities. Nevertheless, nationalisation in such circumstances has its own risks and costs, since eventually, the government will be under renewed pressure to re-privatise these corporations. The government should not be taken advantage of in order to socialise losses and liabilities at the public expense while facilitating the privatisation of profits, lucrative assets and natural monopolies. This process of re-privatisation of "state-owned" corporations or banks can be costly and time consuming if met by strong employee resistance, bureaucratic delays, official reluctance to relinquish power and control, and/or corruption.

Other studies suggest that acquisitions (or takeovers)[24] by "vulture investors" can fulfil the role of taking over financially ailing (cash-strapped) corporations while maintaining employment (usually, with some down-sizing).[25] Hotchkiss and Mooradian (1997) argue that improvements in performance (relative to pre-default times) are greater when a "vulture" joins the board, becomes CEO or chairman, or gains control of the firm. Vulture investors seem to discipline managers of companies in financial distress, thereby minimising moral hazard problems. However, this may also only be due to the vulture capitalists' interest in restructuring assets to maximise short-term financial returns to their investments. However, the "vulture" option is sometimes not as attractive as suggested by their theoretical arguments since potential bidders in the same industry are also likely to be financially distressed and thus constrained in their ability to raise funds to acquire the bankrupt firm.[26] The price bid for a bankrupt firm may be low, as with "fire-sales" of assets. In Shleifer and Vishny's (1992) model, the winning bidder *may* not be the firm that values the assets most (see also Krugman 1998c).

According to Gertner and Picker (1992), asymmetric information may also impede "efficient" acquisitions of distressed firms. Potential bidders, particularly those from outside the target industry, *may* be poorly informed, not only with respect to the firm's value, but also with respect to the best use of its assets. In general, however, even bidders with experience and knowledge of the industry face the "lemons problem". In a "market for lemons", firms available for sale are more likely to be deemed bad. Hence, this option will probably result in undervaluation of asset values.

Stein (1988) argues that takeover *pressure* can be counter-productive if it "induces" managers to sacrifice long-term interests in order to boost current returns to pacify stockholders. If stockholders are imperfectly informed, *temporarily* low earnings may cause the stock to be undervalued, increasing the probability of takeover at an undervalued price. This may switch the management's focus away from enhancing long-term viability to maximising current profitability, i.e. promoting "myopic" — or short-sighted — management.[27]

Corporations that invest in ventures that require long gestation periods (and involve greater uncertainty) are thus more likely to be perceived to be less efficient and profitable, even though they *may* well be very profitable in the longer term.[28] A similar fate could befall a corporation pursuing a "social" objective that may be providing a subsidised service (e.g. infrastructure or public transportation) that improves public or consumer welfare. Distressed corporations are thus more likely to be subject to "ill-informed" and "unfair" takeovers (see also Haan and Riyanto 2000).

Many have argued that bail outs of "large" firms promote "moral hazard",[29] potentially prolonging recovery and increasing the likelihood of crisis recurrence. The managements of these corporations will have little incentive to restructure to enhance efficiency, confident in their knowledge that being "too big to fail" will guarantee subsequent bail outs of future failures. By bailing out firms, the government signals the likelihood of future bail outs, not only encouraging moral hazard, but also incurring costs and reducing resources for future growth. Nonetheless, as pointed out by Frankel (1998), even though the concern for moral hazard is valid, there is a danger of exaggerating it. Actions in one area can generate (partly) offsetting responses in others. However, that is not, in itself, a reason not to take action. For example, while drivers may react to seat belts and airbags by driving faster and less safely than otherwise, that is not a reason to dispense with airbags.

Chang (2000), on the other hand, argues that if the owner or management believes that a financial injection for a bail out is conditional upon change of ownership and top management if the firm continues to do badly, then they have a strong incentive to drastically improve management of the corporation.[30] As such, bailing out "large" firms *per se* need not promote moral hazard. Government bail outs only encourage moral hazard when the bail outs are not accompanied by strict conditions, e.g. punishment for poor management and/or tough terms for financial and operational restructuring. Therefore, bail outs may not promote moral hazard if proper incentive (and disincentive) systems and disciplining mechanisms are in place.

Economic Sovereignty

For some proponents, bail outs are essential for maintaining national sovereignty in the economic sphere. If domestic corporations, especially in developing countries (probably infant industries seeking to achieve dynamic comparative advantage), are allowed to become insolvent and bankrupt, foreign enterprises may come to dominate the national economy.[31] Some would argue that if the "rescued"[32] corporation is not economically viable because the corporation is not able to compete effectively due to operational and managerial inadequacies, then these firms should be taken over by foreign firms, or simply be allowed to die out if, the management is incapable of competing internationally without subsidy or protection. In this case, the firm becomes economically distressed because of inadequate skills, training, learning by doing, lack of competitiveness and other factors. This situation does not involve moral hazard, as is sometimes alleged, since moral hazard occurs when the firm having the capacity to improve performance has an incentive not to do so.

Such operational and managerial inadequacies may be the result of corporations being granted "excessive" protection and privileges (i.e. rents) — high tariffs, subsidies, concessions, monopoly rights, contracts without going through competitive bidding, and so forth — while not being subjected to disciplining mechanisms or performance standards, thereby weakening the imperative to achieve cost and/or quality competitiveness.[33] Hence, bailing out poorly performing corporations simply to avoid losing ownership to foreigners, but with no achievable plan to achieve international competitiveness in the medium term becomes difficult to defend. If (foreign) private investors are interested in acquiring these firms, this may involve injection of private funds and expertise that may be beneficial to the firm and the economy despite the adverse consequences of foreign control of the industry. However, the government or domestic owners have other options, e.g. retain control of the corporation while gaining the services of foreign professionals, experts and consultants where necessary, taking into account the "exorbitant fees" and limited commitments involved.

Some argue that bail outs are necessary in the Malaysian context because allowing Bumiputera or Malay controlled corporations to collapse would negate earlier gains from its New Economic Policy (NEP) inter-ethnic ownership redistribution programme. The NEP's patronage-based redistributive system has involved strong links between ruling politicians and much of the corporate elite (Gomez & Jomo 1999; Nesadurai 1998). Restructuring strategies are likely to be influenced by government leaders wishing to protect their corporate interests, proxies, allies and supporters. The Malay political elite's political and economic interests seem intimately tied to the NEP's ethnic redistributive policies.[34] After three decades, an entrenched system of ethnic patronage and redistribution has meant that the government is *unwilling* to give up this programme and the power as well as privileges it entails.

While the Malaysian ethnic redistribution policies (under the NEP to reduce inter-ethnic socio-economic disparities) may be deemed morally desirable or politically necessary, its benefits have not been evenly widespread among ethnic Malays, but rather, concentrated in the hands of politically well-connected businessmen.[35] Hence, the bail outs justified on such redistributive grounds have similarly benefited even fewer. Many Malaysian bail outs have been abused to mainly benefit the politically best connected distressed few, with the costs socialised. Needless to say, however, the supposed interests of the entire Bumiputera community and employees of these enterprises have been regularly invoked to legitimise and justify the bail outs.

In deciding whether bail outs are indeed welfare increasing or decreasing, we must compare the relevant benefits and costs of undertaking bail outs, which often involve massive public funds and affect national interests and welfare. Focusing only on the costs or problems associated with bail outs, without reference to the potential benefits accruing from bail outs, as well as the costs and benefits of alternative options, will provide an incomplete analysis biased against bail outs, and undermine assessment of the "best" or "optimum" path to take.

If a "corporate rescue" or bail out is to be conducted, it must be well managed to limit undesirable political pressures and to ensure a feasible restructuring programme to ensure corporate viability and to protect the national interest. Bail outs can lead to desirable outcomes if conducted or implemented as part of a viable programme with tough, but feasible conditions. If appropriate negative and positive incentives are in place, economic agents should react positively to incentives, thereby minimising the moral hazard problem.

Bail outs of corporations can lead to adverse consequences if there are no conditions attached to financial, operational or managerial practices to improve corporate performance and to punish managers and owners for failure to improve performance. If these conditions are not strictly enforced, the government will fail to create a credible threat. Balancing the costs against the benefits of a bail out *may* justify the desirability of bailing out some corporations under certain conditions, after considering the costs to society, including negative externalities or spill-over effects. Besides "economic" viability, one also needs to consider the equity impact in assessing policy measures.

Bail outs conducted in a non-transparent manner for political motives, could reduce public and investor confidence as well as policy credibility, thereby undermining medium- and long-term private, including foreign direct investment inflows, adversely affecting economic development in the medium and long term. This calls for the transparency of bail out processes, including the corporations being assisted, and strong arguments, supported with credible evidence, for assisting these corporations. Views of the appropriate government role in dealing with systemic crises are discussed next. (However, detailed discussion of winding-up procedures, bankruptcy proceedings and "break-up basis" liquidation is beyond the scope of this study.)

Concluding Remarks

Given the exceptional and distinct circumstances facing the East Asian economies in 1997/98, it was reasonable for government bail outs to regain control over their respective economy, especially in light of market failures and poorly functioning market mechanisms. Hence, bail outs *per se* are neither "good" nor "bad". They are not necessarily detrimental from an economic perspective as commonly perceived.

Though bail outs are often associated with cronyism, patron-client relations, and moral hazard, they do not apply to all circumstances. To analyse whether bail outs do indeed result in greater socially "acceptably" net economic benefits, one must balance the benefits against the costs of bail outs. It is their nature, implementation and outcome that determine the net effects. Therefore, once a measure is selected, it must be conducted under strict supervision, aided by an effective regulatory framework, disciplining mechanisms and/or penalisation of "irresponsible and ill-management" where necessary, to yield desirable outcomes.

Notes

1. According to OECD (1999), "corporate governance refers to the framework of rules and regulations that shape the extent to which shareholders and other stakeholders can exercise oversight and control over a company. The dominant model in the region is based

on close relationships between corporations, banks and governments, leading to a strong commitment by multiple stakeholders to the survival and growth of companies. Accounting tends to be highly non-transparent, however, and the rights of minority shareholders are weak. This situation was further aggravated by the barriers to mergers and acquisitions, both legal and due to business practices and the nature of stakeholder involvement in Asia." See Oman (2001) for a more comprehensive definition and for an indicative, hypothetical list of the main institutions of corporate governance.

Note that the "closeness" of bank-corporation and bank-government relationships, strength of minority shareholders, degree of "transparency", and so forth of East Asian countries differ from country to country even for those characterised by relationship-based (financial) systems.

2.   See Lanyi and Lee (1999: 20–3) for details.

3.   Yet, full disclosure and transparency of financial information seem impossible. Even if that were to happen, it may actually increase volatility. The degree of transparency and extent of "perfect information" should be looked at from the perspective that being more transparent or having more (complete and accurate) information, will improve social welfare.

   When deciding on more transparency and disclosure of information, one cannot generalise and assume that all forms of information should be disclosed. On the contrary, accurate and timely information about earnings, profits, liabilities, assets, corporate businesses and modes of financing, for example, should be made more readily available. But how much should be made more available to the public and the type of information that is desirable will be subject to much debate — with corporations wanting to maintain a competitive advantage and "element of surprise" from a corporate strategy standpoint.

4.   In North American terminology, this is referred to as "equity" insolvency. In Malaysia, insolvency provisions are mainly stipulated under the Companies Act, 1965. The areas of insolvency provided for under this Act are: arrangement and reconstructions; receivers and managers; and winding up and liquidations (Nor Azimah 1997). Furthermore, procedural aspects are provided for under the Companies (Winding Up) Rules, 1972. Even though there is no legislation that specifically stipulates rescue provisions, some of the provisions of the 1965 Act — for example, provisions under Part VII, under Arrangements and Reconstructions; Part VIII, under Receivership; and Part X, under Winding-Up and Liquidation — may be interpreted as facilitating or relevant for attempting corporate rescue (Nor Azimah 1997). For a definition of corporate rescue, see Campbell (1994).

5. Insolvency Act 1986 ('IA 1986') s 123(1)(e). In the US, it is necessary to show that the debtor is generally not paying debts as they fall due; for this purpose, non-payment of a single debt payment due will not be sufficient (11 U.S.C. § 303(h)(1)).

6. For example, see Belcher (1997: 39–42). Substantial default indicates failure to make a payment (of interest or capital) that is due. This differs from technical default, which connotes breach of any other term of a loan covenant — for example, provisions relating to information provision or maintenance of financial ratios. Belcher also discusses an alternative use of the term, derived from the accounting literature, based on financial ratios.

7. Stone (2000) defines unviable firms as those whose *liquidation value* is greater than their *surplus value as a going concern*, taking into account potential restructuring, at "equilibrium" exchange and interest rates. As such, even after restructuring, with a potential change in management and/or improvement in management incentives (e.g. government gradually or drastically reducing subsidies and protection — depending on the situation — to "coerce" firms to improve efficiency and competitiveness), the firm's value as a going concern is still less than the value of the assets on a break-up basis, then the firm will be considered unviable and hence liquidated. Here, restructuring can encompass many things, and different analysts will have their own interpretations and examples of what constitutes restructuring.

8. Following Stone's (2000) definition of unviable firms, we can deduce that in order for the resources to be put to their highest-valued use, the management must be assumed to be competent enough and to face appropriate management incentives, to identify the opportunities and risks and to make the best decision possible.

9. Armour (2001) notes that if accounting values matched net present values, all economically distressed firms would also be insolvent in the balance-sheet sense. However, accounting measures are based on historic costs, systematically under-valued for prudence in the face of uncertainty or to qualify for depreciation tax allowances. Therefore, many economically viable firms may be insolvent in the balance sheet sense.

10. In the Malaysian context, receivership is generally regarded as a method for enforcing a debenture holder's rights for a loan given to a corporate debtor. Apart from the appointment of a receiver, who usually collects all credit claims and sells property secured by the debenture on behalf of debenture holders and distributes the proceeds to them, a receiver and manager may also be appointed, not only to get and realise the secured assets, but also with powers to run the business. According to Forbes (1992: 121),

a debenture is a document given by a company acknowledging that it owes money to the debenture holder. The money is raised for a fixed period of time. Debentures pay fixed rates of interest. Debentures are usually secured against the property of the company. A debenture holder is a creditor of the company. In the event of winding up of a company, debenture holders are entitled to repayments before any repayments to shareholders are made. The various types of debentures are: (i) Naked or simple debentures are those that are unsecured; (ii) Redeemable debentures are those that are redeemable at some future date; (iii) Irredeemable or perpetual debentures where the loan is not repayable except on liquidation; and (iv) Convertible debentures may be issued with a right to convert the debentures to shares at a future date on specified conditions. In the United States, debentures refer to unsecured long-term debts.

11. In this context, consideration is only given to corporate insolvency procedures.

12. One way to raise finance is to issue ordinary shares, which results in dilution. In the words of Forbes (1992), "ordinary shareholders are the owners of the company. Ordinary shares carry voting rights. Ordinary shareholders receive dividends only after preference shareholders are paid. Since ordinary shareholders are the owners, they bear the most risk. They may not receive dividends when times are bad. In the event of a winding up, they are low down on the priority list of those entitled to repayment of capital." Here, dilution represents "a *reduction* in the earnings per share (EPS) due to the issue of additional ordinary shares" (Forbes 1992: 132). Furthermore, when the firm or bank declares bankruptcy, this implies that the "value" of the firm to the shareholders is now less than before the firm became financially distressed. Therefore, part of the losses will be borne by the shareholders — loss of future dividends, loss in revenue generated due to selling shares at "depressed" prices, and so on.

13. In the case of financially distressed banks, depositors and creditors bear the loss by not being able to recover their deposits in full and the total amount lent (with interest) respectively.

14. This is, of course, the general course of action. If a firm is insolvent, there are two courses of action — either liquidation or undergo restructuring. However, there are certain instances — discussed later on — when the firm is not liquidated for certain national strategic reasons.

15. However, while some observers may see financial assistance given to selected corporations as bail outs, others may not. While the former are likely to see the bail out as unfair, the latter may see the same intervention as socially desirable. This disagreement arises because of the complexities in distinguishing "viable" from "non-viable"

corporations. The identification of non-viable corporations is complicated by poor overall corporate sector performance during and just after the crisis. In such circumstances, there is a greater likelihood for firms to be evaluated as non-viable, especially after a systemic crisis. Furthermore, one has to distinguish between economic distress — which affects profitability due to the poor business environment for the corporations' goods and services — from distress, attributable to poor management because of capability and capacity constraints that obstruct exploitation of favourable business and market conditions — and poor management due to "carelessness", "negligence" and "imprudence", or unwillingness to make the necessary effort to better manage the enterprise, "overextension" or "overdiversification" through acquisition of diverse industries, thereby hampering focus on core competencies and businesses, and deliberately lowered prices to subsidise consumers, e.g. in public transportation.

16. There is a lack of consensus over what, precisely, systemic risk is (Marshall 1998). A systemic crisis has been defined by the IMF (1998a) as "a severe disruption to financial markets that by impairing their ability to function has large and adverse effects on the real sector". According to Claessens *et al.* (2001: 2), "a systemic crisis can be characterised as a situation with large-scale corporate and financial distress". For Steenbeek (1998), "a systemic crisis is a disturbance that severely damages the working of the system and may even cause a complete breakdown". In financial terms, a systemic crisis is a situation in which "a financial institution, typically a bank, fails to settle because another financial institution fails to settle" (Kanda 1992). A crisis may start in any part of the system, but ultimately, it will damage at least one of the three key functions of the financial system: credit allocation, payments, and pricing of financial assets (BIS 1992). *The Economist* (1995) views a systemic crisis as a situation in which "failure of one large financial institution will trigger a *chain reaction*". See Kaufman (1996: 2, 5, endnote 5). Marshall (1998) notes, "while economists may disagree as to the causes and nature of systemic risk, there have been specific events in history that are generally recognised as examples of systemic crisis such as the 1997–98 Asian crisis". According to Marshall (1998), the Asian crisis exemplifies certain characteristics incorporated in most definitions of systemic risk. A systemic crisis originates in, or is substantially magnified by financial markets. It involves *contagion*, a loss of confidence by investors, substantial real *costs* in economic output and/or economic efficiency (not a mere redistribution of wealth from, say, speculators on the losing side to speculators on the winning side), calls for a policy response, and lacks a clear triggering event. For a more thorough explanation of the above characteristics, see Marshall (1998).

17.   Here, we assume that we can ascertain whether or not a corporation
      is viable. Hence, if a bail out is taking place, we assume that the firm
      under consideration is non-viable. However, as highlighted above,
      determination of whether a firm is viable (i.e. present value of the
      firm as a going concern is greater than the value of the firm's assets
      sold for cash and is greater than zero) is complicated since it involves
      a hypothetical sale of the corporation. To quote Bebchuk (1988:
      778), "no objective figure is available for the total monetary value".
      In contrast, "a problem of valuation does not exist in liquidation,
      when an *actual* sale to an outsider takes place. The liquidation results
      in an exchange of the company's assets for cash (or cash equivalents,
      such as marketable securities). Whether or not this cash represents
      the true value of the assets sold, there is no question as to what is
      the total monetary value that is available for distribution" (Bebchuk
      1997: 3).

18.   Assumptions of perfect competition — with many buyers and sellers
      (governed by "greed") of a homogenous product, complete informa-
      tion, perfect mobility of resources, and no barriers to entry and exit
      — should lead to productive and allocative efficiency, eliminating
      producers that are economically inefficient, with only the lowest cost
      and most efficient producers remaining in the market.

19.   In the words of Wijnbergen (1997: 54), "realism and often simple
      humanitarian concern suggest that such drastic actions [straight liqui-
      dation or just closure] may not work for very large enterprises or
      dominant employers in poor regions. Here a *more gradual* approach
      to closure is probably unavoidable."

20.   To quote then Malaysian Finance Minister Daim Zainuddin, "there
      may be some grounds for government assistance for troubled industries
      and companies that fall under the criteria of national and strategic
      interests" (Lee 2000).

21.   Economic viability is more concerned with the future prospects of a
      firm, while bail outs generally try to contain the consequences or
      (present/current) costs of crises. Since borrowing facilities for groups
      are often linked, default by one corporation may trigger problems for
      other group companies; for example, because of cross guarantees,
      rescue procedures may be necessary to preserve the structure and
      financing of companies in a group.

22.   Here, "creative destruction" refers to the "natural" process of selection
      of firms that are not economically efficient, innovative and/or able to
      effectively manage risk, corporate leverage and financing. Joseph
      Schumpeter's definition of "creative destruction" is more focused on
      technology and it refers to the continuous process by which emerging
      technologies push out the old (Greenspan 1999). Caballero and
      Hammour (1994) explain that:

when technology, in the broadest sense, is embodied in capital, skills, and the organisation of work, technical progress puts the economy in a state of incessant restructuring. Its productive structure must constantly adapt to innovations in products, techniques, modes of organisation, and the evolving competitiveness of world markets. Production units that embody new techniques must continually be created, while out-dated units must be destroyed. This process of growth — through Schumpeterian "creative destruction" — results in ongoing reallocation of factors of production from contracting production sites to expanding ones (see Schumpeter 1942).

23. They proved that "if countries had not extended unlimited deposits guarantees, open-ended liquidity support, repeated recapitalisation, debtor bail outs and regulatory forbearance, average fiscal costs in their sample could have been limited to about one percent of GDP — little more than a tenth of what was actually experienced. On the other hand, policy could have been worse: had countries engaged in all of the above policies, the regression results imply that fiscal costs in excess of 60 per cent of GDP would have been the result" (Honohan and Klingebiel 2000: 2).

24. Here, the conglomerate can divest its interests in corporations with rather sound prospects in non-core activities to reduce its debt and free up (financial) resources to be redirected to core activities. This will allow corporations to reassess their style of business and rationa-lise their operations (Ng 2001).

25. However, some parties may put forth arguments relating to national economic sovereignty, discussed later.

26. Consistent with Shleifer and Vishny's (1992) model, Hotchkiss and Mooradian (1997) present evidence of the frequency of takeover activity by buyers without related operations. However, such take-over activity is excluded from their sample, because the acquirers — vulture investors who specialise in the acquisition and management of distressed firms — are financial buyers, and not operating companies.

27. The magnitude of the problem depends on a variety of factors, including the attitudes and beliefs of shareholders, the extent to which corporate raiders have inside information, and the degree to which managers are concerned with retaining control of their firms.

28. It must be noted that it is difficult to ascertain, with certainty, the prospects of a corporation or even an industry as a whole.

29. The definition of moral hazard is available in any standard economics textbook. One general definition is as follows. Moral hazard represents a situation in which one party to a contract has an incentive, after a contract is made, to alter behaviour in a way that harms the other party to the contract. Alternatively, moral hazard arises when one party to a contract passes the cost of his or her behaviour onto the other party to the contract.

30. It is assumed that the management was previously able to manage better, but was unwilling to do so. Hence, given the new "rules of the game", that provide greater incentives and impetus for positive change, they are induced to improve management.

31. Then Malaysian Prime Minister Mahathir Mohamad stated that the government would not divest shares in national corporations to foreigners in a big way because foreign companies will not normally take care of Malaysians' welfare (*The Sun*, 17 July 2001).

32. The term "rescue" here simply implies that the firm is given a lifeline — monetary or other forms of assistance — to keep it going or "afloat". The word "rescue" does not, in itself, imply that the action is "bad" or "undesirable". On the contrary, viable firms that cannot obtain funds from market channels may be "rescued" by the government, and this is not necessarily undesirable. Furthermore, it must be highlighted that in certain legal jurisdictions (of insolvency laws), the rescue process is akin to a liquidation process, while in other jurisdictions, rescue and liquidation are very different (World Bank, 2000d). Furthermore, while certain jurisdictions describe their new statutory regimes under the heading of "rescue", others may utilise the terms "reorganisation", "rehabilitation", "restructuring", "arrangement", "administration", "composition", "reconciliation" and even "merger" or "acquisition" (World Bank 2000d: 75).

33. Here, we assume that the firm operating under lax or "soft" constraints has become "complacent" because the environment proved to be "too favourable and protected". For example, "myopic" corporations that are given protection (hence, like a monopolist) or subsidies would possibly obtain less combined profits in a two period analysis than, say, a monopolist with perfect foresight (who takes advantage of the current situation to learn as much as possible) who would "sacrifice" some profits now in order to earn more in the future through cost reductions that may well yield higher combined or total profits (under certain assumptions). Hence, it is preferable to create a broad regulatory framework that is an environment for firms to react to incentives and disincentives to improve cost and quality competitiveness, as in the North East Asian countries.

34. The pro-Malay distributive policy is presented to other ethnic groups, especially the Chinese, as providing an implicit security guarantee against Malay bitterness over inter-ethnic economic inequalities, which supposedly previously led to ethnic riots in May 1969 (Case 1995: 72–3).

35. It must be acknowledged that not only Malay businessmen were granted privileges. However, the emphasis of the New Economic Policy from 1970 has been to advance the economic situation of the Malays following the May 1969 riots.

CHAPTER 4

Corporate Restructuring Policy Options

WONG SOOK CHING

D ue to the nature of the East Asian financial crisis (with both financial and corporate[1] sectors in distress), banks had to be recapitalised and kept liquid, by taking out "non-performing loans" (NPLs), while corporations had to undergo restructuring. Note that not all financial crises entail general corporate distress. Banks can run into trouble when the domestic currency value of their foreign borrowings balloon due to depreciation, or their lending is overly concentrated in a particularly troubled region or sector of the economy. But where non-performing loans and bad debt are attributable to corporate borrowers, the problem of banks cannot be resolved independently of the factors that impair the capacity of corporate borrowers to service and repay their debts. Easing these constraints will improve the quality of bank assets, bolster their capital and encourage them to resume lending (Asian Development Bank 2000). However, in East Asia, the firms' inability to meet their debt obligations was mirrored by the NPLs on the balance sheets of banks (World Bank 2000d).

The main focus of this study has been on corporate restructuring, with less emphasis on bank recapitalisation and restructuring even though some of the concepts have certain conceptual parallels and are closely linked. The technicalities and details of bank recapitalisation and restructuring will be kept to a minimum, in view of the complexities and breadth of Malaysian bank recapitalisation and restructuring. As such, thorough analysis of the process of bank recapitalisation and restructuring is beyond the scope of this study.[2]

It is important to keep in mind the goal of corporate restructuring, i.e. the timely and orderly transformation and reduction of debt, with a view to enhancing profitability, reducing leverage (deemed "excessive"[3] by some standards and blamed for problems of insolvency during crisis), and restoring credit to viable enterprises (Stone 1998).

This chapter will review the debate on whether government (through the central bank and other government agencies) or markets should lead bank recapitalisation and corporate restructuring programmes. Posing this question implies abandoning the *ex ante* prescription that market processes will always be best for corporate restructuring. The motive is to find solutions or approaches that provide the best results, without ruling out or considering "all" options available. According to Blaustein (2001), "in general, solutions have worked best if the costs to taxpayers were minimised, shareholders were hit hardest, banks did most of the enterprise restructuring, and the government did not end up as the owner of a large number of banks and enterprises".

Following that, some conclusions will be drawn from debates about the desirable type and degree of government intervention in various circumstances. Furthermore, the (immediate and ongoing) "prerequisites" to ensure success of the "corporate restructuring" programme will be highlighted. The success of a restructuring programme may be measured by its "ability" to "minimise"[4] the adverse impacts of systemic crises[5] and financial sector "fragility". The type of financial structure, corporate culture, product market, corporate governance system or framework[6] and other factors that emerge out of the restructuring programme will influence the effectiveness of various economic instruments for handling crises.[7]

However, there are still certain areas where there is no clear-cut answer as to what constitutes "good" corporate governance or strong empirical evidence that supports any one approach. For instance, the issues of independent directors and the dual roles of the chief executive officer (CEO) in affecting corporate performance are subject to tremendous debate (see Donaldson and Davis 1991). Furthermore, there are arguments over IMF policy measures that emphasise corporate restructuring and structural adjustment reforms in the short run, which have dubious, if not negative consequences for the pace of economic recovery.

While corporate restructuring and structural reforms are potentially important for promoting long-term growth, there is growing evidence that the IMF programmes and conditionalities did little, if any, good for economic recovery in the East Asian countries crisis economies. Though this study does not really address the issue of whether a government should focus on macroeconomic policy management, i.e. expansionary fiscal and monetary policies, to help rapid economic recovery, or on corporate restructuring and structural reforms (as argued by the IMF and World Bank) ostensibly to ensure sustained recovery, these issues are briefly considered.

Another important issue that deserves mention, but is beyond the scope of this study, pertains to disagreements over the sequence of bank recapitalisation (and restructuring) and corporate restructuring. Should banks be restructured first, followed by corporations? Or should they be restructured simultaneously? (see Park 2000).

The general sequence of events favoured by the International Monetary Fund and various economists is to recapitalise and restructure the banking sector first, and to then deal with the corporate sector. However, presuming that this is the only right sequence may very well rule out other possibilities that may be more appropriate in the context. Hence, some have highlighted the advantages of conducting bank recapitalisation and restructuring simultaneously. Problems that arise from first conducting bank recapitalisation and restructuring, and then corporate restructuring, do not, in themselves, justify some other alternative sequence. On the contrary, in order for another sequence to be preferred, it must be shown to be viable and better able to minimise the overall cost of the restructuring exercise.

Government or Market-led Corporate Restructuring

A government can employ different approaches to corporate restructuring. The recent debate has involved three approaches to restructuring corporations, namely a market-led approach, a recapitalised bank-led approach, and a government-led approach, with the first approach involving the least "direct" government intervention and the last involving the most.

Three Different Approaches to Corporate Restructuring

The market-led approach mainly relies on market forces and private sector interests to restore enterprise profitability and bank capital. Examples of market solutions to corporate restructuring include bankruptcies[8] of financially insolvent corporations, voluntary restructuring, mergers and acquisitions[9] (i.e. asset sales to [foreign and domestic] investors through competitive bidding or auction), hostile takeovers[10] by private parties, and foreign investment inflows (to buy shares in the corporation or to provide funds in other forms).[11]

A government-led approach, on the other hand, usually uses public resources to finance corporate restructuring. Key decisions in the corporate restructuring programme are made by the government or by government appointed bodies. With a government-led approach, the government or a government agency (e.g. a centralised asset management company, or AMC) takes over a large share of distressed assets from the banks, replacing them with government bonds or other secure assets, thereby recapitalising the banking system (Blaustein 2001). The government then tries to restructure assets to achieve corporate restructuring (by means of voluntary or mandatory special purpose frameworks), including operational restructuring and/or management changes.

In contrast, under the recapitalised bank-led approach, the government recapitalises banks based on an *ex ante* assessment of their losses, with the banks, in turn, taking the lead in corporate restructuring. This involves individual banks or groups of banks working out problem debts and taking charge of the operational and financial restructuring of firms,[12] possibly providing working capital for restructuring.[13]

No approach is perfect or foolproof, suggesting that no one approach is necessarily superior to others in all circumstances. Nevertheless, it is important to understand the various strengths and weaknesses of the above approaches in order to appreciate how each approach may be of benefit or is problematic. In deciding on the appropriate corporate restructuring measure(s), ideological dogma should be rejected in favour of pragmatism, sometimes associated with a "contingency" approach.[14] The relative strengths and weaknesses of the three approaches are now considered.

Market-led Approach

Neo-liberal free market advocates argue that a market-led approach can better achieve economic efficiency, discipline and more resilience in the banking and corporate system. If the insolvent corporation is worth more as a going concern than after break-up, private individuals or firms can then opt to buy the corporation as a going concern (through a takeover, for example). The person or corporation willing to pay the highest price or valuation for a corporation (i.e. through a competitive bid or in an "auction") would obtain control of the corporation, and will then put the corporation and its assets to their highest value use.

If, on the other hand, the firm is valued on a break-up basis, then it would have to undergo liquidation proceedings, since there would not be any interested party to take it over as a going concern. Hence, corporations which "do not deserve" to survive — or are "not fit enough" to survive in the market economy — will be "eliminated" by market forces. This "weeding out" process will thus, argue some, create a more resilient and stronger corporate sector, and consequently, a more resilient banking sector in the long run.[15]

Government intervention is considered counter-productive, and unlikely to achieve these desired outcomes. Furthermore, "the stronger believers of the 'invisible hand' want to show that even if there are some 'market failures', 'government failures' are always larger" (Cui 1999: 9). Therefore, they want to show that the attitude "let the market take care of itself" is always the right one. The role of government, if any, is to enhance the enabling environment, including allowing hostile mergers and acquisitions (takeovers), liberalising rules restricting foreign investment and promoting capital market development.

However, these benefits cannot be (theoretically) presumed *a priori* to materialise since markets (e.g. the capital market) and information are "imperfect" in reality. Furthermore, market approaches (that rely on private funds) may not be viable because of a lack of funds or market players. Market-based methods are only applicable if private capital is available, and private investors are willing to participate in mergers and acquisitions, inject fresh capital, roll over loans, and so forth.

Moreover, competitive auctions may fail to take place because of "financing problems", "absence of competition problems" and/or lack of well-informed bidders.[16] Hotchkiss and Mooradian (1998: 3), referring to Gertner and Picker (1992), highlight the "acquisition problem" that results from asymmetric information. Nevertheless, the fact that market-led approaches can lead to sub-optimal results does not imply total rejection of this approach as every approach has its own deficiencies. Hence, circumstances should determine the most appropriate approach or tool to solve problems at hand.[17]

Unlike the claims of supporters of market-led approaches, Baird (1993) and Bradley and Rosenzweig (1992) argue that Chapter 11 of the US bankruptcy code — as one approach to market-led corporate restructuring which is in fact highly dependent on supportive regulation — fails to provide managers with appropriate incentives to allocate corporate resources to their highest-valued uses. The (indirect) costs involved in maximising the value of assets under Chapter 11 may also be high (which dissipates the value of the assets). According to Bebchuk (1997: 4), "the Chapter 11 process involves substantial administrative costs. Indeed, the fees paid to lawyers, accountants, and other professionals in a Chapter 11 reorganisation of a publicly traded company are often in the order of tens of millions [of] dollars."

Furthermore, some argue that Chapter 11 may not be the most effective or efficient bankruptcy procedure. Bankruptcy proceedings will commence when corporations are unable to pay their creditors or service their debts, or when lenders are unwilling to roll over debts and insist on repayment. However, it would be considered a loss if financially insolvent corporations are considered economically viable.

Market-based approaches also seem to have a liquidation bias. Wijnbergen (1997) suggests that even though bankruptcy proceedings allow for debt restructuring (specifically debt equity conversion), in principle, this rarely occurs in practice. Aghion *et al.* (1992) found that even carefully crafted bankruptcy laws have a strong liquidation bias built in, with 95 per cent of Chapter 11 cases eventually going the liquidation route. Hence the government can ensure that corporations that are illiquid, or even insolvent do not undergo automatic liquidation if they are economically viable even though some may not be profitable in the short term. However, other bankruptcy proceedings could be more effective and "efficient" compared to Chapter 11 (Aghion *et al.* 1992).

The efficiency of other market-based approaches — such as mergers and acquisitions, and hostile takeovers — as disciplining mechanisms remains moot, with considerable empirical evidence and many studies casting doubt over whether these approaches will necessarily correct managerial and other inefficiencies.[18] Referring to the US and the UK, Mayer (1996) found little evidence to support the premise that takeovers were motivated by the poor corporate performance of "target" corporations prior to the takeover bids.

Rather, factors such as changes in corporate strategy or rent seeking were found to be the primary objectives or motivating factors behind takeovers. Other possible motivating factors include increases in firm size and firm growth, and tax benefits (for mergers and acquisitions). But this does not necessarily imply that markets do not play a role in the market for corporate control; existing incentives and regulations may need to be fine tuned to improve the effectiveness of market mechanisms.

The market-led approach claims it would enhance systemic efficiency and safety. These benefits follow if market players who are better capitalised and managed are able to increase their market shares at the expense of those that are weak and potentially threaten systemic stability. This can be aptly referred to as the "survival of the fittest by natural selection" argument. Many market fundamentalist economists — including Friedman, Hayek, Buchanan, Becker and Alchian — invoke the argument of "survival of the fittest by natural selection" as justification for relying on the "invisible hand" (Cui 1999).

However, this change in market structure may lead to greater market concentration (and hence, less competition), that *may* prove to be of concern for the government and the public, in terms of likely reduced competition and consumer welfare. However, this does not imply that "perfect competition" is a real option. Neoclassical economists assume that a market characterised by perfect competition is always the best or ideal form of market structure.

Sloman (1997: 176) notes that "'perfect' competition refers to competition that is total … There is a total absence of power, a total absence of entry barriers, a total absence of product differentiation between producers, and total information for producers and consumers on the market …. Perfect does not mean 'best', however. Just because it is at the extreme end of the competition spectrum, it does not follow that perfect competition is desirable." He further argues that "to say that perfect competition is desirable and that it is a goal towards which government policy should be directed are normative statements". He also points out that "by using perfect competition as a yardstick, and by using the word 'perfect' rather than 'total', economists may be surreptitiously persuading their audience that perfect competition is a goal we *ought* to be striving to achieve". Besides, the "current" bargaining process[19] — say, under Chapter 11 — does not necessarily guarantee an optimal and efficient capital structure after reorganisation (as claimed by market advocates).[20]

It is often claimed that equitable cost sharing arrangements under a market-led approach would help mitigate moral hazard problems and create incentives for more efficient monitoring as all relevant parties would have a stake in the corporation. It is argued that once "ownership" or "property rights" are established, misuse of resources will be minimised. However, the claim of equitable cost sharing assumes that government-led approaches are *necessarily* less equitable, and do not impose costs on debtors or the "party" at fault.

This may not be true, since governments may "force" all parties involved to accept a "haircut" and to share costs. For example, the government may require corporations to sell their non-core assets (to any interested party, including the government) as part of a financial restructuring plan to improve their balance sheet, instead of the government injecting liquidity (by giving them more loans, for example) into corporations to keep them afloat. In that sense, corporations are expected to internalise the costs of their actions and to share the costs of restructuring.

Even if a market-led approach is feasible, moral hazard may not be minimised if the management responsible for causing the problems in the first place is not removed or goes unpunished. This has a greater chance of happening with mergers as the chances of a change in management with mergers are less than with hostile takeovers or acquisitions, *ceteris paribus*. Retaining those responsible for causing the insolvency of the corporation without punishment could signal that future mismanagement and bad performance will be tolerated.

As such, management may not be "threatened" or motivated enough to put in the "required" effort to improve the performance of the corporation. However, removing those with "insider" information, knowledge and experience of the organisation may be counter-productive when facing a limited supply of competent and professional managers. Hence, there need to be some performance criteria and management incentive systems in place to induce better performance, should the old management be retained.

The currently favoured orthodox view among the Bretton Woods international financial institutions, market analysts and much of the profession is that a market-led approach (when feasible) is better than a government-led approach in handling corporate distress. Market-led approaches also seem attractive because they limit the burden on taxpayers since such approaches are more likely to utilise private — rather than public — resources to facilitate restructuring.

However, market-led approach advocates usually underestimate the costs of market-led approaches to the public since they tend to be more time-consuming as they involve "bargaining" and negotiations among various parties — as under US Chapter 11 bankruptcy procedures. This indirectly imposes costs on the public in terms of foregone output[21] during the negotiation and "bargaining" processes. The longer it takes to come to an agreement or consensus — because of the number of creditors and the variety of claims — for example, regarding whether to "reorganise" the corporation, the less attention will be paid to producing goods and services, hence the greater the chances of lower production, *ceteris paribus.*

Market-led approaches, some argue, reduce the likelihood of governments ending up as the principal owners of banks and enterprises. From this perspective, this would distract the government's focus from providing public services and macroeconomic management of the economy to managing corporate enterprises, increasing government expenditure and crowding out access to scarce resources. However, state-owned enterprises may be essential for furthering development objectives or policies. Besides, government owned enterprises are not necessarily less efficient, as critiques of privatisation policies and theories suggest.

Some argue that a market-led approach generally works better in recovering non-performing and bad loans than a bureaucratically administered system. Competition in the acquisition and disposal of assets should eventually make for more efficient debt workouts. However, the market-based approach is unlikely to reduce debt to sustainable levels for many companies, even in the medium term, thereby making them vulnerable to volatility in interest rates and market conditions. Blaustein (2001) cites South Korea as an example. A purely market-based solution in South Korea would have resulted in an average debt-equity ratio of the largest *chaebols* of over 400 per cent in the year 2000. Although the Korean debt-equity ratio has always been high, this would still be above historical levels and much higher than is common in market economies. A government or bank-led approach would face similar difficulties, but to lesser degrees.

Government-led Approach

A government-led approach can be fast since there is a party (the government) ready to undertake the restructuring programme, unlike a market-led approach that relies on the voluntary "availability" of private buyer(s) or investor(s), who may not be sufficient, or may be too difficult to organise to undertake massive financial commitments.[22] However, the World Bank (2000d: 91) argues that "government funds are not required for corporate restructuring and their supply may even hinder private resolution as stakeholders are induced to seek these subsidies". It further stresses that:

> The proper role for governments is to facilitate resolution of financial claims and foster the allocation and mobility of assets. In the absence of efficiently functioning systems to resolve financial claims, governments in all the crisis countries have instituted out-of-court mechanisms to encourage financial settlements. Beyond these immediate measures, also aiding in the short term, are ongoing efforts to achieve effective bankruptcy regimes and improved accounting standards. Once financial property rights have been clarified, the market system and the private sector should be in a position to undertake the required reallocations of productive assets, but governments can play an important role in permitting greater asset mobility.

In other words, the government's role should be limited to creating an *enabling* and *favourable* environment for the functioning of the market and the private sector. However, such measures are usually very time consuming and not necessarily effective, while the severity and urgency of the problems involve generally require quicker, and "direct", even pro-active government interventions.

Even though a government-led approach may be relatively faster than a free-market approach (under certain circumstances), there often are immense fiscal obligations; and costs to taxpayers are likely to be ultimately higher — both in the form of higher taxation in the future to subsidise (past, current and, possibly future) government support for banks and corporations as well as foregone alternative public expenditure. Also, there is a risk that the speed of the restructuring process may be compromised because later re-privatisation of state-owned enterprises (whether financial institutions or corporations) can be costly and time consuming, since it normally meets with strong resistance by employees of state-owned enterprises and can be bogged down by bureaucratic delays and corruption (Park 2000).

Since the centralised AMC takes over the assets of distressed banks and helps recapitalise them, then the distressed banks will not have to force (potentially economically viable, but financially distressed) corporations to undergo liquidation.[23] This ensures that viable corporations can be preserved, and their debts and operations given some breathing space and time to be restructured.

However, centralised AMCs, argue some, are fraught with weaknesses. The most important argument is that even with incentive measures built in, government-owned agencies run the risk of poor management, with a lack of motivation to restructure corporations. Wijnbergen (1997: 48) gives an example of the incentive problem in a "hospital for sick enterprises" to "turned around" enterprises under public sector control: "Its successful implementation of the 'hospital agency' would lead to its quick abolishment. But the jobs and continuing influence of the Agency's officials depend, on the contrary, on it continuing rather than shutting down." He also cites the case of the Italian state holding company Instituto Per La Ricostruzione Industriale (IRI), or Institute for Industrial Reconstruction, that has "overstayed" its statutory obligation to dismantle itself within five years of inception in 1948 to become the largest industrial conglomerate in Italy up till the present.

Haggard (2000: 142) suggests that "if the assets are transferred to a weak asset management corporation and simply 'warehoused', bank balance sheets are cleaned up and borrowers can re-establish relations with creditors, but neither may have incentives to meet their obligations". However, this need not occur and the government can take tough measures to maximise the value of assets, though this is presumed to require a high level of technical capacity and political independence. When a government is involved in corporate restructuring, it may have problems such as weak disciplinary control over corporations to improve operational performance if such corporations have strong influence with the government. According to Haggard (2000: 143), "the closer the political relationship between political leaders and the banks and debtors undergoing restructuring, the more the government deferred to private interests, and the more limited and costly the private restructuring process proved to be".

Simply put, it can lead to acute moral hazard problems. Blaustein (2001) notes, "Past experiences, particularly in countries with weak institutions, suggest that many times an agency 'sits' on its loans, often in fear of antagonising the 'powers that be', the same powers who often contributed to the bad loans in the past." He suggests that large loans — that break the links between banks and corporations, thereby eliminating bank involvement — may reduce the value of assets, as banks have privileged access to "insider" information. In addition, there is the possibility that restructured firms "stigmatised" as "hospital patients" will find it hard to regain access to bank credit (Wijnbergen 1997).

Recapitalised Bank-led Approach

This approach can be relatively fast relative to court adjudication, argue Gray and Holle (1996), and will indicate to the market that problems are being resolved. Some argue that bank leadership offers a more efficient way of debt restructuring (than a centralised AMC) if effective private ownership is established, with debt converted to equity, instead of debt write downs and full collection of what remains.[24] Debt-equity conversion offers a more promising means for the efficient use of assets controlled by enterprises than liquidation into a thin capital market and a depressed economy. However, if banks end up holding large amounts of equity, they can become more vulnerable to stock market fluctuations, thus increasing new uncertainties and risk.

Banks generally play a big role in restructuring because of the unique information they possess about their corporate customers (Fries and Lane 1994). However, even if banks have "insider" knowledge regarding their clients, they may not have the expertise to advise well on the organisational, managerial or operational restructuring of client corporations. Secondly, banks (especially in developing countries) may lack the technical capacity and skills to effectively monitor and restructure a large number of enterprises. As indicated by Blaustein (2001), "although technical assistance is rapidly improving the banks' restructuring capacity, it will take time before they can effectively restructure enterprises".

Advocates of bank-led corporate restructuring argue that banks have the incentives to encourage their clients to restructure their operations to become more viable in the new environment. However, if banks have the incentive to do so, they may not actually be able to act on these incentives and induce the restructuring of corporations. The Polish bank conciliatory procedure suggests that banks had limited power to effect the necessary operational restructuring; in fact, Gray and Holle (1996) found little or no evidence of operational restructuring. Bonin and Leven (2000: 5) argue that state-owned banks in Poland were not effective agents of change for two reasons. First, the banks usually did not have the necessary expertise to design proper business plans and induce the necessary operational restructuring. Second, state-owned banks tend to be influenced by government policy and find it difficult to resist soft lending for political reasons, i.e. by becoming conduits for government subsidies. State-owned banks, they argue, are "particularly vulnerable to incentive problems when dealing with large state-owned enterprises that may be too big or too political to fail".

This approach could ultimately involve lower costs if bank recapitalisation (considered an up-front "investment" by the government) is accompanied by substantive changes in corporate governance and bank operations (Blaustein 2001). Nonetheless, experience shows that governments routinely inject capital into insolvent institutions without effecting sufficient change in bank governance and operations, suggesting that things are always easier said than done. To date, most bank recapitalisation programmes by governments have been unsuccessful. In facing the trade-off between maintaining confidence and preserving incentives for good banking (i.e. minimising moral hazard), most countries favoured maintaining confidence by extending large-scale guarantees or continuing to recapitalise banks, with little guarantee that recapitalisation would either be sufficient or occur only once (Blaustein 2001). Repeated recapitalisation would therefore increase the costs to taxpayers.

Moreover, there is the possibility that in their attempts to retrieve bad and non-performing loans, some banks may exacerbate the situation by: lending into arrears (even when the business is not viable — assuming that banks are given the task of "triage"[25]) to avoid, say, provisioning; rolling over loans to heavily indebted large borrowers [crowding out alternative credit uses]; and/or foreclosing loans and seeking earlier repayments from creditworthy borrowers, undermining their viability or the viability of the resuscitation effort (because firms are constrained from responding to opportunities when faced with a credit crunch).

Another danger arises when incentives meant to promote and accelerate debt repayment become counterproductive. If the time period allowed to clear the old debt of corporations is considered "too short", banks may opt for substantial debt forgiveness, instead of rescheduling such old debt, for fear that their debtors will not be able to meet the tight repayment schedules. Such incentive incompatibilities may ultimately result in higher overall costs. Also, banks may be too weak in restructuring negotiations, compared to corporations, e.g. in the case of corporations considered to be "too big to fail". Dealing with corporations that are too big to fail may result in weak restructuring plans that ultimately result in greater fiscal costs. However, with greater public scrutiny and accountability, such political "abuses" tend to be lower.

The preceding evaluation of the respective pros and cons of market-led, bank-led and government-led corporate restructuring suggests the potential of adopting eclectic approaches, or mixtures of approaches, when dealing with corporate distress, by recognising the relative strengths, weaknesses and problems of each approach. After all, circumstances should determine the most appropriate approaches and tools to solve the problems at hand. As such, the severity of the crisis (in terms of the number of financially distressed firms, the nature and magnitude of their negative externalities for the economy as a whole, systemic impacts on the banking and payments system), the nature of information asymmetries and imperfections, and the legislative, political and bargaining environments should influence the *type* and *degree* of government intervention (including "passive" or "minimalist" government action, e.g. by facilitating or complementing the market, but not leading or supplanting it).[26] It is also important to identify the constraints faced by the government and various economic and non-economic institutions — the quantity and "quality" of financial and human resources available to the government and the private sector.

Hence, the basis for a "one size fits all" approach is moot, at best. Nor does the fact that a crisis has occurred require "direct" government intervention. Furthermore, one must take into account cultural factors. For example, cultural attitudes[27] may facilitate or obstruct dispute resolution, e.g. favouring non-confrontational negotiation and mediation, which is not necessarily bad. Yet, there must exist contingency plans — in the form of formal, supervised, and facilitated processes — and an appropriate insolvency regime (that entails a well-functioning legal system, free of corruption and political interference), in the event that privately negotiated settlements fail (Meyerman 2000).

Circumstances Favouring Particular Approaches

Circumstances Deterring Government Intervention[28]

Government intervention may not be necessary when the number of troubled corporations is small and their macroeconomic significance limited (in terms of negative spill-over or systemic effects), financial information is both sound and sufficient for "good" decision making, private funds are abundant (where the equity market environment is still buoyant enough to attract equity capital), banks have the expertise and resources, and both banks and corporations have incentives to restructure debt — including the credible threat of bankruptcy. As long as there is a credible threat — i.e. the existence of "strong" bankruptcy laws — the incentive for designing or constructing and implementing a "good" restructuring plan or strategy would be greater. A workable bankruptcy law is more likely to induce debtors to cooperate and come up with a restructuring plan, since most corporations would prefer out-of-court solutions to their financial woes — rather than risk "ruining" their reputations with bankruptcy. Since there is little impediment to disrupting the functioning of markets and associated processes, banks (and other creditors) and distressed debtors (financially insolvent corporations) are better able to resolve their financial problems privately without having to resort to "direct" government intervention.

Circumstances Requiring Government Intervention

In contrast, a comprehensive debt restructuring framework[29] involving the government is usually needed when corporate debt problems are widespread or have major macroeconomic consequences, while market failures[30] obstruct debt restructuring, and banks are short of the capital and expertise needed to work out debt on a large scale. See Figure 4.1 on large-scale restructuring. Comparing the suitability of the array of government approaches that can be applied depends on the situation at hand. Debt restructuring frameworks can be divided into four overlapping categories, which may be implemented simultaneously. Types of government involvement (with each category indicating when a scheme may be warranted) — in ascending order of government involvement — are outlined below.

Types of Government Involvement[31]

Government Mediation[32]

Government mediation — between corporations and banks, or among banks — is considered to be the "mildest" form of government intervention, and is justified when market failures or other factors inhibit banks from effectively leading debt restructuring. Factors such as lack of cooperation, excessive negotiating power on either the debtors' or creditors' side, or a lack of incentives for banks or corporations to work out the debt (usually arising from poor supervision and bad governance), can prolong or even prevent debt restructuring, resulting in (avoidable) excessive costs, and even the unnecessary liquidation of debtors. This occurs when such factors impede the close coordination needed for effective restructuring,

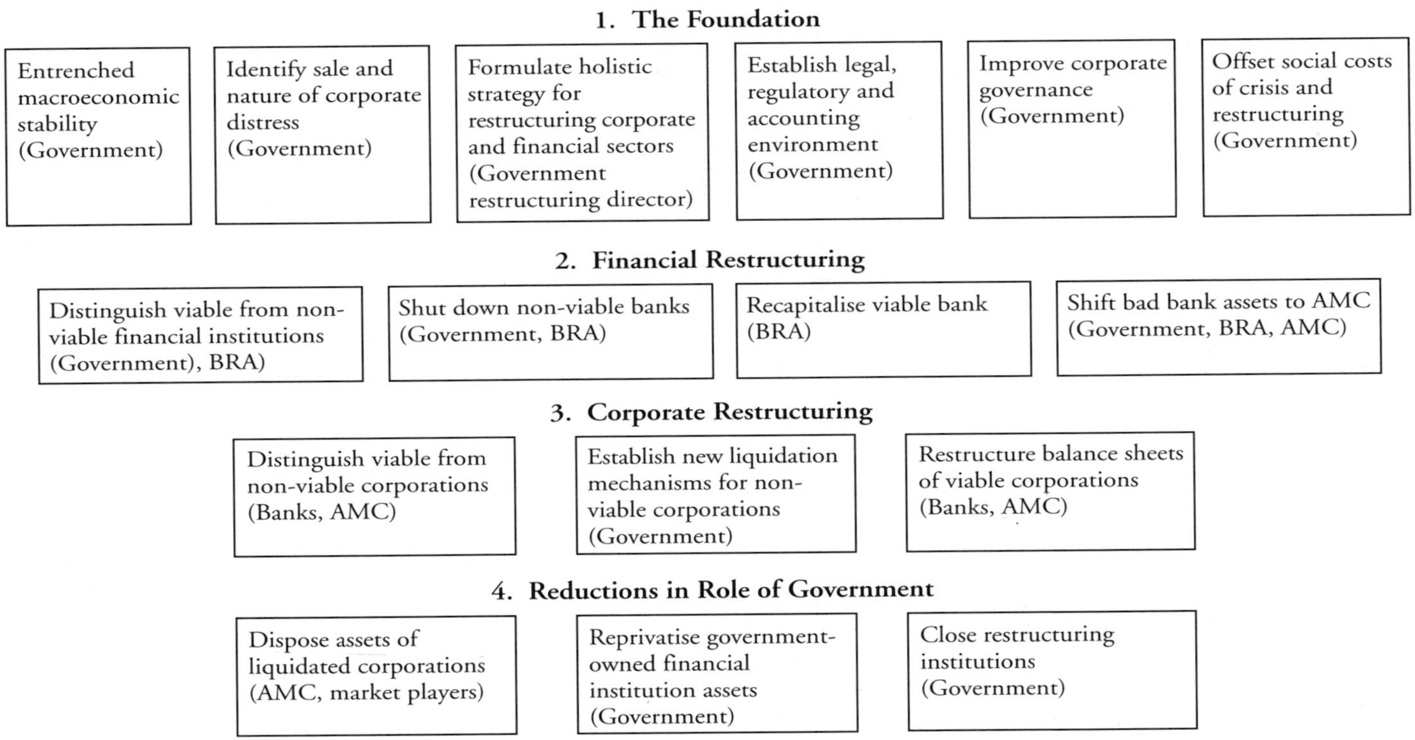

1. The Foundation

| Entrenched macroeconomic stability (Government) | Identify sale and nature of corporate distress (Government) | Formulate holistic strategy for restructuring corporate and financial sectors (Government restructuring director) | Establish legal, regulatory and accounting environment (Government) | Improve corporate governance (Government) | Offset social costs of crisis and restructuring (Government) |

2. Financial Restructuring

| Distinguish viable from non-viable financial institutions (Government), BRA | Shut down non-viable banks (Government, BRA) | Recapitalise viable bank (BRA) | Shift bad bank assets to AMC (Government, BRA, AMC) |

3. Corporate Restructuring

| Distinguish viable from non-viable corporations (Banks, AMC) | Establish new liquidation mechanisms for non-viable corporations (Government) | Restructure balance sheets of viable corporations (Banks, AMC) |

4. Reductions in Role of Government

| Dispose assets of liquidated corporations (AMC, market players) | Reprivatise government-owned financial institution assets (Government) | Close restructuring institutions (Government) |

Source: Stone (2000).

Fig. 4.1 Tasks for Large-scale Corporate Restructuring

including sharing information between banks, formulation and implementation of a common or coordinated strategy, and provision of new credit during the negotiation process.

To ensure a smoother restructuring process, the parties can ask the government to mediate informally, or in a more structured framework. An impartial government mediator can aid bank restructuring by establishing a set of guidelines for triage and financial engineering, providing expertise, facilitating the sharing of information and establishing a more congenial atmosphere for negotiations.

Government Schemes

Financial support to facilitate debt restructuring — through a pre-set government-financed scheme — can be useful if corporate debt problems are pervasive and impose negative externalities on the economy at large. Financial support is usually required when there are too many distressed corporations for banks to handle, and when corporate debt levels are too high, resulting in negative externalities, such as squeezing credit to viable borrowers, or an unsustainably high level of foreign corporate debt that curtails capital inflows.

Government schemes usually involve "insurance" provision or subsidised incentives made available to creditors and debtors on a voluntary basis. These incentives include compensation to creditors for lengthening debt maturities and grace periods, interest rate and exchange rate guarantees, and equity injections. In order for the incentives to be effective, additional government policies — including adjustments to fiscal and monetary policy stances to provide a supportive macroeconomic environment — and improvements in supervision, governance, and the legal system must be in place. However, the benefits of such schemes (which include more expedient debt restructuring for the relevant parties and mitigation of negative externalities) must be weighed against the fiscal costs of the scheme before deciding how far to go.

Direct Bank Recapitalisation

Direct bank recapitalisation by the government would be appropriate when corporate debt problems are pervasive enough to undermine the health of the banking system, and banks are willing and able to work out the debt problems on their own. The severity of the problem would be reflected in the widespread interruption of corporate loan payments. Given backward and forward linkages in various industries and of corporations throughout the economy, the inability of one "node" in the payment linkage to settle its debt — e.g. due to "severe" loss of revenue — will inadvertently mean that their suppliers will not be paid, affecting the balance sheets of industrially linked corporations and their banks. This would most probably translate into macroeconomic instability, exacerbating the banking crisis. In their attempts to rebuild their balance sheets, decapitalised banks may widen the spread between deposit and lending rates — thus subsidising "highly" unsuccessful corporations by "taxing" other corporations — or cut back on new lending to creditworthy borrowers, thus further exacerbating the situation.

If the only thing preventing banks from restructuring debts and working out loans is the lack of new capital (where banks have both the incentives and capacity to work out loans and restructure debts), then government involvement can be limited to restoring bank capital. However, before public funds are used to capitalise banks, existing shareholder equity should be written down, including for loan provisioning, to ensure taxpayers do not bear more than they need to.

The clearest way for governments to recapitalise banks is by buying new equity, although recapitalisation can and does take many forms.[33] Banks can then narrow interest rate spreads, and reduce unsustainably high levels of debt through write-offs. Recapitalisation is more effective if linked to specific measures to restructure debt. The fiscal costs of bank recapitalisation can be very large, and again, must be gauged carefully against the benefits.

Government Asset Management Company

A new government asset management company (AMC) is called for if the number of troubled corporations is large and there are microeconomic factors that severely inhibit the likely efficacy of debt restructuring. The most important of these factors are decapitalised and poorly managed banks, a shortage of bank expertise needed to work out bad debts, an uneven balance of power between banks and corporations, lack of corporate capacity and willingness to provide reliable financial information, and, again, systemic negative externalities such as a credit squeeze or unsustainably high foreign debt.

A government-financed asset management company can buy bad loans, provide equity to banks and corporations, negotiate with debtors and take an active financial and operational role in restructuring. An asset management company can serve as an out-of-court bankruptcy mechanism when bankruptcy courts are ineffective, since passing legislation and building institutional infrastructure for effective bankruptcy procedures can be time consuming (Stone 2002). The debt taken on by the asset management company is usually written down (though in Malaysia's case, corporate borrowers do not seem to have been penalised at all), and can be converted to equity and eventually sold to the public. The asset management company realises economies of scale in the specialised area of corporate debt restructuring and can develop secondary debt markets. Banks benefit from greater capital, while corporations can expect to have their debt restructured more quickly.[34]

Governments, investors and the general public must realise that bank recapitalisation and corporate restructuring comes at a price. In the words of Chung (1999: 28), "trying to ignore the costs of restructuring or attempting to suppress them directly cannot be good policy. Rather, the right approach for government will be to acknowledge the costs [of the restructuring programme] and proceed decisively with reform while asking for the public's forbearance regarding the unavoidable costs". It is important to estimate the amount of funds needed for alternative programmes, ensuring that the burden borne by taxpayers is neither onerous nor likely to be seen as unfair, besides being growth enhancing in the long run (though not profitable in the short term). If restructuring programmes are seen to be "transparent" and "fair", thereby garnering public support and limiting public opposition or dissent, then the required funds can be quickly and effectively channelled to resolve bank and corporate distress without too much delay.

Similarly, it is important to have a clear picture of what one expects from a corporate restructuring programme in the short and medium term. Generally, the short run costs of corporate restructuring — due to slower economic growth (in terms of output and employment) — are higher than in the long run because firms are more focused on debt restructuring, and probably on firm downsizing (thereby diverting the focus temporarily away from profitability and new capital investments). Hence, the gains from corporate restructuring are unlikely to be significantly felt in the short term. Instead, the benefits of corporate restructuring are more likely to be felt in the medium and long term — after corporations have refocused on their core competencies and businesses, improved their balance sheets and cash flows, enhanced their operations to maximise objectives (whether profit or shareholder value), and attained better capabilities to make appropriate investment and other decisions, to become more resilient and competitive.

Box 4.1   Advantages and Disadvantages of a Centralised Public AMC

Advantages
- Economies of scale — i.e. consolidation of scarce work-out skills and resources within one agency.
- Can help securitise assets to generate larger pool of assets.
- Centralises ownership of collateral, thus (potentially) providing more leverage over debtors and more effective management.
- Breaks links between banks and corporations, and can thus improve loan collection.
- Allows banks to focus on core business of banking.
- Improves prospects for orderly restructuring of the economy e.g. to use the AMC as an industrial policy tool.[35]
- Can be given special powers to expedite loan recovery and restructuring.[36]

Disadvantages
- Banks have informational advantages over AMCs as they should have good information on their borrowers.
- Leaving loans in banks may provide banks with better incentives for recovery — and for avoiding future losses by improving loan approval and monitoring procedures.

- Banks can provide additional financing which may be necessary for restructuring.
- If assets transferred to AMCs are not actively managed, the existence of an AMC may lead to a general deterioration of repayment discipline and further deterioration of asset values.
- It may be difficult to insulate a public agency against political pressures, especially if the AMC carries a large portion of banking system assets.

Source: Klingebiel (2000: 6).

Effective Corporate Restructuring

The formulation of an appropriate framework is a highly complex part of comprehensive debt restructuring. Conflicts between different measures to achieve various reform objectives and implementation problems are bound to occur. The pace of corporate restructuring can be slowed down due to several factors. (Cho and Pomerleano [2001] discuss factors that slowed down corporate restructuring in the crisis affected countries — to varying degrees — with each factor having varying importance. Changes have since been made to speed up corporate restructuring in Malaysia.)

Conditions

Notwithstanding the approach chosen, the government must create and maintain a stable macroeconomic environment to facilitate and ensure that the restructuring programme can progress and meet its objectives as swiftly and as effectively as possible (Cho and Pomerleano 2001; Mako 2001a). Macroeconomic stability can help provide the confidence needed for effective debt restructuring programmes. Stable prices, interest rates and exchange rates are needed for debtors, creditors and investors to have enough confidence to make transactions. Delays in attaining macroeconomic stability apparently slowed restructuring progress in Chile and Indonesia (Stone 2000).

Even though stable and, preferably, lower interest rates are essential, according to the World Bank (2000d), they are unlikely to

Table 4.1   East Asian Four: Corporate Distress, Past and Projected, 1995–2002 (shares of firms unable to meet current debt service payment obligations)

Country	1995 Total	1996 Total	1997 Total	1998 Total	1999 (Q2) Total	1999 (Q2) Manufacturing	1999 (Q2) Services	1999 (Q2) Real Estate	2000– 2002ᵃ Total	2000– 2002ᵇ Total
Indonesia	12.6	17.9	40.3	58.2	63.8	41.8	66.8	86.9	52.9	60.8
S. Korea	8.5	11.2	24.3	33.8	26.7	19.6	28.1	43.9	17.2	22.6
Malaysiaᶜ	3.4	5.6	17.1	34.3	26.3	39.3	33.3	52.8	13.8	17.4
Thailand	6.7	10.4	32.6	30.4	28.3	21.8	29.4	46.9	22.3	27.1

Notes: a. Estimates based on the assumption that interest rates stay at their current level throughout the period.

b. Estimates based on the assumption that interest rates regain their 1990–95 averages.

c. Malaysian firms in agriculture and utilities brought down the average for all firms in 1999.

Growth rates assumed through 2002 are based on IMF (1998) projections.

Sources: Claessens *et al.* 1999a; sectoral estimates provided by Claessens, Djankov and Klingebiel for World Bank (2000d).

be sufficient for eliminating distress. The World Bank's estimates of the ability of Asian firms in the four crisis hit countries to meet their current interest payment obligations are given in Table 4.1. Caution is needed in interpreting these figures, as they are based on a small sample of publicly listed firms. Table 4.2 provides a comparison of non-performing loans (NPLs) and recapitalisation requirements.

In addition, as mentioned above, a supporting legal, regulatory and accounting environment is necessary for successful corporate restructuring. Important legal aspects of restructuring include foreclosure standards, foreign investment rules, and merger and acquisition policies. Regulations governing debt-equity conversions and asset sales often need to be changed to enable possible novel and complex restructuring transactions, as in Thailand. Financial disclosure standards should be raised to international levels and enforced to promote more transparent restructuring transactions,[37] but this should not be done in the midst of a crisis, as in Malaysia, as it will only exacerbate the crisis. One must therefore be cautious in deciding when and by how much to raise these standards for this could result

Table 4.2   East Asian Four: Non-Performing Loans and Recapitalisation Requirements

	Indonesia	South Korea	Malaysia	Thailand
NPLs as % of total	60–75[b]	8.5[c]	22[d]	46.5[e]
Bank loans[a]	(58.7)	(12.2)	(23.2)	(34.8)
Current capital[f]	−15.1	−1.0	1.8	−4.5
Capital shortfall[g]	18.5	4.0	1.7	8.1
Gross costs	45	15	12	32[h]
Fiscal recapitalisation costs to date	37.3	15.8	10.9	17.4
Expected additional fiscal costs	12.7	10.7	5.5	15.4

Notes: a. Figures in parentheses are estimates for end-June 2000 (World Bank 2000e).
　　　b. Radelet (1999).
　　　c. End-March 1999.
　　　d. End-July 1999.
　　　e. End-June 1999.
　　　f. As percentage of total bank assets.
　　　g. Assumes a 40 per cent recovery rate on non-performing loans, a constant ratio of loans to deposits, and loan growth in line with GDP growth. The capital shortfall is applied to the entire banking system.
　　　h. As of November 1998, IMF *World Economic Outlook: Interim Assessment,* December 1998.
Sources: Claessens *et al.* (1999b), Baliño *et al.* (1999), and World Bank (2000a, 2000e). Cited by Park (2000).

in negative side effects or harmful secondary effects especially in an already financially distressed and tight credit environment. The World Bank (2000c: 90) proposes that other measures — such as "liberalising foreign investment rules, revamping merger and acquisition policy, opening up markets, and further tax reforms" — should be adopted.[38]

Timing[39]

Issues of corporate governance cannot be isolated from corporate restructuring matters because the two are very much related and both need to be addressed to create the basis for continued economic recovery and to improve long-term economic prospects. There is less debate over the need for implementing corporate restructuring as an "immediate" measure, as long as it is accompanied or complemented by expansionary policy,[40] as discussed later.

There is, however, more contention over the desirability of simultaneous implementation of corporate restructuring and institutional (including corporate governance) reforms. Specifically, there is contention as to *when* "stricter" explicit (or formal) and/or implicit (or informal) rules and regulations should be implemented. There has been debate over whether "orthodox" IMF policy measures — ostensibly for crisis management and promoting sustainable long-term growth — have been effective in meeting their objectives. Park (2000) has summarised the IMF's recommended policy measures for economic recovery.

Like many others, Park (2000) argues that the strategies proposed by the IMF are neither acceptable nor justifiable,[41] for two main reasons. Firstly, though the World Bank (2000d: 7) has claimed that "assertive structural adjustment helped restore credit flows and boosted consumer and investor confidence", it is unclear whether and how much financial and corporate restructuring contributed to the economic recovery of the East Asian economies. Most of the serious structural problems said to be the major causes of the crises in Indonesia, South Korea, Malaysia, and Thailand could not have been resolved within two years (Park 2000). In fact, banks are still holding a large volume of non-performing loans on their balance sheets and remain undercapitalised in all four countries (see Table 4.2).

If restructuring efforts cannot be credited with the 1999–2000 recovery and may not even have catalysed, let alone supported the upswing, what factors and developments provided the impetus for the recovery?[42] In brief, counter-cyclical fiscal policy clearly contributed to recovery in South Korea, Thailand and Malaysia. Second, both South Korea and Malaysia benefited from renewed global demand for electronics. Third, it seems likely that the determined government responses in both countries improved both consumer and investor confidence, contributing to positive changes in the economy. Earlier pessimism induced domestic consumers and investors to greatly cut spending and investment during the early stages of the crisis. Such perceptions have a tendency to become self-fulfilling prophecies.

Over time, the sweeping criticisms of East Asia in the immediate aftermath of the crisis diminished and gradually gave way to bolder thinking and measures as well as more optimism, confidence and recovery in most crisis economies. As the realisation that the crisis was temporary started sinking into the minds of consumers and investors, spending and investment resumed, enabling a V-shaped recovery.

Park (2000: 48) also points out that "in the IMF programmes, many of the institutional reforms, including the reform of government bureaucracy and the legal system, were prescribed as medium-term priorities". Yet, at the onset of the crisis, institutional reforms were said to be critical to winning back the confidence of foreign lenders and investors in the crisis economies, and thus stabilising domestic financial markets, rather than addressing the structural weaknesses of the economy over a longer period. In other words, even though the IMF acknowledged that corporate restructuring and structural reforms were medium-term objectives, in reality, it emphasised corporate restructuring and structural reforms as short-term priorities. Privately, IMF officials argued that unless something was done about structural weaknesses — which, in their view, contributed to, caused and perpetuated the crisis in the first place — the chances of economic recovery were remote or slim.[43] Hence, restructuring and institutional reforms were carried out simultaneously from the start, without making any distinction between, say, a short-run liquidity management priority and, presumably, a preference for avoiding and preventing future crises.

This process frustrated implementation of institutional reforms in two ways. First, rushed institutional reforms were often formal and superficial. Second, with recovery, market pressures to sustain the reforms faded.[44] Furthermore, the IMF programmes underestimated the consequences of possible conflicts between operational restructuring of financial institutions and corporations on the one hand and institutional reforms on the other. For example, the three IMF financed crisis countries of South Korea, Thailand and Indonesia could not be sure whether the planned regulatory improvements (in loan classification, loan loss provisioning and bank capital adequacy) could be completed within the stipulated three-year period and the extent to which this might slow the recovery process.[45]

Malaysian Special Purpose Vehicles

As noted in Chapter 2, the Malaysian authorities radically changed course in early December 1997 when then Finance Minister Anwar promulgated a series of conventional macroeconomic policy measures after five months of declining confidence in response to the regime's early counter-cyclical but quixotic policy measures. Several weeks later, the then Prime Minister Mahathir created the National Economic Action Council (NEAC) led by him to address the crisis. Former Finance Minister Daim Zainuddin was soon put in charge of the NEAC although his earlier policy advice was considered to be even more pro-market and pro-IMF, e.g. in favouring an even larger fiscal contraction.

By the second quarter of 1998, the NEAC had come out with an Action Plan and Anwar reversed his December 1997 policies by trying to reflate the economy with counter-cyclical public spending measures, particularly favouring small businesses and farmers, perhaps in anticipation of the party's annual convention in late June when he came under strong attack from his enemies, including Mahathir, ostensibly for being homosexual and having favoured family members and political allies. By this time, however, he had announced the creation of several special purpose vehicles to save and recapitalise the banking system, and to restructure large corporations considered deserving of special governmental support. These three new creations — Danaharta, Danamodal and the CDRC — are introduced below.

Malaysia's Asset Management Company, Syarikat Pengurusan Danaharta Nasional Bhd, or Danaharta[46]

Syarikat Pengurusan Danaharta Nasional Bhd, or Danaharta, the national asset management company[47] was set up on 20 June 1998, in the aftermath of the 1997–98 Asian financial crisis, under the Ministry of Finance to acquire non-performing loans from banks, or to put it differently, to carve out bad debts from local banks.[48] Unlike the asset management companies in South Korea and Thailand, Danaharta is neither a rapid disposition agency nor a warehousing agency. Rather, it was granted a wider range of restructuring options, with the only stipulation being maximising recovery value. Furthermore, Danaharta could not only take legal action[49] to recover security through the bankruptcy process and sell the loans to a third party, but could also take a more active role in rehabilitating companies since Danaharta's powers include the power to force management and ownership changes within the companies.

Nonetheless, given the risks associated with such a strategy (as highlighted in Box 4.1), Danaharta outlined strict loan restructuring guidelines to avoid many problems of moral hazard.[50] Refer to <http://www.danaharta.com.my/> for its asset acquisition guidelines, framework for acquisition methodology, background to and summary of The Pengurusan Danaharta Nasional Berhad Act 1998 and other information. Tables 4.3 to 4.5 compare the special administration and other workout opportunities used as general guidelines for developing countries.

Danamodal Nasional Bhd, or Danamodal[51]

The second institution established for managing the crisis was the bank recapitalisation agency, Danamodal Nasional Bhd, incorporated on 10 August 1998 with an anticipated life span of five to seven years.[52] The rationale for establishing Danamodal was three pronged:

(1)   to ensure that the banking sector recapitalisation process is commercially driven and that investment decisions are made according to market-based principles;

(2)   delays in addressing recapitalisation and non-performing loans issues will have a drag effect on the financial system and economic recovery; and

(3)   direct capital injection by the government into banking institutions is not desirable and would lead to conflicts of interest in the future.

To address problems of moral hazard inherent in such an exercise, Danamodal operated on the first-loss principle, under which losses arising from past credit decisions are born by shareholders. See the BNM website: <http://www.bnm.gov.my/danamodal/ff_vital.htm> for an overview of Danamodal's vision and mission statement, guiding principles, and operating guidelines, as well as the stabilisation measures undertaken by Danamodal and the financial system.

Table 4.3 Comparison of Debt Workout Arrangements

Area of comparison	Special Administration (Danaharta)	Administration (Australia)	Administration (UK)	Chapter 11 (USA)
Affected person	Corporate borrower of Danaharta Group and its security providers only	Any company	Any company	Any company
Who can appoint	Danaharta • At request of owners or management; or • On own initiative, but subject to approval of Oversight Committee	Company itself, chargee or liquidator/ provisional liquidator	Court of petition by the company, its directors or creditors	Generally, company remains in possession, but court may appoint trustee — on its own or on petition by an interested party
Oversight Committee	3 members appointed by Minister of Finance, one each from Ministry of Finance, BNM and SC	None	None	None
Criteria	Inability or likelihood of inability to pay debts or fulfil obligations to creditors	Insolvency or likelihood of insolvency	Inability or likelihood of inability to pay debts	Generally, inability to pay debts as they become due
Purpose	Survival as going concern, more advantageous realisation than winding up, or public interest	Maximises chances of survival, or results in better return than winding up	Survival as going concern; more advantageous realisation than winding up; voluntary arrangement or deed of compromise	Reorganisation results in creditors receiving at least as much as they would from liquidation

(contd overleaf)

Table 4.3 *Continued.*

Area of comparison	Special Administration (Danaharta)	Administration (Australia)	Administration (UK)	Chapter 11 (USA)
Duration	From appointment until termination (generally upon implementation of workout proposal)	From appointment until termination (generally upon approval of workout proposal)	From appointment until termination in accordance with court order	Generally not applicable, debtor remains in possession
Role	Control and management of assets and affairs: • Powers of existing officers suspended • No dealings without Special Administrator's consent	Control and management of assets and affairs: • Powers of existing officers suspended • No dealings without administrator's consent	Control and management of assets and affairs: • Powers of existing officers suspended • No dealings without administrator's consent	Generally not applicable, debtor remains in possession
Status	Agent of company under administration	Agent of company under administration	Agent of company under administration and court officer	Generally not applicable, debtor remains in possession
Protection	12 month moratorium on all claims and proceedings, subject to extension	Moratorium on all claims and proceedings for duration of administration	Moratorium on all claims and proceedings for duration determined by court	Moratorium on all claims and proceedings for duration of Chapter 11
Functions	Investigates assets and affairs and, as soon as reasonably practicable, submits workout proposal to Independent Advisor and Danaharta	Investigates assets and affairs, and within 21–28 days (unless extended), recommends workout, termination of administration or winding up to creditors	Investigates assets and affairs, within 3 months (unless extended), submits proposal to creditors and reports outcome to court	Company has 4 months to file plan of reorganisation though period is usually extended. A trustee, if appointed, investigates assets and affairs, commences action against third parties and files a plan of reorganisation

Area of comparison	Special Administration (Danaharta)	Administration (Australia)	Administration (UK)	Chapter 11 (USA)
Independent Advisor	Approved by Oversight Committee to review reasonableness of workout proposal, taking into account the interests of all creditors and shareholders	None	None	None
Workout proposal	Requires approval of Danaharta and majority in value of secured creditors, and subject to regulatory approvals	Requires approval of majority in number and value of creditors	Requires approval of 75% of creditors	Requires approval of impaired creditors (2/3 in value and 50% in number of each class)
Binding nature	Once approved, workout proposal binds the company, its shareholders and creditors	Once approved, workout proposal binds the company, its shareholders and creditors (except secured creditors who opt out)	Once approved, workout proposal binds the company, its shareholders and creditors	Once approved, reorganisation plan binds the company, its shareholders and creditors
Modifications	Must refer to Independent Advisor who will review reasonableness and decide whether to seek approval of secured creditors	Requires approval of creditors	Major modifications require agreement of administrator and creditors' approval	Only permitted if not yet substantially consummated and with court approval
Qualifications of Special Administrator	Individual who is an approved company auditor or has requisite experience or ability	Individual who is an accountant or has requisite experience or ability	Insolvency practitioners	Not applicable
Qualifications of Independent Advisor	Merchant bank, accounting firm or other entity with the requisite experience or ability	Not applicable	Not applicable	Not applicable

Source: Danaharta's website: <http://www.danaharta.com.my/>.

Table 4.4   Purpose of Special Administration, Receivership & Liquidation

Special Administration	Receivership	Liquidation
Workout for purpose of achieving: • survival of company under administration as going concern, or • more advantageous realisation of assets than would be achieved on winding up	To deal with assets of the company by enforcing security of a particular creditor chiefly for that creditor's benefit	Winding up leading to eventual dissolution of the company in liquidation

Source: Danaharta's website: <http://www.danaharta.com.my/>.

Corporate Debt Restructuring Committee (CDRC)[53]

The government also addressed the problems of the corporate sector (i.e. to restructure corporate debt over RM50 million) through the formation of a Corporate Debt Restructuring Committee (CDRC), a non-statutory body, in October 1998, under Bank Negara Malaysia

Table 4.5   Major Differences Between Special Administration and Section 176 Scheme

Special Administration	Section 176 Scheme
• Initiated by Danaharta on its own initiative or at request of company's management or shareholders • Requires approval of Oversight Committee • Special Administrator prepares workout proposal • Independent Advisor reviews reasonableness of proposal • Requires approval of majority in value of secured creditors • Automatic 12-month moratorium on all claims and proceedings	• Initiated by the company, shareholders, creditors or liquidator • No equivalent • Person initiating the scheme prepares it • No independent review, but court sanction required • Requires approval of majority in number representing 75% in value of creditors • Moratorium with court approval

Source: Danaharta's website: <http://www.danaharta.com.my/>.

(BNM). The CDRC was formed to provide a platform for both borrowers and creditors to work out feasible corporate debt restructuring schemes[54] without having to resort to legal proceedings, especially for large debtors. Put differently, the objective of the committee, like its counterparts in Indonesia, South Korea, and Thailand, was to minimise losses to creditors, shareholders, and other stakeholders through coordinated voluntary workouts that sidestep the formal bankruptcy procedure.[55]

Existing insolvency legislation in Malaysia was clearly more institutionalised than in either Indonesia or Thailand. Nonetheless, it was unpopular with creditors and did not provide the range of solutions to preserve value for other stakeholders in complex corporate groups with multiple creditors.[56] The purpose of the committee was thus to persuade financial institutions not to precipitate insolvency.[57]

In August 2001, the CDRC, under new leadership, announced three new measures to spur corporate restructuring which included: (1) a revamp of CDRC membership to include representatives from Pengurusan Danaharta Nasional Bhd and the Federation of Public Listed Companies; (2) changes to the framework and approach of the CDRC to accelerate restructuring efforts;[58] and (3) an increase in the frequency of financial disclosure, i.e. regular disclosure and quarterly reporting to keep the market abreast of the progress of restructuring (*The Star*, 10 August 2001).

The CDRC now has the authority to implement management changes. Furthermore, the agency can now appoint liquidators to settle non-performing loans (NPLs). Previously, the CDRC had merely acted as a mediator with limited authority between creditors and borrowers (*The Star*, 13 August 2001). For a detailed look at the principles of the CDRC framework, its objectives, terms of reference, key principles governing the corporate workout process, processes and guidelines, revised debt restructuring guidelines, and revised framework, refer to the CDRC website, <http://www.bnm.gov.my/CDRC/>.

Concluding Remarks

Since financial restructuring determines the allocation of current losses, ownership distribution and future control of the economy, "sound and proper" financial restructuring is crucial. However, developing an appropriate and effective plan is easier said than done. In this connection, there are numerous lessons to be learnt from the past experiences of countries in crisis, including those in East Asia.[59] Enoch *et al.* (1999: 37) suggest that "one cannot specify in advance how banks [and corporations] will be handled. Decisions will depend upon the financial position and prospects of each institution. The restructuring agency is equipped with a toolbox of measures that it can use. Full diagnosis of the state of the banks [and corporations] will determine which set of tools in the box will be appropriate in each case." In other words, different tools may be appropriate in different circumstances. Hence, no appropriate policy response can be specified *ex ante*.

Marshall (1998) points out that since a systemic crisis (which involves an externality — where individuals do not fully internalise the costs or benefits of their actions — leading to "market failure") must result in sub-optimal economic performance, government action could lead to improved economic performance. Experience suggests that government action with appropriate policies based on accurate diagnosis and intended to achieve effective implementation has been invaluable in times of systemic crises.

In light of the extraordinary and unique circumstances facing the East Asian economies in 1997/98, it was imperative for the governments to facilitate, if not lead, economic recovery. Government intervention may well be the key to initiating change and could stimulate growth during a systemic crisis, especially in a situation characterised by market imperfections,[60] through well-conceived policies and measures. In fact, the crises have emphasised the need for appropriate, well-conceived and well-implemented policies and pre-emptive actions. Being in a *strategic position* (borrowing a term from Chang and Rowthorn 1995), the government may be the only agent who could sensibly make and coordinate certain kinds of decisions at the national level to represent the interests of society.[61]

Henceforth, the debate is no longer over whether the government should intervene, but over how. The questions that need to be addressed and answered include what policies to pursue, how "involved" the government should be in restructuring (the *degree* or *extent* of government involvement, i.e. should the government create a favourable environment, and rules of the game for market-based approaches to work, or should the government lead the restructuring process. This is determined, in turn, by the following questions: how quickly does the government want the restructuring programme to progress, who bears the costs, and what kind of financial system it wants to emerge eventually out of the restructuring programme) and how the government should coordinate its activities. What is imperative is how the government decides which is the highest priority issue to address, since there will always be trade-offs among alternative policy measures, in the face of "limited" financial or fiscal and human resources. Yet, it must be stressed again that there is room for errors of judgment and other risks in every decision-making process, whether made by the private sector or the government.

It is important to stress that the preceding argument does not imply that governments are to be given a green light to simply intervene at will, especially in ways that are not welfare improving. Countries with varying types and degrees of political, judicial, economic and social maturity will employ different strategies, with varying types and degrees of government intervention deemed suitable. The key here is to find the right match or fit between "form and content" (Gourevitch 1993), that is, the form of government (e.g. ranging from authoritarian to democratic systems) and content of economic policy, or in this case, of the corporate restructuring programme.

Moreover, the solution to the bad debt — or non-performing loan — problem cannot be an isolated policy, but rather should involve a comprehensive economic strategy or programme that considers macroeconomic factors.[62] One cannot hope to have a successful corporate restructuring programme without considering government macroeconomic policies — both fiscal and monetary (both very much influenced by political economy factors) — to ensure macroeconomic stability and a favourable environment for corporate restructuring, or in short, to ensure "good" "macroeconomic governance".[63] Besides creating a favourable environment for corporate restructuring, the speed at which macro-stability can be achieved is important, as this will determine the viability of corporations, which in turn will affect the success of financial restructuring. Yet, as pointed out by Stone (1998: 5), "macro stability will often require progress in financial and corporate restructuring [as these factors affect say, investor confidence and capital flows], and thus cannot be seen independently from the restructuring process".

Furthermore, since no one approach is necessarily superior to another,[64] there is no *a priori* reason to reject a "hybrid" approach — a comprehensive, but eclectic approach involving the market, financial and non-financial institutions and the government — to manage a financial crisis, such as the 1997–98 Asian crisis.[65] Such a "contingency approach" would offer specific solutions to particular problems, depending on the particular situations at hand. The efficacy of each approach is contingent on several important factors (including constraints). The appropriate role of the government will also be influenced by the nature, phase and severity (impact) of the crisis, the laws (especially with respect to bankruptcy, anti-trust, mergers, acquisitions and takeovers), the macroeconomic, business and information environment, and the government's fiscal and financial constraints.

Hence, "a one size fits all" approach — that may even have proved "successful" in certain circumstances — cannot be adopted blindly or wholesale. It would be wiser to selectively adapt policies (short-term, medium-term and long-term) of "successful" corporate restructuring approaches from other crisis countries that are suitable or tailored to other political, institutional, social and economic conditions. The need for "effective" and "timely" execution of policies and programmes also cannot be over-emphasised.

Notes

1. Corporations that underwent liquidation proceedings will not be reviewed in the case studies.

2. Corporate and bank restructuring differ in several regards, e.g. the loss recognition process in the corporate sector takes longer; no central supervisory agency exists; there are many more different types of corporations, requiring diverse responses; policymakers are less knowledgeable about the corporate sector; there is no magic bullet for corporate restructuring (bank restructuring is generally regarded as the responsibility of the government), highlighting the fact that complementary government measures and private sector initiatives are required (Pomerleano 2000). See also Dziobek and Pazarbasioglu (1997), Enoch *et al.* (1999), Fries and Lane (1994), Dziobek (1998) and Klingebiel (2000) on bank restructuring.

3. To reiterate, there is no objective determinant of what debt leverage is deemed too "high".

4. Not totally or completely eliminating or preventing crises from occurring, since adjustments (improvements) in the internal structure cannot effectively prevent "external shocks" from affecting the domestic economy.

5. More specifically, factors such as the financial structure of the firm and market structure after restructuring — in terms of the size and number of firms in the industry, and the profitability of the firms and the industry as a whole after restructuring, including returns on equity (ROE), returns on assets (ROA), etc.

6. Better corporate governance should improve "corporate performance" (e.g. cost, productivity, quality, efficiency, and "profitability") by ensuring that non-performing loans and bad debts are kept to a minimum.

7. This seems to agree with Yee's (1999) view that "Corporate governance is important not only for protecting investors' interests but also for reducing systemic market risks, ensuring the stability of the market environment where corporations conduct business, and preventing financial crisis and the consequent social destruction as experienced by some counties in the region." However, to avert crisis, a confluence of factors — including "good" fiscal, monetary, investment and industrial policies, conducive and "competitive" business culture and environment — must also be in place.

8. For instance, the "reorganisation" of a financially insolvent — but economically viable — corporation, as provided for by Chapter 11 of the US Bankruptcy Code.

9. After a private acquisition, the new controlling party can push for operational restructuring (part of corporate restructuring) of the enterprise to improve efficiency and profitability. Not all "fire-sale FDI" is necessarily undesirable in certain circumstances, i.e. in a pure "moral-hazard" version of a crisis, a drop in asset values is basically appropriate, and fire-sale FDI — involving transfer of ownership to foreign firms — can improve resource allocation (Krugman 1998c).

10. The major benefits of takeovers include "correction of managerial failures" or getting rid of under-performing managers or those not properly exercising their functions. Empirical studies reveal that shareholders of acquiring firms in hostile takeovers enjoy greater returns than in friendly ones because hostile acquirers tend to have more clarity of purpose and better planning and implementation, being under greater shareholder pressure to "get it right the first time", resulting in greater care and discipline. Yet, impediments include higher transaction costs, inability to conduct due diligence, less cooperation from management, and higher opportunity costs. Hostile

takeovers are easier if there are dispersed shareholdings, with no one party holding a decisive block. Under-performing companies (e.g. where the aggregate value of the individual companies is greater than the group's value), under-priced companies and cash rich companies are also more likely to ensure more profitable hostile takeovers (*The Star*, 8 Nov. 2001).

11.   This point is related to two previous points. Mergers and acquisitions by (both foreign and domestic) firms already in the national economy would not bring in foreign exchange. However, foreign firms coming in to acquire a corporation bring in foreign exchange.

12.   Banks can set up their own AMCs, known as decentralised AMCs.

13.   In Poland in late 1993, the state was only involved in one step, i.e. the initial recapitalisation of the banks. Subsequently, banks were given the task of cleaning up sub-standard loans in their asset portfolios by requiring the financial restructuring of indebted enterprises (Belka 1994).

    In the Polish bank reconciliatory procedure (BCP), a lead bank acted as an agent representing all creditors, designed a financial restructuring plan (which included rescheduling total debt, mainly by partial refinancing at a lower interest rate, partial cancellation, i.e. writing-down the face value of the loan, and swapping some debt for equity) and arranged the enterprise's "revitalisation" or business plan for operational restructuring (Bonin and Leven 2000).

14.   "The 'contingency approach' takes the view that there is no one best, universal form of organisation. There are a large number of variables, or situational factors, that influence organisational performance. Contingency models can be seen as an 'if-then' form of relationship. If certain situational factors exist, then certain organisational and managerial variables are appropriate" (Mullins 1996: 87).

15.   See also Krugman's (1998c) analysis of so-called "fire sale FDI".

16.   For more on these issues, see Aghion *et al.* (1992).

17.   According to Cui (1999: 8), Hayek would argue that "when 'market failures' are identified by pointing out violations of the assumptions of the First Theorem, the 'survival of the fittest' argument could be used against government regulation to correct these 'failures'. According to Hayek and Coase, private dealing and 'spontaneous order' can always resolve these 'market failures' in a better way. To Hayek, the 'survival of the fittest' argument should not only be applied at the individual firm level, it should also be applied to the natural selection of 'rules and institutions'. This is why Hayek criticises 'social Darwinism', because it wrongly 'concentrated on the selection of the individuals rather than that of institutions and practices' (Hayek 1982: 23). It is the natural selection of the fittest institutions that provides the strongest argument for the 'invisible hand paradigm'."

18. See Maher and Andersson (2000: Section IV.3), and the various studies referred to by them for a review of the debate over the effectiveness of market mechanisms, specifically hostile takeovers.

19. See Bebchuk (1988; 1997) and Hart (1999) for an explanation of the bargaining procedure in Chapter 11.

20. Roe (1983) — as quoted by Bebchuk (1997: 5) — "suggests that the nature of the existing bargaining process often leads to an inefficient choice of structure for the reorganised company — and, in particular, to excessive debt in the capital structure". Hotchkiss (1995) empirically supports this argument — many corporations subsequently have to undergo financial restructuring within a few years after reorganisation.

21. This foregone output is calculated as the difference between "normal" output levels — output levels when the enterprise is conducting "business as usual" and is not facing bankruptcy proceedings — and the lower production level during the "bargaining" process, when the firm "temporarily" ceases production.

22. See Aghion *et al.* (1992) for an illustration of the "financing problem" using IBM as an example.

23. Wijnbergen (1998) notes the liquidation bias of Chapter 11 of the US Bankruptcy Code. Also see Aghion *et al.* (1994).

24. See Wijnbergen (1997) for an analysis of the kind of incentives needed to "persuade" the banks to undertake corporate debt restructuring of state-owned enterprises (SOEs) in Poland. From the Polish experience, one can draw some insights into private corporate debt restructuring programmes.

25. According to Enoch *et al.* (1999: 46), triage is defined as "the division of institutions between those that need no help, those that are worth helping, and those that are beyond help". According to Claessens *et al.* (2001: 7), a triage involves a separation of "corporations into viable, not financial distressed corporations, viable, but financial distressed corporations, and unviable corporations".

26. When it comes to developing a voluntary framework along the lines of the London Approach, Meyerman (2000: 304) points out the "the relationship between business and government, the nature of corporate debt, the extent to which debt was denominated in foreign currency, how much debt was held domestically — all influenced the particular framework adopted".

27. There appears to be a distinct aversion (for fear of "loss of face") to the use of strictly legal processes (which require somewhat rigid adherence to the legal system) to resolve commercial disputes and problems. The heightened stigma in relation to financial or business collapse — which results in "loss of face" — *could* be the motive for undertaking desperately ill-conceived measures, such as denial, avoidance, escape, cover-up, secretiveness, or manipulation. However, this is not only true of East Asian countries. On the contrary, it

must be said that the stigma associated with insolvency is part of most cultures, albeit to differing degrees. Corporations are increasingly pressured to meet "market expectations". This probably induces corporations to give the impression of "success", to engage in "creative accounting" to inflate profits, to under-report costs and liabilities, and to hide losses — as in the Enron case.

28.   This discussion draws from Stone (1998). Also see Mako (2001a; 2001b).

29.   According to Stone (1998), a comprehensive corporate debt restructuring plan can be divided into four parts:
   •   Establishment of an appropriate macroeconomic, tax, and legal environment.
   •   Formulation of a debt restructuring framework.
   •   *Triage*, or separation of viable corporations for debt restructuring (i.e. those whose value as a going concern, taking into account potential restructuring at "equilibrium" exchange and interest rates, exceeds its salvage value) from non-viable corporations that should be shut down.
   •   "Financial engineering", involving debt reduction and debt-equity conversions.

30.   For instance, too little private capital is available since private parties are either unable or unwilling to lend or invest in corporations or banks.

31.   This discussion draws from Stone (1998).

32.   In general, "mediation involves the engagement of an independent person for the purpose of reaching a possible resolution of a dispute or issue. The resolution is reached through a consensus of the persons involved in the dispute or issue or having an interest in its resolution. The mediator has virtually no powers (other than as may be agreed to by the parties) and certainly no power to determine the dispute or issue other than by consensus or agreement between the parties. The mediator acts more like a conciliator, endeavouring through meetings and discussions to focus on central and material matters and to encourage the parties to reduce and distil their differences to the point where they may be able to come to a mutually satisfactory determination" (World Bank 2000f: 82).

33.   There are other ways by which the central bank or the government can help banks "financially". See Dziobek (1998: 9–12).

34.   For a summary of the advantages and disadvantages of a centralised public asset management corporation or company, see Box 4.1. Klingebiel (2000: 5–6) offers a more critical view of the various strengths and weaknesses of public AMCs. According to Mako (2001b), public AMCs are ill-suited for corporate operational restructuring [but that does not necessarily imply that they cannot

and will always fail], even though, under special circumstances, public asset management companies may be able to play a useful role in financial stabilisation and resolution of some assets (for more details, see Mako 2001b).

35. However, this may be tricky for two reasons: (i) it is not necessarily obvious that the government has better information, than the private sector, about overcapacity and future growth areas; and (ii) involving government agencies may provide the scope for political interference.

36. For example, Danaharta had the power to demand management changes where deemed necessary to improve the operations of the corporation. This could improve the profitability and financial position of the corporation, thereby increasing the likelihood of the corporation repaying its loans.

37. In Hungary, the enactment — in 1991 and 1992 — of new loan provisioning laws furthered bank restructuring, and contributed to gradually tightening corporate budgets (Stone 2000).

38. According to the World Bank (2000f: 90), "investment in financial and corporate sectors needs to be liberalised as foreign investment can provide much-needed capital and expertise. Tax and regulatory changes to facilitate debt-to-equity conversions and ease asset sales can also be necessary. Over the medium term, biases in the tax treatment of debt versus equity often need to be redressed."

39. The arguments here draw from Park (2000).

40. Chung (1999) notes that with the economic downturn, the view that the restructuring programme should be implemented concurrently with a stimulus package gained support. The supposed reasoning behind this is that lack of a restructuring programme may cause high levels of unemployment and undermine the economy's industrial base, also causing social disruption and political instability, with long-term consequences and problems. A more cynical view would be that after blaming the banks and corporations for the financial crisis, neo-liberals pushed through their reform agenda for corporate restructuring while blaming its adverse consequences on the crisis and its alleged culprits.

41. He does acknowledge, however, that the IMF should not be criticised for failing to develop a comprehensive framework *ex post facto*, because the IMF did not have the luxury of spending many months designing a coherent programme as the crisis was deepening in the crisis countries. "The programme packages therefore had to bring in various reform measures that were presumed to help restore market confidence, reduce the likelihood of a recurrence of crisis, and improve the long-term economic performance of these countries without much thinking about the possible conflicts between different measures for different reform objectives" (Park 2000: 44–5).

42.   To answer this question, one needs to conduct an empirical study
      gauging the relative importance of a number of factors. Yet, the data
      and information required for such a study are not available. As such,
      one can only make a qualitative assessment at best, with available
      evidence on the effects of various factors on recovery.

43.   Note that with "limited" financial and fiscal resources, there will
      always be trade-offs among alternative policy measures. As such, the
      government must decide which is of highest priority.

44.   Park (2000: 49) suggests that, "the rush to introduce new corporate
      governance, a new regulatory and supervisory structure, and new
      accounting standards, and even to initiate legal and judicial reform
      in disregard of the difficulty of assimilating a set of alien institutions
      has resulted in many cases in cosmetic reform. Worse yet, once the
      recovery got underway, it has become difficult to maintain the
      momentum of reform, because the recovery has diminished the need
      to improve foreign investors' confidence in the crisis countries. On
      their part, foreign investors and lenders have been losing interest in
      monitoring whether these countries are moving in the right direction
      in carrying out the planned reforms. There is little market pressure
      on these economies to stay on course with the initial reform pro-
      gramme. In adjusting the sovereign ratings of the crisis countries, for
      example, the rating agencies appear to attach more weight to
      improvement in the external liquidity position and macroeconomic
      variables than the progress in restructuring. This lack of foreign pressure
      has given a false impression to the crisis countries that the international
      community is satisfied with the progress in economic reform they
      have achieved."

45.   Park (2000: 48) found that "in many cases, banks were trying to
      reduce their exposure to those weak but viable borrowers, while the
      policy authorities were busy in providing special credit facilities and
      credit guarantees to the same borrowers".

46.   Sources for this appendix are Haggard (2000) and Danaharta's website:
      <http://www.danaharta.com.my/>.

47.   A definition of an asset management company as provided by
      Danaharta can be obtained from its website: <http://www.danaharta.
      com.my/default.html>. "Assets" here refer to both loans and tangible
      assets, with the preferred source of repayment being realisation of
      gain through reconstruction and rehabilitation of the asset while
      other forms of repayment include identified cash flows from acquired
      assets, existing business operations and disposal of collateral.

48.   With paid-up capital of RM250 million (approximately US$65 million
      [US$1 = RM3.8]), Danaharta raised RM25 billion in working capital
      in zero-coupon government-guaranteed bonds.

49.   Danaharta has the legal authority to conduct liquidation procedures.

50.   These included the ability to displace management and appoint "special administrators" to manage distressed companies, the requirement that shareholders take appropriate "haircuts" in any loan rescheduling, and the provision that borrowers are provided only one opportunity to implement a restructuring plan (Thillainathan 2000).

51.   This appendix draws from Haggard (2000) and the Danamodal website: <http://www.bnm.gov.my/danamodal/ff_vital.htm>.

52.   Danamodal fell under the central bank (Bank Negara Malaysia, or BNM), and was to be funded by capital raised in the form of equity and hybrid instruments, or debt, in both domestic and international markets, to minimise the use of public funds. The central bank provided the initial seed capital of RM3 billion, and another RM2 billion on a standby basis.

53.   This section draws from Haggard (2000) and the CDRC website: <http://www.bnm.gov.my/CDRC/>, *The New Straits Times*, 9 Aug. 2001, *The Star*, 10 Aug. 2001, and *The Star*, 13 Aug. 2001.

54.   The CDRC thus acts as an advisor and mediator between creditors and debtors in debt restructuring.

55.   With the formation of the CDRC, companies have opted for this friendlier arrangement to resolve their debt problems, instead of going to court to defend themselves against the creditors.

56.   For the most part, the usual receivership and liquidation administrations do not discriminate between viable and non-viable businesses, resulting in the inevitable closure of affected companies (in most cases). Section 176 has proven to be very unpopular with the financial institutions.

57.   A CDRC workout includes initial meetings between debtors and creditors, appointment of independent consultants to design a restructuring program for the debtor, an initial review of business viability, a formal standstill among creditors if the restructuring exercise proceeds, and oversight of restructuring plans. Even then, the arrangement is informal, has no legal status and can be called off by either side at any time. In the beginning, before certain changes were made and the power of the CDRC increased, it did not have Danaharta's power to force management and ownership changes within companies (*The New Straits Times*, 9 Aug. 2001).

58.   Under the revised restructuring guidelines, a borrower must have a minimum aggregate debt of RM100 million (compared with RM50 million previously), exposure to at least five creditor banks, an ongoing, viable concern, and sufficient cash generation to cover operating expenditure, to be eligible for CDRC assistance. Furthermore, companies can be referred to the CDRC by corporate borrowers or

bank creditors accounting for at least 25 per cent of total debt. To speed up the restructuring process, deadlines would be set for each of the debt restructuring processes and each case should be completed within six to nine months, with debt reorganization agreements to be signed within the first three months. In the first month, the CDRC would evaluate the case, form a creditors' steering committee and prepare an interim standstill agreement. In the subsequent three months, scheme advisors and solicitors would be appointed, and the workout proposal would be implemented after creditor approval had been secured (*The Star*, 10 Aug. 2001).

59.   See Mako (2001a), Stone (1998), and Dobrinsky *et al.* (1997), to name a few. Needless to say, no particular analysis represents "the whole truth", but rather, interpretations of what is considered important and "right" by the author.

60.   Markets, especially in developing countries, rarely function perfectly, and are usually characterised by incomplete or asymmetric information and other market imperfections, and perhaps more influenced by sentiments, rather than fundamentals.

61.   However, there are always errors of judgment and other risks in all decision making.

62.   As Stone (2000: 4) notes, "successful restructuring is not possible without a strong foundation established by government actions that span the entire spectrum of economic policies".

63.   "Macroeconomic governance" (following the definition employed by Lanyi and Lee 1999: 14) here refers to "the political and administrative processes by which macroeconomic policies are formulated, implemented, and evaluated. From a technical standpoint, the same policies can be carried out with equal effectiveness by either an autocratic or a democratic government." The main questions or issues for any government, according to Lanyi and Lee (1999: 16) are (1) "how to organise macroeconomic governance in a way that is technically competent, coordinated, sensitive to international developments relevant to the home country, and accountable to the political authority, and (2) whether the nature of political governance matters in this regard: witness the contrast between the once fashionable notion that authoritarian governments may be more effective in 'getting the job done' in the macroeconomic realm, and the current, equally fashionable notion, that democratic governance may after all work better in dealing with a major macroeconomic crisis".

64.   In practice, a mixed approach is often followed, even where a market-led strategy might otherwise be favoured. In developing economies especially, there are usually a number of constraints that limit options. For example, the highly qualified, skilled and experienced personnel needed to steer banks out of their difficulties are often in short supply.

In these circumstances, punishing managers and owners for their earlier mistakes may deprive the process of needed expertise. Likewise, markets are unlikely to work well in the midst of a financial crisis. Disposing of NPLs at fire-sale prices — that bearish post-crisis markets dictate — only serves to increase the costs of restructuring. Also, the private sector may have neither the resources needed to recapitalise illiquid banks nor an adequate appetite for risk. In these circumstances, public capital and other incentives may be needed. Furthermore, a government-led approach may be more effective than a market-led approach in resolving corporate and banking sector distress in certain circumstances, while the converse may be true in other circumstances.

65. The task of managing a systemic crisis, such as the 1997–98 Asian financial crisis, is extremely complex and challenging given the "high" level and structure of corporate debt, the "large" number of debtors and creditors involved, the weak legal environment and scarce financial resources (in light of the distressed banking system and depressed stock market), not to mention the varying political, economic, social, cultural and historical characteristics of the various East Asian countries.

CHAPTER 5

Bank Restructuring in Malaysia

CHIN KOK FAY

Since the onset of the financial crisis in July 1997, efforts have been made to ensure that Malaysia's financial sector will become sound, robust and ready for greater international financial liberalisation. Bank reform and restructuring have been undertaken, ostensibly to address weaknesses in the sector that had rendered them vulnerable following huge currency depreciation sparked by sudden and massive international capital outflows.

Although banking sector weaknesses were not the proximate cause of the financial crisis in Malaysia (see Chin and Jomo 2003), the next section argues that bank restructuring is necessary and has been an important element of the Malaysian crisis management programme. Hardly a year after the initiation of restructuring efforts, there was a lot of self-congratulation in the Malaysian media, proclaiming the success of its "unorthodox" financial restructuring. The euphoria was understandable as rehabilitation of the financial system had been proceeding well and the economy recovered strongly in 1999–2000. However, the smugness was worrying for two reasons, as Lim Say Boon (1999) argues: "One, it presumes the fight is over. Worse, there appears to be a fatally flawed belief that success in stabilising an economy under assault means there was never anything wrong with the 'Malaysian way' of doing business."

Hence, this chapter examines progress of government efforts to restore financial stability and to restructure the banking system in Malaysia, as well as some critical underlying issues. Based on available data, it examines what has been accomplished thus far, and to what extent the Malaysian bank restructuring experience has helped build a more robust banking system, not only to avoid another financial crisis, but also to meet future challenges, especially imminent international financial liberalisation.

Why Bank Restructuring?

Unlike in the other East Asian crisis economies, foreign bank loans did not figure as significantly in the Malaysian crisis; rather, capital market flows, especially those into and out of the stock market, figured more prominently. Malaysia's prudential financial regulation — though somewhat weakened prior to the crisis by pressures due to financial liberalisation — remained better than in most other Southeast Asian countries besides Singapore, thus saving Malaysia from some of the worst excesses elsewhere in the region. Although the Malaysian banking system contributed to asset price inflation by lending for property and share purchases, Malaysian banks and corporations were allowed far less access to foreign borrowings than their counterparts in the other crisis economies in the region. Hence, exposure to private bank borrowings from abroad did not figure as significantly in the Malaysian crisis as elsewhere. The ratio of short-term debt to reserves in Malaysia was far less than in Indonesia (1.704), Thailand (1.453) and South Korea (2.073) (Radelet and Sachs 1998b: Table 3), while domestic interest rates were lower as well.

As a consequence of its reduced exposure to private bank borrowings from abroad, Malaysia was not in a situation of having to go cap in hand to the International Monetary Fund (IMF) or to others for emergency international credit facilities. Unlike its neighbours, Thailand and Indonesia, as well as South Korea, that had to adopt IMF conditionalities attached to their rescue packages due to their huge external commitments requiring foreign credit, Malaysia enjoyed the freedom to prescribe its own recovery plans. After a series of unorthodox policy initiatives exacerbated the situation between July and November 1997, the Malaysian authorities pursued somewhat similar — but less contractionary — macroeconomic policies than the IMF rescue packages of the three crisis-affected economies. Such policies were intended to stem the capital flight facilitated by Malaysian capital account liberalisation, though there is little real evidence of success on this score. Official policy as well as market pressures served to push up interest rates, though the rise in the

Table 5.1   Malaysia: Loan Classification and Reserve Requirements, 1997–98

	Old (since Sept 1997)	Revised (since Sept 1998)
Classification of NPLs		
General	Overdue for 3 months	Overdue for 6 months
BA's, trade bills	Dormant for 6 months	Dormant for 6 months
Credit cards	3 months in arrears	Unpaid 1 month after maturity
Reclassification of NPLs to Performing Status		
General	Full settlement of arrears on interest and principle	Total period in arrears less than 6 months
Rescheduled/ Restructured	Complies with rescheduling terms for 12 consecutive months	Complies for 6 consecutive months
Provisioning		
General provisioning	Minimum 1.5%	Minimum 1.5%
Specific provisioning		
Substandard	20% (3 to 6 months overdue)	20% (3 to 6 months overdue)
Doubtful	50% (6 to 12 months overdue)	50% (6 to 12 months overdue)
Bad	100% (12 months and more)	100% (12 months and more)

Source: Fitch IBCA cited in *The Edge* (1999).

nominal rate was higher than the real increase, owing to contemporaneous inflationary pressures.

With the onset of the financial crisis, emphasis was given addressing the high exposure of banking institutions to the property and stock markets as well as consumption credit. Stricter regulations, which include stricter guidelines on loans to selected categories of property were enforced. At least three other developments after the currency crisis had made things worse for the banking system. First, the authorities adopted a tighter definition of non-performing loans (NPLs) in late 1997, reducing the grace period from six to three months, thus increasing the number of NPLs by redefinition in the midst of the crisis (see Table 5.1). Second, banks were obliged to meet higher statutory reserve requirements, which must have played some

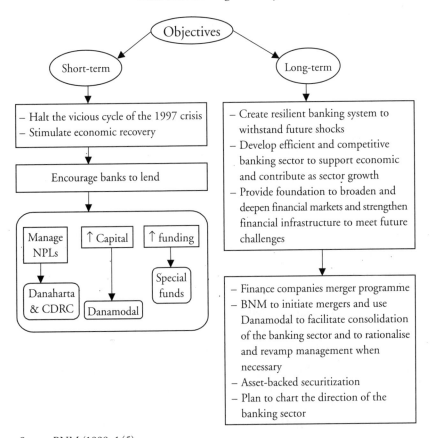

Source: BNM (1999: 145).

Fig. 5.1 Malaysia's Banking Sector Restructuring Plan Objectives

part in raising the cost of funds. Third, credit growth slowed down and did not rise after September 1998 despite central bank directives to increase credit growth by eight per cent per annum in both 1998 and 1999. Hence, tighter monetary policy from late 1997 exacerbated deflationary pressures due to government spending cuts from around the same time.

The full brunt of the crisis was felt in 1998 when NPLs began to rise rapidly. Hence, bank restructuring was necessary to restore the integrity of the banking system. As shown in Figure 5.1, these efforts comprised short-term stabilisation measures and medium to longer-term strategies to develop and strengthen the banking sector

Table 5.2   Malaysia: Estimated Funding Requirements for Economic Recovery, 1998–2000

Programme	RM bn
Danaharta	15
Danamodal	16
Infrastructure Development Fund	5
Additional 7th Malaysia Plan Allocation*	26
Overall balance	62

Note: *including financing deficits in the Federal Government budget.
Source: NEAC (1999: 51).

(BNM 1999: 421). To contain the looming banking crisis and to restore liquidity, the government set up Pengurusan Danaharta Nasional Bhd (Danaharta) — a state-established and financed asset management company (AMC) — to ensure that the level of NPLs in the banking system remained manageable, and Danamodal Nasional Bhd (Danamodal) to recapitalise banking institutions. These two agencies were further complemented by setting up the Corporate Debt Restructuring Committee (CDRC) to provide a mechanism for banks and debtors to reach mutually acceptable feasible debt work-out solutions. The IMF-like policies introduced in late 1997 were subsequently replaced, by reflationary fiscal measures from mid-1998, lengthening the NPL classification period to six months and selective capital controls beginning 1 September 1998, pegging the Malaysian currency at RM3.80 per US dollar, imposing a year-stay on proceeds from the sale of shares by foreigners, which could be substituted by early exit levies from February 1999.

As shown in Table 5.2, the government estimated the costs of purchasing the banking system's NPLs and recapitalising the banking system at RM15 billion and RM16 billion respectively — very different from the actual expenses. The total cost of bank restructuring as a percentage of real GDP during the crisis period has been estimated at 17 per cent, compared to 5 per cent (Hawkins and Turner 1999: Table 6) for the previous banking crisis in the late 1980s. Of the total funding required by Danaharta, RM1.5 billion was the initial contribution from the government,[1] RM3.5 billion was obtained through loans from the Employees Provident Fund (EPF) and Khazanah, while the remaining RM10 billion was sourced from bond issues (NEAC 1999: Appendix 2).

Cleaning Up the NPLs

Following the prolonged crisis and worsening economic conditions, banks became increasingly reluctant to provide new lending. Rising NPL levels encouraged them to be more cautious with new lending to avoid incurring more bad loans. To relieve banks of their NPLs prior to merger, Danaharta was set up in June 1998 to purchase and manage NPLs from banking institutions with a gross value of at least RM5 million (NEAC 1999: 34), or in other words, Danaharta sought to carve out bad debts from local banks.[2] This was to enable them "to refocus on lending to viable business and economic activities which can support economic recovery, without being burdened by the task of managing their non-performing assets" (NEAC 1999: 34).

Unlike the asset management companies in South Korea and Thailand, Danaharta was neither a rapid disposition agency nor a warehousing agency. Rather, it was granted a wider range of restructuring options, with the only stipulation being maximising recovery value. Furthermore, Danaharta could not only take legal action[3] to recover security through the bankruptcy process and sell the loans to third parties, but could also take a more active role in rehabilitating companies since Danaharta's powers included the power to force management and ownership changes in the companies.

By the end of 1999, Danaharta had acquired RM45.5 billion of NPLs from the financial system, of which RM35.7 billion were loan rights acquired (LRA)[4] from the banking system (BNM 2000). This constituted 42 per cent of the NPLs in the banking system then, and reduced the residual NPL level from its peak of 9 per cent in November 1998 to 6.6 per cent in December 1999 (based on the old 6-month arrears classification). Danaharta accumulated the NPLs in two ways (Danaharta 2002: 3):

(1)   Acquiring NPLs from almost 70 financial institutions at an average discount rate of 54.4 per cent, with payment made either by issuing zero-coupon Danaharta bonds to the selling

financial institution or in cash (especially when purchasing
Islamic loans or loans from development financial institutions).
The total cost involved using this mode of acquisition was
RM9.03 billion.

(2)   Being assigned, at no cost to Danaharta, the NPLs of the now
defunct Sime Bank and Bank Bumiputera Malaysia to manage
on behalf of the government which had decided to let them be
acquired by other banks.

Having completed this loan acquisition phase by 2000,
Danaharta then focused on the management and resolution of loans
and assets under its administration in 2001. Vested with the legal
powers to facilitate and expedite this enormous task, Danaharta
adopted various asset management techniques to maximise recovery
values, including active restructuring and rescheduling, and schemes
of arrangement[5] for viable loans, foreclosure[6] and appointment of
special administrators for non-viable loans. The Pengurusan Danaharta
Nasional Berhad Act of 1998 confers on Danaharta the power to
appoint special administrators to manage the affairs of distressed
companies. A special administrator is a company auditor or person
who has the requisite experience to revive a distressed company and
come up with a workout proposal aimed at maximising the recovery
value on the business.

Danaharta has acquired and managed RM47.7 billion of total
loan rights in its portfolio. Of these loans, Danaharta expects a recovery
rate of 57 per cent (50 per cent for acquired loans and 63 per cent
for managed ones) from the outstanding value of the loan rights
acquired (inclusive of accrued interest). Before winding up its
operations in 2005, Danaharta expects total recovery of RM30.19
billion. It had already collected and received RM18.93 billion in cash
and non-cash assets by the end of 2002 (see Table 5.3).

Danaharta has been fully funded by the government (see Table
5.4). As at the end of 2002, it had total capital and outstanding
liabilities of RM14.54 billion. With most of its government-guaranteed
bonds maturing in 2004,[7] Danaharta needs to generate enough cash
to redeem all its bonds when they fall due. As changes in the value
of non-cash assets (securities and properties) due to market uncertainties affect recovery receipts, the ability to quickly realise non-cash

Table 5.3   Malaysia: Danaharta's Recovery Proceeds by Asset Group, 31 Dec. 2002 (RM bn)

Asset Group	Expected Recovery* Excluding Defaults	Pending Implementation	Received Recovery
Cash	13.53	6.82	6.71
Restructured Loan	9.82	1.70	8.12
Securities	5.38	1.97	3.41
Properties	1.46	0.77	0.69
Total	30.19	11.26	18.93

Note: *Expected recovery does not include interest or adjustment gains or losses arising from the recovery process.
Source: Danaharta (2002a: 9).

assets during the remaining lifespan of Danaharta will have an important bearing on its success. Danaharta has two options that could cause taxpayers to bear the burden if it fails to redeem the bonds as scheduled. It could roll over the bonds for up to five years, by turning the zero-coupon bonds into interest-bearing bonds, or the government guarantee could be invoked to bear any shortfall in the bond redemption exercise.

Table 5.4   Malaysia: Danaharta's Funding Sources and Outstanding Liabilities, 31 Dec. 2002 (RM bn)

Funding Sources	Purpose	Maximum Amount Allocated	Capital & Outstanding Liabilities
Government contribution	Initial capital	3.0	3.0
Loans from EPF & Khazanah Nasional Bhd	Draw down for working capital	2.0	0.4*
Zero-coupon bonds issued to selling financial institutions	For loan acquisition	15.0*	11.14**
TOTAL		20.0	14.54

Notes: *Total loans drawn down were RM1.3 billion.
        **Refers to nominal value/face value of total bonds issued.
Source: Danaharta (2002a).

Banking on immunity from legal challenges to its sale of property, stock and other assets, Danaharta has been recovering value from the bad debts it bought from Malaysian financial institutions after the 1997 Asian financial crisis. However, its legal immunity was threatened in late November 2002 after the Malaysian Court of Appeal ruled that the provision in the law (Section 72 of the Danaharta Act) giving Danaharta immunity from injunctions was "unconstitutional and void" (Jayasankaran 2003: 45). Several outstanding legal suits involving applications for injunctions not only slowed down its operations, but also threatened its credibility. Two years later, the Federal Court set aside an injunction granted by the Court of Appeal to a private firm to stop Danaharta from selling its land — charged to Danaharta for a non-performing loan — to a third party even though it was now willing to pay a higher price than the third party for recovery of the charged land (*The Star*, 16 January 2004).

Recapitalising Malaysian Banking Institutions

Recognising the constraints facing banking institutions in raising capital on their own in adverse financial circumstances, Danamodal was established with an anticipated life span of five to seven years to recapitalise banking institutions in order to restore their capitalisation to healthy levels. The rationale for establishing Danamodal was three-pronged: (1) to ensure that the banking sector recapitalisation process is commercially driven and that investment decisions are made according to market-based principles; (2) to avoid delays in addressing recapitalisation and non-performing loan issues which would have a drag effect on the financial system and economic recovery; and (3) to avoid direct injections of government capital into banking institutions, which were deemed undesirable and could lead to conflicts of interest in the future.

To address problems of moral hazard inherent in such an exercise, Danamodal operated on the first-loss principle, under which losses arising from past credit decisions were born by shareholders. The capital injections have been in the form of equity or hybrid instruments. Incorporated on August 1998 as a wholly owned subsidiary of the central bank, Bank Negara Malaysia (BNM), it received RM3 billion as initial seed capital. Anticipating a worst case scenario, BNM had estimated that RM16 billion would be required to bring the risk weighted capital ratio of all domestic banking institutions to at least 9 per cent (NEAC 1999: Appendix 3).

To minimise the use of public funds, and hence the taxpayers' burden, Danamodal's operations have been based on commercial or market principles. In identifying the banks needing recapitalisation, Danamodal used objective guidelines developed by BNM. The steps to be followed included, but were not limited to:

- in-depth analysis of the competitive position and financial standing of each banking institution;
- quantification of potential synergies to be realised through consolidation;
- CAMEL (capital, assets, management, earnings, liquidity) analysis.

Danamodal only recapitalised viable banking institutions based on assessments and due diligence reviews conducted by reputable, international financial advisors. After the capital injections, Danamodal instituted reforms through its nominees appointed to the boards of these banking institutions.

Besides expediting the consolidation of more capitalised domestic banking institutions, Danamodal — as a strategic shareholder in recapitalised banking institutions — has been in a better position to facilitate the rationalisation of banking institutions in conjunction with their consolidation. Thus, Danamodal complemented Danaharta and other financial restructuring and economic recovery measures. Although there is no obligation for any banking institution to enter into an agreement with Danaharta, banking institutions that receive capital assistance from Danamodal have been required to sell their eligible NPLs to Danaharta to reduce their NPL ratio below 10 per cent.

No capital injections have been made into financial institutions since December 1999 as the capital position of banking institutions has continued to improve (BNM 2002: 134). Total capital injections into ten banking institutions declined from RM7.5 billion to RM2.1 billion on 22 December 2001 following repayments by

Table 5.5   Malaysia: Danamodal's Recapitalisation of Banking Institutions, 22 Dec. 2001 (RM bn)

	Injection	*Repayment*	*Outstanding Balance*
RHB Bank Bhd	1,500	500	1,000
Arab-Malaysian Bank Bhd	800	340	460
MBf Finance Bhd	2,280	1,600	680*
United Merchant Finance Bhd	800	800	0
Oriental Bank Bhd	700	700	0
Arab-Malaysian Finance Bhd	500	500	0
BSN Commercial Bank (M) Bhd	420	420	0
Arab-Malaysian Merchant Bhd	400	400	0
Sabah Bank	140	140	0
Perdana Merchant Bankers	50	50	0
TOTAL	7,590	5,450	2,140

Note: * Subordinated term loan.
Source: Danamodal (2001).

three of the banking institutions (see Table 5.5). With recapitalisation completed, Danamodal focused on managing its surplus funds and ensuring sustainable returns to its assets before ceasing operations in 2003. With net tangible assets of RM2.3 billion, Danamodal was able to redeem its RM11 billion bonds in October 2003.

Resolving Corporate Debt

Since the health of the corporate and banking sectors was inter-related, bank restructuring may not be complete without the restructuring of corporate debt, which impinges on the level of NPLs in the banking sector. Together with Danaharta and Danamodal, the Corporate Debt Restructuring Committee (CDRC) was set up in 1998 as part of the government's three-pronged approach to deal with the crisis. Its aim was to facilitate the restructuring of large corporate loans, enabling both borrowers and creditors to work out feasible debt restructuring schemes without having to resort to legal action and/or liquidation.

Without legal or statutory powers, the CDRC could only act as an advisor and mediator between debtors and their creditors for

Table 5.6 Progress of Corporate Debt Restructuring in the Four Asian Crisis Economies, 1999

Country	Corporate Debt Cases Resolved (%)	Corporate Debt Restructured, by value (%)
South Korea (September 1999)	78	50
Malaysia (December 1999)	22	35
Thailand (December 1999)	14	15
Indonesia (August 1999)	1	13

Source: Binamira and Haworth (2000: 143).

each restructuring exercise. The CDRC had to rely on cooperation, persuasion and a consultative approach to reconcile the interests of the financial institutions and the borrowers (CDRC 2002). Given the large number of creditors involved in the debt restructuring exercises and the difficulties in obtaining the necessary 100 per cent consensus from the parties involved, the progress of the corporate debt restructuring exercises under its purview was relatively slow at the outset. The restructuring efforts involving corporate firms linked to powerful political personalities were even more complicated (Ranawana 2001a). Although Malaysia has made better progress in restructuring corporate debts than Thailand and Indonesia, it has trailed significantly behind South Korea (see Table 5.6).

With the global economic slowdown, especially in the US in 2001, Malaysia could no longer count on fast growth to allow its corporations to recover and to pay off their debts. Meanwhile, the lacklustre performance of capital markets also hampered implementation of some debt restructuring schemes. Thus, Malaysian corporate debt restructuring needed greater private sector involvement, but that was unlikely to be forthcoming until there was stronger evidence that the government was serious about debt restructuring and greater transparency (Ranawana 2001a).

Recognising the need to toughen its approach, on 9 August 2001, CDRC unveiled three new initiatives aimed at expediting the resolution of debt restructuring under its purview. The initiatives were:

(1)   Expanding the CDRC to include representatives from Danaharta

Table 5.7   Malaysia: Status of CDRC Cases, 31 Dec. 2002

	Total Debt Outstanding* (RM m)	Number of Accounts
Total referred to CDRC	67,644	87
Cases withdrawn/rejected	12,615	28
Transferred to Danaharta	2,470	11
Cases accepted	52,559	48
Resolved	52,559	48
Implemented	35,969	32
Pending implementation	16,590	16

Note: * Including non-banking and offshore institutions.
Source: BNM (2003: 116).

and the Federation of Public Listed Companies to ensure that the relevant sectors were better represented. The CDRC began to utilise the legal powers of Danaharta to hasten the restructuring process (Gabriel 2001). The CDRC passed some cases to Danaharta, with borrowers losing control with the appointment of special administrators or with liquidation.

(2)   Changing the framework and approach of the CDRC to accelerate restructuring efforts. Hence, for example, restructuring could take place with the approval of 75 per cent — rather than 100 per cent — of the creditors.

(3)   Establishing a schedule — with clearly identified deadlines — for resolution of each case handled by the CDRC.

During its four years of operations, the CDRC resolved 48 cases with total debts amounting to RM52.6 billion, representing approximately 65 per cent of the total cases under its auspices (see Table 5.7). Of the resolved cases, 32 have been fully implemented. The recovery profile of the resolved cases shows that 83 per cent of recovery proceeds were in the form of cash, redeemable instruments and rescheduled debt. The closure of the CDRC on 15 August 2002 marked the conclusion of the debt restructuring efforts undertaken, after which resolution of the remaining 16 cases — involving debt of RM16.6 billion — would be monitored by their respective Creditors Steering Committees and Danaharta.

Bank Mergers

Bank Negara Malaysia has been attempting to consolidate the fragmented banking industry for some time. However, past calls since the late 1980s for banks to merge voluntarily have largely been ignored. Only one merger between two ailing banks — i.e. Bank of Commerce and United Asian Bank — took place in mid-1991. Lucrative oligopolistic bank profits, largely assured by banking regulation, have meant that the desire to maintain banking licences remains strong.

A new two-tier regulatory system (TTRS) was introduced in December 1994 to provide incentives for smaller banks to merge. To qualify for privileged first tier status, banks must have equity of at least RM500 million.[8] These privileged first-tier banking institutions were subject to less regulation, engaging in a wider range of activities previously denied to all institutions such as opening foreign currency accounts. Rather than resorting to bank mergers, shareholders often chose heavy short-term borrowings to inject more capital into the banking institutions in their zeal to meet the TTRS requirements. This exerted undue pressure on bank managements to generate the requisite returns to the newly injected capital in order to service their loans (see BNM 1999: 210). Consequently, this new regulatory system led to a sharp increase in aggressive and imprudent lending activities, which eventually resulted in poor asset quality, which increased the risk of the banking system as a whole. Given these adverse developments, the TTRS was subsequently abandoned in April 1999.

The financial crisis has given the BNM greater powers to implement its merger programme for domestic banking institutions. In response to the earlier failures to achieve mergers voluntarily, in July 1999, the government unveiled a tough plan to have only six "anchor banks" remain after the proposed mergers (see Table 5.8). All banking institutions were given two months to sign a Memorandum of Understanding (MOU) and eight months to complete the exercise.

Few dispute the rationale for bank mergers in Malaysia. There have been too many bank branches (see Table 5.9) competing for depositors with the extensive branch networks of other savings institutions (including the National Savings Bank and credit cooperatives including Bank Rakyat), resulting in socially wasteful duplication

Table 5.8 Malaysia: Milestones in Domestic Banking Institution Mergers, 1998–2000

1998

2 January[1]   Merger programme for finance companies announced by the BNM. 31 March 1998 deadline set for finance companies to identify merger partners and agree in principle to terms and conditions of merger.

1999

29 July[1]   Merger programme for domestic banking institutions announced by BNM. Programme aimed at creating six large domestic financial groups to reduce number of domestic commercial banks, finance companies and merchant banks to six each, one for each group. All banking institutions required to sign Memorandum of Understanding (MOU) by end September 1999 and given until end March 2000 to complete exercise.

3 August[2]   Six anchor banks identified, i.e. Malayan Banking, Perwira Affin Bank, Multi-Purpose Bank, Bumiputra-Commerce Trustee Bhd, Public Bank and Southern Bank.

12 August[1]   Three broad valuation guidelines to be used for the bank consolidation programme released by BNM.

20 October[1]   Prime Minister announces that all banking institutions would be given flexibility to form their own merger groups and to choose their own group leaders to lead the merger process by the end of January 2000. Upon BNM approval of the new groupings, domestic banking institutions were allowed to terminate MOUs signed with earlier partners.

2000

14 February[1]   Approval granted for formation of 10 banking groups, selection of anchor banks and their respective partners.

31 July   BNM decided to extend tax incentives for bank mergers by one month.

1 September[1]   All banking institutions involved in the merger programme signed S&P agreements by 31 August to take full advantage of the merger incentives granted by the government.

31 December[1]   50 of 54 banking institutions consolidated into 10 banking groups. For the four remaining banking institutions, the agreement between Malayan Banking and PhileoAllied Bhd for the acquisition of PhileoAllied Bank was extended by 21 days to secure the regulatory approval. Approval was also granted for Multi-Purpose Bank and MBf Finance, as well as for the Arab-Malaysian Banking Group and Utama Banking Group Bhd (comprising Bank Utama and Utama Merchant Bank) to mutually terminate their respective Sales & Purchase (S&P) agreements.

Sources: Compiled from:
   [1] BNM press releases.
   [2] Taing (1999).

Table 5.9   Malaysia: Number of Banking Institutions, Branch Networks, ATM Networks and Persons Served Per Office, 1995–2002

	As at end							
	1995	*1996*	*1997*	*1998*	*1999*	*2000*	*2001*	*2002*
Number of	89	89	86	80	68	62	47	45
Commercial banks	37	37	35	35	33	31	25	24
Domestic banks	23	23	22[a]	22	20[c]	17	11[e]	11
Foreign banks	14	14	13[b]	13	13	14[d]	14	13[f]
Finance companies	40	40	39	33	23	19	12	11
Merchant banks	12	12	12	12	12	12	10	10
Branch Networks	2,438	2,689	2,839	2,811	2,749	2,713	2,557	2,403
Commercial banks	1,433	1,569	1,671	1,690	1,767	1,758	1,664	1,631
Finance companies	988	1,096	1,144	1,099	630	933	874	755
Merchant banks	17	24	24	22	22	22	19	17
ATM Networks	2,632	2,851	3,150	3,309	3,904	3,607	3,992	4,028
Commercial banks	2,230	2,326	2,528	2,647	3,317	3,004	3,386	3,477
Finance companies	402	525	622	662	587	603	606	551
Persons served/office								
Commercial banks	14,024	13,492	12,966	13,124	12,854	13,256	13,959	15,040
Finance companies	20,341	19,314	18,939	20,182	23,659	24,920	26,474	32,490

Notes: [a] DCB Bank and Kwong Yik Bank were merged in 1997.
  [b] Chung Khiaw Bank merged with United Overseas Bank in 1997.
  [c] Sime Bank was taken over by RHB Bank and Bank Bumiputera Malaysia Bhd was absorbed by Bank of Commerce in June and September 1999 respectively.
  [d] Bank of China is the new foreign bank operating in the country.
  [e] Bank Utama's two attempts to merge with Arab-Malaysian Banking Group and EON Bank were not successful.
  [f] Overseas Union Bank merged with United Overseas Bank on February 2002 following the merger of their parent banks based in Singapore.
Sources: BNM (2000; Table A.64; 2002: Table A.55; 2003: Table A.59).

of services, which also undermines achieving economies of scale in the provision of banking services. Although there were 39 finance companies in 1997, more than 70 per cent of the finance company business was concentrated in five or six of the larger finance companies (<http://www.bnm.gov.my/pa/1998/0102.htm>).

Table 5.10 Malaysia's Resilient Mid-sized Banks, 1998

Bank	Pre-Tax Profit (RM m)	NPL Purchases by Danaharta as of 31.12.98 (RM m)	Accounting Period
Ban Hin Lee Bank	45.9	Nil	31.12.98
Hong Leong Bank	72.9	Nil	31.12.98*
Southern Bank	78.5	Nil	31.03.99

Note: *Accounting period for Hong Leong Bank is half-year ended.
Source: Tan (1999).

Although the cost of banking services should decrease following some rationalisation of branches and staff relocation, it is far from clear that the Malaysian approach to bank consolidation will bring about a much more efficient banking sector. Concerns have been raised about the speed and scale of the mergers and the somewhat biased selection of anchor banks. Of the six anchor banks selected, the choice of Maybank and Public Bank was uncontroversial as they are not only the country's largest but they are also reasonably well run. The selection of Southern Bank, despite its relatively smaller size, was uncontroversial as it was well managed and did not need any government bail out (see Table 5.10).

Most controversial was the inclusion of two unimpressive smaller banks — i.e. Multipurpose Bank and Perwira Affin Bank — apparently due to political influence (see Jayasankaran 1999a). Multipurpose Bank is controlled by businessmen viewed as close to former Finance Minister Daim, while Perwira Affin Bank is controlled by the Armed Forces Fund Board (LTAT). Ironically, some efficient, but smaller banks — owned by ethnic Chinese interests[9] — were not selected, particularly Hong Leong Bank which has never lost money or needed any government bail out. It has been well managed with no NPLs purchased by Danaharta. It made profits, even during the financial crisis. Bank mergers may thus produce bigger banks without significantly enhancing their efficiency and competitiveness.

It is not clear why efficient mid-sized banks should be taken over by bigger, but weaker banks. More than half the RM39 billion in bad loans absorbed by the government came from two big domestic banks, i.e. the now defunct Sime Bank and Bank Bumiputera, rescued by RHB Bank and Bank of Commerce respectively via mergers (Jayasankaran 1999a). As pointed out by *The Economist* (1999):

... bigger banks are not necessarily any safer than smaller ones ... Bank for International Settlements (BIS) worries that the current restructuring of the banking industry could cause strains, as "competitive pressures interact with stubborn cost structures and heighten incentives for risk-taking". That is especially dangerous since bigger banks are more likely to be considered "too big to fail", and hence to carry a greater implicit government guarantee.

Due to the strong objections to the number and composition of the proposed banking groups, short time frame for consolidation, ensuing negative market reaction and appeals by affected parties, Prime Minister Mahathir decided to allow ten — instead of six — banks to remain in a revised merger plan announced in October 1999. To speed up the merger process, various tax incentives[10] were granted to domestic banking institutions that signed sale and purchase (S&P) agreements or conditional S&P agreements on or before the end of August 2000.

The revised merger policy did not, however, address the fear of likely concentration of banks in the hands of a few closely connected to the government. For example, the merger plan between Arab-Malaysian Banking Group, one of the selected anchor banks, and Utama Banking Group Bhd (UBG), a small bank with dispropor-tionate political influence based in Sarawak, "encapsulates the pitfalls of merger politics" (Jayasankaran 2000). The deal was opposed by UBG's controlling shareholder, Cahya Mata Sarawak Bhd (CMS), linked to the state's powerful, long-serving Chief Minister. Sarawak remains politically vital to the ruling National Front coalition; e.g. in the 1999 general election, the Chief Minister led the ruling National Front to a clean sweep of the state's 28 parliamentary seats, repre-senting almost 15 per cent of the total number of parliamentary seats. In late December 2000, the merger exercise failed, apparently due to differences over management control and pricing. UBG's second attempt to merge with EON Bank also met with a similar fate in early February 2001. UBG then made no secret of its intention to become an anchor bank (Jayasankaran 2001) and eventually took over the RHB financial group and bank, apparently after its founder, and principal shareholder Rashid Hussain, fell foul of then Finance Minister, Daim Zainuddin.

On 2 February 2001, then Finance Minister Daim rejected RHB Capital's proposal to buy back RHB Bank's irredeemable non-cumulative preference shares from Danamodal, even though Rashid offered to pay Danamodal a 38 per cent premium over the one billion ringgit outstanding balance (Jayasankaran 2001). After helping banks get back on a sound financial footing, Danamodal was supposed to eventually dispose of its stakes in the banks into which it had injected funds. As Rashid's offer would clearly benefit Danamodal, the move to block the deal that would have re-established Rashid's control over RHB Bank sparked off speculation that the Finance Minister wanted to oust Rashid from control of the bank.

Bank Utama was given approval in a letter dated 19 April 2001 from the then Finance Minister to the UBG and Rashid Hussain Bhd to begin merger talks. The merger between RHB Bank and Bank Utama was finally signed on 20 March 2002. The plan was for UBG to buy over Malaysian Resources Corporation Bhd (MRCB)'s 22.7 per cent stake as well as Rashid Hussain's 23.9 per cent stake in RHB, which held a 55.4 per cent stake in RHB Capital Bhd (the immediate holding company of the group).

Other Bank Restructuring Efforts

With the institutional arrangements put in place to clean up problem loans and strengthen the capital position of the banking system, banks are expected to refocus on lending to viable business and economic activities that can support economic recovery. While a third of the 36 commercial banks in Malaysia then registered negative loan growth, only five had a loan growth rate of more than 8 per cent (Taing 1998). To urge banks to extend loans, the BNM set an annual loans growth target of 8 per cent to be met by the end of 1998. The BNM sent a circular to all financial institutions issuing guidelines for their lending activities, warning that the chairmen and chief executive officers of banking institutions would be held accountable if their banking institutions did not show serious commitment to meeting

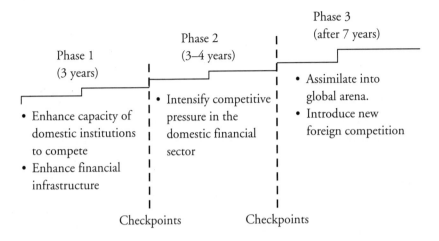

Source: BNM (2001).

Fig. 5.2 Implementation of Recommendations in the Financial Sector Masterplan, 2001–10

the 8 per cent loan growth target. Many bankers construed this as a threat of getting the sack if their banks failed to comply with the circular (Taing 1998).

Against the backdrop of an increasingly globalised, liberalised and a more complex domestic economy, Malaysia sees the need to focus on the medium and longer term agenda to build a financial sector responsive to changing economic requirements and a strong and resilient financial system for facing future challenges in the new environment. Thus, in the first quarter of 2001, the government adopted the Financial Sector Masterplan (FSMP) (see Figure 5.2) that outlines strategies over a ten-year period for the development of the financial sector. Under the FSMP, the change programme, involving 119 recommendations to be implemented over the next ten years, will undergo three phases of implementation, subject to achieving certain milestones and various safeguards. The first phase is focused on building the domestic capacity, the second phase involves increasing domestic competition, and the third phase sets the pace for integration with the international market.

Assessing Progress

As discussed above, the institutional arrangements put in place since 1998 to restore financial system stability have achieved significant milestones. During its four years of operation before closing in August 2002, the CDRC had successfully resolved approximately 65 per cent of the total cases under its purview. Since completing its loan acquisition phase by 2000, Danaharta has focused on implementing recovery strategies, collection, and conversion of non-cash recovery assets into cash for distribution until its closure originally targeted for 2005. Danamodal had redeemed its entire RM11 billion five-year zero-coupon unsecured redeemable bonds, which matured on 21 October 2003. With the completion of the first round of the merger programme at the end of 2002, the domestic banking system has been transformed from one that was highly fragmented with 71 institutions before the Asian crisis, to 30 banking institutions under 10 domestic banking groups.

With a moderate economic rebound supported both by exports and domestic demand, as well as progress in financial restructuring, it was reported in BNM's 2002 Annual Report (2003: 142) that the banking system continued to show improved performance characterised by:

- Continued strong profitability, owing to high recoveries, lower provisioning requirements and higher revenue from fee-based activities;
- Narrowing of interest margins on lending activities due to increased competition especially in the household sector;
- Higher lending activities with strong growth recorded in lending to households and small businesses;
- Improving asset quality, particularly in the latter half of 2002, as non-performing loans began to trend downwards on account of the lower incidence of new NPLs and greater reclassification of NPLs as performing loans;
- Ample liquidity following large trade surpluses and inflows of foreign direct investments;
- Manageable level of exposure to market risks;
- Strong capitalisation levels attributable to higher profits and capital injections; and

Table 5.11 Malaysia: Banking System Risk-weighted Capital Ratios, 1996–2002

	As at end						
	1996	*1997*	*1998*	*1999*	*2000*	*2001*	*2002*
Risk-Weighted Capital Ratios (%)	10.7	10.5	11.8	12.4	12.3	13.0	12.8
– Commercial Banks	10.8	10.3	11.7	12.6	12.1[1]	12.8[1]	12.8[1]
– Finance Companies	9.8	10.3	11.1	10.8	11.6	12.1	11.4
– Merchant Banks	11.7	13.3	15.2	14.5	16.6	19.6	18.4

Notes: [1] Excludes Islamic banks.
[2] Excludes bad debt provisions.
Source: Bank Negara Malaysia (2003).

- Consistently strong risk-weighted capital ratios (RWCRs) of the banking system, above 12 per cent from 1999 (see Table 5.11).

Since their establishment, Danamodal had injected a total of RM7.6 billion into ten banking institutions while Danaharta had spent RM15.44 billion to fund its operations. These expenses were significantly lower than the initial budget allocations of RM16 billion for Danamodal (see Table 5.2) and the maximum allocation of RM20 billion for Danaharta (see Table 5.4).

The infusion of public funds also gave the government more leverage over the banking sector. There has been considerable concern about political interference in Malaysian bank restructuring, particularly the bank consolidation programme since 1999.

The bank consolidation exercise seems to have been influenced by powerful politically connected business interests, with much suspicion focused on then Finance Minister Daim. Even at the outset, the selection of anchor banks was subject to much criticism. The then Finance Minister's rejection of RHB Capital's offer to buy back RHB Bank's preference shares from Danamodal at a high premium raised the larger issue of the integrity of the bank restructuring programme. The final lap in the first round of bank consolidation was completed when UBG — associated with the family business interests of the long-serving Sarawak Chief Minister Taib Mahmud, and which was not among the original ten short-listed anchor banks — ended up

Table 5.12 Malaysian Banks: Overhead and Staffing Costs, 1999–2002

	1999	*2000*	*2001*	*2002*
Cost/Income Ratio	38.2	39.6	41.7	43.8
Staff Cost Per Employee (RM)	41,900	52,300	54,800	55,300

Source: *The Asian Banker* (2003).

with control of one of the country's largest banks following the RHB-Utama Bank merger.

Still digesting the first round of bank consolidation, the immediate pressing issue confronting the remaining ten anchor banking groups includes their ability to reap and use the synergies arising from the mergers to enhance their competitiveness and to improve their efficiency in intermediation. Pre-tax profit of the banking system rose by 34.5 per cent to RM9.3 billion in 2002 despite the marginal (2.2 per cent) increase in the gross operating profit before provisions. Thus, banking profitability growth in 2002 was mainly due to lower provisions for NPLs, rather than organic expansion. The significantly lower loan loss provision (by 38 per cent) from the preceding year was due to the combined effects of lower provisions charged for loan losses, which fell by 19.2 per cent, and higher recoveries of RM3.4 billion (by 69.9 per cent) (BNM 2003: 142). As Table 5.12 shows, overhead and staffing costs are still high with the industry's cost-income ratio increasing by a constant 5 per cent annually since 2000.

Although the average interest margin of the commercial banks fell in 2002 to 3.87 percentage points from 4.14 percentage points in 2001 (BNM 2003: 143), the narrowing of the interest margin should not be misconstrued as improving the efficiency of intermediation by the banks. The interest margin refers to the difference between the interest rate charged on loans and advances granted (average lending rate, or ALR) and the rate paid by banking institutions on deposits and borrowed funds (average cost of funds, or ACF). It can be used to reflect the gross returns to banking institutions from their lending activities before taking into account operating costs as well as regulatory costs such as compliance with statutory reserve requirements.

The narrowing of the average interest margin was driven by the larger decline in ALR than ACF due to intense competition in the consumer loan market. The ambitious loan growth target led to attractive housing loan packages offered by banks competing intensely for such low risk lending.[11] Apart from offering competitive mortgage rates with flexible repayment schemes and high financing margins of up to 90 per cent, the "mortgage war" also included other innovative lures such as waivers of or exemptions from legal and processing fees. Loan growth in 2002 had mainly been driven by lending for the purchase of cars and residential properties (BNM 2003: 145). Amidst strong demand for household spending on consumer goods and passenger cars, and investment in houses, loans to the household sector soared by 15.6 per cent in 2002.

The removal of substantial non-performing loans from the banking system by Danaharta and the injection of capital into under-capitalised banks by Danamodal has contained the banking system's asset quality problems and reduced the potential for systemic risk. The banking institutions were, therefore, expected to concentrate on lending activities and thus contribute to real recovery, rather than be pre-occupied with recovery and rehabilitation of delinquent loans. Also, the BNM went further to set an 8 per cent annual loans growth target for 1998 and 1999. However, these measures not only failed to ensure increased productive sector bank borrowing, but instead encouraged the recurrence of a build-up of loans for unproductive activities, as shown in Table 5.13. The broad property sector received

Table 5.13 Malaysia: Commercial Bank Lending and Advances to Selected Sectors, 1995–2003 (% share)

Sector	1995	1996	1997	1998	1999	2000	2001	2002	2003
Manufacturing	23.3	21.0	19.0	18.8	18.5	18.2	17.6	16.8	15.9
Agriculture[a]	2.1	2.0	2.0	2.0	2.4	2.9	3.0	3.0	2.6
Broad Property[b]	29.3	30.3	34.9	35.8	36.7	37.3	39.7	42.7	45.0
Consumption credit	3.5	3.6	6.2	5.5	6.0	6.0	6.3	6.9	7.2
Purchase of securities	4.5	4.3	8.3	8.0	7.1	6.7	6.2	4.6	4.1

Notes: [a] Includes agriculture, hunting, forestry and fishing
 [b] Comprises construction, real estate and housing.
Sources: BNM Annual Report, various issues.

a much greater proportion of 45 per cent of total commercial bank loans in 2003 — in contrast to manufacturing, which had experienced a consistent decline even before the crisis. Lending to the broad property sector as well as for the purchase of securities and for consumption purposes has made up more than 50 per cent of the total loans extended by the commercial banks since 2000. Government intervention in the banking sector in the post-crisis period has hardly sought to achieve industrial policy goals, as in the pre-crisis period (see Chin 2001).

Even before imminent international financial liberalisation begins to bite, stiff competition in consumer loans has started to eat into the profit margins of the banking institutions. As envisaged in the FSMP, the financial market will open up to incumbent foreign banks by 2004, and is expected to be fully opened to new foreign players by 2007/8. While much attention has been paid to which of the ten anchor banks will survive the next consolidation phase, the real challenge concerns the ability of Malaysian domestic banks to prepare themselves to withstand the impending international liberalisation of the financial sector. Notwithstanding various restrictions such as branching by incumbent foreign banks in Malaysia, they have been able to increase a significant banking sector market share, controlling about 25 per cent of total assets and total deposits at the end of 2000 (BNM 2001: 34).

Furthermore, time is running out for local banks that have yet to update their risk management practices as they have been preoccupied thus far with post-consolidation integration issues. A survey cited in *The Asian Banker* (2002) found that only 31 per cent of respondent banks in Malaysia had a risk strategy document in place, which defines the operational risk tolerance of the banks. Less than 10 per cent of the banks that have such a document have comprehensively addressed the different areas involved in operational risk management, from strategy and management structure, to measurement tools and operational issues. Only 12.5 per cent of commercial and merchant banks surveyed have developed plans to meet the requirements and recommendations of the Basel Accord pertaining to capital charges on operational risk. In an increasingly competitive environment, there is a pressing need for banks to beef up operational efficiency and risk management to sustain or enhance profitability.

Concluding Remarks

Bank restructuring on a large scale is not easy, especially in developing countries which lack the institutional capacity to address both market and government failures. Unlike Indonesia, Thailand and South Korea, where state capacities were often undermined by neo-liberal reforms and policy conditionalities imposed by the IMF, Malaysia has had freer rein in determining its own policy responses, hence avoiding some of the problems associated with the IMF rescue packages. Malaysia's pro-cyclical IMF-like policies from late 1997 exacerbated contractionary tendencies until the second quarter of 1998, when they were replaced by reflationary fiscal measures. Financial restructuring efforts to deal with the banking crisis helped strengthen the banking system. The removal of NPLs by Danaharta and bank recapitalisation by Danamodal significantly strengthened the banking sector.

Nevertheless, self-congratulation on the supposed Malaysian success with its unorthodox financial restructuring may be a little premature. While Danamodal and Danaharta made significant progress in strengthening the banking system, government-imposed bank restructuring measures in Malaysia have not effectively addressed some weaknesses, especially in regulatory enforcement and interference by powerful interest groups in decision-making. The bank consolidation programme from 1999 may not resolve the fundamental problems of the Malaysian banking system. A select group of cronies continues to receive handsome rents. There is a lack of disciplinary mechanisms to force rentiers to achieve greater efficiency, as Malaysia continues to suffer from institutional drawbacks that restrict industrial upgrading. There is little evidence that banking sector reforms have significantly enhanced economic recovery, let alone created the financial basis for sustained economic growth and structural transformation. The external economic environment facing developing countries has become less favourable. With much cherry-picking, and (often more efficient) foreign banks waiting at the gates with international financial liberalisation, it is also not clear that the recent banking reforms have successfully prepared the sector for such foreign competition.

Notes

1. Danaharta adopted the approach of receiving capital from the government, as and when required.
2. With paid-up capital of RM250 million (approximately US$59 million), Danaharta raised RM25 billion in working capital through zero-coupon government-guaranteed bonds.
3. Danaharta has the legal powers to conduct liquidation procedures.
4. Loans outstanding from financial institutions at the point of acquisition. It comprises both principal outstanding as well as interest.
5. This refers to schemes, voluntarily negotiated by borrowers and creditors, to restructure the loans.
6. This refers to the sale of property and securities.
7. The first tranche of bonds were due on 31 December 2003.
8. The minimum shareholder funds for commercial banks were subsequently increased to RM1,000 million in December 1998.
9. The number of banks under ethnic Chinese control will shrink from 11 to 2.
10. These tax incentives —— which comprised exemptions from stamp duty and real property gains tax, as well as tax credit for 50 per cent of the accumulated losses of banking institutions acquired —— were intended to reduce acquisition costs and enhance the value of the merged entities <http://www.bnm.gov.my/pa/2000/0731.htm>.
11. Particularly residential properties costing RM250,000 or less.

CHAPTER 6

Corporate Debt Restructuring in Malaysia

WONG SOOK CHING

Bank recapitalisation and restructuring exercises alone were considered insufficient to ensure a strong and sustained economic recovery. A comprehensive solution to Malaysia's banking and corporate woes required implementation of corporate restructuring programmes. While this study recognises various flaws and abuses in the Malaysian bank and corporate restructuring programmes, this does not imply automatic rejection of the need for government-led bank and corporate restructuring exercises to address some consequences of the 1997–98 Asian financial crises.

Rather, the key lesson to be drawn is that such government-led and publicly financed exercises need to be fair, transparent, accountable and judiciously executed, e.g. by ensuring objectivity in the acquisition and recovery criteria used in restructuring exercises. More market-based approaches utilised elsewhere proved to be relatively "sluggish" and ineffectual, and hence, more deleterious for the economies concerned in the long run. This was especially true of Indonesia, and to a lesser extent, Thailand, but the process in Korea has also been subject to critical scrutiny (Shin and Chang 2003).

From Privatisation to Corporate Restructuring and Renationalisation

The Asian financial crisis has indeed exposed weaknesses especially those entrenched in poorly privatised corporations that were previously operating in a relatively comfortable business and financial environment. It cannot be denied that financially prudent and economically sound corporations were also greatly tested, with some exiting the market. Nonetheless, a select few of privatised entities embarked on ambitious expansion programmes that left them over-extended and over-leveraged, thus increasing vulnerability to abrupt credit crunch and adverse business conditions.

The privatisation[1] of Malaysia's national sewerage system, airline, car project, and light rail transit (LRT) system was part of the government's attempts to improve efficiency and increase investment through owner-managed enterprises. This was achieved through some form of subsidy, given the high capital costs, low margins (at least in the medium term), and large externalities. State support was also required because the owners could not charge high tariffs or fares to cover their costs. In the case of Perusahan Otomobil Nasional Bhd (Proton), the national car project, protection was desperately needed, ostensibly to provide "learning rents"; "high" import tariffs raised the relative prices of unprotected vehicles, thereby helping Proton's growth.

Ironically, the gains from privatisation, i.e. improved efficiency and competitiveness, and meeting of long-term targets by privatised entities were generally "patchy". This was partly due to weak regulatory framework — which was imperative to ensure that incentives were in place to induce the owners to improve efficiency and invest — and *ad hoc* intervention by the government through various ministries. Moreover, these failures can be attributed to institutional failure that led to incorrect privatisation choices, poor screening and selection, and weak regulation.

An example of an incorrect privatisation choice was the privatisation of the sewerage system that proceeded without sufficient information on the performance, assets and condition, and customer base of the existing system, or an adequate legal framework. This led to the operator having to take over and maintain more assets than originally agreed, three tariff revisions following consumer opposition, and bill collection problems, which raised operating costs and reduced revenue and cash flow. The government's privatisation of public transit systems was also unfeasible to begin with without some form of state support given the cost of infrastructure and general inability of such systems to cover operating costs. For instance, fares only covered 30 to 40 per cent of operating costs in the US and 55 per cent in the

UK (Hakim *et al.* 1996). In the case of the two operational LRT systems, this figure was 44 per cent (STAR) and 22 per cent (PUTRA) in 1999 (Halcrow Consultants 1999).

While most countries underwrite the costs of construction and subsidise such public transportation operations, the Malaysian government chose to leave the financing of the LRT system largely to the private sector. According to the former head of the government's Corporate Debt Restructuring Committee (CDRC), infrastructure projects required state funding as only the state, and not banks, could provide long-term funds given the long gestation period (FinanceAsia.com, 24 July 2000). The government provided long-term, low interest loans directly (in the form of government and infrastructure support loans) and through state institutions (e.g. the Employees Provident Fund and the Development and Infrastructure Bank). Moreover, in order for the company to even have a chance to breakeven or generate profits without adversely affecting consumer demand and welfare, huge fare subsidisations were required.

In the case of Malaysian Airline System Bhd (MAS), the poor purchase structure and industry problems would have made it difficult for private ownership to address the airline's long-term capital investment requirements. The purchase was financed entirely through loans, but low profit margins, large externalities, and regular bankruptcies inherent to the industry meant that revenues could not be guaranteed to generate sufficient profits to repay the loan, let alone increase investment.

Proton, on the other hand, was probably not viable to begin with. An ambitious project to spearhead Malaysia's industrialisation process, it was closely modelled after the Korean car industry's success but failed to take into account the different global market conditions, necessary scale economies (which were beyond the domestic market), high capital costs, and excess global capacity due to intense competition. Despite the government postponing the lowering of tariffs — as part of the Common Effective Preferential Tariff programme under the ASEAN Free Trade Agreement (AFTA) — from 2003 to 2005 (*The Sun,* 21 June 2000), Proton's alternative (Japanese) director has suggested that Proton might still not be competitive by 2005 (*The Sun,* 25 July 2000). It was therefore unlikely that privatisation would have made a difference. Apparently, cross subsidisation — relatively higher domestic price compared to export price with better quality for export markets — helped Proton penetrate the overseas market, though their market share is miniscule.

High import tariffs were used to protect the domestic carmaker and ensure the viability of the cross-subsidisation strategy. Since Proton and Perodua are ostensibly "national carmakers", both have enjoyed a 50 per cent discount on excise duties. Proton's vehement stalling to include automobiles in the ASEAN Free Trade Agreement (AFTA) has raised doubts about their ability to compete successfully without such advantages. Anticipation of lower prices for non-national car models, especially from Japanese and South Korean carmakers, since 2003 has apparently discouraged consumers from buying the "national cars". As a result, Proton's market share shrank to 49 per cent in 2003 from 59 per cent in 2002 as its car sales fell by 27.5 per cent to 155,420 units in 2003. Proton's declining market share — and sales revenue — resulted in a net loss of RM42 million in the third quarter of the financial year ending 31 March 2004, compared with a profit of RM197 million in the corresponding quarter the previous year (*The Star*, 24 April 2004). However, for the financial year ending 31 March 2004, the group reported a net profit of RM510.1 million, down significantly from the RM1.1 billion recorded in 2003. The significant drop in pre-tax profit — from RM1.36 billion for the financial year ending 31 March 2003 to RM592 million for the subsequent financial period — reflected the sharp decrease in sales from RM9.27 billion in 2003 to RM6.47 billion in 2004, also reflected in Proton's share price (*The Star*, 29 May 2004).

The absence of open bidding in all four cases can be said to have compromised the quality of awardees. With the exception of one LRT operator and Proton's owner, none of the major awardees had much relevant experience. STAR was a consortium formed and headed by Taylor Woodrow (a UK housing, property development, construction and engineering company) and Adtranz (a train manufacturer owned by Daimler Chrysler, which was later sold to Canada's Bombardier Transportation in 2000). Although Taylor Woodrow and Adtranz had a majority of 30 per cent share in the consortium, state institutions had a combined share ownership of 50 per cent. Berjaya Group, the company that headed Indah Water Konsortium (IWK — the consortium awarded the sewerage treatment concession), had no experience in public works aside from some small road-building projects (Gomez and Jomo 1999). The owner of MAS had never run an airline or been associated with similar business, having made his fortune from a cellular (mobile) telephone monopoly. The remaining two LRT operators[2] did not have experience building or operating public transport systems. Proton's owner was an automotive engineer with some relevant experience, but the government chose to bypass the rest of the existing car assembly industry.

Poor choice of awardees exacerbated by political patronage may be a major explanation for the failures of privatisation in Malaysia that greatly increased the cost of government-led "bail outs" which reversed mostly the one-time gains from the privatisation programme. The owners of IWK, MAS, Proton and the LRT system were all closely linked to the United Malays National Organisation (UMNO) leadership at the highest level, and patronage can be said to have influenced the poor choice of awardees, weakening incentives to increase efficiency and investment. The choice of awardees was important given the national significance of many of these projects, and the government was aware of the risks percentage and need for careful assessment of track records, credit ratings, and intentions: "They must not be the kind of people who would sell their shares for quick gains" (Mahathir 1998a: 29). The prime minister defended this by arguing that successful awardees "had already proven their ability to run big operations" (*New Straits Times*, 27 November 1995) and were already rich and successful businessmen (Mahathir 1998b).

The poor choice of awardees was not only reflected by the financial difficulties of these companies (with the exception of Proton, which remained protected and profitable), but also in the performance of the owners' other businesses, all of which were debt-ridden. This reduced the ability of the owners to continue financing the privatised projects, and the government was forced to re-nationalise them when the owners clearly could not break even, even in the medium term. According to the new head of the CDRC in 2001, the subsequent replacement of these owners with professional managers was to separate the powers between chairman and chief executive officer in order to "alleviate the problems of owner-managers who have their own debt problems" (*Far Eastern Economic Review*, 18 October 2001).

Regulatory failure, on the other hand, is perhaps best exemplified by the government's "arbitrary administrative action" when it revised tariffs, not once, but three times, in the case of IWK. The privatisation of the sewerage and LRT systems sought to facilitate capital accumulation through the allocation of short-term (construction) and long-term (concession) rents. The concessionaire can thus earn profits at the end or at the beginning, by overstating construction costs.[3] The 60-year concession period for the LRT privatisation can be seen as providing long-term monopoly rents, while the decision to privatise infrastructure construction, instead of underwriting capital costs and privatising operations, as elsewhere, offered further rents. This was also consistent with growing investments in the country involving construction.

Similarly, by creating a monopoly from an essentially decentralised sewerage system run by 144 local authorities, potential efficiency gains from privatising to several different operators were ignored to ensure monopoly rents. For example, the government could have privatised sewage treatment to more than one operator along the lines of the 19 urban centres outlined in the national sewerage development programme (see Pillay 1994). According to Ridzuan Halim, there is "no advantage organising sewerage works on a national basis since there is little sense centralising or collecting sewerage on a national basis" (*The Edge*, 1 June 1998).

Hence, while regulation is normally needed to limit monopoly rents, this may not be the case where the state seeks to create such rents to promote capital accumulation. The government also effectively failed to regulate the LRT system by not accounting for the large externalities that necessitated some form of state support. The unlikelihood of repaying the capital costs meant that the operators had lost the incentive to be efficient (Halcrow Consultants 1999). Moreover, the owners of both operating LRT companies had little incentive to improve efficiency given their debt burdens and government guaranteed incomes, which made the prospect of breaking even unlikely.

In the case of MAS, this was partly due to the externalities inherent in the airline industry. In addition, previous management decisions on fleet expansion added to the new owner's debt burden and the government continued to limit domestic airfares and require MAS to fly to unprofitable destinations that impinged on the airline's revenue stream. The picture that emerges then is one of entrepreneurial failure, compounded by poor investment decisions and inappropriate regulation, which eventually led to re-nationalisation in some cases. Persistent policy failure was partly due to a combination of a highly centralised, insulated, non-transparent and unaccountable political executive, and the country's rich natural resource endowment (e.g. see Bowie 1988; Jesudason 1989) that diluted imperatives for economic efficiency.

Effectiveness of the Special Purpose Vehicles

With the benefit of hindsight, it is easier to see the severity of the problems affecting Malaysia's banking and corporate sectors, and the need for some form of government intervention to control the NPL situation and to resolve corporate distress. Interestingly, a lion's share of government (hence taxpayers) funds have been concentrated in restructuring and assisting, directly or indirectly, previously privatised entities. Financial or other forms of government assistance *per se* are not counterproductive. *Net* positive outcomes or "return on taxpayers' monies" can be achieved with proper selection, appropriate and reasonable terms and conditions for restructuring, disciplining mechanisms and "performance" targets in a favourable macroeconomic environment. Hence, the greater tendency of the restructuring programmes to deviate from such conditions will probably result in sub-optimal results. As such, our objective here is focused on the flaws of the corporate restructuring and bail out programmes,[4] so that appropriate lessons can be drawn to improve on debt restructuring programmes and outcomes in future.

There are two levels of analysis in "measuring" or determining the "success" of a corporate restructuring programme: (1) whether the policy measures (e.g. setting up special purpose vehicles) adopted by the government were "appropriate" and justified, given the conditions thought to be facing the banking and corporate sector; and (2) whether the corporate restructuring plans were "well thought through", "appropriate" and well in order to improve the corporations' and stakeholder interests. This includes assessing the implementation or execution of plans, that is, whether the corporations under review used their improved debt situation to implement socially desired reforms including changes in management where necessary. The latter tends to be ignored when business resumes as the economy improves.

Successful corporate restructuring is measured here in terms of successfully averting or minimising systemic crises, the recoverability of assets through sales, capabilities and efficiency enhancing operational restructuring and greater competitiveness (short-, medium- and long-term). Effective implementation reduces restructuring costs and use of public funds, which improves social welfare. Other desired outcomes include creating conditions for economic recovery, sustained growth and technological progress. Also of importance is whether the government conducts bank or corporate rescue measures or bail outs in the public interest or principally in favour of politically influential business interests.

The Corporate Restructuring Programme

With the severe impact of the crisis on the banking and real sectors,[5] the government created special purpose vehicles (SPVs) — Pengurusan Danaharta Nasional Bhd (Danaharta), Danamodal Nasional Bhd (Danamodal) and Corporate Debt Restructuring Committee (CDRC) — to check, reduce and manage NPLs (Table 6.1 summarises the NPL situation in Malaysia from December 1998 to September 2003), recapitalise the banking sector, and restructure corporate debt.

Ministry of Finance, Incorporated (MoF Inc.) — which already existed prior to the 1997–98 financial crisis — helped to take over financially ailing (but according to MoF Inc., "economically viable") corporations on behalf of the government, which enabled the government to directly restructure them. MoF Inc. has several investment arms responsible for managing assets held by the government and for undertaking strategic investments (meaning acquisitions of shares and takeovers of corporations it deems appropriate in the contemporary situation). Syarikat Prasarana Negara Bhd (SPNB) and Khazanah Nasional Bhd (Khazanah) are wholly owned subsidiaries of MoF Inc. Khazanah was incorporated under the Companies Act 1965 on 3 September 1993 as a public limited company. Syarikat Danasaham Nasional Bhd (Danasaham) is a wholly owned subsidiary and special purpose vehicle of Khazanah (another Treasury investment arm) (see Chapter 4 for a description of Danaharta, Danamodal and the CDRC).

Given the breadth and depth of the crisis, the government was probably right in creating various SPVs with their objectives and

Table 6.1   Malaysia: Banking Industry Non-Peri ›rming Loans, Dec. 1998 to Sep. 2003

		NPLs (3 months)				*NPLs (6 months)*			*Loan Growth*	
		Gross	*Net[1]*	*Gross Ratio*	*Net Ratio*	*Gross*	*Net[1]*	*Gross Ratio*	*Net Ratio*	*(mom)*	*(yoy)*
		RM bn	*RM bn*	*(%)*	*(%)*	*RM bn*	*RM bn*	*(%)*	*(%)*		
1998	Dec	77.0	52.9	18.6	13.6	52.4	31.7	12.7	8.1	–	1.3
1999	Dec	65.5	40.6	16.6	11.0	46.8	23.8	11.8	6.4	–	–4.3
2000	Mar	64.9	39.4	16.4	10.7	47.1	23.6	11.9	6.3	–	–1.8
	Jun	65.0	39.3	16.2	10.4	48.4	24.6	12.0	6.5	–	0.9
	Sep	65.5	38.6	16.1	10.1	50.5	25.9	12.4	6.7	–	–2.9
	Dec	64.3	37.7	15.4	9.7	49.0	24.7	11.8	6.3	–	5.3
2001	Mar	67.6	41.4	16.2	10.6	52.1	28.0	12.5	7.1	–	5.6
	Jun	73.4	45.7	17.2	11.4	58.3	32.3	13.6	8.0	–	6.2
	Sep	77.3	47.2	17.9	11.7	61.6	33.0	14.3	8.2	–	5.9
	Dec	76.8	46.2	17.7	11.5	61.8	32.8	14.3	8.1	–	3.8
2002	Jan	78.5	46.9	18.1	11.7	63.4	33.5	14.7	8.3	0.1	4.0
	Feb	78.9	47.0	18.1	11.6	63.7	33.3	14.6	8.2	0.7	4.6
	Mar	79.2	46.8	18.1	11.5	64.3	33.5	14.7	8.2	0.5	5.0
	Apr	79.0	46.1	18.0	11.4	64.9	33.6	14.8	8.2	0.2	4.8
	May	77.8	46.0	17.6	11.2	64.5	34.0	14.5	8.2	1.0	4.6
	June	76.5	45.6	17.2	11.0	63.4	33.9	14.2	8.2	0.3	4.1
	July	76.6	45.7	17.2	11.0	63.4	33.9	14.2	8.1	0.1	3.6
	Aug	74.9	44.1	16.8	10.6	62.2	32.8	13.9	7.9	0.4	3.9
	Sep	74.5	44.1	16.6	10.5	61.9	32.5	13.8	7.7	0.6	4.1
	Oct	74.2	42.8	16.4	10.2	61.8	32.3	13.7	7.7	0.5	4.1
	Nov	74.7	43.6	16.5	10.3	61.4	31.8	13.5	7.5	0.4	4.9
	Dec	71.7	43.1	15.8	10.2	58.9	31.7	13.0	7.5	–0.3	4.7
2003	Jan	71.7	42.4	15.8	10.0	59.2	31.3	13.0	7.3	0.6	5.1
	Feb	73.7	44.2	16.2	10.4	59.7	31.7	13.1	7.4	–0.1	4.2
	Mar	70.6	42.1	15.6	9.9	57.0	30.0	12.7	7.0	–0.2	3.5
	Apr	70.2	42.8	15.4	9.8	56.7	30.1	12.5	7.0	0.3	3.6
	May	70.5	42.0	15.4	9.8	57.2	30.2	12.5	7.0	0.5	3.1
	June	69.0	41.6	14.9	9.5	55.7	29.6	12.0	6.8	1.5	4.3
	July	68.2	40.8	14.6	9.3	55.8	29.6	11.9	6.7	0.7	4.9
	Aug	67.7	40.3	14.4	9.1	55.3	29.2	11.8	6.6	0.7	5.2
	Sep	67.1	40.3	14.2	9.0	54.5	29.2	11.5	6.5	0.4	5.1

Note: [1] Net NPL = NPL — interest-in-suspense-specific provisions.
Sources: Bank Negara Malaysia, *Monthly Statistical Bulletin,* June 2000, Dec. 2001, April 2002, Sep. 2003.
RHB Research Institute (2002).

Table 6.2   Malaysia: Gearing of Selected Government Related Companies, 1996–2001

Selected Companies	1996/97 %	1998/99 %	2000/1 %
MAS	153	323	467
UEM	297	378	585
Proton	Net cash	Net cash	Net cash
DRB-Hicom	2	73	105
Renong	80	280	579
Tenaga	62	177	185
Telekom	11	57	45

Source: CIMB Securities as reported by the *The Star*, 1 October 2001a.

functions to help resolve the NPL problems facing the banking sector, as well as the debt and operational restructuring challenges facing the corporations. Table 6.2 on the gearing[6] of selected government related companies provides some indication of the magnitude of the problem faced by some key corporations which have accumulated relatively large fixed charge capital (preference shares and debts) to equity. However, there is dispute as to whether or not the resources of these SPVs were "effectively" and "properly" utilised to reduce corporate debts to sustainable levels, improve corporate performance and enhance corporate governance, thereby helping corporate survival and economic recovery.

Government Agencies Involved in Private Sector Restructuring

The Malaysian government has clearly taken a pro-active stance in trying to resolve the non-performing loans (NPLs) problem in the banking system, and to facilitate and/or lead corporate restructuring, especially of large conglomerates and their main constituent corporations. This section will examine and evaluate the rationale and justification for government assistance or bail outs since the measures undertaken cannot be assumed *a priori* to have improved net welfare.

The progress and performance of these programmes so far are then briefly reviewed. Here, we assess whether these corporations have taken the necessary steps or were pro-active in resolving their debt and liquidity problems. One particularly controversial issue is the purchase prices of shares and assets in takeovers. Haggard (2000: 166) suggests the Malaysian corporate restructuring experience has been distinct from those of its East Asian counterparts:

> In contrast to other countries in the region, a distinguishing feature of the Malaysian response to the crisis has been to extend support directly to a number of firms. These interventions do not exhibit a single pattern. Not all were straightforward bail outs; some involved indirect forms of support. In others, a proposed bail out was either rejected or modified, suggesting some of the checks that operate on the government. Others, however, suggest the socialisation of private risk and the presence of moral hazard, including forbearance toward shareholders and management of ailing firms. Some actions could have been predicted by government efforts to use companies to fulfil social and foreign policy objectives.
>
> The Malaysian government's strategy toward financial and corporate restructuring appears to have two faces. On the one hand, the government established institutions with clear mandates and professional staff to address the problems of bank recapitalisation, non-performing loans, and corporate debt restructuring, and launched an aggressive plan of mergers in the banking sector. On the other hand, the government's strategy has relied heavily on an interventionist approach to asset restructuring that runs the risk of shifting losses onto Danaharta and the government.
>
> A common pattern in these cases is for the government to initiate projects, either directly through state-owned enterprises or through policy decisions, and then to privatise those efforts in whole or in part to favoured private partners. It is impossible to say whether these partners were selected on the basis of political criteria alone; all had some prior experience in business. But it is possible to say that the discretionary and non-transparent means of allocating assets and contracts, as well as the personal connections to government officials, created risks.

Danaharta

As noted earlier, Pengurusan Danaharta Nasional Bhd, or Danaharta, the national asset management company[7] was set up under the Ministry of Finance on 20 June 1998 in the aftermath of the 1997–98 financial crisis to acquire non-performing loans from banks. Rather than allow the "normal course" of foreclosure and bankruptcy proceedings,[8] the Malaysian government resorted to extending "indirect" support to some corporations, most notably,

United Engineers (M) Bhd (UEM), Renong Bhd (Renong), Malaysian Airline System Bhd (MAS), Projek Usahasama Transit Ringan Automatik Sdn Bhd (PUTRA) and Sistem Transit Aliran Ringan Bhd (STAR). The government bought or took over bad loans, saving corporations from liquidation and associated "market discipline". Such bail outs may not necessarily be bad under certain circumstances or conditions. But government leniency with errant corporations, banks, directors or managers implies poor governance or worse, abuse. The question then arises: How can the corporate (or banking) sector be properly restructured if some "large" corporations (or banks) do not fully or adequately internalise or bear the costs and consequences of their actions? To answer this question, four issues are important.

Firstly, two issues that come to mind in the banking sector are (1) why the banks allowed only 15 corporate groups to account for 20 per cent of total loans (*freeMalaysia*, "Bank Bail outs? More Like Buddy Bail outs") in the first place? and (2) did banks extend credit to non-creditworthy borrowers[9] of their own free will, or were they "coerced"[10] to do so?

With regards to the banking sector, Moody's Investor Service forecasted that Malaysia's NPLs would peak at 30 per cent of total loans, or RM125 billion, twice the latest official figures of 15 per cent — based on a three-month classification standard (*freeMalaysia*, "Bank Bailouts? More Like Buddy Bailouts"). In July 1998, Standard and Poor estimated that net NPLs would reach 30 per cent within a year, and that banking system recapitalisation costs would reach 40 per cent of GDP. However, the NPL problem had been contained, and according to the National Economic Action Council (NEAC 2001), net NPLs only reached a peak of 14.9 per cent (3-month classification) in November 1998. In gross terms, NPLs reached 20 per cent of outstanding loans. According to the NEAC (2001), the cost of banking system recapitalisation amounted to RM7.1 billion, or 2.4 per cent of GDP. Total financial sector restructuring costs have not exceeded 7 per cent of GDP.

One can obtain some answers to these questions by looking at past public policies such as the New Economic Policy (NEP) and the Malaysian privatisation policy[11] (see e.g. Gomez and Jomo 1999; Gunasegaram 2001b and *freeMalaysia*, 2001). It appears that Danaharta has helped resolve or absorb NPLs while helping to bail out or rescue politically well-connected individuals, most memorably, the three billion ringgit worth of loans by Malaysian banks to Hottick, owned by a lawyer of Halim Saad of UEM-Renong.

Was the government justified in bailing out banks and corporations in the name of protecting "national interest" and preserve jobs? Would doing otherwise have led to the collapse of Malaysian corporate capacities and capabilities embodied by these enterprises? And why did the government rescue politically influential major shareholders, rather than the corporations themselves?

The government has invoked "national interest" in providing "relief" to certain corporations (or, more specifically, to particular shareholders). The government had used a privately held corporation (Hottick Investment, registered in Hong Kong) to take over private Malaysian interests (of Joseph Chong, then Member of Parliament of the ruling coalition in the National Steel Corporation of the Philippines), which had apparently embarrassed the government leadership. What was achieved by taking over the Hottick loans at 100 sen to the ringgit?[12] The full compensation of the banks in this notable, if exceptional case suggests that the banks had been "directed" by the authorities to finance the Hottick takeover of NSC. The RM3 billion takeover of Hottick Investment's NPL by Danaharta was widely criticised. NSC was on the brink of liquidation, reducing the RM3 billion loan to near scrap value, leaving banks with almost worthless NSC stocks as collateral (Ng 2001).

Clearly, the acquisition of NSC was certainly not in the national interests unless this is equated with the personal whims and reputation of government leaders. Hottick had no relevant management and technical expertise and experience. Hottick's nominal owners — including a lawyer of then UEM-Renong boss Halim Saad — were thus "covered" by the authorities, wasting public money for a politically motivated corporate acquisition. Such decisions clearly involved resource misallocation, "crowding out" others, and increasing the fiscal burden to the government and, ultimately, to taxpayers.

As Quek (2000: 2) notes: "If Danaharta had not stepped in to take over the bad loans, the lending banks would be bound by law to pursue Halim to recover the debts as the latter would have been customarily a personal guarantor to these loans. And that would deplete or bankrupt Halim but would not cause the collapse of his conglomerate Renong. So, how would that cause unemployment as alleged by Mahathir?" By taking over the loan, Danaharta was effectively saving Hottick's major shareholders and guarantors and those who had directed them to take over NSC. By taking over the loan without any discount, Danaharta was contributing to the partial recapitalisation of the lending banks, which had presumably been directed by the authorities to finance the NSC takeover. Such directed credit suggests other possible abuse of credit policy.

The third issue is whether the price of the loan was fairly determined (since Danaharta claims to practise "strict market valuation").[13] Clearly, the loss in collateral value was not factored into the price for acquiring these NPLs.[14] It appears that Danaharta was otherwise reasonably consistent and proper in dealing with shareholders and creditors in resolving bad debts. According to Danaharta executive chairman Dato' Azman Yahya, at the Chief Financial Officer (CFO) Summit 2001 on "Corporate Restructuring: The Malaysian Experience": "If needed, shareholders and creditors would have to take a bigger 'haircut' to resolve the companies' debt problems." He noted that in order to mitigate the possibilities of "social dislocation", Danaharta was reluctant to "trim 100 per cent of the fat" during the first round of corporate restructuring. However, he indicated that Danaharta would further "trim fat" in the second stage and, if required, would proceed ruthlessly, as evidenced by foreclosure of about a quarter of the NPLs under its management (*The Star,* 9 November 2001). Dato' Azman Yahya was appointed by the Minister of Finance as Danaharta's chairman on 1 August 2001. He succeeded Danaharta's first chairman, Dato' Chellappah Rajandram. Dato' Azman Yahya's tenure ended on 31 July 2003. He was succeeded by Dato' Zainal Abidin Putih on 1 August 2003, whose term will end on 31 December 2005 (Danaharta, press release, 30 July 2003).

In various six-monthly operations reports, from 30 June 1999, Danaharta has noted that discounts on its purchased loans have been above 50 per cent on average. However, this may not reflect the discounts of NPLs purchased in the overall banking system. For instance, as at 30 June 1999, Danaharta was assigned by the government to manage Sime Bank Bhd and Bank Bumiputera Malaysia Bhd (BBMB) groups' NPLs (RM14.459 billion and RM7.082 billion respectively)[15] on its behalf (i.e. at no cost to Danaharta) (Danaharta 1999b; 2003b). *freeMalaysia* (1999b) argues that Sime Bank Bhd and BBMB groups' NPLs were acquired by the government at *full face value* (i.e. exempted from taking "haircuts") even though their loan collateral (mainly stocks[16] and commercial property) had obviously lost much market value by the time of acquisition. While other financially troubled banks accepted an average discount of 57 per cent on NPLs sold to Danaharta (and others), the Sime Bank Bhd and BBMB groups unloaded a massive total of RM21.5 billion[17] in bad loans to the government at full face value. Put differently, the authorities could have saved some RM12 billion if the two banking groups had taken the average 57 per cent "haircut" other institutions had to.

Since the government has guaranteed the bonds issued by Danaharta, this means that the burden of financial and corporate restructuring will ultimately be borne by the public (taxpayers),[18] and not mainly by the "reckless" and/or imprudent financial institutions and corporations — or their shareholders — who should be held responsible. According to *freeMalaysia* ("Bank Bailouts? More Like Buddy Bailouts"), "fifty-seven financial institutions in Malaysia were forced to subscribe to these bonds, using cash released from cuts in liquid reserves maintained at the central bank". By doing so, this crowded out financial resources available for smaller corporations. Nonetheless, a distinction should be made between poor performance due to internally-led and externally-caused factors. If private enterprises are not to be held responsible for the negative impacts of adverse external factors or shocks on the business environment and real economy, government assistance in mitigating their adverse effects and preserving Malaysian economic capabilities can be defended to ensure economic development and "catching-up".

The fourth key issue involves the inequitable treatment of financial institutions or creditors, especially exceptions to loan acquisition and criteria policies. Danaharta, Danamodal, and others have been rather selective about which bad loans to buy and restructure, and on what terms they were acquired. It appears that not all banks and financial institutions were treated "equally". According to *freeMalaysia* (1999b), of the RM8.3 billion paid by Danamodal and Khazanah to help revive debt-stricken banks and corporations, RM5 billion, or 60 per cent, went to four institutions: MBf Finance Bhd, RM1.6 billion; BBMB, RM1.1 billion; RHB-Sime Bank Bhd, RM1.5 billion, and Oriental Bank Bhd, RM850 million. Of the

RM31.4 billion in bad loans acquired [and managed on behalf of the government] by Danaharta, 85 per cent of the total — nearly nine out of every RM10 paid by the agency [and the government] for bad-loan buy-outs — went to only five institutions, namely Sime Bank Bhd group, which was relieved of RM12 billion; BBMB group, RM9.5 billion; MBf Finance Bhd, RM4 billion; Oriental Bank Bhd, RM1 billion; and Commerce Asset-Holdings' Bank of Commerce (M), about RM800 million. There is no clear evidence that these were the only banks in need of such massive intervention.

As noted earlier, only 15 corporate groups accounted for 20 per cent of all Malaysia's bank loans at the start of the economic crisis. The three biggest borrowers, in descending order, were the corporate groups associated with Halim Saad (around RM30 billion), Tajudin Ramli (RM16.5 billion) and Vincent Tan (RM7 billion), with combined loans totalling over RM53 billion. Most of the remaining borrowers were friends (and children) of the then Prime Minister Dr Mahathir Mohamad and then Finance Minister, Daim Zainuddin (*freeMalaysia*, "Bank Bailouts? More Like Buddy Bailouts"). Needless to say, fears of likely abuse in granting government assistance are generally higher with such evidence of cronyism and nepotism in business-government relations.

Much criticism has been directed at the banks for lending such huge amounts to so few corporations, while the NPLs bought by the government have been less controversial. However, such concentrated lending — coupled with politicised, cronyistic and nepotistic corporate as well as financial governance and external shocks — increased the vulnerability to financial crises and led to the problems faced by the banking sector. As such, it came as no surprise when the government bought over both BBMB and Sime Bank Bhd groups' NPLs. Both were government-controlled institutions, either directly or indirectly, with the former taken over by the Commerce Asset group and the latter by the RHB group after the government NPL buyout. Both banks held the bulk of the NPLs (Ng 2001) involving financially battered corporations such as UEM/Renong and MAS.

Even though Danaharta had the power to force changes in management to promote operational restructuring to increase the probability of NPL recoverability through loan restructuring[19] or settlement[20], these powers were rarely exercised in practice.[21] This cast doubt on the independence of Danaharta and its ability to consistently handle the NPLs free from political considerations. By resolving the banks' NPL problems without consistently demanding appropriate discounts or stern disciplinary action against mismanagement, the government reinforced the perception that abuse and mismanagement would not be punished as corporations were rescued from foreclosure or liquidation proceedings while some banks got to unload their NPLs without penalty. The leeway given to creditors involved public subsidisation of bail outs for those at least partly responsible for the financial distress. Thus far, Danaharta has been able to restructure the NPLs and successfully dispose of assets (received as loan collateral) at favourable prices, and to recover the prices paid for bad loans in order to redeem the bonds issued to finance Danaharta.

One important factor determining the performance of an AMC is whether it can maximise the value of assets, either by "turning them around", or by disposing of them judiciously. Klingebiel (2000) suggests the following two dimensions for evaluating the success of centralised AMCs: (i) whether they achieve the objectives for which they were set up, which may include (a) rapid asset disposal and liquidation agency assets as measured by the speed of asset disposal, usually considered a success if completed within five years; and (b) accelerating corporate restructuring which is considered successful if the AMC sells off 50 per cent of its assets within a five-year time frame (this "benchmark" is the norm, largely due to lack of data and counterfactual); and (ii) whether the banking system return to solvency or if banking problems reappear (i.e. whether the financial system/ banks experienced repeated financial distress), whether credit operations resumed as banks were cleaned up, and whether the problem of recovering bad loans was decoupled from making fresh loans (i.e. did credit to the private sector really resume, and was there positive credit growth?).

Based on the above criteria, Danaharta has done a relatively good job by selling half its "assets" by the end of December 2001, thus meeting its 50 per cent asset disposal requirement (see Table 6.3). Moreover, the average recovery rate above the 50 per cent level has been commendable. According to Danaharta's senior general manager (property division), Johan Ariffin, since November 1999, Danaharta had taken 644 properties to the market and sold 83 per cent of them,

Table 6.3   Restructuring and Recovery of Non-Performing Loans (NPLs) by Danaharta

As at:	NPLs Acquired and Managed by Danaharta so far* (RM bn)	NPLs Restructured by Danaharta so far* (RM bn)	% of Total Portfolio of NPLs Resolved	Expected Recovery Value* (RM bn)	Expected Average Recovery Rate (%)
31/12/1998	19.728	8.106	–	–	–
31/12/1999	45.521	17.607	38.7	12.064[c]	80.2[d]
31/12/2000	47.49	35.83	75.4	23.80[c]	66
31/12/2001	47.72[a]	47.69[b]	99.9	28.51[c]	56
31/12/2002	52.52	52.52	100.0	30.19[c]	57
31/03/2003	52.30	52.30	100.0	29.46[c]	56
30/06/2003	52.30	52.30	100.0	30.42[c]	58
31/12/2003	52.44	52.44	100.0	30.63[c]	58
31/03/2004	52.44	52.44	100.0	30.86[c]	59
30/06/2004	52.44	52.44	100.0	30.99[c]	59

Notes: * Figures are based on gross value, unless specified otherwise.
[a] The figure was based on loan rights acquired (LRA) value.
[b] If the figure was based on gross value, the figure would be LRA of RM47.69 billion plus accrued interest of RM3.25bn.
[c] This assumes a zero recovery rate for default cases.
[d] Recovery rate (excluding those under "SA — pending approval"). SA = Special Administration.

Sources: Danaharta 1999a.
Danaharta 2000.
Danaharta 2001a.
Danaharta 2002b.
Danaharta 2003b.
Danaharta 2003c.
Danaharta 2003e.
Danaharta 2004a.
Danaharta 2004b.

with an average recovery rate of 95 per cent against valuation (*The Star*, 10 April 2002). This represented good progress in property disposal since Danaharta managed to clear some 83 per cent of the assets under its management with a high average recovery rate within two years.[22] As at 30 June 2003, Danaharta had disposed of 748 — valued at RM1.48 billion — out of 892 properties — worth RM2.42

billion; i.e. it had cleared approximately 84 per cent of the properties under its responsibility (Danaharta 2003e).

Danaharta's declared intention of wrapping up its operations within the targeted time frame of seven years, i.e. by 2005 (*The Star*, 5 September 2001), has also enhanced credibility.[23] This helps ensure expeditious resolution of NPLs, reducing the drag on the banking sector, its lending activities and the real economy. Out of the RM48.03 billion in Danaharta's NPLs portfolio (acquired managed) as at June 2001, 66.5 per cent was from commercial banks, 11.1 per cent from offshore banks, 7.3 per cent from merchant banks, and 0.1 per cent each from discount houses and insurance companies (*The Star*, 5 September 2001). This gives an idea of the severity of the NPL problem in the commercial banking sector. As of 31 December 2001, Danaharta had restructured — or approved for restructuring — an impressive 99.9 per cent of its total portfolio of NPLs, with an average expected recovery rate of 56 per cent (Table 6.3). However, as of 31 March 2003, Danaharta had managed to restructure or had approved restructuring of 100 per cent of its total NPLs portfolio, with an average expected recovery rate of 56 per cent. As at 30 June 2003, the average expected recovery rate increased to 58 per cent, largely due to the "high" expected recovery rate from managed NPLs — BBMB and Sime Bank groups' NPLs managed by Danaharta on behalf of the Malaysian government. Besides the high percentage of restructured or managed NPLs, the somewhat high average recovery *value* rate had also been impressive.

As at 31 March 2003, Danaharta's NPL portfolio of loan rights acquired (LRA) totalled RM47.40 billion, consisting of RM19.73 billion in acquired NPLs (from financial institutions) and RM27.97 billion in managed NPLs (of the now defunct BBMB Group and Sime Bank Group). For the same period, Danaharta acquired and managed a total of 2,903 accounts involving 2,564 borrowers. As at 31 March 2003, the expected recovery value of NPLs stood at RM30.86 billion, up from RM30.63 billion for the financial year ended 31 December 2003. The expected recovery rate as of 31 March 2004 increased to 59 per cent from 58 per cent as of 31 December 2003. Danaharta expected to recover a total RM30.86 billion from its portfolio of NPLs during its lifespan due to end in 2005. Danaharta has been making steady progress in the recovery process involving cash, restructured loans, securities and properties. Danaharta managed to collect RM24.01 billion, or 78 per cent, as of 31 March 2004, an increase of RM1.61 billion from the previous quarter up to 31 December 2003.[24]

As at 30 June 2004, Danaharta has managed to recover RM24.70 billion or 80 per cent of the expected targeted total asset recovery of RM30.99 billion. Of the RM24.70 billion assets recovered, Danaharta recovered RM11.82 in cash, RM7.57 in the form of restructured loans, RM3.98 billion in securities and RM1.33 billion in properties. Compare this against the 58 per cent and 73 per cent of assets recovered out of the targeted figure as at June 2002 and June 2003, respectively, we can deduce that Danaharta is pushing hard to resolve matters and tie-up its operations by end 2005. These developments have enabled Danaharta to fully redeem RM8.647 billion bonds or approximately 78 per cent of RM11.14 bonds issued as at 30 June 2004 (Danaharta 2004b).

To reiterate the point made at the beginning of this chapter, despite initial reservations with regards to relatively more favourable "discount" and "haircut" conditions for certain banks, Danaharta has managed to remain focused on its main objectives of resolving NPLs and maximising recovery value within a stipulated timeframe. Danaharta through its continued efforts some six years after the crisis have overcome the general tendency of AMCs to simply "warehouse" their loans. Nonetheless, the identification of weaknesses in the acquisition, management and recovery process can ensure greater transparency and accountability as well as improvements in future bank restructuring workouts. Despite significant flaws in Malaysia's government-led bank restructuring, the process is still generally judged to have had a generally favourable net outcome.

CDRC: Corporate Debt Restructuring Committee

The government also addressed the problems of the corporate sector (i.e. to restructure corporate debt over RM50 million) through the formation in October 1998 of a Corporate Debt Restructuring Committee (CDRC), a non-statutory body under Bank Negara Malaysia (BNM). The CDRC was formed to provide a platform for both borrowers and creditors to work out feasible corporate debt restructuring schemes without having to resort to legal proceedings, especially for large debtors. In other words, the objective of the committee, like its counterparts in Indonesia, South Korea, and Thailand, was to minimise losses to creditors, shareholders and other stakeholders through coordinated voluntary workouts while bypassing the formal bankruptcy procedure.

Existing insolvency legislation in Malaysia was clearly more institutionalised than in either Indonesia or Thailand. Nonetheless, it was unpopular with creditors and did not provide the range of solutions to preserve value for other stakeholders in complex corporate groups with multiple creditors. In effect, the principal purpose of the committee was thus to persuade financial institutions not to precipitate insolvency.

In August 2001, the CDRC — under new leadership — announced three new measures to spur corporate restructuring, which included: (1) a revamp of CDRC membership to include representatives from Pengurusan Danaharta Nasional Bhd and the Federation of Public Listed Companies; (2) changes to the framework and approach of the CDRC to accelerate restructuring efforts; and (3) an increase in the frequency of financial disclosure, i.e. regular disclosure and quarterly reporting to keep the market abreast of restructuring progress (*The Star*, 10 August 2001).

The CDRC now has the authority to implement management changes. Furthermore, the agency can now appoint liquidators to settle non-performing loans (NPLs). Previously, the CDRC had merely acted as a mediator, with limited authority, between creditors and borrowers (*The Star*, 13 August 2001). [For a detailed look at the principles of the CDRC framework, its objectives, terms of reference, key principles governing the corporate workout process, processes and guidelines, revised debt restructuring guidelines, and revised framework, refer to the CDRC website, <http://www.bnm.gov.my/CDRC/>.]

The CDRC has played a proactive role in the resolution of the bad debt problem.[25] The progress in corporate restructuring — among other factors, such as the country's strong balance of payments and external liquidity positions, due to its modest external debt burden — probably helped improve Malaysia's currency rating, with international rating agency Fitch Ratings' positive outlook on Malaysia's long-term foreign and local currency ratings of *BBB* and *A* respectively (*The Star*, 19 April 2002). The "quicker pace of corporate restructuring has received positive remarks from investment analysts,

Table 6.4   Malaysia: Major Corporate Restructuring Exercises in 2001

Company	Debt (RM bn)
Malaysian Airline System Bhd (MAS)	7.80
Technology Resources Industries Bhd (TRI)	3.80
Malaysian Resources Corp Bhd (MRCB)	1.28
United Engineers (M) Bhd (UEM)	30.30

Source: *The Star*, 20 December 2001a.

particularly foreign-based financial groups such as JP Morgan, Credit Suisse First Boston and Hongkong and Shanghai Banking Corporation (HSBC)" (*The Star*, 4 February 2002: 3). HSBC Fixed Income Research Head, John Woods, commended the progress in corporate restructuring: "We like what we see in Malaysia in terms of corporate restructuring compared with South Korea. We are impressed with the pace. The government makes a positive effort to ensure that corporate governance and transparency are demonstrated in corporate restructuring. It is different now compared with previously" (*The Star*, 4 February 2002: 3).

Table 6.4 shows the four major corporate debt restructuring exercises (with some still yet to be resolved) in 2001, which accounted for a sizeable share of the bad debts in the system. From its inception in 1998 until 31 December 2001, the CDRC resolved 37 cases with debts amounting to RM34.5 billion.[26] (See Table 6.5 for a summary of debt restructuring from 1998 to 2002.[27]) Of the 37 cases, eight — with debts totalling RM8.845 billion — were successfully resolved, with an impressive average recovery rate of 95 per cent between 1 August 1998 and 31 December 2001 (*The Star*, 31 January 2002).[28]

With its renewed commitment to accelerate the pace of progress and to close down operations as soon as possible, the committee made several changes — including setting specific timelines or schedules to complete restructuring,[29] besides enhancing disclosure and reporting requirements for debt restructuring (*The Star*, 21 March 2002) — and has been given the authority to implement management changes for effective operational restructuring to ensure the viability of the corporation over the long term and to appoint liquidators to resolve NPLs (*The Star*, 13 August 2001; *The Star*, 21 March 2002).

Table 6.5 Cumulative Progress Summary of the Various Stages of Corporate Restructuring by the CDRC, 1998 to 2002

Quarter	Application Received (cumulative)	Total Debts (RM m) (cumulative)	Withdrawn/ Rejected Cases (cumulative)		Transferred to Danaharta (cumulative)		Completed		Resolved with Assistance of Danaharta (cumulative)		Cases Outstanding (cumulative)	
			No	Amount (RM m)	No	Amount (RM m)	No	Amount (RM m)	No	Amount (RM m)	No	Amount (RM m)
3Q/1998	20	5,350.20									20	5,350.20
4Q/1998	36	11,028.15					2	344.50			34	10,683.65
1Q/1999	52	26,018.52	4	849.85			4	1,153.30			44	24,015.37
2Q/1999	62	33,039.64	8	2,053.05			10	10,249.40	2	954.30	42	19,782.37
3Q/1999	63	35,024.65	14	3,259.35			11	11,234.89	2	954.30	36	19,576.11
4Q/1999	66	35,652.77	15	3,504.35	8	2,764.70	13	11,778.29	2	954.30	28	16,651.13
1Q/2000	68	36,519.20	13	2,760.45	10	3,298.44	17	13,106.84	2	954.30	26	16,399.17
2Q/2000	71	39,643.01	16	3,822.63	9	1,813.54	23	17,392.49	2	954.30	21	15,660.05
3Q/2000	75	45,938.82	18	4,072.57	9	1,813.54	28	23,085.17	2	954.30	18	16,013.24
4Q/2000	75	47,209.75	21	7,825.89	9	1,813.54	31	25,476.92	2	954.30	12	11,139.10
1Q/2001	75	47,209.75	21	7,825.89	9	1,813.54	33	25,816.82	2	954.30	10	10,799.20
2Q/2001	75	47,378.75	21	7,825.89	9	1,813.54	33	27,576.92	2	954.30	8	9,208.10
3Q/2001	84	65,899.00	22	9,516.00	11	2,470.00	29*	26,310.00	2	954.30	20	26,649.00
4Q/2001	86	66,813.00	23	10,069.00	11	2,470.00	35	33,535.00	2	954.30	15	19,785.00
1Q/2002	87	67,644.00	25	10,606.00	11	2,470.00	42	37,398.00	2	954.30	9	17,170.00
15 Aug 2002	87	59,060.00	28	12,620.00	11	2,470.00	47	43,971.00	2	954.30	1	8,600.00

Note: * Decrease principally due to some schemes requiring renegotiation needing lenders' approval.
Sources: CDRC 2002a, CDRC 2002b.

Datuk Azman Yahya announced three new measures to spur corporate restructuring as of 1 August 2001. First, a revamp of the CDRC membership to include representatives from Pengurusan Danaharta Nasional Bhd and the Federation of Public Listed Companies; second, changes in the CDRC framework and approach and third, increased frequency of information disclosure with regular disclosure and quarterly reporting to keep the market abreast of the restructuring progress. Under the revised restructuring guidelines, a borrower had to have a minimum aggregate debt of RM100 million (compared with RM50 million previously) to be eligible for CDRC assistance and had to have exposure to at least five creditor banks.

The business must also be a viable on-going concern, and the borrower must have sufficient cash generation to cover operating expenditure. Furthermore, corporations could be referred to the CDRC by corporate borrowers or bank creditors accounting for at least 25 per cent of total indebtedness. From then, deadlines were set for each debt restructuring process, with each case to be completed within six to nine months, with debt reorganising agreements to be signed within the first three months (*The Star*, 10 August 2001). This should bode well for the corporate and banking sector, and for shareholders in the long run.

The CDRC has estimated that banks only took an average two per cent discount (*The Star*, 13 August 2001) prior to the new guidelines, leading to concerns — as with Danaharta — as to whether shareholders and creditors were being "sufficiently" punished for bad lending decisions and management. The impression that the CDRC had been too lenient has since been offset by the second CDRC chairman, Datuk Azman Yahya, who indicated that the CDRC would force corporations to dispose of non-core assets, and that funds thus realised would not be used to make new purchases that would not augment the value of the corporation. For instance, MAS and UEM made efforts to divest non-core businesses. On the creditors' side, Azman stressed that non-compliant (with respect to unapproved delays in producing a restructuring plan and making other necessary agreements) banks would be reported to the central bank (*Asiaweek*, 7 September 2001).

Nonetheless, one must distinguish between the positive impact of corporate restructuring proposals and their implementation on the firm itself, and their effects on the economy, the public (e.g. taxpayers) and the government. For instance, even though the UEM/Renong restructuring proposals have been beneficial for the conglomerate itself (improving balance sheets, reducing debt and focusing on core businesses)[30] and have been well received by most analysts, the generous restructuring terms and conditions for the conglomerate adversely affect the government and the public who will bear their costs.

To fulfil its declared commitment to dissolve the agency within an appropriate and acceptable timeframe, the CDRC indicated that it would stop accepting new cases at the end of March 2002 and would close its (four-year) operations by 31 July 2002, after resolving the remaining cases (*The Star*, 5 February 2002). As shown in Table 6.5, between its inception in July 1998 and 31 March 2002, the CDRC had resolved 42 cases, with debts totalling RM37.398 billion, and intended to resolve the remaining nine cases, with total corporate debt of RM17.170 billion, by 31 July 2002. By 15 August 2002, the CDRC managed to resolve all cases (with total debt of RM43.971 billion) except the debt restructuring of the Lion Group amounting to RM8.6 billion.

The CDRC's reputation for speed in handling corporate debt cases is evident in its official closure on 20 August 2002 with a press conference chaired by Tan Sri Dato' Dr Zeti Akhtar Aziz, Governor of Bank Negara Malaysia, and attended by Dato' Azman Yahya, the Chairman of the CDRC, members of the CDRC Steering Committee and officials of Bank Negara Malaysia (CDRC 2002b). Even though the closure was slightly later than the expected date of 31 July 2002, the delay of only half a month is highly commendable especially when compared to the Italian case (see Wijnbergen 1996). As at 15 August 2002, CDRC had resolved 47 of 48 cases, with debts totalling RM43.971 billion, the exception being the Lion Group with debt amounting to RM8.6 billion (see Table 6.5 and CDRC 2002b).

The Instituto per la Riconstruzione Industriale (IRI), or Institute for Industrial Reconstruction, was originally created by the Italian government to manage the large portfolio of companies controlled by the Banca Commerciale, Credito Italiono and Banco di Roma (Aganin and Volpin 2003). However, IRI's "temporary" function of bailing out troubled corporations (and later re-privatising the companies) was eventually expanded to acquiring sound companies and making direct investments in all industrial sectors, thus becoming a state holding company. However, during the 1990s, IRI faced huge losses and debt. IRI's losses amounted to US$540 million in 1991. By 1992, IRI's losses reached a staggering US$3.4 billion with consolidated debt of US$58.3 billion. From 1992–93, IRI focused on debt repayment by asset sale to reduce its debt-to-equity to 0.9:1 in 1999. In 2000, IRI was liquidated with its remaining shares transferred to the Treasury (Mako and Zhang 2002).

Table 6.6   Malaysia: Recent Policy Reversals Involving Privatisation

1970–85 Public Sector Expansion	*1985–96 Privatisation*	*1997/98 Economic Crisis*	*2000/1 Nationalisation*
Massive expansion of public sector to achieve NEP inter-ethic redistribution and rural poverty reduction (equated with development) objectives.	Both privatised projects and privatisations. The most common of the former were toll road projects and independent power producers (IPPs), while the latter involved companies like Proton, MAS and Hicom to private interests sold at massive discounts.	Rising interest rates and a depreciated ringgit raised debt levels. NPLs in the banking system rose to 16%.	Government (including Petronas) bought back previously privatised assets. In 2000–1, 6 major acquisitions — MAS, UEM, STAR, PUTRA, PROTON and IWK — were completed.
Encouraged by increased oil export revenues from mid-1970s.		Outstanding cases remain with the CDRC and Danaharta.	
Further state owned enterprise (SOE) investments for heavy industrialisation in early and mid-1980s.		Some 80–90 publicly listed companies faced de-listing due to reduced shareholder funds below KLSE Practice Note 4 (PN4) requirements.	The restructuring of other companies/debt has generally been slow.
	Among the names that emerged were Halim Saad, Tajudin Ramli, Francis Yeoh, the late Yahya Ahmad and Vincent Tan.		

Sources: CIMB Securities, as reported by *The Star*, 1 Oct. 2001a; Jomo and Tan (1999).

MoF Inc: Ministry of Finance Incorporated

Ministry of Finance Incorporated or MoF Inc. — through Syarikat Prasarana Negara Bhd (SPNB), Khazanah Nasional Bhd (Khazanah) and now Permodalan Nasional Bhd (PNB) as well as Syarikat Danasaham Nasional Bhd (Danasaham) — has taken over (i.e. "nationalised") financially ailing corporations to "turn them around" for later return to the market and to private hands. Table 6.6 provides a summary of various related developments in Malaysia over the past three decades. According to CIMB Securities, re-nationalisation is only for assets of national "strategic importance" (*The Star*, 1 October 2001a), though such claims are often vague and, arguably, quite subjective and even inconsistent. Table 6.7 presents a list of corporations that have been

Table 6.7   Malaysia: Some Recently Completed Nationalisation Exercises

Date	Private co.	Vendor	Acquirer	Valuation	Consideration
Completed in July 2000	Indah Water	Prime Utilities	Ministry of Finance	RM193m	Cash
Ongoing General Offer closing 14 Sep. 2001	UEM	All shareholders	Khazanah/ Danasaham	RM3.7bn	Cash
Completed in Dec. 2000	Proton	DRB-Hicom	Petronas	RM981m	Cash
Completed in February 2001	MAS	Naluri	Ministry of Finance	RM1.8bn	Cash
1 Sep. 2002	PUTRA LRT	Renong	Government	RM5bn (estimate)	Bond issue
1 Sep. 2002	STAR LRT	EPF, Taylor Woodrow plc & other state-run funds	Government	RM5bn (estimate)	Bond issue

Note: Prasarana took over the assets and operations of the Light Rail Transit (LRT) systems from STAR and PUTRA on 1 Sep. 2002. The RM1.0 billion in redeemable guaranteed Coupon-Bearing Bonds (CBBs) was issued on 6 Sep. 2002 to partially finance the acquisition costs of the STAR and PUTRA LRT systems, for general working capital purposes and/or future capital expenditure of the STAR and PUTRA LRT systems (RAM 2003).

Source: CIMB Securities, as reported by the *The Star*, 1 October 2001a.

recently nationalised.[31] The following analysis will centre on whether such takeovers (which invariably constitute bail outs) of MAS, PUTRA, STAR and UEM/Renong were appropriate, justifiable and above board, and whether the public (taxpayers) are bearing more costs than necessary to simply save or bail out these corporations and their owners (i.e. whether the "bail outs" were conducted in a "fair" and "reasonable" manner).

On 14 May 2004, Prime Minister Abdullah Badawi announced that the government intends Khazanah to become the biggest and most dynamic investment house in the region, and that would entail remaking "Malaysia Incorporated". This would involve shifting the public sector reform strategy away from the earlier emphasis on government-linked company (GLC) privatisation to improving GLC performance (*The Star*, 15 May 2004a, and *The Edge Daily*, 14 May 2004, available from <http://www.theedgedaily.com/>). Part of the rationalisation strategy involves transferring shares currently held by MoF Inc. — worth billions of ringgit in more than 30 publicly-listed companies including substantial stakes in key blue-chip companies such as Tenaga Nasional Bhd (TNB), Telekom Malaysia Bhd (Telekom), and majority stakes (over 50 per cent) in companies such as Malaysia Airports Holdings Bhd (MAHB) and MAS — to Khazanah. See Figure 6.1 for group of companies in which Khazanah has a stake. As of May 2004, the combined market value of 40 GLCs — approximately RM232 billion — accounted for 34 per cent of the total market capitalisation of Bursa Malaysia Bhd, i.e. more than half of Malaysia's gross domestic product (*The Star*, 15 May 2004b; *The New Straits Times*, 15 May 2004a).

To facilitate better management and monitoring of the various GLCs, Khazanah itself has been making changes to its top management and board of directors,[32] beginning with the appointment of Azman Mokhtar[33] as chief executive officer (CEO) of Khazanah Nasional from 1 June 2004 (*The Star*, 15 May 2004b; *The Star*, 18 May 2004a). In September 2004, Khazanah appointed Ganen Sarvananthan as director of investments while Shahnaz Al-Sadat was appointed as director and chief financial officer (*The Star*, 25 September 2004). Another reform slated to take effect by 1 January 2005 is full implementation of Key Performance Indices (KPIs) and performance-linked compensation (*The New Straits Times*, 15 May 2004a) to try to encourage the GLCs to be more performance- and profit-oriented; it

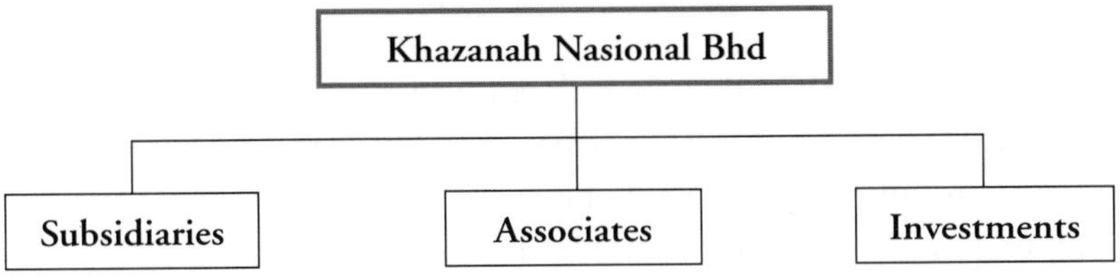

Khazanah Nasional Bhd		
Subsidiaries	**Associates**	**Investments**
• BBMB Securities Sdn Bhd	• Tenaga Nasional Bhd	• Putrajaya Holdings Sdn Bhd
• STLR Sdn Bhd	• BI Waden Venture Ketiga Sdn Bhd	• MSC Venture One Sdn Bhd
• Syarikat Danasaham Sdn Bhd	• Telekom Malaysia Bhd	• Motosikal dan Enjin Nasional Sdn Bhd
• Silterra Malaysia Sdn Bhd	• Valuecap Sdn Bhd	• Commerce Asset-Holding Bhd
• Crystal Clear Technology Sdn Bhd	• Spring Hill Bioventures Sdn Bhd	• Megasteel Sdn Bhd
• Malaysia Technology Development Corporation Sdn Bhd	• Perusahaan Otomobil Nasional Bhd	• The Royal Mint Exchange Sdn Bhd
	• RHB Bank Bhd	• Westport Holdings Sdn Bhd
	• TIME dotCom Bhd	• Edaran Otomobil Nasional Bhd
	• Bank Muamalat Sdn Bhd	• DRB-HICOM Bhd
	• Arena Target Sdn Bhd	• Malayan Banking Bhd
	• AIC Technology Sdn Bhd	• YTL Power International Bhd
	• AIC Microelectronics Sdn Bhd	• Maxis Communications Bhd
	• Malaysia Airports Holdings Bhd	• Malaysia International Shipping
	• D'nonce Technology Bhd	
	• ASTRO All Asia Networks plc	
	• PLUS Expressways Bhd	
	• Northern Utility Resources Sdn Bhd	

Source: "Group of Companies". Available from <http://www.khazanah.com.my/>.

Fig. 6.1 Khazanah Nasional Bhd's Group of Companies

is often noted that the GLCs have been under-performing the stock market by 21 per cent in the last five years (*The Star*, 18 May 2004b).

Apparently, some analysts believe that the tide is turning in favour of key GLCs, most notably Telekom. According to CIMB Securities, efforts by Telekom's top management to come up with a better-conceived business plan that articulates clearly the strategies and general direction of its restructuring plan have been rewarded by the market; with its share price having risen 30 per cent year-to-date. Also, greater foreign shareholding of 19 per cent in the company as at July 2004, from a mere 3.2 per cent a year ago appears to signal greater foreign investors confidence. (*The Star*, 25 September 2004) On a broader front, GLC heavyweights such as Telekom, TNB, Maybank Bhd and Sime Darby Bhd have been trading at their 52-week highs (*The Star*, 25 September 2004).

Table 6.8   Reform of GLC Boards

Board composition	• Small effective board, around six to ten directors; • Balance between executive and non-executive directors; • Independent non-executive directors constitute majority; • Board members have no conflicts of interest, e.g. no regulators; • Board members should be persons of high calibre, credibility, and experience; and • Chairman and CEO roles are separated and clearly defined.
Board role	• Challenging and guiding top management in corporate strategy; • Defending shareholder value; • Selecting, developing and compensating senior management; and • Overseeing board governance issues.
Board interaction	• Regular interactions with management on business performance, talent management and governance issues; • Annual review of corporate strategy as well as corporate and management performance appraisal; and • Dedicated board committee to engage with regulators and policy markers to clarify and quantify costs to national development agenda on period basis.

Source: Booz Allen Hamilton, as reported in *The Star*, 15 May 2004c: 3.

Changes to GLC board structures and managements as well as greater emphasis on suitable candidates to hold key strategic positions in GLCs should bode well in the long run, especially with improved decision making processes, greater emphasis on fiduciary responsibilities/duties in checking mismanagement or poor management as well as conflicts of interest, and greater transparency as well as accountability (see Table 6.8). On 19 May 2004, the government announced the appointments of Datuk Abdul Wahid Omar and Che Khalib Mohamad Nor as the CEOs of Telekom and TNB respectively, effective 1 July (*The Star*, 20 May 2004). The appointment of these ostensible technocrats to hold key management posts in Khazanah, Tenaga and Telekom[34] has apparently been well received by the market.[35] However, it remains to be seen whether these corporate figures can improve the financial health and earnings of the GLCs they take over. For instance, it will not be easy to turn things around in many GLCs such as TNB — with around RM30 billion in debt

Table 6.9 Reform of Government-linked Companies: Objectives and Strategies

---

Objectives:
- To ensure that GLCs, especially "natural monopolies", provide better services to customers, i.e. the public; and
- To ensure that GLCs act as catalysts for economic growth.

Strategies:
- Introduction of KPIs, which will be monitored monthly by a steering committee headed by Second Finance Minister Nor Mohamed Yakcop;
- Senior management of GLCs will be rewarded with bonuses and stock options depending on results;
- Fixed term contracts for senior management, renewable with achievement of targets;
- Smaller boards of between 6 to 10 members to enhance focus and effectiveness;
- Government representatives involved in regulation can no longer serve as directors of companies they regulate;
- GLCs encouraged to go global and to forge links with global players; and
- Khazanah Nasional to become the biggest and most dynamic investment house in the region. Its board will be restructured and streamlined. Azman Mokhtar appointed new CEO of Khazanah. Transfer of GLC shares belonging to MoF Inc. to Khazanah.

Source: *The Star*, 15 May 2004a: 1; *The New Straits Times*, 15 May 2004a: 1.

(49 per cent ringgit-denominated, 34 per cent US dollar-denominated, and 20 per cent yen-denominated) (*The Star*, 26 May 2004).

The above reforms among others outlined in Table 6.9 may be timely in view of improved macroeconomic stability and general financial sector improvements. Moreover, the Prime Minister's intention to reduce support for "infant industries" has strengthened the new government's image and inspired the confidence of local and international investors. The appeal of such market-friendly reforms is contingent on the reforms being "deep" and permanent, not merely cosmetic and/or temporary. These changes are considered imperative as many GLCs hold key strategic assets in core areas such as transportation, energy, telecommunications, and financial services (*The Star*, 15 May 2004b).

These reforms are intended to signal to both domestic and international market participants the serious intentions of the government to improve efficiency, corporate governance and confidence in government-linked companies (GLCs). By monitoring Key Performance Indices (KPIs), the government hopes to rationalise the entire structure of performance and standards reporting of GLCs, which have been largely protected from market forces by minimal transparency, implicit or explicit government guarantees, subsidies, soft loans and guaranteed lifelong employment.

However, as suggested by *CLSA Asia Pacific Markets*, the benefits of these strategic plans are not immediate, with much room still left for improvement. CLSA has pointed out that KPIs had still not been introduced by the 19 major GLCs it monitors. Similarly, performance-linked remuneration has yet to be implemented. Commerce Asset came out tops in the CLSA survey, having introduced or implemented nine of the 18 key points viewed by the government as necessary changes to their boards and managements for becoming performance-linked corporations. Interestingly, Khazanah itself scored particularly poorly on transparency as it provides almost no information on its board and audit committee, as most public companies are required to. Like PLUS and Time dotCom Bhd, it had only implemented 5 of the 18 points (*The Star*, 25 May 2004) (see Table 6.10).

Perhaps most importantly, the proposed reforms do not seem to have fully taken into account critical commentary on recent trends in corporate governance discussed earlier, which have gained added significance after the Enron and other corporate scandals in the West.

Table 6.10   CLSA Scorecard on How Some GLCs Fared

	Khazanah	Telekom	TNB	Proton	MAS	MAHB	Bintulu Port	Commerce Asset	PLUS	Time dotCom
Appointed new CEO	✓	✓	✓		✓	✓				
Introduced key performance indicators (KPIs)										
Introduced performance linked remunerations										
Employee Share Option Scheme in place		✓	✓	✓				✓		
CEO on fixed term contracts, renewable on target achievement	✓	✓								
Forged strategic links to global players										
Formal dividend policy		✓								
Separation of roles and duties of CEO and chairman	✓	✓	✓	✓	✓	✓	✓	✓	✓	✓
Succession policy in place										
Board of directors: 6 to 10 members	✓	✓		✓		✓	✓	✓	✓	✓
Removal of industry regulators as directors		✓								
Balance between executive and non-executive director	✓	✓	✓	✓	✓	✓	✓	✓	✓	✓
Independent directors constitute majority			✓		✓					
Chairman is an independent non-executive director							✓	✓		
Audit committee — chaired by independent director		✓	✓	✓	✓	✓	✓	✓	✓	✓
Audit committee — majority members are independent			✓	✓	✓	✓	✓	✓	✓	✓
Remuneration committee — chaired by independent director					✓	✓	✓	✓		
Nominating committee — chaired by independent director						✓	✓	✓		
Total score	**5**	**8**	**7**	**6**	**7**	**8**	**8**	**9**	**5**	**5**

Source: CLSA, as reported in *The Star*, 25 May 2004.

Despite reservations and uncertainties over the direction and likelihood of success of the reform measures, these new developments are especially interesting as the rationalisation programme and strategic measures are pre-emptive in nature and differ from the corporate restructuring bail out programmes initiated in 1998 following the 1997–98 Asian financial crisis.

Concluding Remarks

In the absence of attractive and proven effective market mechanisms and solutions to address Malaysia's corporate sector crisis, government intervention was deemed necessary to control economic contraction and expedite economic recovery and growth. As such, the decision by the Malaysian government to act proactively — by providing a working framework to facilitate the proper and effective functioning of market options as well as for "re-nationalisation" — may have been commendable in so far as they served to "correct" market failure given the lack of capital markets, overly depressed asset prices, and so forth. However, the terms of restructuring, re-nationalisation and other related programmes have been fraught with abuses and weaknesses, suggesting government failure.

Furthermore, financial difficulties, exacerbated by the 1997–98 regional crisis that led to state bail outs and re-nationalisations, highlight the problems of political patronage closely associated with its privatisation programme. Poor privatisation design, selection and regulation led to inappropriate candidates for privatisation as well as awardees, and weakened incentives to increase efficiency and investment, increasing the vulnerability of poorly privatised entities to external shocks. The poor privatisation of relatively gargantuan corporations — in terms of capitalisation and corporate structure — have likely exacerbated the overall magnitude of Malaysian banking and corporate distress, which required direct and indirect government (financial) assistance and offset any possible benefits of privatisation. This painful experience underscores the abuse of Malaysia's privatisation programmes, and its adverse consequences for the overall health of the Malaysian corporate and banking sector. Careful analysis suggests that such failures could easily have been avoided if policy making had not been compromised from the outset. Social resources were thus not efficiently utilised to generate a *socially* optimal and desirable outcome.

Hence, it was right for the Malaysian government to step in to ameliorate the consequences of the crisis for the real economy, including the financial distress adversely affecting Malaysian corporations. This is especially relevant given the intricate links between the Malaysian financial system and corporate sector. In so far as the financial, operational and management problems of the corporations were not well addressed, the potential benefits of bank and corporate restructuring cannot be fully realised. Prompt action and effective institutions helped banks resolve their NPL problems and improve liquidity.

Financially distressed corporations — due to negative external shocks and/or internal factors — cannot borrow in order to continue otherwise viable operations, given their already high debt burdens and financial distress. Moreover, heavily indebted or leveraged corporations understandably tend to focus on improving their financial situation, rather than on achieving efficiency or productivity gains, in the near term. As such, these firms are unlikely to take on additional debt even if these are considered necessary and desirable to enhance long-term competitiveness. Even if corporations want to borrow, banks — including those flush with liquidity — will be reluctant to lend to financially distressed corporations, however economically viable, thus further exacerbating the situation during a crisis. Given this scenario, the loss in current and potential output may well outweigh the costs of "speedier" government-led or government-mediated corporate restructuring programmes, even if properly conducted.

Notes

1. The definition of "privatisation" in Malaysia is so broad that it includes cases where private enterprises are awarded licenses to participate in activities previously the exclusive preserve of the public sector, as in the case of television broadcasting from 1984. Contracting out of services, especially by municipal authorities (e.g. involving garbage disposal and parking), and private ownership or even contracted leasing of public properties — e.g. enabling the imposition of tolls on roads previously built by the Public Works Ministry or the Malaysian Highway Authority (Lembaga Lebuhraya Malaysia, or LLM) — are

also frequently considered to be cases of privatisation. In Malaysia, when a state-owned enterprise (SOE), legally formed as a government department or statutory authority, is privatised, it necessarily entails corporatization, or the formation of a limited company incorporated under the Companies Act, 1965. On the other hand, the privatisation of an SOE that has been constituted as a limited company would merely entail a transfer of share ownership from the public to the private sector without any change in the legal form of the enterprise.

2.   PUTRA and KL Monorail (formerly Rapid People Mover).

3.   See interview with Chellappah Rajandram, the former head of the CDRC (FinanceAsia.com, 26 July 2000).

4.   Even if a policy is perfect at the conception stage, it may run into problems during implementation. It is therefore imperative that proper assessments be made so that appropriate policies can be designed to address the "actual underlying" or root causes of the problems, and not the symptoms. Without this, effective and efficient execution and implementation of a policy would still be insufficient to yield "optimum" results.

5.   Klingebiel (2000: 10) notes that "Since the level of non-performing loans is a reflection of the performance of the real sector this number can also be used as a rough proxy for the extent of corporate distress." Mako (2001b) views non-performing loans as a good indicator of financial sector distress, but an imperfect proxy for corporate distress.

6.   The ratio of a company's debt to its equity, more commonly referred to as leverage in the US.

7.   A definition of an asset management company as provided by Danaharta can be obtained from its website: <http://www.danaharta. com.my/default.html>. "Assets" here refer to both loans and tangible assets, with the preferred source of repayment being realisation of gain through reconstruction and rehabilitation of the asset while other forms of repayment include identified cash flows from acquired assets, existing business operations and disposal of collateral.

8.   Action taken by banks against corporate loan defaulters (or, more specifically, borrowers who fail to pay interest on loans after several months, which results in bank action).

9.   This includes those without good profitability prospects or with poor past financial and performance records.

10. This applies more to private banks. The government will find it relatively easier to channel funds to various parties and activities if the banks are public or government-owned.

11. The NEP objectives are to reduce poverty and inter-ethnic economic disparities. However, policy abuse and waste have contributed significantly to the severity of the NPL problems faced by the financial sector today. Privatisation (which merely represents a change in

ownership from public to "private") does not automatically guarantee efficiency.

12. The problem faced by Hottick Investment was aggravated due to poor management as a result of incapable and inexperienced management, further exacerbated by the 1997–98 Asian financial crisis.

13. This query arises because of doubts as to whether Danaharta was given sufficient autonomy and independence to conduct its operations as fairly and expeditiously as possible, free from political pressure.

14. As highlighted by *freeMalaysia*, "Bank Bailouts? More Like Buddy Bailouts". Is the underlying collateral collectible? Are the loans worth what the government paid for them?

15. According to Wain (1999), "to make Bank Bumi attractive to the listed Commerce Asset, the government said it would take over all the nonperforming loans currently in the bank's books at face value".

16. The Kuala Lumpur Composite Index (KLCI) fell in 1998 to a low of 262.70 points on 1 September 1998. In 1999, the KLCI fell to a low of 494.45 on 24 March, but managed to regain ground to 829.72 on 29 June and ending the year at 812.33, still below the pre-crisis level, which was well above 1,000 (Bank Negara, *Stock Market Indices Daily Updates*).

17. As at 30 June 1999, Danaharta managed RM 21.541 billion of NPLs on behalf of the government (Danaharta 1999b).

18. If Danaharta defaults in repaying its bond obligations five to ten years later, e.g. if they cannot raise sufficient funds from selling collateral or by successfully restructuring NPLs.

19. Plain loan restructuring refers to restructuring which may include rescheduling loans, partial cash settlements or asset disposal (Danaharta website: <www.danaharta.com.my>).

20. Settlement refers to cases where loans have been disposed outright, or settlement has been agreed upon and payment has been received or is pending (Danaharta website: <www.danaharta.com.my>).

21. As mentioned earlier, Mako (2001b) is sceptical of the suitability and effectiveness of public or centralised AMCs in operational restructuring.

22. For a more in-depth look at updated key portfolio statistics covering loan management activities — including recovery rates, assets accumulated, asset movements and payments to financial institutions for surplus recovery — refer to the Danaharta website: <http://www.danaharta.com.my/>. Refer also to *The Star*, 5 September 2001, for a summary of recovery rates, methods of recovery and how proceeds were utilised and distributed as of 30 June 2001. See *The Star*, 10 November 2001, and *The Sun*, 10 November 2001, for summary updates as of 30 September 2001; see *The Star*, 13 March 2002, and 21 March 2002 for summary updates as of 31 December 2001; see Danaharta 2003b for updates as of 31 December 2002; and Danaharta 2003e for updates as of 30 June 2003.

23. The speed of asset disposal and the maximisation of the recovery value and the recovery rate are very much dependent on the country's economic recovery (dependent, to an extent, on the speed of resolution of the NPL problem), liquidity in capital markets, the state of the capital market, the availability of "market" and "non-market" participants, and others. Real estate agents can help accelerate the sale of property (*The Star*, 10 April 2002).

24. The default rates assigned as of 31 December 2003 and 31 March 2004 were 3.2 per cent and 2.6 per cent respectively.

25. According to Liau Y-Sing, "Debt accumulation began during the heady days of the early 1990s when there was a surge in credit expansion and many companies embarked on aggressive plans to widen their reach. The crunch came with the 1997 Asian financial crisis and many players found the carpet pulled from under their feet. When payback time came, many companies were found wanting" (*The Star* [Business], 20 December 2001a: 1).

26. The CDRC noted that the improvement in business sentiment and overall performance of the stock market augured well for debt restructuring.

27. For an update on the quarterly progress of CDRC cases up till the fourth quarter of 2001, refer to Appendix III of the CDRC Status Report as of 31 December 2001. According to RHB Research Institute (RHBRI), the CDRC had successfully completed the restructuring of 41 cases, involving RM35.2 billion, which represented 61.7 per cent of the total debt it had accepted for restructuring by the end of January 2002. See Table 9 (page 16) of RHBRI's Economic Outlook report for Malaysia dated 22 March 2002 for the statistics.

28. The eight companies were Gadek (M) Bhd, Hai Ming Holdings Bhd, Tanco Holdings Bhd, Idris Hydraulic Bhd, Sistem Transit Aliran Ringan Sdn Bhd (STAR), Projek Usahasama Transit Ringan Automatik Sdn Bhd (PUTRA), Cygal Bhd and Nam Fatt Corp Bhd (*The Star*, 31 January 2002).

29. In August 2001, the CDRC set a one-year deadline to clear the backlog of corporate debt totalling RM29 billion (*The Star*, 20 December 2001a). While commending the speed and confidence shown by the CDRC to restructure the corporate debts to the banking system, some analysts felt the timeframe of a year to complete the corporate restructuring ambitious, as some cases were complicated (*The Star*, 10 August 2001).

      In addition, incentives — in the form of an extension of the stamp exemption and a tax deduction for corporate debt restructuring expenses — would help motivate faster restructuring. Stamp duty exemption for all instruments involved in corporate debt restructuring schemes (an extension on the 31 December 2000 deadline) could be approved by the CDRC or Danaharta up to 31 December 2001. Furthermore, professional fees for expenses incurred in corporate debt restructuring certified by the CDRC or Danaharta between 30 October 1999 and 31 December 2000 were also tax deductible. *The Star* (19 October 2001) also considers incentives analysts were hoping to hasten restructuring.

30.   For an evaluation of the progress of UEM/Renong's corporate restructuring, see the subsection on "Evaluation of Corporate Restructuring".

31.   CIMB Securities explained that "excluding the Petronas related deals, the government has paid/will be paying out nearly RM12 billion. This would represent approximately 14 per cent of the federal government's total expenditure — not such an alarming number. Even if the government were to spend another RM2 billion on other acquisitions, the percentages will not rise significantly, circa 16 per cent of total expenditure. One would, of course, have to weigh this slight negative against the positive implications on the banking sector. On a broad assumption that the entire amount paid by the government (including the Petronas acquisitions) are repaid to banks and that the loans are all classified as NPLs (non-performing loans), we estimate that the banking sector NPLs could drop to circa 11 per cent from 13.8 per cent gross (as at July 2001)" (*The Star*, 1 October 2001a).

      Even though this amount was not considered to be of great significance by CIMB Securities, nonetheless one should at least evaluate whether the 14 or 16 per cent of the budget utilised was getting a "reasonable" and "fair" "return", even if "government assistance" was not justified in the first place.

32.   As at 18 May 2004, Khazanah's board comprises nine representatives from the public and private sectors, with the Prime Minister as the chairman. The other eight directors of Khazanah are Second Finance Minister Tan Sri Nor Mohamed Yakcop; Finance Minister Secretary General Tan Sri Dr Samsudin Hitam; Bank Negara Malaysia Governor Tan Sri Dr Zeti Akhtar Aziz; Economic Planning Unit Director-General Raja Datuk Zaharaton Raja Zainal Abidin; Proton Holdings Bhd and United Engineers (Malaysia) Bhd (UEM) chairman Datuk Abu Hassan Kendut; KUB Malaysia Bhd chief executive Che Khalib Mohamad Noh; Negri Sembilan Menteri Besar Datuk Mohamad Hasan; and, Khazanah's outgoing managing director, Datuk Anwar Aji. Effective 1 June 2004, Anwar was replaced by Azman Mokhtar (*The New Straits Times*, 18 May 2004b).

33.   Azman Mokhtar was the founder and managing director of Binafikir Sdn Bhd, the lead consultant in the restructuring of MAS that applied the widespread asset unbundling (WAU) programme. Azman had years of experience as an investment analyst, as director and research head at Salomon Smith Barney in Malaysia, after a decade as an

accountant with Tenaga Nasional Berhad, which corporatised the National Electricity Board (*The Star*, 18 May 2004a; *The New Straits Times*, 15 May 2004c).

34.   Azman Mokhtar (Khazanah's chief executive officer) and Datuk Nur Jazlan Mohamad were appointed non-executive directors of Telekom Malaysia Bhd effective 1 June 2004, replacing Datuk Dr Munir Majid and Tan Poh Keat. Telekom's board size has been downsized to nine members comprising chairman Tan Sri Ir Mohd Radzi Mansor, Datuk Abdul Wahid Omar, Azman, Nur Jazlan, Datuk Dr Abdul Rahim Haji Daud, Datuk Abdul Majid Hussein, Datuk Lim Kheng Guan, Prabahar N.K. Singam and Rosli Man (*The Star*, 27 May 2004; *The New Straits Times*, 27 May 2004).

35.   Datuk Abdul Wahid Omar was managing director/CEO of United Engineers (M) Bhd (UEM), while Che Khalib Mohamad was managing director/CEO of KUB Malaysia Bhd (*The Star*, 20 May 2004).

CHAPTER 7

Corporate Restructuring: Case Studies

WONG SOOK CHING

F ollowing the 1997–98 Asian financial crisis, Malaysian corporations, particularly those politically well-connected, busily prepared and revised corporate restructuring plans to turn around their loss making corporations, reduce debt and other liabilities, and improve long-term prospects. A first step in evaluating the corporate restructuring plans of the corporations, conglomerates or groups under review, was to look at the proposed sequencing and actual implementation of the restructuring plans.

Then one should ascertain whether the underlying corporate weaknesses existed prior to the crisis. However, if corporate distress was precipitated by the currency and financial crisis, there is more basis for the claim that weak corporate performance was induced by the systemic crisis rather than microeconomic problems. By uncovering and identifying other problems and their contribution to corporate distress, one can better evaluate whether the corporate restructuring or "turnaround" plans (which should encompass both debt and operational reforms) will be able to turn the corporations around and ensure their long-term viability.

Malaysian Airline System Bhd (MAS)

Government Role in MAS Corporate (Debt) Restructuring

After buying over the 29.09 per cent stake in MAS from Naluri Bhd (controlled by Tan Sri Tajudin Ramli) in December 2000, MoF Inc. became the largest shareholder.[1] In December 2000, Naluri had indicated that it would sell its entire issued and paid-up share capital in MAS, comprising 224 million ordinary RM1 shares (*Daily Express,* 21 December 2000). The total proceeds to Naluri Bhd amounted to RM1.792 billion (*The Sun,* 15 February 2001). Apart from questioning whether the MAS "bail out"[2] was justifiable — which did not reprimand, but instead, benefited Tajudin Ramli who was largely responsible for the poor performance of a viable corporation — criticism of the government has focused on the payment of RM8.00 per share, i.e. more than double its market price then and more than quadruple the price of RM1.80 in November 2001.

The MAS bail out underscores the distinction between rescuing a major shareholder and rescuing a corporation. If MAS was considered potentially economically viable after proper corporate restructuring, then there would be a strong case to salvage it. The restructuring has changes in management, debt and operational restructuring through some form of consolidation with a strategic partner. Having done this, the corporation can improve business prospects, hopefully returning to profitability as soon as possible in better times. However, the cost to the government of the MAS bail out has been well beyond what would be considered necessary. To make matters worse, it was the party responsible for MAS's mismanagement and failure who was generously "rescued" without "reprimand".

The government argued that MAS was viable[3] and would recover its value once it was successfully restructured and tied-up with a "strategic partner", besides serving and furthering strategic national interests. The government claimed optimism about MAS's prospects and that after "spring-cleaning", MAS stock would sell for RM10.00 per share, i.e. at 25 per cent premium over its acquisition cost, in an attempt to justify it against the popular perception that the acquisition price was to bail out Tajudin and the interests he represented (Ho 2001). Then Finance Minister Daim Zainuddin also claimed that some international investment houses — such as UBS Warburg — had valued MAS at above RM8.00 per share.

Nonetheless, despite such claims, many doubt the government can recoup the RM8.00 per share that it paid. With a relatively buoyant stock market, which breached the 800-point index level on 22 April 2002, MAS's stock price rose from RM1.80 in November 2001 (*The Star,* 28 February 2002b) to close at RM4.16 on 26 April

2002 (*The Star*, 29 April 2002), i.e. still barely over half the purchase price. Most observers still believe the price was not justified. Ong (2001a) notes that the RM8.00 per share Tajudin obtained when the deal was signed and sealed on 20 December 2000 was more than twice the market price of RM3.6[4] and twice the value of the carrier's net tangible assets.[5] Moreover, starting from 1998, MAS had four consecutive years of losses, and accumulated debt of almost RM10 billion. Based on MAS's unaudited accounts for the year ending 31 March 2001, available on its website, many maintain that Tajudin did not deserve the handsome price since the previous MAS management headed by him was mainly to blame for its financial woes before 11 September 2001 or even the 1997–98 crisis, which undoubtedly made things worse for MAS. [For details, refer to the section on MAS's "Corporate Restructuring Plan".]

Abdul Rahman Othman (2001) argues that (then Finance Minister) Daim's claim that MAS's net tangible assets (NTA) per share were RM8.00 was grossly inaccurate, to say the least, when even MAS itself had declared its NTA per share at RM1.23! According to his calculations, MAS's NTA per share were only worth RM0.66 as it should exclude the deferred income of RM453 million appearing in the same balance sheet as "intangible" — its assets totalled RM11.44 billion, long-term borrowings came to RM8.61 billion, and deferred charges were RM1.87 billion. Rahman further argues that, "with NTA [per share] of RM1.23 and a loss after tax of RM852.7 million [for the same period], how much premium can you give? At premium 50 per cent of NTA per share is only worth RM1.84 (*sic*). Isn't a market price of RM3.60 sufficient premium for the share?" (also see *FAC News*, 28 March 2001). While Tajudin is believed to have "upgraded" the MAS fleet, he had sold off planes and other assets, acquired non-profitable assets and greatly increased MAS debt. Hence, while the government emphasised that it was paying the share price Tajudin had paid to acquire MAS, the premiums over the market price as well as NTA value were much higher, giving rise to great public outrage.

On a different note, Syed Husin Ali (2001) has argued, "The Government or Finance Ministry has always been ever so keen to bail out ailing cronies or crony companies. Why are they not equally concerned about the plight of much less fortunate sections of the population? For example, the oil palm smallholders are now facing difficulties because the price of their produce has plunged from over RM300 per tonne at the beginning of the economic downturn to merely RM80 per tonne now." Similarly, rubber tappers and other farmers were also suffering from low prices, reduced subsidies and other problems.

There continued to be discontent over the RM6.1 billion MAS restructuring proposal involving asset sales to enable the national carrier to retire some of its debt and to secure RM820 million of working capital to hasten recovery (*The Star*, 8 January 2002). [For more details, see Box 7.1.] Injecting cash into MAS by buying assets using SPVs has raised the question of why the government did not consider alternatives to paying RM1.8 billion, or RM8.00 per share to Tajudin Ramli for his 29.09 per cent stake in MAS. Lim (2002) has described the MAS bail out as probably the first "double government bail out" in the world of a troubled company as well as of its principal shareholder. Taxpayers are not only bearing the costs of bailing out MAS (which would be less unacceptable to the public), but also of personally bailing out Tajudin by paying well above its run-down NTA value or even the market price. The bail out has thus served to fuel suspicions that Tajudin was a proxy for other more powerful political interests. Even though Tajudin lost his executive position in MAS on 14 February 2001, he has never been reprimanded for mismanagement. More importantly, as mentioned above, he managed to gain substantially from the sale of MAS shares.

The government "rescue" of MAS was further extended on 28 January 2002, with the MAS board approving the reorganisation proposal[6] of taking MAS private (retaining control of domestic operations) — with the MoF Inc. owning 100 per cent of MAS — and transferring its listed status to a newly-incorporated company (Newco), with its international and cargo operations separated from its domestic operations (*The Star*, 29 January 2002).[7] (Figure 7.1 shows the corporate structure of MAS before and after the proposed, but aborted reorganisation.)

Even with the later restructuring plan — Widespread Asset Unbundling (WAU) plan (see Box 7.1) — approved by the board and announced on 30 July 2002, similar concerns to those raised by the previous restructuring plan still need to be addressed. The government

MAS CORPORATE STRUCTURE

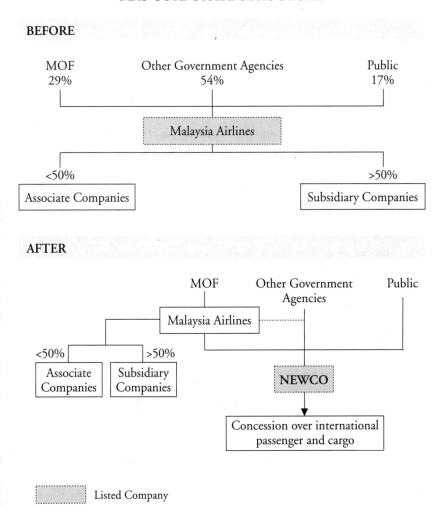

Fig. 7.1 MAS Corporate Structure Before and After Initial Proposed Reorganisation

must ensure that: assets will be transferred at "realistic" prices; the concession valuation[8] and pricing of the operating lease to MAS will be transparent; the cost of the government's contribution to MAS's recovery — in terms of reduced financing charges and so on — should be quantified and made transparent; the debt-equity swap

Box 7.1 Turnaround Measures/Strategies Proposed by MAS

Objective

- The new management intends to improve on profitability by reducing costs, setting new targets for achieving higher overall yields, shortening ground turn-around time, maximising "belly utilisation" by optimising loads and yields for cargo operations. It will also review domestic services, sales and distribution, in-flight services, corporate content, IT, subsidiaries as well as (current) policies and processes.

Proposed Measures (Prior to the September 11 Terrorist Attacks in the US)

- Installation of a new system for computing yields (MAS had been operating with a semi-computerised system) to improve operating procedures.
- Increase domestic fares to improve revenue.[9]
- Reorganise into nine divisions (or adopt a new organisational structure) for greater efficiency. The nine divisions envisaged were marketing services, sales and distribution, support operations, information (IT division), finance, cargo, flight operations, corporate services, and engineering & maintenance, where all the divisions would be headed by senior personnel who will report directly to the newly appointed managing director, Datuk Mohd Nor Yusof (*The Star*, 2 June 2001).[10]
- Set up an audit unit directly under the purview of the managing director to ensure greater accountability.
- Introduce a "hub and spoke strategy" to simplify its domestic network and reduce unnecessary staging costs. It plans to enhance the frequency of domestic flights and align current traffic flows with 90 per cent of the traffic channelled through the three main hubs of Kuala Lumpur, Kuching and Kota Kinabalu.
- It would not split its loss-making domestic operations from its international operations as such a move would be very complex and would eliminate commercial advantages and efficiency gains.
- Consider pulling back capacity from unprofitable long-haul routes and redeploying aircraft to reach critical frequency to popular destinations in order to raise high yield traffic and maximise profits.
- Improve the position balance sheet as well as cash flow and gearing problems, possibly by disposing off certain assets.

Proposed Measures (Post-September 11)

- MAS secured RM1.2 billion in loans and would seek additional funding to take delivery of five new aircraft in 2001 and 2002 (as reported by Bloomberg).
- To cope with increased insurance premiums and lower "coverage", MAS decided to impose an insurance surcharge of US$1.25 (RM4.75) per passenger on all international and domestic flights except rural air services on tickets issued on or after September 28 for travel on or after 1 October 2001.[11]
- To offset the impact of the slowing economy, in October 2001, MAS proposed to withdraw from 12 international destinations,[12] cut jobs through a proposed voluntary separation scheme (VSS) and dispose non-core assets.[13]
- Management change has been ongoing. (See Box 7.2 for changes in top management.) MAS appointed three new independent, non-executive directors — Datuk Mohd Azman Yahya, Datuk N. Sadasivan and Datuk Kee Mustafa.[14]
- To deal with the ballooning debt problem, to pay for new aircraft and to improve profitability of core businesses with additional working capital, MAS announced an asset sale exercise to raise a massive RM6.1 billion to retire part of its debt and provide RM820 million in working capital.
- The following were the measures announced to improve finances (*The Star*, 8 January 2002):
- The national carrier raised RM3.9 billion from a financing package involving the proposed sale and leaseback of eight aircraft — five new and three old — to a government (Ministry of Finance Incorporated or MoF Inc.) special purpose vehicle (SPV), Penerbangan Malaysia Berhad (PMB) or Aircraft Business Malaysia Bhd (ABMB).
- Disposal of properties worth RM2.2 billion to a government SPV. The properties included its headquarters in Jalan Sultan Ismail; 34 office and workshop buildings forming the MAS office complex in Sultan Abdul Aziz Shah Airport in Subang, its Kelana Jaya complex, which has the MAS Academy; and 21 buildings forming the MAS complex located at the Kuala Lumpur International Airport (KLIA); and
- The start of negotiations with a consortium comprising Fahim Capital Sdn Bhd, Advent Group Management Sdn Bhd and LSG

SkyChefs for the proposed sale of 70 per cent equity in MAS Catering Sdn Bhd.

- MAS intended to complete the sale and lease back its aircraft by May, and to dispose of the properties by June 2002. From the RM6.1 billion to be raised, roughly RM2.4 billion would be used to take delivery of five new aircraft; RM1.58 billion to repay yen bonds due in 2002; RM1.3 billion to repay short-term debt, and RM820 million to be used as working capital.

- On 28 January 2002, MAS announced that it would be made private and its listed status transferred to a newly incorporated company (Newco)[15] as part of a plan to reorganise the airline's operations and to pare debt, reflecting poorer market conditions post-September 11, 2001. With this move, international and cargo operations would be separated from domestic operations, with Newco being awarded the concession to manage international passenger and cargo (both domestic and international) operations.[16] MAS currently has four business units, with the remaining three being domestic, engineering & maintenance, and ground handling.

Revised Restructuring Plan and Business Model (Widespread Asset Unbundling — WAU)

Financial Restructuring

- MAS unveiled a new business model — widespread asset unbundling (WAU) — that entailed it transferring all its remaining 73[17] aircraft — worth RM5.1 billion — and liabilities of RM6.96 billion to Penerbangan Malaysia Bhd (PMB) — a wholly-owned unit of the Ministry of Finance Inc (MoF Inc.) — and leasing back the aircraft for its inter-national passenger and cargo (domestic and international) operations.

- Once the entire process is completed, MAS would still manage domestic operations on a fee basis for the government (who will assume responsibility for the performance of domestic operations), as in the previous restructuring plan. MAS will now be a conces-sionaire — given a three-year contract, renewable yearly — and will be able to earn profits as long as revenue generated exceeds the fee it pays the government via PMB to operate the national carrier.

- The thus restructured MAS would maintain its listed status, with the major stakeholder PMB owning 69.4 per cent stake while the investing public would hold the remaining 30.6 per cent after MAS issues 482.5 million new shares at RM3.85 per share to PMB for assumption of its net liabilities of RM1.85 billion (transferred liabilities minus value of aircraft). The previous plan to transfer MAS's listed status to Newco was considered unsuitable as it was fraught with numerous legal problems.

- However, the initial MAS plan of unbundling, transferring and disposal of assets[18] to reduce its debt of RM8.9 billion remains intact.

Operational Restructuring

- MAS's new focus on developing and penetrating markets with high yields is in line with its desire to increase profitability. Previously, emphasis was placed on high visibility and international presence.

- MAS's operational restructuring was thus conceived to reflect this shift in business focus to maximise profitability by:

  (i) improving passenger and cargo yields by reconfiguring its network — increasing frequency, exploring new destinations (MAS is aiming to reach 60 international destinations directly by adding Chengdu (China), Lahore (Pakistan), Stockholm (Sweden) and Bahrain to its list), revisiting destinations such as Canada, and Boston and Chicago in the United States, pro-viding convenience and connectivity with improved scheduling;

  (ii) keeping costs down by reviewing inventory management and installing a better revenue management system (RMS); and

  (iii) enhancing marketing by differentiating its services from rival airlines such as Singapore Airlines, Cathay Pacific and British Airways, through improving service standards and quality, and upgrading its aircraft cabins.

Sources: Announcement by MAS to the KLSE, available from: <http://www.mas.com.my/>.
The New Straits Times, 27 Sep. 2001.
The Star, 30 May 2001; 31 May 2001; 2 June 2001; 10 July 2001; 19 July 2001; 26 Sep. 2001; 31 Oct. 2001; 6 Dec. 2001; 8 Jan. 2002; 29 Jan. 2002; 30 Jan. 2002b; 31 July 2002; 1 Aug. 2002a; 5 Aug. 2002b; 8 Aug. 2002.

Box 7.2   MAS Management Overhaul

Appointed	*Resigned/Retired*
• Dave Condit General Manager (Sales Division) (Effective November 2001)	• Datuk Bashir Ahmad Executive Vice President (Airline) (Resigned October 2001)
• Kim J. Kelly Assistant General Manager (Yield and Inventory Management Division) (Effective November 2001)	• Rodzlan Akib Abu Bakar Executive Vice President (IT & Corporate Planning) (Resigned October 2001)
• Paul Mooney Senior General Manager (Network and Revenue Management Division) (Appointed in June 2001)	• Datuk Abdullah Mat Zaid Executive Vice President (Corporate Services) (On leave prior to retirement)

Source: *The Star*, 31 Oct. 2001.[19]

arrangement and pricing are "fair". Unfortunately, the generous terms of the initial bail out for Tajudin Ramli undermined the credibility of the CDRC corporate restructuring exercises just as the Hottick NPL buyout at face value undermined Danaharta's reputation.

Corporate Restructuring Plans

One key element of a good corporate restructuring programme or turnaround plan is the ability to adjust, modify and improve with new information or changes in the business environment are evident or anticipated. Apart from favourable market and other conditions, flexibility, timely execution, patience and vision can help ensure the success of restructuring plans. The MAS turnaround plan has taken numerous twists and turns with changes in the business, policy and political environment, both nationally and internationally.

Box 7.3   Urgent Priorities for MAS

Financial

Objective 1: Improve liquidity position

- Closer management of yields on seats sold on international routes.
- Review domestic fares.
- Raise additional working capital.
- Pre-plan US dollar cash needs for delivery of aircraft. MAS started discussions with several investment bankers on possible options.
- Pre-pay term liabilities were due. MAS received a firm proposal from an international investment bank.

Objective 2: Normalise leverage and capital structure compared to peers

- MAS took a first step by raising quasi capital with the proposed issue of RM800 million of Redeemable Convertible Preference Shares.
- MAS formulated other action plans, including pruning its balance sheet and reviewing its fleet replacement programme with key suppliers and financiers.

Strategic

Objective 1: Prepare new strategic plan to make MAS a profitable national carrier

- Rationalise international network, with focus on the profitable Asian region and selected long haul destinations to set foundations for future network growth.
- Improve domestic network with hub & spoke strategy.
- Secure alliance membership/bilateral cooperation.
- Achieve industry standards in operational productivity, service levels and cost.
- Fill key capability gaps within new organisational structure.

Objective 2: Position MAS to compete in the "premier league"

- Rally employee support to achieve competitiveness. Ensure employees' contribution towards restoring pride and confidence in the organisation.

Source: MAS; *The Star*, 30 May 2001.

Prior to the September 11, 2001 terrorist attacks, an initial turnaround plan — involving financial and strategic aspects — was unveiled on 29 May 2001. The objective of the plan, according to the new MAS managing director, Datuk Mohd Nor Yusof, was to improve MAS's liquidity, improve its balance sheet, raise additional working capital, enhance MAS's competitive position, and ensure MAS profitability as national flag carrier by FY2004. At that time, Mohd Nor said MAS expected to get about RM1.5 billion in net income, and to return to profitability, earning an expected pre-tax profit of RM341 million by FY2004 with full implementation of the turnaround plan (*The Star*, 30 May 2001). [See "Evaluation of Corporate Restructuring" for a review of MAS's corporate performance after the 1997–98 Asian financial crisis. Box 7.3 provides a summary of the financial and strategic objectives of MAS's turnaround plan.]

By February 2002, MAS had accumulated about RM9.2 billion in debt (*The Star*, 28 February 2002a). Some measures to improve MAS's profit position included reducing costs, setting new targets for achieving higher overall yields, shortening ground turnaround time, as well as maximising belly utilisation by optimising cargo operations' loads and yields. MAS also planned to review domestic services, sales and distribution, in-flight services, other subsidiaries as well as policies and processes. To improve its balance sheet and financial position, MAS proposed to dispose of and lease back aircraft and to sell off certain non-strategic assets. [Box 7.1 summarises various measures before September 11 as well as additional and modified measures post-September 11.]

The predicament faced by MAS has by no means been solely attributable to the Asian financial crisis and other fortuitous factors, including September 11, 2001, as claimed by the government (in providing its rationale for the bail out). In fact, weaknesses before the 1997–98 crisis were already clear under the previous MAS management headed by Tajudin Ramli. Many believe the previous management, under Tajudin, had been overly ambitious and had borrowed heavily to expand operations. But trying to expand and diversify when the industry was fraught with overcapacity, proved disastrous.

For a comparison of the proposed and implemented turnaround plans, see Table 7.1. While some similar measures — e.g. revamping senior management, scrapping unprofitable international routes and

Table 7.1 Tajudin Ramli's and Mohamad Nor's Turnaround Plans Compared

Turnarounds: Comparing the Last Two MAS Master Plans

On 14 February 2001, Naluri, a listed holding company controlled by Tajudin, announced that it had sold its controlling 29 per cent stake in MAS back to the Ministry of Finance (MoF). As Tajudin and his management team made their exit amid controversy about the price the government paid, the government appointed Mohd Nor Yusof the airline's managing director. Mohd Nor's experience is in merchant banking — a strong indication that the main task at hand is to improve MAS's battered balance sheet and return the company to financial health.

On 29 May 2001, 104 days after the government formally took control of MAS, the airline announced a RM1.3 billion net loss — its largest ever — for the financial year ended 31 March 2001. Mohd Nor sought to reassure investors by announcing a series of initiatives that he promised would return MAS to profitability by financial year 2003.

	Part of 2001 strategy?	Part of 1997 strategy?	Remarks
Revamp senior management	Yes	Yes	Normal for new management to have its own team. Reporting lines also changed on both occasions.
Seek domestic fare increase	Yes	Yes	Last increase was in 1992. Politically sensitive, need government approval.
Scrap unprofitable international routes	Yes	Yes	A logical move, but also politically sensitive because many such routes were initiated by then PM Mahathir.
Realign international routes	Yes	Yes	2001 strategy focused on shorter, higher yielding routes in Asia.
Secure strategic alliances	Yes	Yes	Involves code share agreements and other airline alliances.
Review yields on seats sold	Yes	Yes	Following route realignment and pricing. 1994 strategy had tried to attract more first- and business-class travellers.
Increase aircraft utilisation	Yes	Yes	In 1994, methods included charter, leasing and new routes. See also following comments for costs reduction.

(cont'd overleaf)

Table 7.1   Continued.

	Part of 2001 strategy?	Part of 1997 strategy?	*Remarks*
Reduce costs	Implied	Yes	In 1994, this included shorter aircraft turnaround times; the heavier workload resulted in staff dissatisfaction.
Improve liquidity position	Yes	No	Severe balance sheet deterioration made this imperative from 2001.
Consolidate of unprofitable subsidiaries	Yes	No	In 1994, new subsidiaries were created to turn non-flight operations into "profit centres". They remained loss making and are likely to be merged again.
Aggressive fleet expansion	No	Yes	Fleet expansion in the mid-1990s was overly ambitious and became a major reason for MAS's subsequent financial predicament.

Note: This table shows that the 1994 corporate restructuring proposal and its 2001 counterpart bear striking similarities. Indeed, the Boston Consulting Group, which helped draw up the latest plan, also conducted studies for Tajudin's team when he took over in 1994.

Source: The Edge, July 2001. Analyst and press briefings by MAS management.

increasing aircraft utilisation — were employed by both Tajudin's and Mohd Noor's management teams, the latter did not expand fleet size, but instead focused on improving yields and reducing debt in his haste to expand, while Tajudin quickly accumulated massive debts. This left Mohd Noor and his management team the daunting task of trimming a huge debt of about RM9.2 billion. To make problems worse, MAS had four consecutive (financial) years of losses beginning from 1997/98, i.e. with the financial crisis. Tajudin had taken MAS's net debt-to-equity ratio to 4.7 in 2001, i.e. more than twice the 1.9 at the end of 1995 (*The Edge,* 9 July 2001: 4). This large debt burden meant that the company's net income from operations was not sufficient to service its debt obligations without selling some aircrafts.

Even though Tajudin was "forced" to resign from MAS as chairman and president, he was not reprimanded for mismanagement. Instead Tajudin was given a "golden parachute" when the government bought his 29.09 per cent Naluri stake at RM8.00 per share, which earned him RM1.792 billion. This suggested that Tajudin could take, on hindsight, excessive risks (e.g. rapid and massive expansion of MAS's fleet which increased debt burden and interest payments) and be greatly rewarded if the strategy was successful. On the contrary, if the strategy "failed", Tajudin would still earn a sizeable remuneration as chairman of MAS and cite unfavourable external factors (which was partially justifiable) for the strategy failure.

Evaluation of Corporate Restructuring

Aviation and financial analysts responded positively to the 2001 proposed measures and seemed to feel that the plan was a step in the right direction in the airline's quest for profitability by 2004. For example, the corporate restructuring proposals announced on 8 January 2002 convinced OSK Research analyst Hilmi Mokhtar that the airline would be profitable by its financial year ending March 2004, the target set by the management though he believed further efforts were also required (*The Star*, 9 January 2002).

Analysts seemed to be in agreement that debt reduction (thereby reducing interest payments due) and staff reduction measures were required to ensure MAS's return to profitability. According to them, MAS's gearing level will be reduced from 4.5 times to slightly over 2.5 times with the sale and leaseback of aircraft and property, and the sale of MAS's 70 per cent stake in MAS Catering Sdn Bhd. Asset disposal will eliminate maintenance charges and boost cash reserves to enable it to expand its network and operations.[20] Meanwhile, selling MAS Catering should relieve the airline of a loss-making subsidiary and indirectly reduce staff[21] (*The Star*, 8 January 2002; *The Star*, 9 January 2002).[22] Furthermore, the divestment of non-core assets will further enhance the group's focus on its core competencies, thereby improving its chances of viability and survival in the highly competitive, but oligopolistic industry.

On 25 September 2003, MAS finalised the sale of MAS Catering Sdn Bhd (MCSB) to Gubahan Saujana Sdn Bhd — a joint venture comprising Bumiputra food entrepreneur Fahim Capital Sdn Bhd (Fahim) and LSG Lufthansa Service Holding AG (LSG Sky Chefs), the world's largest provider of in-flight catering, through its subsidiary LSG Asia GmbH. The signing of formal agreements for operational handover to Gubahan Saujana Sdn Bhd was completed by early December 2003. With the completion of the deal, MAS's equity stake in MCSB would decline from 100 per cent to 30 per cent (MAS 2003q).

While some analysts viewed the reinstatement of 12 previously scrapped routes as an attempt by the management to take advantage of the post-September 11 fallout in the global aviation industry, most believe that the uneconomic step was due to the then Prime Minister's orders, which will only undermine MAS's viability. Undoubtedly, many analysts are still cautious about the prospects for MAS[23] and prefer to wait to see how the measures affect its profit and loss account (*The Star*, 9 January 2002). Market analysts say the earlier corporate reorganisation proposal involving a Newco seemed promising, but lacked crucial details, especially with respect to valuation of MAS's international cargo and domestic operations (*The Star*, 29 January 2002). Analysts believe (based on available information) that the new arrangement will augur well for the MAS group,[24] minority shareholders[25] and potential investors.

Analysts expected Newco to rake in net profits of RM250 million to RM300 million a year, based on the airline's recently released third-quarter 2001 results. The Centre for Asia-Pacific Aviation's outlook report for 2002 noted that the next three months would be critical in deciding the long-term prospects of airlines. It added that "Net revenue drops of 15 to 20 per cent [combining traffic and yield decreases] simply cannot be corrected by even the fiercest of conventional cost reductions." MAS's third-quarter 2001 revenue fell by 13.8 per cent to RM1.9 billion due to the decline in long-haul passenger loads after September 11. Meanwhile, revenue from its cargo division dropped 16.5 per cent due to declining demand for electronic components (Gabriel 2002). However, MAS believed that if all financial and operational restructuring measures were fully implemented, the group would be able to turn around and register a pre-tax profit of RM341.0 million in financial year 2004 (see Box 7.4 and Table 7.4).

Box 7.4   MAS Corporate Performance After the 1997–98 Asian Financial Crisis

MAS, the Malaysian national airline carrier, faced operational losses, falling revenues and mounting debts following the 1997–98 Asian financial crisis. The situation was further exacerbated following the September 11, 2001 terror attacks in the USA. MAS's losses since the 1997–98 Asian financial crisis continued into the year 2002. Tables 7.2, 7.3 and 7.4 summarise earnings estimates of the MAS group following the 1997–98 Asian financial crisis.[26] The pre-September 11 projected earnings' numbers (in Table 7.2) and post-Sept 11 revised earnings estimates (Tables 7.3 and 7.4) highlight the impact of September 11 on the national carrier and the sensitivity of the "industry" to such external shocks.

Tables 7.2 and 7.3 show MAS's group performance steadily deteriorating after the Asian financial crisis. Prior to the crisis, MAS posted a net profit of RM33.02 million for the financial year ending 31 March 1997. For the financial year ending 31 March 2000, the group recorded a net loss of RM258.6 million. The situation worsened the following year with a net loss of RM417.428 million and losses per share rising from 33.6 sen to 54.2 sen. According to Table 7.4, the situation was not expected to improve dramatically for the financial year ending in 2002, with an estimated net loss of RM1.11 billion.[27] Quarterly figures in Table 7.3 suggest generally weaker corporate performance through 2001 compared to the previous year, with slight improvements from one quarter to the next.[28]

MAS's Annual Report for 2001 showed a marked improvement over initial estimates. Table 7.5 suggest that MAS's financial performance was expected to improve dramatically from a net loss of RM835.6 million for the financial year ending 2002 to a net profit of RM94.2 million for the financial year ending 2003 after successful implementation of the Widespread Asset Unbundling restructuring plan. If not, MAS would incur a net loss of RM357.3 million. The WAU scheme appeared to be effective as it propped up MAS's net profit after tax and minority interest for the financial year ending 31 March 2003 to RM339.1 million, higher than the earlier estimate of RM94.2 million, despite the weak external economic climate.

Table 7.2 MAS Earnings and Earnings Projections from Financial Year 1996/97 to 2003/4[1] Under the First Restructuring Plan as of Mid-2001

	FY96/97	FY97/98	FY98/99	FY99/00	FY00/01	FY01/02P[2]	FY02/03P[2]	FY03/04P[2]
Operating profits/(losses)[3] (RM m)	–	–	–	–	–	(363.9)	(97.5)	312.6
Net profits/(losses) after tax & exceptional items (RM m)	333.02[4]	(259.85)	(700.05)	(258.6)	(417.428)	(604.0)	(455.3)	(17.6)
EPS (sen)	43.8	(33.7)	(90.9)	(33.6)	(54.2)	(78.4)	(59.1)	(2.3)
NTA per share (RM)	–	2.81	1.68	1.74	2.14	0.63	0.56	1.05

Notes: [1] MAS's financial year ends on 31 March.

P = Projection

[2] Note that these projections were made without taking into account the September 11, 2001 terrorist attacks on the US, which had not occurred at the time the estimates were announced.

[3] Includes depreciation and forex costs, but excludes interest costs and income from aircraft sales and non-flight operations.

[4] Before transfer of profits to general reserves.

Source: Analyst and press briefings by MAS management in *The Edge*, 9 July 2001.

Table 7.3   MAS Earnings for Financial Year 2000/1 as of May 2001

	FY00/01 ending 31 Mar. 2001[1]	FYQ1 ended 30 June 2001[2]	FYQ2 ended 30 Sep. 2001[2]	Cumulative basis for 6 months ending 30 Sep. 2001[2]	FYQ3 ending 31 Dec. 2001[2]	Cumulative basis for 3 quarters ending 31 Dec. 2001[2]
Pre-tax profits/ (losses) (RM m)	(1330.0)	(413.35)	(359.15)	(772.50)	(354.83)	(1,127.33)
Net profits/ (losses) (RM m)	(1333.8)	(413.82)	(358.98)	(772.80)	(340.05)	(1112.85)
Earnings/(losses) per share (sen)	(173.2)	(53.74)	(46.62)	(100.36)	(44.16)	(144.53)

Source: [1] *The Star*, 30 May 2001.

[2] Announcements of quarterly reports of unaudited consolidated balance sheets by MAS.

The revised restructuring plan — widespread asset unbundling (WAU) — has received "positive" feedback from the MAS board and financial analysts. Once the WAU plan had been implemented, MAS's debt to equity ratio of more than 700 per cent on its total debt of RM8.96 billion at end March 2002 was expected to be eliminated, resulting in a projected net cash position of more than RM670 million by the end March 2003 (*The Star*, 31 July 2002). In addition, the

Table 7.4   MAS Earnings Projections for Financial Years 2001/2, 2002/3, 2003/4, as of Late 2001

	FY01/02	FY02/03	FY03/04	FY03/04
Pre-tax profits/(losses) (RM m)	(1320.0)[1]	(255.0)[1]	341.0[3]	–
Net profits/(losses)(RM m)	(1110.0)[2]	(628.3)[2]	341.0[4]	200.0

Sources: [1] Revised estimates provided by MAS, as reported by *The Star*, 9 Jan. 2002.

[2] Based on Multex consensus figure in *The Sun*, 27 Nov. 2001a.

[3] Revised estimates provided by MAS, as reported by *The Star*, 9 Jan. 2002.

[4] Revised estimates provided by MAS, as reported by *The Star*, 2 Jan. 2002.

Table 7.5   MAS Earnings for 2000/1, 2001/2, 2002/3 and Earnings Projections for 2002/3 for FY Ending 31 March Before & After Implementation of the Widespread Asset Unbundling (WAU) Restructuring Plan and Business Model

	FY2000/1	*FY2001/2*	*FY2002/3 Projections Before Restructuring*	*FY2002/3 Projections After Restructuring*	*FY2002/3*
Net profits/(losses) after tax and minority interests (RM m)	(417.4)	(835.6)	(357.3)	94.2	339.1
Earnings/(losses) per share (sen)	(52.1)	(108.5)	(46.41)	9.31	38.95
Net debt/cash (RM m)	–	8,552	8,629	676	–
Net gearing ratio (%)	–	704	757	Net Cash	–

Note: Assuming completion of restructuring on 30 September 2002, based on five-month pro rata
          P = Projection
Sources: *The Star*, 30 July 2002; 31 July 2002.
          MAS 2002.
          MAS 2003g.

RM1.6 billion proceeds from the sale of MAS Catering and the properties expected to be fully received by 31 December 2002 would generate quite a significant cash flow for MAS. However, such an amount in the aviation industry is neither "highly" significant nor sufficient to sustain MAS for long. As such, an operational restructuring plan to improve marketing and yield, as well as to reduce costs was conceived.

By managing both yield and revenue while containing cost, the likelihood of MAS returning to profitability was raised as it is no longer burdened with the need to service high interest rate charges on loans for aircraft purchases and depreciation costs. However, the maintenance costs that MAS will incur currently and in future due to over-expansion of its aircraft fleet in 1994 and 1995 remain a cause for concern (*The Star*, 5 August 2002). However, such optimism is justifiable if demand for aviation services improves with a more buoyant global economic environment and reduced security concerns. Furthermore, MAS must implement its plans and embark on a sustained and disciplined cost cutting strategy while forming desirable and appropriate strategic alliances to maximise reach, connectivity and load.

While some doubt if MAS will ever be commercially profitable, the current debate is not on whether MAS will be able to make a profit, but when MAS will get out of the red and by how much. Some analysts believe that it would take at least two years for the full benefits of the operational restructuring exercises to be felt. Nonetheless, MAS's un-audited financial statement for the financial year ending 31 March 2003 suggested a net profit after tax and minority interest of RM339.1 million, with earning per share of 38.95 sen. This result is attributable to the reduction in finance costs, gain from sale of property and from the execution of the WAU plan including sale of aircraft and engines, and realisation of deferred income (MAS 2003g). Since gains from disposal of assets are a one-time event, MAS's future performance will depend on its operational restructuring plan (outlined in Box 7.1) to increase yield and revenue, and to cut operations costs.

With respect to the MAS's concessionaire term under the WAU scheme, the three-year contract, renewable yearly, should provide sufficient "incentive" and impetus for its management to achieve "financial discipline" and focus on improving performance, rather than "empire-building" or expansion. However, whether this will remain a binding and effective constraint on MAS's future behaviour and financial performance is still unclear. If political factors that impede the proper and efficient allocation of resource are allowed to influence decisions as to whether to extend the contract or impose additional conditionalities such as management changes where appropriate, then the contract will not have serve one of its intended purposes of imposing performance discipline.

Since the implementation of the WAU strategies, MAS has continued to come up with various operational and strategic measures to help strengthen profitability and performance. However, airlines worldwide, especially Asian carriers, were severely affected by the severe acute respiratory syndrome (SARS) following the earlier collapse of the industry after September 11, 2001. MAS was no exception. The total number of passengers carried declined by 22 per cent to 3.12 million passengers, while the number of international passengers dropped by 33 per cent to 1.26 million passengers after the SARS panic during the second quarter of 2003. MAS posted a RM225.472 million operating loss and RM164.512 million net loss after tax for the first financial quarter ending 30 June 2003 (MAS 2003i; 2003o).

By the second financial quarter ending 30 September 2003, MAS's accumulated second quarter net loss after tax had shrunk to RM63.445 million — attributable to a net profit after tax of RM101.068 million. The recovery after the SARS panic in the first financial quarter was largely due to a steady return of travel confidence. MAS's resilience and proactive measures have ensured their ability to capitalise on the increased confidence and renewed demand for air travel. The second quarter saw RM102.971 million in operating profit against the first quarter's dismal RM225.472 million operating loss (MAS 2003i; 2003u; 2003v). Following initial government assistance, a variety of external factors — the more favourable aviation environment after the SARS scare receded as well as the generally improving domestic and global economies — and company-driven strategies/measures (some mentioned below) have contributed to MAS's improving performance.

In January 2003, Penerbangan Malaysia Bhd (PMB), the new holding company for MAS, signed a memorandum of understanding (MOU) with Airbus to acquire six Airbus A380–800 passenger aircraft for delivery scheduled to commence in 2007. According to Dato' Gumuri Hussain, the managing director and chief executive officer of PMB, since the 555-seater A380 will use state of the art technology, operating costs per seat kilometre will be reduced by up to 20 per cent. Greater comfort and customer satisfaction are expected, given the A380's full upper deck with additional 49 per cent cabin space and approximately 35 per cent more seats compared to existing aircraft.[29]

In line with such fleet expansion and strategic growth, MAS's senior general manager for sales, distribution & marketing, Dato Ahmad Fuaad Dahlan unveiled its route expansion programme expected to increase passenger seats per week to identified routes by 28,650 to 150,346. This is expected to further boost yields, competitiveness and make KLIA a primary international aviation hub, supported by secondary hubs in East Malaysia[30] and Northern Peninsular Malaysia as well as tourism, through increased connectivity, especially in regional and domestic routes. This strategic and commercial programme was envisaged on the basis of improved performance and yields following the restructuring exercise and turnaround programme. (For details, see MAS, media release, 30 January 2003.) However, the costs of route expansion need to be seriously factored in. Another concern is whether KLIA can effectively compete with international airports such as Singapore, Bangkok and Hong Kong, the busiest cargo airport in the region with high passenger traffic.

For most of 2003, MAS had been implementing its route expansion and reach programme for greater coverage through charters and direct services.[31] MAS has signed numerous agreements and memoranda of understanding (MOUs) with other airlines to enhance market presence and service quality — through a Master Agreement and MOU with Garuda Indonesia — as well as improved and promoted KLIA airport services, such as ground handling, and maintenance, repair and overhaul — involving Royal Dutch Airlines (KLM), Jet Airways, Air China, Air Atlanta (MAS 2003p; 2003r). To boost domestic tourism and revenue, MAS unveiled a new marketing package — Golden Holidays Great Getaways — involving 22 specially selected destinations within Malaysia in May 2003 (MAS 2003h).

To further enhance in-flight service competitiveness, in August 2003, MAS unveiled plans of a RM700 million programme to upgrade its 32 long and medium haul aircraft fleet to "provide the ultimate in contemporary global air travel". This was to be achieved by entirely revamping First and Business class cabin accommodation, and the in-flight entertainment system by introducing cutting edge style and design (MAS 2003n).

If winning international awards are testaments to or reflections of operational efficiency, customer satisfaction and competitive pricing, then MAS's financial performance after restructuring has been steadily improving. MAS broke into the top five spots in the "Airline of the Year 2003" rankings in an international airline survey conducted by Skytrax Research of London. In addition, it was voted the second best international airline for the "Best Economy Class 2003" and was in third position for Asia's "Best Airline 2003" award (MAS 2003e).

Meanwhile, the Kuala Lumpur International Airport (KLIA), which houses Malaysia Airlines Cargo Sdn Bhd (MASkargo), bagged first place in the Emerging Airport category (less than 500,000 tonnes per year) at the Asian Freight and Supply Chain Awards 2003 (AFSCAs) in March 2003 (MAS 2003f). MAS's appointment as the official airline for Real Madrid's Asia Tour 2003 by Asia Sports Development Limited of Hong Kong in August 2003, and for the inaugural FA Premier League (FAPL) Asia Cup tournament by ESPN STAR Sport in July 2003 have further enhanced its reputation (MAS 2003j; 2003l).

These achievements should augur well for MAS in a highly brand and image competitive industry. MAS has been out of the red since the third quarter of 2002, except in the second quarter of 2003 — when the SARS situation reached a climax — and third quarter of 2003, when losses dropped sharply. For the quarter ending 31 December 2003, MAS recorded a net profit of RM230.535 million. Improvement in MAS's financial year third quarter results of RM230.535 million outweighed MAS's accumulated financial year second quarter loss of RM63.445 million to help push it back into the black, recording a three quarter accumulated profit as of 31 December 2003 of RM166.637 million (MAS 2003x).

Despite recording lower operating revenue — down RM83,600 from the previous financial year — MAS registered net profit after tax of RM461.143 million for financial year ended 31 March 2004 — up 37 per cent from the previous financial year — due partly to lower operating costs and finance costs as well as "negative" tax expense for the year. Basic earnings per share however, dropped from 38.7 sen per share to 36.8 sen per share for FY2004 (MAS 2004a).

For the first quarter ended 30 June 2004, thanks mainly to operating revenue outstripping operating costs and reduced finance costs, MAS recorded a net profit after tax of RM26.589 million; a stark contrast from the RM164.512 million net loss after tax during the same period last year (MAS 2004b). Given the relatively optimistic forecast for worldwide air travel and air travel in Asia — growing at four per cent and six per year respectively — MAS may be en route to a relatively sustainable and healthy financial position despite the absence of Dato' Md Nor bin Md Yusof — whose term ended effective 1 April 2004 — who is arguably largely responsible for the turnaround success of MAS when he took the helm in 2001.

These developments should boost morale and provide further incentives for proper operational and financial restructuring and management, especially with respect to fleet expansion and debt management by PMB. Proper financial, economic, capability, competition and strategic analyses are necessary when undertaking costly investments. On the other hand, there is a need to anticipate changing business conditions and to try to gain first mover advantage in anticipation of increased air travel or cargo demand by expanding aircraft fleet. This would be in line with a supply driven, rather than a demand led approach, with the latter generally associated with lack of capacity, bottlenecks and longer turnaround time.

The United Engineers (M) Bhd/Renong Bhd (UEM/Renong) Group

The privatisation of the North-South Expressway was hailed as one of the most successful ever, ostensibly proving that the private sector could accomplish what the government could not, while furthering the development of a Bumiputera, entrepreneur class. Projek Lebuhraya Utara-Selatan Bhd (PLUS) became the cash cow of the Renong/UEM (United Engineers (M) Bhd/Renong Bhd) empire. Rapid expansion, over-diversification into areas demanding resources generating low returns, high debt levels and lack of business focus eventually drove the group to the brink of bankruptcy (Gunasegaram 2002b).

Government's Role in UEM/Renong Corporate (Debt) Restructuring

The government intervened to take over UEM in 2001 after the Renong/UEM empire under Tan Sri Halim Saad unravelled after the 1997–98 Asian financial crisis became "the straw that broke the camel's back". It is beyond the scope of this study to unravel the complex intricacies of the UEM/Renong saga. Instead, we focus on the CDRC debt-restructuring scheme involving the issuance RM8.4 billion of zero coupon bonds by PLUS. [See Box 7.5 for details.] This followed the default on loan repayments totalling some RM8.4 billion by Renong and UEM (*freeMalaysia* 1999a). The CDRC designed a debt-restructuring plan to prevent the consequent liquidation of Renong and UEM (and thus preserved the country's largest business conglomerate — in distress due to the crisis — and thus, jobs).

According to the CDRC, the restructuring plan represented a private sector solution, without any financial support from the Government, of immense benefit to the economy, especially the banking sector, and in the best interests of the creditors and shareholders of Renong and UEM. From Renong's standpoint, the CDRC's proposal (by avoiding the immediate liquidation and sale of its assets at depressed market prices), would allow Renong to realise more fully the value of its investments, and to capture the upside potential of the anticipated national recovery, thereby putting Renong in a better position to service its liabilities and to return value to shareholders (CDRC 1999).

Moreover, according to the CDRC, successful restructuring will ease the NPL burden on banks, thereby improving the overall financial health of the system, which should improve confidence in Malaysia. Since the entire Renong group accounted for 7 per cent of all Malaysia's bank loans, the restructuring plan should significantly reduce NPLs in the banking system (*freeMalaysia* 1999a). Without such a bail out, it was claimed, the Renong group's debts would put the Malaysian banking system under great stress. Even if this argument was true, the key question remains: how and why did Renong rack up such a huge debt in the first place? It is difficult not to suspect that the government actually provided indirect financial support to Renong, thus bailing out the group[32] — previously controlled by the ruling party, United Malays' National Organisation (UMNO) — and then by Halim Saad, long believed to be a proxy for UMNO and its then Treasurer, then Finance Minister Daim Zainuddin.[33]

Further, there were other ways of resolving the problem that would duly punish — not compensate — those responsible for the mess. The proposed bail out was thus against a clear principle of the NEAC's 1999 National Economic Recovery Plan, i.e. that culprits would not be allowed to get away without penalty. Under the proposal, no penalty would be imposed on either the top management or the

Box 7.5 Outline of UEM/Renong Group Corporate Restructuring Plan

Financial Restructuring

Initial Debt Restructuring Plan, October 1998

- In October 1998, Renong proposed that the government guarantee a RM10.5 billion bond issue to refinance overdue loans (*freeMalaysia* 1999a). It was rejected because creditors would receive as little as half their money back. However, the proposal implied another government-funded bail out of a politically well-connected business group, with no penalty on Renong's management (Lopez 1999).
- On 13 October 1998, Renong announced a restructuring of its corporate structure into four business areas of construction and engineering, expressways, transportation, and property development.

Revised Proposal, March 1999

- The second proposal, announced on 8 March 1999, involved UEM subsidiary, PLUS, issuing RM8.4 billion of zero-coupon bonds (present day value),[34] yielding 10 per cent per annum, which would mature in seven years. PLUS would then lend RM5.4 billion to Renong and RM3.0 billion to UEM to settle creditors' claims (CDRC 1999).[35]
- All creditors' claims would be settled in full (either in cash or bonds). All UEM creditors and Renong's secured creditors would receive cash repayment, while Renong's unsecured creditors would receive 50 per cent repayment in cash, with the 50 per cent balance in PLUS bonds.[36]
- Under the revised plan, PLUS would repay the bonds with untaxed revenue from its highway tolls (Lopez 1999).
- However, according to Renong on 13 March 2000, the PLUS bonds would only bear an annual yield of 9.4 per cent. Although no coupon payments would be made, if Renong and UEM allowed the full seven-year term to run, with accumulated interest, these PLUS bonds could be redeemed in 2006 for a total of RM16 billion (Renong 2000).
- Also, in 1999, the Renong group issued RM4.3 billion (present value at date of issue) Renong SPV (special purpose vehicle)

bonds back-to-back with part of the RM8.4 billion PLUS bonds. The Renong SPV bond would yield of 9.4 per cent per annum compounded on a semi-annual basis, which would grow to RM8.2 billion upon maturity in September 2006 (Renong 2001a).

Takeover of UEM by Khazanah via Danasaham, July 2001

- In July 2001, the government offered to "nationalise" UEM (*The Star*, 21 September 2001a).[37]
- In August 2001, Danasaham made a Conditional Voluntary Offer (CVO) to purchase the entire shares and warrants of UEM, which included Renong's 37.9 per cent interest in UEM (Renong 2001a).
- On 15 September 2001, the government got 90 per cent control of UEM (Renong 2001b).[38]
- In October 2001, Khazanah took control of UEM, and now controls 100 per cent of UEM equity following a successful voluntary takeover offer (Renong 2001b).
- After the RM3.8 billion takeover, analysts expected disposal of the group's assets and resolution of Renong boss Halim Saad's RM3.2 billion debt to UEM (*The New Straits Times*, 30 July 2001).
- On 1 October 2001, UEM appointed the former Chief Financial Officer of Telekom Malaysia Bhd, Abdul Wahid Omar, as its Managing Director and Chief Executive Officer (Renong 2001b).
- With the UEM takeover, Abu Hassan Kendut was appointed UEM chairman and Datuk Dr Ramli Mohamad executive director effective 8 October 2001. Renong appointed Tan Sri Mohd Sheriff Mohd Kassim as non-executive chairman and Abdul Wahid Omar as executive vice-chairman, while Datuk Izham Mahmud, Datuk Hamzah Bakar and Oh Chong Peng were appointed independent and non-executive directors with effect from 8 October 2001(*The Star*, 9 October 2001).
- Since then, there have been several management and board changes. Ahmad Pardas Senin was appointed managing director and CEO of the UEM group and UEM World effective 1 July 2004.[39] He succeeded Datuk Abdul Wahid Omar, who was appointed as CEO of Telekom Malaysia Berhad effective 1 July 2004. (*The Star*, 2 June 2004; *Bernama*, 21 May 2004).

Debt Restructuring Under Government Stewardship, December 2001

- In December 2001, under government stewardship, UEM announced a major corporate and debt restructuring plan to trim the group debt of RM30.3 billion to RM14 billion by mid-2002 (*The Star*, 2 May 2002).
- The plan involved streamlining operations into six units and divesting stakes in six companies to reduce its huge debts of some RM30 billion.
- One immediate priority was to reduce PLUS's debt level by RM11.5 billion, to a relatively comfortable debt level (to match its cash flow with its debt obligations) of around RM7 billion, prior to its listing (*The Star*, 2 May 2002).
- Other outstanding issues included resolving loans for previous projects undertaken by Renong and UEM, and defaults in loan repayments by some companies within the group such as Elite (*The Star*, 21 September 2001a).
- According to HLG Research head Yee Yang Chien, one way to resolve the huge debt would be via asset sales after Danasaham identified its core business, what it intended to keep, areas needing strengthening or downsizing, and non-core assets (*The Star*, 21 September 2001a).

Possible Ways to Resolve the RM8.5 billion Zero Coupon Bonds Issued in 1999 (worth RM16 billion upon maturity in 2006) to Pay Some Renong and UEM Loans

- The quickest way to resolve this issue would be to pay bondholders with government bonds. Then, PLUS would be in a more favourable financial position and could attract market capitalisation of RM15 billion minus borrowings. According to Yee Yang Chien, with this option, Danasaham would only need to hold a 51 per cent stake in PLUS and could sell the remaining 49 per cent to recoup its investment (*The Star*, 21 September 2001a).
- As part of PLUS's debt restructuring scheme to enhance its valuation upon listing, on 7 May 2002, Renong approved the transfer of the RM8.2 billion zero coupon bonds from PLUS to UEM (*The Star*, 8 May 2002). The Securities Commission (SC) had agreed on 3 May to transfer the guarantee for Renong bonds to UEM. This transaction would not affect Renong's share capital,

substantial shareholders' shareholdings, earnings and net tangible assets.

- PLUS intended to issue between 800 and 900 million[40] PLUS shares at between RM2.50 to RM3.00 each, thus raising between RM2.0 to RM2.7 billion (Ismail 2002), i.e. less than the RM3.5 billion mentioned in earlier reports (*The Star*, 2 May 2002).[41] On 17 July 2002, PLUS was listing on the KLSE Main Board; issuing five billion ordinary shares at RM2.65 each.

UEM-Renong Group Proposed Restructuring Plan, March 2003

- 27 March 2003, the UEM-Renong group announced that Renong would be taken private with its listed status transferred to a new company, UEM World Bhd (UEM World), whose operations would be streamlined into four core business units or activities, namely engineering & construction, healthcare, environmental services, and property.
- Renong's five-step restructuring plan below is expected to see: (i) UEM World buying UEM's entire interest in Pharmaniaga Berhad (Pharmaniaga), Intria, Kuality Alam Holdings Sdn Bhd, Cement Industries Malaysia Bhd (CIMA) and Kinta Kellas Public Limited Company (Kinta Kellas) from UEM for a total amount of RM944.9 million via a share swap of 591 million new UEM World shares at an indicative issue price of RM1.60 each to UEM; and (ii) the UEM group — the rebranded UEM-Renong group — having a 60.8 per cent to 61.6 per cent stake in UEM World.
- The UEM group planned to be listed on the KLSE in September 2003.
- The final outcome of the restructuring plan would culminate (as mentioned earlier) in UEM World having four distinct core businesses comprising:
  - (a) engineering and construction led by Intria Berhad, to be renamed UEM Builders Berhad;
  - (b) healthcare headed by Pharmaniaga Bhd;
  - (c) environmental services under Kualiti Alam Holdings Sdn Bhd, to be renamed UEM Environment Sdn Bhd; and
  - (d) property spearheaded by Renong, to be renamed UEM Land Sdn Bhd.

Final Five-Step Restructuring Plan

(i) Renong to be taken private via a share swap of one UEM World share of RM1.00 for every four Renong shares held at 50 sen each. Renong will be renamed UEM Land and will own Prolink.

(ii) Reduction of the Renong SPV (special purpose vehicle) bonds from RM3,695.4 million to a manageable level of RM1.9 billion to be repaid over an extended period of 10 years at an interest rate of 2 per cent per annum from 9.6 per cent. Annual interest savings is expected to be approximately RM278.6 million per annum. In part settlement of its SPV bond, Renong would offset the amount payable to UEM with its holdings of 11.1 per cent in Commerce Asset-Holdings Bhd (CAHB), 44.4 per cent in Park May Bhd (Park May), 48.4 per cent in Faber Bhd (Faber), 3.2 per cent in Camerlin Bhd (Camerlin) and 46.8 per cent in Time Engineering Bhd (Time) (see Figure 7.2 and Box 7.6).

(iii) UEM World would buy equity stakes in several companies for a total of RM945 million via the issuance of 591 million new shares at RM1.60 each to UEM. It would buy 30.9 per cent interest in Pharmaniaga for RM124.9 million, 48.9 per cent of Intria Bhd for RM391.8 million, 100 per cent of Kualiti Alam Holdings Bhd for RM180 million, 54 per cent of CIMA for RM170.2 million, and 62.4 per cent of Kinta Kellas for RM78 million.

(iv) Spearheaded by Intria (renamed UEM Builders Bhd) the UEM group's engineering and construction unit would be strengthened and duplication of business activities eliminated. Intria will own stakes in UE Construction Sdn Bhd (UEC), Projek Penyelenggaraan Lebuhraya Bhd (PROPEL), Pati Sdn Bhd (PATI), Constain, Penang Bridge and Intria Bina. Intria will be 48.9 per cent to 55.3 per cent owned by UEM World (see Figure 7.2). Under Intria's plan, UE Construction will divest Kualiti Alam to UEM for RM83.7 million and buy the 50 per cent remaining stake in PATI from UEM for RM55 million. Intria will then acquire 100 per cent equity interest in UEC (and hence PATI) from UEM for RM156.3 million, to be settled by Intria assuming the inter-company loans of RM110.7 million currently owed by UEM to PROPEL and the issuance of RM45.6 million Intria shares at the issue price of RM1 each.

Intria will also acquire PROPEL which would be delisted from the Main Board of the Kuala Lumpur Stock Exchange (KLSE).

(v)   UEM will offer 10 per cent of the equity in UEM World to eligible employees of UEM Group to meet the 25 per cent public spread requirement for UEM World under the KLSE listing rules.

Status of UEM-Renong's March 2003 Restructuring Plan

- UEM World Berhad (UEM World) was initially incorporated on 11 March 2003 under the name of Global Converge Sdn Bhd. The Company changed its name to UEM World Sdn Bhd on 8 September 2003, and subsequently became a public limited company and assumed the name of UEM World Berhad on 12 September 2003. Pursuant to the Scheme of Arrangement (SOA) — under section 176 of the Companies Act, 1965 — of UEM Land Sdn Bhd (UEM Land, formerly known as Renong Bhd), UEM World became owner of the entire shareholding in UEM Land through an exchange of shares, and assumed UEM Land's listing status on the Main Board of Malaysia Securities Exchange Bhd (MSEB) or Bursa Malaysia Bhd on 14 November 2003 (UEM World 2004a).

- On 29 July 2002, UEM Land announced the change of the end of its financial year from 30 June to 31 December. The audited financial statement for the preceding period was prepared for a period of 18 months from 1 July 2001 to 31 December 2002.

- The above SOA was in line with the proposed March 2003 restructuring exercise and involved:

   (i)   Restructuring and partial settlement of the entire RM8,197.6 million nominal value zero coupon redeemable secured and guaranteed bonds due in 2006 (SPV Bond) issued by Renong Debt Management Sdn Bhd (RDM), a subsidiary of UEM Land, with an accreted (accumulated) value to 31 October 2003 of approximately RM2,899.1 million;

   (ii) Cancellation and exchange by existing UEM Land shareholders of their respective UEM Land shares of RM0.50 each for new ordinary shares of RM1.00 each in UEM World Berhad, on the basis of four UEM Land shares held for one new UEM World share (the exercise has been known as the "privatisation of UEM Land");

(iii) A reduction in the issued share capital of UEM Land after the privatisation of UEM Land from RM1,561.9 million, comprising 3,123.7 million shares of RM0.50 each, to RM780.9 million, comprising 1,561.9 million shares of RM0.50 each;

(iv) The acquisitions of the following core businesses and designated investments by UEM World from UEM:

- 71,194,325 ordinary shares of RM1.00 each in CIMA for a purchase consideration of RM170.1 million;
- 498,315,593 ordinary shares of RM1.00 each in Intria Berhad (now known as UEM Builders Berhad, UEM Builders) for a purchase consideration of RM418.4 million;
- 20,000,000 ordinary shares of RM1.00 each and 44,307,740 5 per cent redeemable cumulative preference shares of RM1.00 each in Kualiti Alam Holdings Sdn Bhd (now known as UEM Environment Sdn Bhd, UEM Environment) for a purchase consideration of RM180.0 million;
- 98,795,600 ordinary shares of 25 sen each in Kinta Kellas plc, for a purchase consideration of RM78.0 million; and
- 30,980,466 ordinary shares of RM1.00 each in Pharmaniaga for a purchase consideration of RM124.9 million.

- On 27 March 2003, UEM World entered into a Heads of Agreement (HOA) with UEM Land, UEM and UEM Builders to implement the above SOA involving the privatisation of UEM Land, restructuring of the SPV Bond and acquisitions of core businesses and designated investments (known as the Scheme).

- As mentioned earlier, UEM World changed its name from Global Converge Sdn Bhd to UEM World Sdn Bhd and subsequently became a public limited company and assumed the name of UEM World Bhd on 8 and 12 September 2003 respectively.

- Trading of UEM Land shares was suspended on 17 October 2003 after the Order of the High Court of Malaya sanctioning the SOA obtained on 6 October 2003.

- On 27 October 2003, the privatisation of UEM Land was finalised with the cancellation of all existing issued and paid-up share capital of UEM Land comprising 3,123,729,124 ordinary shares of RM0.50 each pursuant to Section 64 of the Companies Act, 1965, and the issue by UEM Land to the company of 3,123,729,124 new UEM Land shares credited as fully paid up.

- As planned earlier, on 28 October 2003, UEM Land transferred the following listed securities to UEM as consideration for partial redemption of the SPV bond:
  (i) 50,000,000 shares in CAHB;
  (ii) 9,000,000 shares in Camerlin Group Berhad;
  (iii) 97,242,268 shares in Faber Group Berhad;
  (iv) 18,637,800 shares in Park May Berhad;
  (v) 349,112,731 shares in Time; and
  (vi) 31,737,521 warrants in Time.
- As part of the finalisation of UEM World's listing, UEM Land was removed from the Official List of MSEB, and UEM World admitted — in place of UEM Land — with effect from 9.00 a.m., 14 November 2003. UEM World's entire issued and paid up capital of RM1,388,087,086 — comprising 1,388,087,086 UEM World shares — arising from the above Scheme was admitted to the Official List of MSEB, with the listing and quotation of UEM World Shares on the Main Board under the "Construction" rubric.

Sources: CDRC 1999.
　　　freeMalaysia 1999a.
　　　Lopez 1999.
　　　PLUS 2003.
　　　Rabindra Nathan Shearn Delamore & Co, "Insolvency Law Reform: Case study from Malaysia", available from: <http://www.insolvencyasia.com/>.
　　　Renong 2000.
　　　Renong, *Annual Report*, 2001a.
　　　Renong 2001b.
　　　Renong 2003b.
　　　The New Straits Times, 30 July 2001.
　　　The Star, 13 July 2001; 21 Sep. 2001a; 21 Sep. 2001b; 9 Oct. 2001; 11 Dec. 2001; 2 May 2002; 8 May 2002; 28 March 2003.
　　　UEM World 2004a.

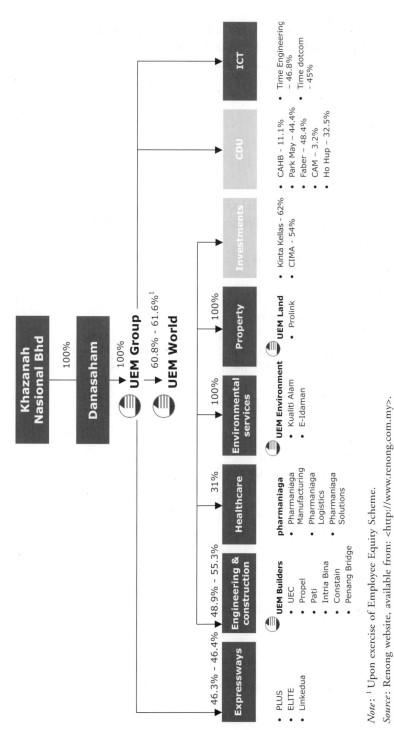

Note: [1] Upon exercise of Employee Equity Scheme.

Source: Renong website, available from: <http://www.renong.com.my>.

Fig. 7.2 UEM-Renong Group Eventual Structure (after Re-branding), as at 30 April 2004

Box 7.6 Comparison of UEM's Effective Equity Interests Held, as at 30 April 2003 and 31 March 2004 (%)

UEM had effective equity interests in the following companies:	As at 30 Apr 2003	As at 31 Mar 2004
UEM World Bhd*	NA	51
Expressways		
• PLUS Expressway Bhd*	46	46
• Projek Lebuhraya Utara Selatan Bhd	NA	46
• Expressway Lingakaran Tengah Sdn Bhd (ELITE)	100	100
• Linkedua (Malaysia) Bhd	100	100
Engineering and Construction		
• UEM Builders Bhd (formerly known as Intria Bhd)*	45	26
• UEM Construction Sdn Bhd (formerly known as UE Construction Sdn Bhd, UEC)	100	26
• Projek Penyelenggaraan Lebuhraya Bhd (PROPEL)	56	26
• Pati Sdn Bhd (PATI)	100	26
• Penang Bridge Sdn Bhd	NA	26
• UEM Development India Pvt. Ltd	100	26
Healthcare		
• Pharmaniaga Bhd*	31	16
Environmental Services		
• UEM Environment Sdn Bhd (formerly known as Kualiti Alam Holdings Sdn Bhd)	100	51
Property Development		
• UEM Land Sdn Bhd (formerly known as Renong Bhd)	49	51
• Prolink Development Sdn Bhd	NA	33

Information and Communications Technology

- Time Engineering Bhd*   46.8   46
- Teras Teknologi Sdn Bhd   100   100
- Krisbiz Sdn Bhd   100   100
- Infrared Advanced Technologies Sdn Bhd   75   75
- Rangkaian Segar Sdn Bhd (RSSB)   31   38
- Time dotcom Bhd*   45   20

Others

- United Services & Automotive   100   100
  Industries Sdn Bhd
- Kuad Sdn Bhd (Kuad)   70   70
- UEM Genisys Sdn Bhd (UEG)   51   51
- Faber Group Bhd*   48.4   46
- Gapima Sdn Bhd   37   37
- Kinta Kellas Public Limited Company*   62   32
- Cement Industries of Malaysia Bhd*   54   27
- Park May Bhd*#   44.4   25
- Ho Hup Construction Company   32   17
  Bhd*

Notes: * Public listed companies.
        # Company pending divestment.
Source: UEM World website, "Corporate Profile", available from:
        <http://www.uemworld.com/>.

major shareholders of the Renong group. To aggravate matters, many benefits of the bail out would have gone to the Renong group's foreign creditors, to whom at least billions of ringgit were owed. Furthermore, since many major shareholders of Renong and UEM were foreigners (often using nominees), the Renong group bail out proposal would benefit them as well. In short, Malaysian public funds would be used to allow the owners of Renong, including its foreign shareholders, to walk away with their asset value partly restored at public expense, and to pay off their creditors, including foreigners.

      The government had already agreed to the CDRC-approved bail out in the late 1990s proposed by Renong — prepared by Renong consultants, Credit Suisse First Boston (CSFB) merchant bank — to, among other things, extend the North-South Highway toll concession by five years (albeit at slightly lower toll rates), at great cost to the Malaysian government and, ultimately, to the public. Even though the revised plan removed the government (i.e. sovereign) guarantee for the bonds, a banker involved in the restructuring noted that the government was still indirectly lending support by allowing higher toll-rates, writing off government loans and waiving tax payments due (Lopez 1999).

First, the government would postpone taking over the North-South Highway, UEM's main cash cow, as well as the revenue stream from it, by five years. Under its original build-operate-transfer (BOT) arrangement, the Highway was supposed to revert to the government 25 years after the anticipated completion date specified in the contract. However, PLUS succeeded in completing the Highway ahead of time, but at considerably higher cost. Hence, PLUS was able to begin collecting tolls earlier than anticipated, though the additional revenue from early completion is unlikely to have covered the additional costs incurred. The concession extension was partially mitigated by some modest reduction of the toll rates to be imposed.

Second, the government agreed to transfer the RM824 million soft loan provided to finance completion of the Second Link from PLUS to Linkedua, who are unlikely to be in a position to pay back, while the Renong group would get to keep the contiguous 27,000 acres it received at a nominal price of just over RM1 per square foot to cross-subsidise the Second Link. Although the Second Link was not expected to be profitable in the short term, Renong had made a bid for it with a view to lucrative profits from the surrounding land obtained at a specially discounted price. The government gave the group more than 42 square miles (26,880 acres) of what became much more valuable land around Gelang Patah on the Malaysian side of the new bridge to Singapore. The CSFB proposal suggested that a new Infrastructure Development Corporation (IDC) take over the Second Link, while the Renong group would get to keep the land, some of which it had already resold for more than RM10 per square foot, i.e. ten times the price it paid for it! Also dominant in the consortium that took over Keretapi Tanah Melayu (KTM), the peninsula's railway, Renong also suggested that IDC take over the generally unprofitable railway services while Renong and other consortium members would retain the lucrative railway land for itself.

Third, the government agreed to forego future tax payments by PLUS of RM4.5 billion, although the government already had a large budgetary deficit and had cut public spending for health, education and welfare, among others.

The proposal thus sought to "nationalise" or "socialise" the Renong group's debts and liabilities, while allowing Renong to retain its profitable privatised assets, enhanced by a valuable tax exemption. Thus, the case is a bail out as the group was unable to repay its debt. Clearly, it could not generate sufficient revenue without either government subsidy or other financial assistance.

Despite not formally guaranteeing the bonds, the government virtually or implicitly guaranteed the RM8.4 billion in zero-coupon bonds to replace the Renong group's debts to lenders; the main bondholders are Malaysian banks and insurance companies as well as the Employee Provident Fund (EPF), i.e. a public fund under government control. Hence, the RM8.4 billion zero-coupon bond issue *could* lead to a government bail out in the future (Lopez 1999). At a 9.4 per cent compound interest rate, one "bullet" repayment of RM16 billion will be made for the zero coupon bonds when due.

UEM then generously terminated Halim Saad's "put option" to buy back the shares he sold to UEM in late 1997 for RM3.2 billion, which came due in February 2001 (Gunasegaram 2001a; Lim 2002; KLSE 2001), on 21 November 2001. Renong Berhad claimed that the put option on the Renong shares granted by UEM to Halim was a matter between UEM and Halim only. Obviously, it raises questions as to why the option was not exercised to alleviate UEM's financial situation. Thus, the socialisation of corporate debt indirectly involved the socialisation of private debt. Exempting Halim from honouring his put option not only "cheats" those who invested on the basis of his commitment, but more generally undermines the credibility of such commitments, and thus, investor confidence. According to a report by Affin-UOB Research, "Terminating the put option however is a major disappointment for it again raises the issue of corporate governance in Malaysia, which was perceived to have improved of late. This could affect near-term market sentiment" (Jalil 2000; see also Gunasegaram 2001a; *The Star*, 28 June 2001).

Also, will PLUS (which guaranteed the bond), Renong and UEM be able to make the bullet repayment due when the bond is due? According to C. Rajandram (CDRC chairman up to 30 June 2001), repayment should not be problematic owing to PLUS's strong cash flow and other assets. Rajandram noted that Prolink Development Sdn Bhd (Prolink) [the group's big property developer in Johor] and Commerce Asset-Holdings Bhd (CAHB) [Malaysia's second largest banking group] were worth RM4.5 billion and RM2 billion respectively in 2000[42] (Tharmaratnam 2000). Bondholders seem to be securely covered since both Renong and UEM have pledged assets worth more than the current value of PLUS bonds issued as collateral for these bonds, and the assets would belong to PLUS, which could then "unlock" the value of the assets to repay bondholders if both companies do not repay bondholders (*The Star*, 21 September 2001a).

According to *freeMalaysia* (1999a), "the value of the assets of the Renong group [were] worth RM8 billion and that's before deducting the several more billion [owed] in debt remaining by other group affiliates like PUTRA, Prolink, Time Engineering Bhd and Faber. Watch for their bail outs, too." However, these arguments were made before the government took over UEM and listed its cash cow, PLUS, to raise funds to redeem the bonds before 2006, and PUTRA was taken over by the government in November 2001 after the government had effectively taken over UEM. Valuing PLUS at RM15 billion, listing PLUS and selling 30 per cent of its shares, should generate about RM4 billion in cash. Thus redeeming RM4 billion of the RM8.4 billion bonds, instead of waiting until 2006, would save on "interest" payments (Tharmaratnam 2000).[43]

In October 2001, through Danasaham, a wholly-owned subsidiary of Khazanah, the government took control of UEM and now controls 100 per cent of UEM's equity (UEM, in turn, has a 32 per cent stake in Renong[44]) following a successful voluntary general offer (*The Star*, 11 December 2001). UEM was officially de-listed from the KLSE (now known as Malaysian Securities Exchange Bhd) (MSEB) on 15 October 2001 (Renong 2001b). With this "nationalisation" of UEM, the government is now in a position to restructure UEM and Renong.[45] [For a look at the various debt-restructuring efforts planned and undertaken by the government, see Box 7.3.]

In December 2001, UEM, now directly controlled by the government, announced a major corporate and debt restructuring plan to reduce the group's debts of RM30.3 billion to RM14 billion by the middle of 2003 (*The Star*, 2 May 2002). The strategies include selling non-core and non-strategic assets — PUTRA being one — and listing corporations such as PLUS, Time dotCom Bhd and Prolink.

Trying to raise funds, Renong resorted to listing Time dotCom Bhd (Time dotCom). If things had been left to "private market players", the share would have been undersubscribed. However, another bail out had been arranged; it managed to raise the money it wanted because the Employees' Provident Fund (EPF) and the civil servants' pension fund had paid over RM1 billion to underwrite the deal (Ong 2001b). With an initial public offering (IPO) price of RM3.30, justified by the earlier tech boom, the company saw its share price plunge nearly 30 per cent with its market debut in mid-March 2001. The civil servants' pension fund (Kumpulan Wang Amanah Pencen, KWAP) paid nearly RM1 billion (US$270 million) to take a 10.8 per cent share in the company while the EPF took a 3.2 per cent share (Ong 2001a).

On 29 January 2002, Khazanah submitted an offer to Bumiputra-Commerce Trustee Bhd, the trustee for the USD bonds to buy the outstanding US$162 million principal of Time Engineering Bhd's US$250 million zero-coupon USD bonds 1996/2001 at a 10 per cent discount (*The Star*, 30 January 2002c). Danasaham — a unit of the government investment arm, Khazanah — now owns UEM, which in turn holds a controlling stake in Time Engineering. Hence, it comes as no surprise that Khazanah decided to step in to repay the bondholders. As such, Khazanah — instead of the bondholders — now has the right to sell the collateral, in the event of any payment default by Time Engineering. Will Khazanah indeed press for the sale of assets by Time Engineering at an opportune time to redeem the bonds? Doing otherwise would once again lead to accusations of a bail out with taxpayers again expected to bear the costs of a bond default.

There is now concern as to whether the government will carry out asset sales to reduce the debts, and not merely resort to issuing long-term government debt, and whether the government will take over default papers (i.e. bonds that corporations are unable to redeem)

Box 7.7   Selective UEM-Renong Asset Disposal Plans and Exercises

Prior to Khazanah's Takeover of UEM in July 2001

- Prior to Khazanah's takeover of UEM via Danasaham, Renong disposed several smaller assets, including its interests in UB Co-Management Sdn Bhd, and all subsidiaries of Renong Solution (M) Sdn Bhd (Renong 2000).

Post-UEM Takeover by Khazanah in July 2001

Asset Disposal Plans

- In its December 2001 disclosure, UEM said it would divest six non-strategic assets, namely PUTRA, Park May Bhd (Park May); Cement Industries of Malaysia Bhd (CIMA); Ho Hup Construction Bhd (Ho Hup); Commerce Asset-Holdings Bhd (CAHB), in which Renong has a 12.1 per cent equity stake); and Crest Petroleum Bhd (Crest) (*The Star*, 25 February 2002).
- Confusion may arise since these corporations were previously identified in Renong's corporate structure, or are direct subsidiaries of Renong, but are only considered as part of cross-shareholdings by UEM. With the takeover of UEM by the government, Renong no longer had any stake in UEM, while UEM still had a 31 per cent stake in Renong. As such, the UEM restructuring plan encompasses the restructuring of Renong and includes the disposal of Renong subsidiaries.
- Analysts had speculated earlier that the fund-raising programme "to unlock the value of various assets under the UEM/Renong group" (to retire some PLUS bonds) would most likely come from divesting (in the first stage) stakes in CIMA (54 per cent), Pharmaniaga Bhd or Pharma (31 per cent) and Ho Hup (32.5 per cent) — all subsidiaries or affiliates of UEM. The companies in the Renong stable to be sold in the first tranche were Crest (38.6 per cent Renong stake) and CAHB (12.4 per cent) (*The New Straits Times*, 30 July 2001).
- According to UEM chief executive officer (and managing director) and Renong (executive) vice-chairman Abdul Wahid Omar, Renong planned to sell CAHB (the country's number 2 lender); oil and gas company, Crest; bus operator, Park May; phone unit, Time

Engineering Bhd (Time Engineering)[46] and hotel operator, Faber Group Bhd (Faber) to cut RM8.7 billion in debt (*The Star*, 17 January 2002).

Asset Disposal Exercises

- PUTRA was the first company to be divested and taken over by SPNB in November 2001 as part of the government's plan to rationalise the transportation system in the Kelang Valley (*The Star*, 25 February 2002).
- Park May was the second asset disposed off — by way of a reverse takeover by Kumpulan Kenderaan Malaysia Bhd (KKMB), that acquired a 63.7 per cent stake in Park May for RM128 million via a share swap (Barrock 2002).[47]
- Prolink Seaview Sdn Bhd — a wholly-owned subsidiary of Prolink Development Sdn Bhd, which in turn, was a 64 per cent owned subsidiary of Renong Bhd — completed the disposal of 91.104 ha of freehold land held under PTD 71047 and PTD 71065 in Mukim Pulai, Johor Baru, for RM80,957,556.35 to Ho Hup Jaya Sdn Bhd on 9 May 2002 (*The Sun*, 11 May 2002).
- The Wisma Time building was sold in October 2002 to Khazanah for RM62.05 million, 7 per cent above the valuation price of RM58 million (*The New Straits Times*, 5 November 2002; YY Property Solutions 2002).
- Ranhill Bhd proposed to acquire EPE Power Corp Bhd (EPE) — in conjunction with EPE's proposed corporate and debt restructuring exercise, and Ranhill's desire to expand into the power generation business and related construction & engineering business — in December 2002 by first, buying 60 per cent stake, or 2.94 million ordinary shares at RM1.00 each, in Penjanaan EPE-Time Sdn Bhd (PET), a 40 per cent stake or 4 million shares at RM1.00 each in Powertron Resources Sdn Bhd (PRSB), and PRSB's RM11.6 million (nominal value) of outstanding Convertible Unsecured Loan Stocks (CULS), all for RM54.35 million, and then selling these assets to EPE for RM54.35 million to be satisfied by the issuance of 54.35 million new ordinary shares at RM1.00 each in EPE. This would enable Ranhill Bhd to own a 90.06 per cent equity interest in EPE (Ranhill Bhd, Announcement, 27 December 2002). PET and Powertron are both owned by EPE's parent, Time Engineering Bhd (*The New Straits Times*, 30 December 2002).

The above proposals were approved by Ranhill's shareholders on 25 August 2003 (Ranhill 2003).

- The proposed disposal of UEM Land's entire 29,222,203 ordinary shares, or approximately 38.56 per cent equity interest in Crest Petroleum Bhd to Sapura Telecommunications Bhd (Sapura), announced on 15 January 2003, was completed on 21 April 2003 for RM105.2 million (KLSE 2003). Moreover, Sapura had obtained shareholder approval to proceed with a full 100 per cent acquisition of Crest (*The Star*, 9 April 2003). The proceeds from the disposal were utilised by UEM Land to partially redeem the SPV bond.
- The disposal by UEM Land of 1,637,500 ordinary shares of RM1.00 each in Malaysian Technology Development Corporation Sdn Bhd (MTDC) to Khazanah for a cash consideration of RM212,875.00 was completed on 4 April 2003.
- TimeCel Sdn Bhd, a subsidiary of Time dotCom Bhd, was sold to Maxis Communications Bhd for RM1.47 billion in May 2003 (Disini Network website, 13 May 2003).
- On 8 July 2003, Renong Bhd via wholly owned subsidiary, Fleet Group Sdn Bhd, disposed of its 6.17 per cent stake in Commerce Asset-Holding Bhd (CAHB) to various institutional investors for RM3.76 per share and raised RM594.08 million in the process. Renong will gain RM236.986 million from the sale and save on interest expenses of approximately RM56.1 million annually after redeeming part of its SPV bonds (*The New Straits Times*, 9 July 2003; *The Star*, 9 July 2003).

Sources: Barrock 2002.
Disini Network 2003.
KLSE 2003.
Ranhill Bhd 2002; 2003.
Renong 2000.
The New Straits Times, 30 July 2001; 5 Nov. 2002; 30 Dec. 2002; 9 July 2003.
The Star, 25 Feb. 2002; 9 Apr. 2003; 9 July 2003.
The Sun, 11 May 2002.
UEM World 2004a.
YY Property Solutions 2002.

which could have been resolved via market solutions (i.e. letting the private bondholders issue a petition to sell assets pledged in case of default). The latter measures imply "socialisation" of the bail out costs — via the government — to taxpayers *if* insufficient value is obtained from the assets upon maturity. So far, the government claims to be sticking to its plan to dispose of non-core and non-strategic assets to resolve the UEM/Renong group debt. As at 31 May 2003, major assets that had been divested by Renong include PUTRA, Park May, EPE Power, Crest Petroleum Bhd and TimeCel Sdn Bhd. [Box 7.7 reviews progress so far.]

Evaluation of Corporate (Debt) Restructuring

The debt restructuring plan for the UEM/Renong group sought to pare debt to a more sustainable level and to enable Renong to return to profitability. For a brief chronology of the group's debt restructuring plan, see Box 7.5 above. The operational restructuring measures for individual subsidiaries or affiliates of UEM and Renong will not be discussed here.

The main objective of the UEM/Renong group restructuring exercise has been to pare its huge debt, thereby reducing interest costs and improving its balance sheet and profitability. [See Box 7.8 for a summary of Renong's earnings for financial year 1997, 1998, 1999, 2000, 2001 and a brief review of its corporate performance from 1998 till 2001.] The group resorted to two main strategies, namely asset disposal[48] and listing subsidiaries with the potential to generate cash to repay debt and to secure working capital. In January 2002, the Renong group expected to turn a profit in fiscal 2003 by selling assets and focusing on its property unit (Prolink Development Sdn Bhd, Prolink), one of the nation's biggest landowners (*The Star*, 17 January 2002).[49] The group managed to post an unaudited net profit of RM538 million for the 18 months ending 31 December 2002 (Table 7.6). Renong's return to profitability was largely due to channelling the entire proceeds of RM1.39 billion from disposal of its stake in United Engineers (M) Bhd (UEM) to partially redeem the Renong SPV bonds. This move contributed to interest savings of RM159 million for the 18-month period (*The Sun*, 1 March 2003).

Box 7.8   Renong-UEM   Group   Post-crisis   Corporate Performance[50]

The performance of the Renong group deteriorated following the Asian financial crisis, except in the financial year ending 30 June 2000. The generally depressed stock and property markets, and weaker overall macroeconomic performance affected final demand, contributing to the group's poor financial performance. From a pre-tax profit of RM703 million for the financial year ending 30 June 1997, the group recorded a pre-tax loss of RM812 million for the following financial year ending 30 June 1998.

The group attributed the poor performance to the credit squeeze that had severely constrained the group's property development projects under Prolink Development Sdn Bhd (Prolink), while tight liquidity adversely affected Prolink's two major land sales totalling RM1.2 billion, with two others aborted. Another factor contributing to weak financial performance was foreign exchange losses due to depreciation of the ringgit against the US dollar, which caused US denominated debt to balloon. Moreover, the increase in interest rates — from 7.46 per cent on 15 August 1997 to 11.04 per cent on 26 June 1998 (Bank Negara Malaysia, *Interbank Interest Rates*)[51] — raised the burden of debt and exacerbated cash flow problems for highly leveraged companies within the group such as PUTRA. The poor performance of the stock market resulted in losses from the sale of investments and the need to make provisions for further diminution in the value of investments, and delayed the IPO of new companies.

The group's financial performance deteriorated further in the financial year ending 30 June 1999, with the group registering a pre-tax loss of RM1.26 billion, up by 84 per cent from RM0.81 billion in the previous year. Troubled companies, such as Faber, have contributed to this scenario. In addition, the need to make provisions for the loss in value of assets such as property (whose value had fallen due to depressed property market values), especially Prolink assets, contributed to the group's losses.

Group performance improved considerably in the financial year ending 30 June 2000, with the group registering a pre-tax profit of RM380 million, compared to the huge pre-tax loss of RM1.3 billion for the previous year. This improvement is attributable to restructuring efforts in 1999, which greatly benefited from the improved economic climate in the form of better property values and stock market conditions — making the sale of property by Prolink and IPOs more feasible.

However, the group sank into the red again in the financial year ending 30 June 2001 by recording a large pre-tax loss of RM1.549 billion on the back of provisions for Renong's investments in PUTRA — a write down of PUTRA's value of RM1.032 billion in contingent loss — then expected to be taken over by the government by June 2002. The takeover of PUTRA's asset would result in an estimated net realised value of RM577 million (the difference between the carrying value of the assets of RM1.609 billion and an exceptional loss of approximately RM1.032 billion). Furthermore, the change in status of Faber and Park May from subsidiary to associate companies resulted in a loss due to dilution of RM106 million. Further provision for diminution in the value of quoted warrants of RM83 million also contributed to the loss (Renong 2001a).

For the 18 months ended December 2002, Renong made a net profit of RM538 million from the huge loss of RM1,652 million for financial year ended 2001. Renong's improved financial results were largely attributable to interest savings of RM159 million when Renong channelled the entire proceeds of RM1.39 billion from disposal of its stake in UEM to partially redeem the Renong SPV bonds.

After the privatisation of UEM Land (previously Renong Berhad), restructuring of the SPV bond and acquisitions of core businesses and designated investments, UEM World managed to maintain a healthy profit level of RM314.326 million for the financial year ended 31 December 2003, partly due to its ability to reduce its finance costs substantially to RM194.56 million from RM623.666 million in the previous 18 months ended 31 December 2002. The finance costs "savings" were offset by the reduced gains from disposal of investments, which recorded RM310.682 million, as opposed to RM1,322.196 million for the 18 months ending 31 December 2002. Nonetheless, UEM World gained' RM287.983 million after being exempted from paying interest on its SPV bond. All in all, UEM World's revenue generating capability has remained relatively stable, registering RM359.817 million for the financial year ending 31 December 2003, when compared with the 18 months to 31 December 2002 revenue figure of RM356.175 million (UEM World 2004a). UEM World continues to show steady progress by registering a net profit of RM25.511 million for the first quarter ending 31 March 2004 (UEM World 2004, *Quarterly Report on Consolidated Results for the First Quarter Ended 31 March 2004*).

Table 7.6   Renong Earnings/Losses for Financial Years 1996/97 to 2001/2*

	FY96/97	FY97/98	FY98/99	FY99/00	FY00/01	18 mths ended 31.12.02
Operating Profits/ (Losses) (RM m)	342	(806)	(1,533)	(23)	(1,678)	793
Profits/(Losses) before Tax (RM m)	703	(812)	(1,265)	380	(1,549)	591
Profits/(Losses) after Tax (RM m)	550	(948)	(1,352)	280	(1,647)	543
Profits/(Losses) to Shareholders (RM m)	470	(782)	(1,411)	249	(1,652)	538
Net Earnings/(Loss) per Share (sen)	21.6	(35.2)	(63.2)	10.8	(71.1)	22.70
Dividend per Share (sen)	–	–	–	–	–	–
Net Tangible Assets per Share (*sen*)	173.6	93.1	45.1	54.4	(55.6)	5.9

Note: * For financial year ended 30 June.
Sources: Renong, *Annual Report*, various years.

These improvements in Renong's corporate performance can partly be attributed to the various financial and operational restructuring exercises undertaken to pare down the Renong/UEM group debts and improve its financial standings. For example, in early 1999, PLUS issued RM8.4 billion of zero-coupon bonds and then lent the proceeds of RM5.4 billion to Renong and RM3.0 billion to UEM to settle creditor claims (CDRC 1999) (see Box 7.5 above). When Khazanah took over UEM and, hence, PLUS in 2001, the immediate objective was to reduce group debt — mainly the RM8.5 billion PLUS bonds issued to refinance debt — to a more sustainable level, and to improve PLUS's valuation before seeking listing. According to then UEM Managing Director, Dato' Dr Ramli Mohamad, "it makes no sense for UEM to allow the PLUS bonds to run to full maturity in 2006 if we can afford to reduce debt by repaying them earlier, particularly as UEM and Renong will jointly owe a total of RM16 billion if we allow interest accumulation to run over the full seven-year term ... If we are successful in refinancing the PLUS debt, depending on the discount rate, the total equity value of PLUS could be in excess of RM15 billion. The size of the IPO has not yet been determined, but as an example, a 25 per cent divestment through listing could yield as much as RM3.75 billion. Since UEM's total PLUS bond debt is currently only RM3 billion, there are therefore obvious benefits to be gained in settling the Bonds as early as possible" (Renong 2000). [For details, see Box 7.5.]

The listing of PLUS in mid-2002, was expected to be popular, as the investing public could buy stock in Malaysia's largest expressway operator, which regularly generated large cash flows, had low risk and yielded steady growth (see also Gunasegaram 2002b). PLUS had been the most successful toll concession in Malaysia; in the UEM stable,[52] PLUS's growth has been between 1.5 to 2 times Malaysia's GDP growth rate (*The Star*, 2 May 2002). However, with the relatively slow progress of UEM's asset divestiture, as part of the group's debt restructuring programme, the listing of PLUS was postponed until after mid-2002, since its huge outstanding debts would adversely affect PLUS's valuation (see Nuryushida 2002). By deferring listing, PLUS could benefit from a stock market recovery after mid-2002.

PLUS's listing on the Main Board of the KLSE materialised in 17 July 2002 when it listed all five billion ordinary shares at RM2.65 each. Malaysian and foreign institutional investors got an institutional offer price of RM2.55 per share, which gave them a 10 sen premium per share, while retail investors subscribed at a 35.5 sen premium at RM2.295 per share (PLUS 2003). The listing of PLUS Expressway Bhd made it the sixth largest company on the KLSE and the biggest highway operator in Southeast Asia (*UEM-Renong Group Corporate Newsletter*, Inaugural issue, January 2003). More than a year later, PLUS's share price closed roughly 3 per cent lower than its initial public offer price of RM2.65 at RM2.57 on 12 September 2003 (*The Star*, 15 September 2003).

In 1999, Renong had issued Renong SPV bonds as part of its debt restructuring plan, or refinancing strategy, facilitated by the CDRC. (See Box 7.5 above.) However, considering the high interest burden, early redemption of the Renong SPV bonds — via structured and systematic disposal of group assets — was considered desirable and has been actively pursued. However, the slowdown from 2001 and depressed stock market has delayed pursuing this line of action. The Renong group debt of RM9.9 billion as of 30 June 2001 was mainly due to the Renong SPV bonds of RM5.1 billion and PUTRA's RM4.1 billion debt (Renong 2001a).[53]

Renong has fared relatively well in terms of asset disposal as it has managed to dispose of two large assets, namely PUTRA and Park May, besides other smaller ones, including its interests in UB Co-Management Sdn Bhd and all subsidiaries of Renong Solution (M) Sdn Bhd, to help alleviate Renong's debt situation. (See Box 7.7 for additional information.) The nationalisation of PUTRA seemed inevitable since the mammoth project with a long gestation period, had entailed huge investment outlays, and hence, financing costs as well as fare subsidisation.

PUTRA's nationalisation has helped reduce NPLs in the banking system and trimmed Renong group debt, possibly hastening its return to profitability. With the takeover (and management of assets) of PUTRA by Syarikat Prasarana Negara Bhd (SPNB), the Renong group debt of around RM10 billion, as at June 2001, would be reduced by RM4.1 billion. Following the partial redemption of the SPV bonds issued by PLUS, and the takeover by SPNB, debt would decline to just over RM4.5 to RM4.6 billion (*The Star*, 28 December 2001).

While the disposal of Park May did not involve any cash inflow,[54] the group should still benefit by relinquishing the loss-making Park May to KKMB whose core competence is in transportation. KKMB got a listed vehicle,[55] while Park May increased its chances of enhancing cash flow and future earnings in the long term.

Apart from deciding on how best to settle the RM8.5 billion PLUS bonds, most corporations under the Renong umbrella are loss-making and debt-laden, with many having defaulted on their debt service payments. For example, Time Engineering Bhd defaulted on the second third[56] and fourth tranches of its US$250 million bond, which matured on 5 December 2001 (*The Star*, 30 January 2002c). Failure to redeem the remaining US$162 million bonds would result in penalty interest of two per cent per annum and give lenders the right to foreclose on loan collateral — the collateral pledged by Time Engineering to secure the bonds include 55 per cent of power producer EPE Power Corp (EPE), 16 per cent of Renong and 15 per cent of cellular network operator, Time dotCom Bhd[57] — worth about RM1.2 billion (*The Star*, 20 December 2001b).[58]

Time Engineering Bhd and its controlling company, UEM fought hard to avoid foreclosure of their loan collateral, but their proposals for an extension — put forth on 4 December 2001 — were flatly rejected by most, if not all bondholders.[59] This led Khazanah to offer to buy all outstanding bonds of US$162 million (or RM615 million) for 90 per cent of their original value (Tan 2002).[60] If the bondholders accepted this, then Time Engineering would not have to sell its assets in the immediate future. However, Time Engineering only intended to seek Khazanah's "assistance" if it failed to reach an agreement with bondholders. In January 2002, Time Engineering unveiled a new plan (superseding the one unveiled on 4 December 2001), involving asset sale in three tranches on 5 December 2002, 2003, and 2004, to redeem the bonds in three years.[61] If the bondholders reject Time Engineering's new proposal — involving a full payment of the amount outstanding — and choose to accept Khazanah's offer to buy over the bonds from them at a "discount", then Time Engineering would probably not have to dispose of more assets in the near future.

Another heavily indebted corporation in the group was Faber. According to Faber chairman, Datuk Anwar Haji, the group would sell its hotels to repay RM1.8 billion worth of bonds maturing in 2005 (*The Star*, 12 December 2001). Renong's listing strategy has been less successful — Time dotCom IPO shares were grossly under-subscribed, but had been underwritten by EPF and KWAP for more than RM1 billion (Ong 2001b).

Construction activity contracted by about 20 per cent on average compared to a year ago from first quarter 1998 through second quarter 1999. In subsequent quarters, the government's pump-priming initiatives presumably contributed to the nascent recovery of the construction sector, which is one of the core businesses of UEM-Renong group. Nevertheless, the construction industry still failed to recover from the pre-Asian-crisis (1992–96) average growth pace of about 15 per cent. During the first three quarters of 2002, construction activity only grew by about 3 per cent on average over a year ago. In the fourth quarter of 2002, however, the growth rate was roughly flat compared to a year ago. To be sure, the pace of recovery, while still lacklustre, was roughly in the 1 to 3 per cent range in the four quarters of 2003 (Bank Negara Malaysia, *Monthly Statistical Bulletin,* September 2004).

For the Renong group to turn a profit by 2003 (as projected), apart from improvements in consumer demand and the economic climate, a confluence of factors — including accelerated disposal of non-core assets (dependent on the economic and stock market environments), focus on core businesses and competencies, and improvements in operational processes as well as management planning and decision making — would be necessary.[62] Renong managed to improve on its own forecast by registering a net profit of RM538 million for the 18 months ended 31 December 2002.

To further consolidate and ensure continued profitability, the Renong-UEM Group announced a new corporate restructuring plan on 27 March 2003. The new plan aims to ensure the long-term viability of the Renong group by addressing Renong's balance sheet, paring down its debt and improve long-term earnings prospects. The plan also avoids duplication and potential conflicts of interest in the group's corporate structure by streamlining the group into four core activities. These activities will include creating a formidable engineering and construction unit headed by Intria Bhd (to be renamed UEM Builders Bhd) and refocusing Renong (to be renamed UEM Land Sdn Bhd) to manage the property business (Renong 2003b). The other two core businesses are healthcare, to be led by Pharmaniaga Bhd, and environmental services, which will be spearheaded by Kualiti Alam Holdings Sdn Bhd (to be renamed UEM Environment Sdn Bhd).

According to one consultant from the Minority Shareholder Watchdog Group (MSWG), the proposed restructuring plan is simply an asset reshuffling exercise that does not involve "significant" injection of funds or projects into companies (*The New Straits Times,* 14 April 2003), in effect transferring the supposed "bad apples" from Renong to parent company, UEM, while the relatively better companies valued at RM944.4 million[63] will go to UEM World. This should augur well for Renong since without the restructuring plan, it (with a change of name or otherwise) would have "ceased to exist".

The new plan appears to be more focused, with only four core business units, instead of six, as proposed under the earlier plan announced in December 2001. However, the sale of Crest Petroleum Bhd to Sapura Telecommunications Bhd for RM105.2 million — announced in January 2003, but completed in April 2003 — could be disadvantageous for Renong in the long run as Crest Petroleum Bhd (Crest) has not been making a loss, but instead, has good business prospects, especially in light of the post-war Iraq war oil situation. Even though the RM105.2 million proceeds from the divestment of Crest would save interest payment expenses by approximately RM10.0 million per annum — if the proceeds are used to partially redeem the Renong SPV bonds — and provide a one-time gain of RM22.2 million (Renong 2003a), this must be balanced against the loss of future revenue due to the disposal of Crest. However, the overall sentiment is positive, given that the group is making tentative steps to reorganise and refocus its business units and dispose of non-core and/or loss-making entities to be handled by other specialised companies, as in the case of Park May.

The Renong group conveniently ignored the option of collecting on the put option due in February 2001 made by Halim Saad to UEM (*The New Straits Times*, 14 April 2003). If the money had been repaid by Halim, it would have provided much needed funds, allowing greater room for manoeuvre and reorganisation of the Group.

The restructuring plan has generally been perceived as a positive and proactive move to reorganise and streamline the group's financial and operational position. Even so, the MSWG argues, from Renong minority shareholders' standpoint, that the move had made minority shareholders worse off — by way off share dilution — compared to Intria and PROPEL (*The Star*, 29 March 2003a; *The Star*, 1 April 2003). With respect to the dilution issue, according to the UEM-Renong group, Renong shareholders will exchange four Renong shares, with a par value of 50 sen each, for one UEM World share, with a par value of RM1.00 each, to be issued at a price of RM1.60, with Renong's listed status being transferred to UEM World. Thus, each Renong share is now valued at 40 sen (*The Star*, 1 April 2003).

Renong's shareholders will now hold shares in UEM World, which has been reorganised into four core activities supposedly capable of generating over RM100 million in net profit (*The Star*, 29 March 2003b). With the four-for-one share swap scheme, Renong's current shareholders' stakes will be reduced by three quarters from 3,123.7

million Renong shares to 780.9 million UEM shares. Moreover, with the additional issue of up to 628.9 million ordinary UEM World shares to acquire targeted companies, there would be a dilution of Renong's current minority shareholders' stakes of over 40 per cent (*The New Straits Times*, 14 April 2003)

Shareholders of Intria and Propel are better off compared to Renong's because they were given the option to either cash out of the companies at a premium or benefit from a healthier engineering and construction business in the future, while Renong's shareholders had to take a penalty discount or "haircut". An investment research house expected Intria's net tangible assets to remain at 50 sen per share, with its borrowings reduced to 1.3 times shareholder funds on expanded capital after the issue of new shares post-restructuring. In addition, Intria's four sen earnings per share in 2002 would rise to roughly eight sen after incorporating the pro forma earnings of UE Construction and PROPEL (*The Star*, 29 March 2003a).

All in all, the most recent restructuring plan announced in March 2003 appears to have alleviated the debt situation in Renong and streamlined the group into a more focused entity. Instead of the initial projected listing of UEM World in September 2003, UEM World took over the listing status of Renong Bhd (later known as UEM Land Sdn Bhd) to become the newly listed flagship of the UEM Group, listed on the main board of Bursa Malaysia on 14 November 2003 (*Bernama*, 21 May 2004). Figure 7.3 shows the UEM Group's interests in UEM World and its holdings in the expressway, and information and communications technology businesses as at 30 June 2004. Box 7.6 shows that the UEM group's stakes in most of its business interests has declined by nearly half from its holdings as of 30 April 2003. This divestment strategy may be an effective method to help reduce the group's overall debt in the medium term.

However, Halim Saad's debt remains unresolved and the performance of the restructured group is unlikely to match that in its heyday in the near or medium term. The construction sector has been somewhat sluggish and is expected to remain so for the foreseeable future. The number of loans approved for construction has not increased with the number of houses built or approved. This suggests that the types of houses built are smaller (and therefore, of lower value), or that companies are finding other means to finance their

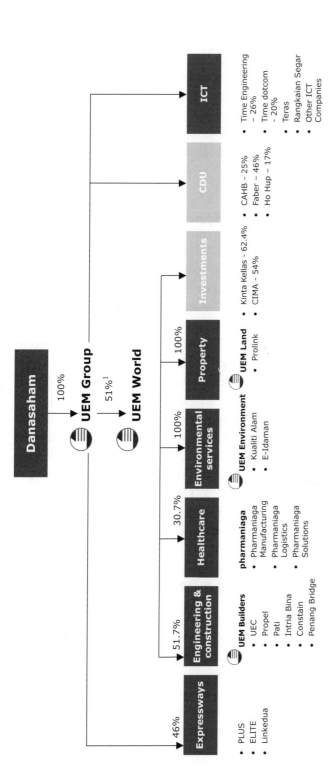

Note: [1] Upon exercise of Employee Equity Scheme.

Source: Renong website, available from: <http://www.renong.com.my>.

Fig. 7.3   UEM Corporate Structure as at 30 June 2004

projects. However, the increase in the number of houses, the growth in cement, concrete, iron and basic steel production and imports of construction materials and mineral products may point to a less anaemic property sector than expected. As such, the respective core businesses will need to strive to further improve cost efficiency and performance, and to reduce (over) reliance on government subsidies and assistance.

The Light Rail Transport (LRT) Systems

Sistem Aliran Ringan Sdn Bhd (STAR) was formed in 1991 to build, own and operate one of three light rail transport (LRT) systems in the Federal Territory of Kuala Lumpur for 60 years, making it the first privately owned LRT company. Construction started in 1994. The two phases were completed for less than the RM3.5 billion budgeted, with the first phase launched in December 1996 and phase two in July 1998 (*The New Straits Times*, 31 August 2001).

Projek Usahasama Transit Ringan Automatik Sdn Bhd (PUTRA) was incorporated in Malaysia on 15 February 1994. The principal activities of PUTRA were to design, construct, finance, operate and maintain the Light Rail Transit (LRT) System 2 and ancillary activities, principally station development. PUTRA began revenue services — as opposed to free trial runs — in (September) 1998, while the city section opened in (June) 1999 (PUTRA, available from: <http://www.subways.net/malaysia/kualalampur.htm>). It now operates the longest line (29km), with a fully automated light rail transit system (*The Star*, 6 March 2002).

Government's Role in STAR and PUTRA Corporate (Debt) Restructuring

According to the government, the takeover of the LRT systems — a reflection of the failure of the privatisation programme — was both necessary and unavoidable because: (1) it involved the public interest (the LRT system being part of the public transportation system); (2) liquidation would allow assets to be divided and sold piecemeal, threatening the transportation system and commuter welfare, and (3) liquidation would mean that employees of STAR and PUTRA would be retrenched. Besides, the public transportation system has been the responsibility of the government through various programmes to provide affordable public services.[64] Also, a government takeover would help reduce the amount of NPLs in the banking system (and the debt of certain conglomerates). PUTRA was a subsidiary of Renong, the centre of the biggest conglomerate with the largest debt in the country (*The Star,* 21 September 2001a; *The Sun,* 2 November 2001).

Besides, the government claimed the 1997–98 Asian crisis[65] and the LRT operators not being allowed to charge higher fares (which would burden the public)[66] were responsible for the failure of the LRT projects to be profitable and financially viable (*Sibexnews,* 29 May 2001). Then Advisor to the Finance Ministry, Datuk Mustapa Mohamed claimed that a thorough analysis and feasibility study had been conducted (taking into account rapid economic growth in the country at that time, traffic congestion in the city, and the likely efficiency and environmental impacts of not improving the traffic situation). The study indicated that the projects were feasible in terms of engineering, finance and profitability. The LRT projects had been undertaken based on these projections. However, the feasibility study had not factored in the possibility of an economic crisis, let alone one of such magnitude, according to him.

Yet, according to a former government minister for the federal territory of Kuala Lumpur, the government was quite aware that the project had a high probability of being unprofitable. To quote Shahrir Samad: "From day one, we knew it wasn't going to be a profitable project. In the end it will be the government that will assume the debts" (Fuller 2000). The government's failure to ensure project viability was compounded by grossly overestimated passenger forecasts (resulting in the operators operating with less than one-third of their forecast demand) and cost overruns (Halcrow Consultants 1999; FinanceAsia.com 26 July 2000). According to the former head of the CDRC, many infrastructure projects did not meet the forecasts, and many were un-bankable, with a wide gap between funding and cash flows (FinanceAsia.com, 27 July 2000).

Moreover, inconsistent policies reduced the chances of the two LRT systems to minimise losses. Prime Minister Mahathir's personal commitment in the car project undermined the viability of the LRT system by promoting personal automobile ownership and construction of privatised highways that have served to limit the use of public transport. The government first postponed and then privatised the LRT system, and did not regulate private vehicle traffic to help create the necessary passenger volume (*The Edge*, 26 August 1996). Consequently, the failure of the LRT system is attributed to poor physical and operational integration into a well-connected public transportation system.

On 1 September 2002, SPNB took over PUTRA's operations and assets (Renong 2003c). [In November 2001, Syarikat Prasarana Nasional Bhd (SPNB) purchased the outstanding debts of STAR and PUTRA totalling about RM5.5 billion[67] (*The Star*, 4 April 2002). In the second phase of the restructuring scheme, SPNB planned to complete the takeover of all assets and operations of STAR and PUTRA by June 2002 (*The Star*, 4 April 2002).[68] For details, refer to Box 7.9.] The bail out [69] of PUTRA helped reduce the huge debt amassed by the UEM-Renong group of more than RM30 billion. Many observers suspect that this represented yet another bail out for its "boss", Halim Saad, and the interests he represents.

Signs of financial weakness (probably reflecting lack of economic viability and/or operational problems) were already apparent when PUTRA defaulted on its RM2 billion loan in 1999. Nonetheless, rather than classify the loan as non-performing, Bank Negara requested creditors — Commerce International Merchant Bankers Bhd (CIMB) and RHB Bank Bhd — to defer labelling the loan "non-performing" in the hope of "containing" the bad debt problem (Ong 2001a). However, such "cover-ups" are difficult to sustain indefinitely, and CIMB eventually served a winding-up petition on PUTRA.

The terms of the PUTRA bail out did not impose any penalty ("haircut") on its shareholders, who had benefited from construction projects worth at least RM1 billion. Hence, a major concern has been the excessive sums spent to save STAR and PUTRA. The initial plan — costing RM6 billion — was met with criticism, especially for reimbursing and even rewarding failure. [Refer to Box 7.5 for details.] The revised plan costing RM5.5 billion seemed less excessive, but apprehensions still abound as actual construction costs are believed to have been much less. An additional concern arises because the existing PUTRA and STAR managements will continue to run the

Box 7.9   Restructuring Measures/Strategies to Renationalise the LRT Systems: Summary

Financial Restructuring

Initial Plan

- On 22 December 2000, the government proposed to issue RM6 billion in bonds to buy the assets of ailing LRT operators, PUTRA and STAR, as part of a plan to overhaul Kuala Lumpur's transportation system (*freeanwar* 2000). According to Fuller (2000), the costs of the bail out were equivalent to about 7 per cent of the entire government budget for the year 2001.
- However, in May 2001, the Finance Minister confirmed that the bail out plan had been put on hold due to a public outcry charging that the assets had been overvalued (*Channelnewsasia*, 29 May 2001) at RM6 billion.

Revised Plan

Phase 1

- On 29 August 2001, the CDRC announced that the government planned to acquire 80 per cent of Kuala Lumpur's light rail systems — run by STAR and PUTRA — leaving Renong Bhd, Taylor Woodrow plc, the state-run pension funds and other shareholders with 20 per cent.
- On 29 August 2001, the CDRC presented a revised plan for the LRT companies to lenders — including Bayerische Landesbank, RHB Bank Bhd, PhileoAllied Bank Bhd and the Employees Provident Fund (EPF). According to a document obtained by Bloomberg News, the government revived a plan to take over two LRT companies and convert US$1.4 billion of their overdue loans into bonds in the nation's biggest ever corporate restructuring (*The Star*, 1 September 2001; 1 October 2001b). SPNB will buy the loans from creditors by issuing bonds to them in four tranches, with maturities of between 5 to 15 years, at coupon rates between 4.00 per cent and 5.40 per cent.[70]
- In November 2001, Syarikat Prasarana Nasional Bhd (SPNB) purchased all the rights to the outstanding debts of STAR and PUTRA, totalling about RM5.5 billion, via the issue of RM5.468 billion of fixed rate serial guaranteed bonds to the two companies' creditors.

- As stipulated in the concession agreement terms, the government would pay PUTRA RM5.2 billion as "project costs", RM4.2 billion of which would be used to settle its debts (*The Star*, 28 December 2001).
- On 7 December 2001, CDRC completed the first phase of the PUTRA/STAR debt restructuring process.

Phase 2

- On 21 February 2002, CIMB filed a winding-up petition to close down STAR for not repaying RM1 billion. CIMB claimed that, together with interest, STAR owed it RM1,051,509,127.16 as of 26 December 2001 under a loan agreement dated 13 August 1993 (*The Sun*, 3 April 2002).
- On 20 March 2002, PUTRA was served two winding-up petitions by Commerce International Merchant Bankers (CIMB) after it failed to pay its RM2 billion loan obligations.[71]
- Both these events prompted the government takeover of PUTRA and STAR. Announcement of the takeover of LRT assets and operations came two days after a winding-up petition dated 21 February 2002 against STAR was filed in the High Court because of its failure to pay in full a loan totalling RM1.05 billion. On 20 March, CIMB also served two winding-up petitions on PUTRA after the latter failed to repay its loan obligations on the RM2 billion commercial financing facilities extended to it (*The Star*, 4 April 2002). SPNB expected to complete the takeover of all assets and operations of STAR and PUTRA by June 2002 (*The Star*, 4 April 2002).
- According to MoF Inc., the assets include all buildings, structures, tracks, electrification, signalling and telecommunications equipment, mechanical equipment, rolling stock, tools, escalators, lifts, safety and power equipment (*The Star*, 4 April 2002). According to MoF Inc., SPNB will take over the entire operating concessions of both companies and will be the sole operator of the country's entire LRT system once the takeover exercise is completed (*The Star*, 4 April 2002).
- On 26 April 2002, the High Court ordered the winding up of PUTRA by appointing liquidators.
- On 1 September 2002, PUTRA's operations and assets were taken over by SPNB.

Differences between the Two Restructuring Phases

- During the first phase, the government did not take over PUTRA or STAR; it merely purchased the loan rights of Star and PUTRA[72] lenders via SPNB (*The Star*, 1 December 2001a).
- During the second phase, the government effectively took over the two LRT systems following their inability to meet their debt obligations after being served winding-up petitions.

Operational Restructuring

- In 2001, STAR embarked on some cost-saving measures, notably to reduce energy consumption and the company's RM10 million annual electricity bills. According to Zainal Abdul Ghani, STAR's target was to achieve a 15 per cent reduction over five years, starting from 2001 (*The Sun*, 12 February 2001).
- According to PUTRA managing director Ridza Abdoh Salleh, PUTRA submitted a proposal to the Government for assistance to double the number of coaches for its trains from 70 (the company then ran 35 trains with two coaches each) to 140 in response to demand,[73] to carry more than 350,000, or even up to 400,000 passengers daily (*The Star*, 6 March 2002).
- With the takeover, the government planned to provide seamless travel for commuters by adopting common ticketing, improving linkages between (stations of) the LRT systems, improving infrastructure, implementing a zoning system and providing a covered walkway at the Masjid Jamek stop (*The Star*, 4 April 2002).
- The government planned to increase the number of carriages on each train from two to three. New lines might be introduced at a later stage in response to increased demand (*The Star*, 4 April 2002).

Sources: *Channelnewsasia*, 29 May 2001.
    CDRC 2001.
    freeanwar 2000.
    Fuller 2000.
    Renong 2001b.
    Renong 2002.
    Renong 2003c.
    The Star, 1 Sep. 2001; 1 Oct. 2001; 1 Dec. 2001a; 4 Dec. 2001; 28 Dec. 2001; 6 Mar. 2002; 22 Mar. 2002; 4 Apr. 2002.
    The Sun, 12 Feb. 2001; 3 Apr. 2002.

LRT systems, seemingly endorsing their performance so far. Some quarters argue that by leasing back the LRT operations to PUTRA and STAR at discounts, the authorities would not have been addressing the basic issues of attracting more passengers and restructuring the loans.

While the managers may know the business better than others, "they should also be made accountable" (*The Sun*, 12 February 2001). The terms of the restructuring plans do not seem to recognise responsibility and demand accountability for past problems. This would be tantamount to socialising losses and liabilities while allowing profits and profitable assets to be privatised. If the managements were not at all to blame for the financial failures, the case can be made to retain them after taking over the companies, rather than lease back the LRT operations to the owners (*The Sun*, 12 February 2001).

By taking over the debts of both PUTRA and STAR, the government reduced the amount of NPLs in the banking system.[74] According to analysts, the discount or "haircut" of RM232 million, or four per cent, for banks that made loans to PUTRA and STAR was relatively small, and the banks got a good deal receiving government-guaranteed debt in return (*The Star*, 1 December 2001b).[75] It is widely believed that the banks got off lightly because they had been encouraged by the government to lend to the LRT companies, raising serious doubts about the privatisation policy, bank lending practices and their implications for the likely accumulation of "contingent liabilities" by the government. However, there is considerable anecdotal evidence that some banks, including foreign banks in Malaysia such as Hong Kong and Shanghai Bank Bhd (HSBC), had been enthusiastic about such lending and needed no encouragement.

Evaluation of Corporate Restructuring

According to Halcrow[76] regional director C. Paul Buchanan, who prepared a report on the weaknesses of the Kuala Lumpur public transport system, the lack of integration among the five public transport operators — PUTRA, STAR, Intrakota, Park May and KTM Komuter — has limited public traffic volume, leading to a shortfall in passengers[77] and revenue, causing financial problems for both PUTRA and STAR, and the other three operators (*Asiafeatures* 2000). Even if passenger volumes increase, the gain in revenue may be offset by lower fares and the burden of financial and depreciation costs.[78] Another transport sector analyst argues that the main problems have been a poor business strategy, unfavourable fare structures[79] and poor integration between the LRT stations and feeder bus (*The Sun*, 12 February 2001).

Moreover, according to the Malaysian Centre for Transportation Studies (MaCTRANS) Research and Consultancy co-ordinator, Zakaria Ahmad, the main problem with KL's integrated public transportation system lies in the fact that the authorities themselves — the Entrepreneur Development Ministry (KPUN), the Ministry of Transport (MOT), the Public Works Department (JKR) and the Economic Planning Unit (EPU) — are not integrated. There are so many authorities — from the KPUN to the MOT, the JKR and the EPU — that they impede proper coordination. According to Zakaria, "The two most important ones, the KPUN and MOT, do not work hand in hand. That is why we proposed to the EPU that there should be only one ministry in charge of public transport, a Ministry of Land Transportation. This new ministry would handle the planning, organisation and regulation of public transportation, as well as the issuing of licences to public transport companies. While this creates the problem of having to establish a separate ministry to cover other forms of transport, a single body to oversee land transport is something all correspondents agreed on. A less radical suggestion made over the last 10 years has been the establishment of a body much like the Land Transport Authority of Singapore." Intrakota Komposit Sdn Bhd chief executive officer Zainuddin Fathodin, added that, "If you look at the Singapore model, they initially had 10 bus companies. Now they have one MRT and two bus consortia" (Damis and Poosparajah 2002).

Therefore, it is imperative to organise, coordinate and realign the various government agencies and departments so that they can effectively organise and direct operators to work together to ensure efficient and attractive services that will increase public transport usage. As long as there is a lack of integrated authority, the ease and attractiveness of LRT use will still be limited even if the various transport operators improve their services.[80]

Lack of revenue, coupled with the burden of making interest payments, proved too much for both PUTRA and STAR as they defaulted on loan repayments due to CIMB, and were served with winding-up petitions in 2002[81] (see also Renong 2002). As C. Paul Buchanan notes that a revamp of government policies on fares, infrastructure and private car use would only enable the LRT operators to pay a "tiny portion" of outstanding liabilities, and would not stop the financial bleeding of LRT operators. The state bailed out these operators, whose commercial debts were backed by the government in line with their concession agreements, by issuing bonds worth RM5.5 billion to take over their loans and, eventually, the assets of both operators.

The rationalisation exercise by the government to integrate and improve the operations of the LRT systems in the Kelang Valley is divided into two phases. (See Box 7.9 for a brief chronology of corporate restructuring or turnaround plans to rationalise the LRT systems.) With the extension of financial assistance and takeover of the system, PUTRA and STAR can now focus on improving their operations and earnings. Aware of the poor integration among public transport operators, the government proposed an integration plan to firstly "merge" PUTRA and STAR, and to then improve auxiliary services. Though this may be a slow process, it should bode well for public transportation users in the long run.

Concluding Remarks

Malaysia's government-led corporate restructuring programmes were not without problems. Concerns abound regarding overly favourable corporate restructuring conditions provided by the government for the restructuring of corporations such as Renong and MAS, associated with cronies. More importantly, why did the government allow the management of select privatised entities of assumed national strategic interest to amass huge and unsustainable debts that increased their vulnerability? Why did the government not intervene earlier to ensure service delivery given the national importance of these privatised enterprises? Mistakes by the government do not explain why it failed to act against non-performing companies, particularly given the Prime Minister's authority. Faced with financial difficulties, the owners of

Proton, MAS, and the LRT system were apparently unwilling to carry out further capital investment, or to repay loans for investments already undertaken, forcing the government to take over the enterprises at great cost.

MAS for example had incurred huge debts following several fleet expansions and the various drops in passenger traffic following 1997–98 currency crisis. The owner also took a large personal debt to purchase the airline, and his other publicly listed (telecommunications) company also faced debt problems. After successive losses and mounting debts between 1998 and 2000, he claimed he could no longer finance MAS (*Business Times*, 28 November 2000), and sold his share back to the government for RM1.79 billion (in 1998, the government pegged the Malaysian ringgit to the US dollar at RM1 to US$0.263) or RM8 per share on 20 December 2000.

The parent company of PUTRA, the less efficient LRT operator, was the country's largest corporate debtor, with over RM25 billion in debt (*Far Eastern Economic Review*, 21 December 2000) and needed to be bailed out by the government. In the case of the LRT system, the operators continued managing operations after re-nationalisation. Even though the government replaced some of these owner-entrepreneurs with professional managers who could be sacked for not performing (see *Asiaweek*, 7 September 2001), this is not a very serious threat in comparison to loss of ownership.

While the ability to monitor informs the principal whether the agent is performing, it does not in itself guarantee that the agent can and will actually deliver. The principal must also be able to enforce discipline to ensure delivery. Regulatory failure thus also occurs when the government is unable to threaten punishment for non-delivery. Elsewhere, the state simply gives the contract or transfers the company to someone else, and the private operator who fails to deliver is allowed to go bankrupt. Since all four projects were deemed to be of national importance the owners were confident that the government would not allow the projects to fail.

But why then did the government not just save the projects and discipline the owners? Instead, the owners were doubly blessed when the government bought back the company. The government paid RM8 per share when MAS shares were trading at RM3.80. The price was justified on the basis of a premium for a controlling stake, although the government already had a "golden share" ensuring ultimate management control and owned 49 per cent of the airline on 12 December 2000 through various state agencies.

Hence, despite possible justification for government assistance to corporations of strategic interest and to minimise the adverse consequences of systemic crises, there is no justification for such favourable treatment of those principally responsible for the abuses that exacerbated their corporate problems. Their corporations could well have been bailed out at much lower social cost. Nevertheless, the government's efforts to resolve the NPL problem and to restructure the corporate landscape — by encouraging and, in some cases, forcing debt and operational restructuring — should help improve corporate governance and performance. To minimise future occurrences of corporate sector distress of such magnitude, improvements or modifications to corporate governance guidelines and effective regulation may be desirable, but since their role in the crisis as well as the record of such reforms are rather ambiguous, these were hardly an immediate priority in handling the crisis, as suggested by influential Western observers. However, as suggested above, the various SPVs should serve the welfare of society as a whole (including other stakeholders such as creditors, debtors, taxpayers and government).

Notes

1. This stake will further increase to 49 per cent assuming that the proposed issue of zero dividend new redeemable convertible preference shares (RCPSs) of RM1 each up to RM800 million by MAS is not redeemed by MAS, and MoF Inc. elects to convert all the RCPSs into MAS shares at a conversion price of RM3.20 each (based on a 10 per cent premium over an assumed market price of RM2.91 per share), resulting in MoF Inc.'s shareholding exceeding 33 per cent (*The Star*, 17 May 2001). This would make it necessary for MoF Inc. to make a mandatory general offer under the Malaysian Code of Takeovers and Mergers (*The Star*, 17 May 2001).

   The proposed RCPSs issue is expected to contribute positively to future group earnings as the capital injection will result in annual interest savings of about RM64 million based on an assumed borrowing cost of 8 per cent per annum. Besides that, OSK Securities senior analyst, Hilmi Mokhtar noted that the issue of RCPSs (zero coupon paper in the case of MAS) will not reduce cash flow since it does not incur any immediate interest expense (*The Star*, 18 May 2001). As of 31 March 2000, the airline's net tangible assets (NTAs) per share stood at RM1.74. However, after the proposed full conversion of the RCPSs, the NTAs per share would be RM1.99. MAS had borrowings of RM10.33 billion at end March 2000, shareholder funds of RM3.22 billion, and a gearing of 3.21 times [gearing = debt-equity ratio = RM10.33 billion/RM3.22 billion]. Upon full conversion of the RCPSs, the MAS borrowings would remain at RM10.33 billion, but its shareholders' funds would increase to RM4.015 billion, with gearing reduced to 2.57 times (*The Star*, 17 May 2001).

2. Bail out here refers to the rescue of MAS's major shareholder, i.e. Tajudin Ramli.

3. Daim Zainuddin denied the government was paying too much for the shares although the price was much higher than the market price. Daim denied any bail out for Tajudin and insisted that MAS's value was well above the market price, as it had good assets and potential (Matthias 2000). See also Heong (2001).

4. This represented a 117 per cent premium above the market price of RM3.68.

5. Naluri said the sale consideration of RM1.792 billion represented a premium of RM854,639,912, or 91.2 per cent over the 29.09 per cent of consolidated MAS's net tangible assets of RM3.222 billion (equivalent to RM937.36 million), based on the audited consolidated accounts of MAS for the financial year ended 31 March 2000 (*Daily Express*, 21 Dec. 2000).

6. The proposal forwarded was intended to reorganise MAS's operations and reduce its debt.

7. This option implies that the more profitable international operations of MAS will benefit minority shareholders, while the government will be left with the (loss-making) domestic operations, with the objective of serving the national interest. For details on the proposed reorganisation, see MAS's announcement to the Kuala Lumpur Stock Exchange (KLSE), available from: <http://www.mas.com.my/pdf/2001/announcement.pdf>; *The Star* (29 Jan. 2002) and *The Star* (30 Jan. 2002a).

8. On the potential difficulties of valuing the concession, see Gunasegaram (2002b).

9. The government approved the proposal for increased airfares and allowed an average increase of 51.8 per cent (while emphasising that the revised airfares would still be among the lowest in the region), taking rising fuel costs, salaries and aircraft prices among other factors into consideration.

10. According to a MAS source, the existing group structure (which includes three executive vice-presidents and several senior vice-

presidents) consisted of eight operating units: cargo, airline, catering, engineering, property and investment, training, information techno-logy, and offshore (*The Star*, 2 June 2001).

11. After the September 11, 2001 incident, international insurance firms cut their compensation ceiling on third party damages related to war and terrorism to a maximum of US$50 million from the previous ceiling of US$2 billion. Noting problems caused by such a drastic action by aviation insurance companies, on 25 September 2001, the Government agreed to help the national carrier bridge the gap of up to US$1.95 billion to cover third-party liabilities in the aviation industry (*The New Straits Times*, 27 Sept. 2001).

12. However, in January 2002, Mohd Nor announced that MAS would resume services to six destinations and continue services to two destinations that it had earlier intended to suspend. In addition, MAS would reinstate services between Kuala Lumpur and Manchester, Rome, Istanbul, Cairo, Beirut and Karachi, and continue to fly to Auckland beyond 26 February 2002 and to Zurich beyond 30 March 2002 (*The Star*, 8 Jan. 2002).

13. The market is speculating that MAS would receive jet fuel concessions similar to Tenaga. This would help MAS shore up operating margins, which were severely eroded by the 61 per cent rise in jet fuel prices in 2000 (Ho 2001). Besides, jet fuel prices made up, on average, 20 to 30 per cent of an airline's total costs, while MAS is said to have only hedged between 3 and 10 per cent of its total jet fuel needs, a dismal ratio compared to the industry average of 40 to 50 per cent (*The New Straits Times*, 27 Sept. 2001).

14. For a brief description of the background of the three new independent, non-executive directors, see *The Star*, 6 Dec. 2001.

15. See Figure 7.1 for the MAS corporate structure before and after the proposed reorganisation.

16. According to MAS managing director Mohd Nor Yusof, Newco would be granted at least a 30-year concession to operate MAS international and cargo operations. The new arrangement will make Newco the first airline in the world to operate with a full operating lease structure (Gabriel 2002).

17. Earlier, MAS had sold eight aircraft for RM3.8 billion to Aircraft Business Malaysia Sdn Bhd, in which PMB has 70 per cent equity stake (*The Star*, 31 July 2002).

18. MAS would sell its 70 per cent stake in MAS Catering Sdn Bhd for RM175 million cash to Gubahan Saujana Sdn Bhd, and dispose of about RM1.48 billion worth of its properties at the KL International Airport, Subang airport, Kelana Jaya complex and MAS head office to Asset Global Network, a company which is 100 per cent owned by the Finance Ministry. Subsequently, MAS would lease back the

properties to operate its business with the leaseback periods ranging from 43 to 57 years.

19.   Danny Condit and Kim J. Kelly, referred in *The Star*, are known as Danny Kondic (General Manager of Sales) and Kym Joylene Clarke (Assistant General Manager of Revenue Management) respectively, in Renong's *Annual Report 2001/2002*.

20.   According to Mohd Nor Yusof, MAS aimed to complete the sale and leaseback of its aircraft by May 2002, and disposal of its properties by June 2002, with a capital gain of RM400 to RM450 million from the sale of three aircraft. By selling the aircraft and subsequently leasing back five new aircraft, MAS would be able to resolve the issue of payment for the new aircraft, for which it had incurred debt of some RM9.2 billion. From the RM6.1 billion to be raised, RM820 million was to be used as working capital (*The Star*, 8 Jan. 2002).

21.   MAS had a staff strength of 21,518 as of 31 March 2001 (*The Star*, 9 Jan. 2002).

22.   Nonetheless, this measure could be offset by lower staff morale, which would affect service, and hence, customer satisfaction.

23.   MAS's share price increased by 128 per cent from a low of RM1.80 in November 2001 (*The Star*, 28 Feb. 2002b) to RM4.10 on 30 April 2002 (*The Star*, 1 May 2002).

24.   MAS managing director Mohd Nor Yusof highlighted this: "We are taking a two-pronged approach to resolve the issue. Right now, MAS, as it stands, has multiple challenges — to repair a massively impaired company in terms of financial capability, and its inability to continue because of that. That impairment has also gone into the structures and that requires a massive amount of work. At the same time, MAS is a going concern and a vital institution of growth for the government in terms if its role in supporting government policies and strategies. To do all that in one location will entail priority issues such as allocation of resources and attention, and that is why we are separating the repair and growth functions" (*The Star*, 29 Jan. 2002). Newco would benefit from this arrangement since (according to the research head of a foreign investment house) foreign investors would now find the company more "quantifiable" as viability and profitability would only involve the international side, and international operations will be subject to market forces (Gabriel 2002).

25.   Minority shareholders stand to benefit from the corporate reorganisation of MAS as they would participate in a growth company, Newco. The company will be debt-free and asset light and it will concentrate on the more lucrative international market, thus placing itself in a better position to reap and reinvest profits, and grow "organically" with the airline's profitable international and cargo business (*The Star*, 30 Jan. 2002a). Mohd Nor Yusof said that the separation of roles —

and the government retaining domestic operations — would provide minority investors an opportunity to "enjoy the upside" of Newco, relieved of being trapped in a company with huge debts and undergoing restructuring (*The Star*, 29 Jan. 2002). The new arrangement would take away the loss-making activities and debt-ridden part of the company (to be owned by the government), allowing minority shareholders and investors to reap the benefits of the debt-free, asset-light and profitable business under Newco. Unfortunately, all this would be at the government's and taxpayers' expense.

26. The earnings figures under review are for 1997, 1998, 1999, 2000, 2001, 2002, and June 2003; the estimated earnings figures are for financial year 2004.

27. For a brief analysis of the profit position of the group, see *The Sun*, 27 Nov. 2001a.

28. For instance, for the second quarter ending 30 September 2001, MAS incurred a net loss of RM359 million compared to a net loss of RM270 million previously, attributing the loss to lower passenger and cargo carriage as well as weakening currencies. The national carrier saw net loss widening by 49 per cent to RM772.8 million in the next half year, from RM398 million in the corresponding first half of the previous financial year (*The Sun*, 27 Nov. 2001a).

29. Dato' Mohd Nor Yusof, the Managing Director and Chief Executive Officer of MAS, believes that the acquisition of such aircraft of technologically superior quality will help MAS sustain and improve its position as a premier carrier with the latest aircrafts on offer. He adds that given MAS's strategic position in the Asia Pacific region, flagship long-haul routes' traffic growth, slot constraints in key destinations and the A380s' expected cost advantage, the acquisition will be both economically rational and timely (MAS 2003a; 2003b).

30. For the Borneo state capitals of Kota Kinabalu and Kuching, MAS expects to profitably increase intra-Asia traffic flows as well as long haul flights, and thus also accelerate the Borneo states' economic development and integration into the region. Geographically distant from Peninsular Malaysia, MAS expects to link Kota Kinabalu and Kuching with newly affluent destinations such as Hong Kong, Guangdong (Canton), Shanghai, Taipei, Kaohsiung and Seoul among others. It also hopes to promote them as natural gateways to the vast hinterland of the Brunei Indonesia Malaysia Philippines-East ASEAN Growth Area (BIMP-EAGA) region, especially to poorly served destinations in Indonesia such as Balikpapan and Manado (MAS 2003d).

31. These include, among others, flights to Italy (e.g. Milan from Langkawi), China (e.g. Xiamen and Guangzhou from Kota Kinabalu), London (from Langkawi and Penang) and Indonesia (e.g. Balikpapan

from Kota Kinabalu, Manado in North Sulawesi from Kuala Lumpur via Kota Kinabalu, Medan from Ipoh) (MAS 2003m; 2003s; 2003t; 2003w).

32.   Once again, distinctions must be made between (i) extending "direct" or "indirect" (financial) support to economically viable and "well managed", but financially distressed (due to circumstances beyond the corporations' control) businesses, requiring some breathing space to restructure debt and exploit market conditions as they improve; (ii) extending "direct" or "indirect" (financial) support to economically viable, but "poorly managed" and financially distressed (due to poor business strategy and management, exacerbated by external factors beyond the corporation's control) businesses, and (iii) "rescuing" major shareholders responsible for poor management — in the form of incompetence, negligence or plain greed — resulting in poor corporate performance and financial insolvency even prior to the 1997–98 Asian financial crisis.

33.   *freeMalaysia* (1999a) argues that "If the proper course of bankruptcy were allowed to run, Renong (which is already in default on a number of loans) would already be in receivership by now; liquidators would be conducting asset sales (perhaps back to the Malaysian government at attractive prices); and Halim Saad would be jobless — if not exactly poor. If the asset sales fell short of covering total liabilities, Renong's creditors would take the haircut. In this story, the potential winner is the Malaysian government (that's you and me), which gets back cheaply assets of national importance. The losers are Halim Saad, his benefactor Daim Zainuddin and foolish lenders".

34.   The PLUS bonds are rated A3 and secured against a basket of securities, Renong's corporate guarantee, and ultimately, PLUS's cash flow (*The Star*, 13 July 2001).

35.   See CDRC (1999) for details of PLUS offerings to UEM and Renong.

36.   See CDRC (1999) and Rabindra Nathan Shearn Delamore & Co, "Insolvency Law Reform: Case Study from Malaysia".

37.   On Monday, 23 July 2001, Danasaham proposed to buy all UEM shares for RM4.50 each and warrants for 40 sen each, and to make the group private. The offer price for the shares were 26 per cent higher than UEM's last traded price of RM3.56 prior to the offer on Friday, 20 July 2001, and 53 per cent higher than the stock's weighted average price of the previous three months of RM2.94. The offer price for the warrants was 52 per cent lower than its last traded price of 53 sen (*The New Straits Times*, 30 July 2001). Even though the offer price of RM4.50 per share was 26 per cent higher than the market price on 20 July 2001, it closed at RM4.24 on Monday, 15 October 2001. As such, the "premium" paid by Danasaham actually fell to only 6.1 per cent (*The Star*, 15 Oct. 2001).

38. This was after some 90.72 per cent of UEM shareholders accepted the conditional voluntary general takeover offer by Danasham at RM4.50 per share — exceeding the 90 per cent minimum stipulated in the offer document. Danasaham had also received an acceptance level of 60.45 per cent for the UEM warrants at 40 sen per warrant (*The Star*, 21 Sept. 2001b; *The New Straits Times*, 30 July 2001).

Abdul Wahid Omar was appointed managing director and chief executive officer of UEM on 1 October 2001; he has been heading the restructuring exercise (*The Star*, 11 Dec. 2001; UEM World website, available from: <http://www.uemworld.com>).

39. Prior to his executive position in UEM and UEM World, Pardas was executive director of Silterra Malaysia Sdn Bhd, a subsidiary of Khazanah Nasional Bhd.

40. Of this, between 200 and 300 million would be allocated for a foreign tranche, while the remainder would be offered to the Malaysian public (*The Star*, 2 May 2002).

41. The initial public offer (IPO) will be lead-managed by JP Morgan Chase & Co and RHB Sakura Merchant Bankers Bhd (Maisara 2002).

42. According to Renong, the CAHB securities formed part of the collateral pledged by Renong for revenue from PLUS bonds. Other listed and unlisted securities made up the remainder valued at around RM10 billion in 2000, exceeding revenue from its PLUS bonds of RM4.50 billion (Renong 2000).

43. However, bankers may refer to hold paper earning 9.4 per cent, as this would represent a higher return on assets, than the current low interest rate (Tharmaratnam 2000).

44. With the success of Khazanah's bid, the agency now will emerge as Renong's controlling shareholder, ahead of Halim who held 16.5 per cent of the company (*The New Straits Times*, 30 July 2001).

45. Acceptance of the Conditional Voluntary Offer (CVO) by Renong and other shareholders of UEM resulted in Danasaham effectively becoming a substantial shareholder of Renong by virtue of UEM's 31 per cent stake in Renong (Renong 2001a).

46. Renong group managing director and Time Engineering director, Ahmad Pardas Senin, suggests that the future of Time Engineering and Time dotCom — including whether or not Time Engineering would be sold to repay PLUS bondholders — would depend on the government's plans to consolidate the telecommunications industry. In reports on the telecommunications industry consolidation, Time Engineering and Time dotCom were reported as linked to Maxis Communications Bhd (Maxis) (*The Star*, 12 Dec. 2001).

47. For additional details on Park May, see *The Star* (19 Feb. 2002b) and Barrock (2002).

48. Disposal of assets includes sale of shares and sale of fixed or physical assets.

49. For a summary of the Renong group's performance for first quarter ending 30 September 2001, refer to *The Sun* (27 Nov. 2001b).

50. This box draws from the annual reports of Renong for the financial years ending 30 June from 1998 until 2001.

51. The interest rates are based on three-month daily average of interbank deposit rates at the Interbank Money Market in Kuala Lumpur.

52. For the year ended 31 December 2000, PLUS recorded a 12.8 per cent increase in traffic volume to 10.26 million passenger car unit km compared with the previous year (*The Star*, 2 May 2002). Toll collection rose 3.6 per cent to RM1.15 billion from RM1.11 billion in 1999, while pre-tax profit increased by 11.9 per cent to RM712.50 million from RM636.58 million previously. The government has allowed PLUS to raise its toll rate by 10 per cent instead of the 33 per cent agreed to earlier (Nuryushida 2002). This should augur well for the toll operator's revenue.

53. The disposal of Renong's 37.9 per cent stake in UEM under the CVO enabled Renong to quickly raise RM1.4 billion. On 30 October 2001, the entire RM1.4 billion was utilised to partially redeem the Renong SPV bond. By doing so, the company will save at least RM159 million per annum on financial charges until the maturity date of 2006 (Renong 2001a).

54. Even though the deal is a non-cash transaction (share swap), nonetheless, as part of the deal, Park May's parent, Renong, has to make a restricted offer for sale that will see RM27 million cash flowing into its coffers. Following this, Renong would end up with a 2.4 per cent stake in Park May after the exercise, down from its current 32.4 per cent (Barrock 2002).

55. The acquisition of Park May would give KKMB the opportunity to list the nine companies through Park May when Park May acquired the entire equity stakes of Express Nasional Bhd, Kenderaan Langkasuka Sdn Bhd, Kenderaan Klang Banting, Kenderaan Labu Sedayan Sdn Bhd, Starise Sdn Bhd, and Syarikat Rembau Tampi Sdn Bhd; 99.1 per cent of the equity in Transnational Express Sdn Bhd; 95.6 per cent of Syarikat Kenderaan Melayu Kelantan Bhd (SKMKB) and 200,000 cumulative redeemable preference shares of RM1 each in SKMKB and 98.2 per cent of Syarikat Tanjong Keramat Temerloh Utara Omnibus Bhd (Keramat) (*The Star*, 19 Feb. 2002b). However, there are some quarters who believe that the valuation of KKMB's nine companies was on the high side.

56. The second tranche was due on 5 August 2001 and the third on 5 December 2001 (Ho 2002).

57. Time Engineering Bhd held a 45 per cent stake in Time dotCom Bhd, of which a third had been charged to bondholders. However,

even though the Time dotCom shares account for about 70 per cent of collateral value, both Time Engineering Bhd and its bondholders were prohibited from selling those shares until newly-listed Time dotCom Bhd had two consecutive years of profit, as required by the IPO conditions set by the market regulator (*The Star*, 20 Dec. 2001b).

58.   There are extensive cross-holdings within the UEM/Renong group, with UEM controlling Time Engineering through its 31 per cent stake in Renong, as Renong owned 46.7 per cent of Time Engineering, which in turn held a 20.48 per cent stake in Renong (*The Star*, 21 Dec. 2001).

59.   The bondholders had rejected a proposal put forward by Time Engineering on 4 December 2001, which would involve 100 per cent repayment with interest of its obligations over a three-year period. Sources said the 4 December proposal entailed a plan for disposal of assets to help Time Engineering redeem the bonds, and superseded an earlier proposal dated 21 August 2001. The bondholders rejected the second proposal on 12 December 2001, and served notice on Time Engineering, demanding payment of US$162 million, which were due on 19 December 2001. Part of the reason the bondholders were so hard on Time Engineering was because the issue was supposed to have been resolved as part of Time Engineering's RM5 billion debt restructuring plan announced in January 2000. While the other creditors were paid in full, the bondholders were left in the lurch — after redeeming the first tranche of bonds in February 2001, Time Engineering had defaulted on the second, third and fourth tranches. Furthermore, the bondholders did not see why they needed to wait another three years to be repaid (*The Star*, 21 Dec. 2001).

60.   In other words, the bondholders would have to accept a 10 per cent discount (or "haircut"), or a combined loss of RM61.5 million, in return for being paid (Tan 2002).

61.   Under the new scheme, Time Engineering Bhd proposed that the final maturity date for the bonds be extended to 5 December 2004, and that the *entire* outstanding amount of US$162 million be redeemed in three tranches through the sale of assets on 5 December 2002, 2003, and 2004. The group would pay US$44.5 million (27.5 per cent of the total) on 5 December 2002, a similar amount on 5 December 2003, and US$72.9 million (45 per cent) on 5 December 2004. The assets, which Time Engineering proposed to sell over the next three years included those pledged as collateral to the bondholders, its stakes of 16 per cent in Renong Bhd, 55 per cent in EPE Power Corp Bhd, and 15 per cent in Time dotCom Bhd, and its building, Wisma Time (*The Star*, 30 Jan. 2002c).

62.   Poor management — manifestations of incompetence, complacency and/or pure recklessness, resulting in hasty expansion of the conglo-

merate into non-core business areas — had in fact played a huge role in the conglomerate's debacle. As such, to just blame the 1997–98 Asian crisis for the financial woes of the group would be incorrect since weaknesses were already apparent prior to the crisis.

63.   This figure was given in a presentation by the group to the MSWG.

64.   According to Sebastian Chang, research head of Vickers Ballas Research (M) Sdn Bhd, "With this kind of infrastructure it's difficult to make money. It should be in the hands of the government" (*The Star*, 1 Sept. 2001).

65.   Daim claimed: "The economic crisis has made it difficult for them to inject new capital or to pay back their loans, as the development and upgrading costs for a LRT are very high" (Fuller 2000).

66.   According to Mahathir, if the LRT operators were allowed to charge full cost-covering fares, they would be very profitable because the usage of PUTRA was very high (almost three million passengers used the service every month). He complained the public wanted a world class LRT service, but was unwilling to pay commensurate fares (*Sibexnews*, 29 May 2001). His claim does not acknowledge the counter-claim (by an ex-minister for the Federal Territory) that the LRTs were never commercially viable because LRT usage would decline with high commuter charges.

67.   Outstanding loans stood at approximately RM5.7 billion on 29 November 2001 (CDRC 2001). The bail out (or complete takeover) would be cheaper than the one initially planned (announced in December 2000, but deferred to June 2001) because by guaranteeing the bonds, it would pay creditors a lower coupon rate (*The Star*, 1 Oct. 2001b; *The Star*, 1 Sept. 2001).

68.   However, profitability would also be affected by managerial, operational and business strategy considerations.

69.   In normal circumstances, PUTRA and STAR would have undergone winding-up and liquidation, with a high possibility that no *private* firm would undertake to buy the corporation as an entity. Both have been unprofitable because of high interest costs and reduced fare rates, falling well short of their passenger and revenue projections (Lee 2000). Hence, both corporations can be considered non-viable in the short and medium term. Without the government taking over debts and providing subsidies, PUTRA and STAR would still be unprofitable, and hence, considered commercially unviable, since low traffic volume will not generate sufficient revenue to service the loans. However, PUTRA and STAR are performing fairly well if one just looks at operational costs versus revenue. When financing and depreciation costs are factored in, the firm will be in the red even if ridership increases (assuming reduced fares). See "Government's Role in STAR's and PUTRA's Corporate (Debt) Restructuring" on PUTRA and STAR for details.

70. The rates were lower than the previous 5.8 per cent and 7.2 per cent because the government would guarantee the bonds. Guaranteed by the government, the bonds would be in four tranches, the first, a five-year issue of RM546.815 million at a coupon rate of 4 per cent a year, the second, a seven-year issue of RM820.223 million at 4.55 per cent a year, the third, a 10-year issue of RM2.187 billion at 4.85 per cent a year, and the fourth a 15-year issue of RM1.913 billion at 5.40 per cent a year (*The Star*, 1 Dec. 2001a). For details of the bond issues, see CDRC (2001).

71. For details, see *The Star*, 22 Mar. 2002, and Renong, Announcement, 26 Apr. 2002.

72. According to Renong, this implied that the federal government, through SPNB, had effectively become a creditor of PUTRA, but had not taken over the company (*The Star*, 4 Dec. 2001). However, according to the Renong statement, the government's acquisition of PUTRA debt would enable it to effect the takeover of PUTRA's LRT assets by initiating PUTRA's liquidation process (*The Star*, 4 Dec. 2001).

73. After two and a half years, PUTRA managed to surpass the target of 170,000 passengers each day within 7 to 8 years from the time it began operations in 1999 (*The Star*, 6 Mar. 2002).

74. According to Sebastian Chang, research head of Vickers Ballas Research (M) Sdn Bhd, the takeover of debt by the government will help reduce the amount of NPLs in the banking system, which will help restore banking system stability (*The Star*, 1 Sept. 2001).

    According to the CDRC, successful debt restructuring of STAR and PUTRA was expected to reduce the level of non-performing loans — on a net six-month basis in the banking system — by RM2.9 billion, or 0.7 per cent (excluding loans extended by offshore banks, development finance institutions and other non-bank institutions) (*The Star*, 1 Dec. 2001b; CDRC 2001).

75. According to a banking analyst, a discount ("haircut") of less than 10 per cent is "no big deal" and one would expect banks to take small "haircuts" to recoup their money, given the size of the NPLs. In fact, analysts agree that the banks got a good deal since they received government-guaranteed bonds yielding higher rates (a coupon rate of 4.0 to 5.4 per cent, depending on the maturity of the bonds) than traditional Malaysian government securities. A research head of a local broking house noted that the banks received an extremely good deal as the banks had swapped bad debt for gilt-edged bonds (*The Star*, 1 Dec. 2001b).

76. Halcrow is a UK-based railway system consultant.

77. During the third quarter of 1999, 60,000 passengers used STAR daily, while 75,000 passengers used PUTRA daily. However, these

figures fell short of forecasts by 20 and 40 per cent respectively, with PUTRA charging lower fares than planned as well (*Asiafeatures* 2000).

78. In the first half of 2001, STAR's average number of passengers —. around 2.7 million monthly — exceeded forecasts. It transported 2.8 million passengers in March and was expected to increase ridership to three million a month (*The New Straits Times*, 31 Aug. 2001).

79. For instance, according to Zainal Abdul Ghani, STAR was not only unable to increase fares since it started operations [in 1996], but had resorted to price cuts (with average fares dropping from RM2.03 to RM1.63) to attract more passengers. This had resulted in increased ridership — the number of passengers increased from 1.3 million a month in January 1997 to 1.57 million in January 1998, 1.58 million in January 1999, 2.07 million in January 2000 and 2.6 million in January 2001 — but not revenue. Revenue was merely RM4.23 million a month (with RM1.63 as the average fare multiplied by 2.6 million users), insufficient to even service interest on loans. STAR chief executive officer Zainal Abdul Ghani pointed out that the consultants had over-estimated the number of LRT users, projecting 230,000 riders daily in 1997 and 590,000 in 2001. STAR's trains were under-utilised, though it had capacity for 66,600 passengers per hour per direction. In January 2001, 94,000 to 120,000 users on average utilised the service during weekdays, while only 45,000 people used it during weekends (*The Sun*, 12 Feb. 2001).

80. According to Zainal Abdul Ghani, the STAR LRT system had achieved 99 per cent reliability — disembarking and embarking on schedule as a result of very minimal breakdowns — equivalent to international standards, and thus ensuring that consumers had great confidence in utilising its services (*The New Straits Times*, 31 Aug. 2001).

81. In 1999, PUTRA defaulted on interest payments of RM44.6 million on a RM2 billion loan, after passenger traffic fell and revenue did not cover expenses (*The Star*, 1 Sept. 2001). This prompted the CDRC to meet with creditors of PUTRA and STAR for discussions on how to resolve the debt woes of the two companies (*Asiafeatures* 2000).

CHAPTER 8

Conclusion: From Financial Crises to Economic Recovery

JOMO K.S.

Less than two years after the East Asian crises first broke out in Thailand in mid-1997, the East Asian countries, including Malaysia, recovered strongly in 1999 and 2000, before facing new contractionary pressures owing to the US recession slowdown following the end of the "dotcom bubble". Growth rates have been positive since, but not at the levels preceding the crises except during the early recovery phase after the sharp contractions of 1998, i.e. in 1999 and 2000. In other words, export growth has recovered, but more modestly, and signs of deindustrialisation are to be seen. Social and political unrest was kept to a minimum, except in Indonesia, with new challenges appearing.

As indicated in Chapter 1, the 1997–98 crises in East Asia gave rise to new debates and insights into how this generation of currency and financial crises happened. Most importantly, the crises happened in one of the fastest growing regions in the world during the early and mid-1990s with few signs of macroeconomic fundamentals — e.g. public sector deficits, balance of payments problems — being seriously at risk. The earlier generations of currency crises theories were found wanting in East Asia, with their policy prescriptions actually exacerbating rather than ameliorating the crises.

Even the IMF has slowly come to acknowledge errors in its policy responses to the crises. The IMF's initial policy prescriptions and conditionalities attached to emergency financial aid to Thailand, Indonesia and South Korea included pro-cyclical macroeconomic policies — these are now widely acknowledged to have been based on misdiagnoses. Such erroneous policies and reforms clearly worsened the crisis. From around mid-1998, the IMF reversed its position on budgetary contraction, and approved counter-cyclical fiscal — but not monetary — measures. Only much later, while visiting Malaysia in September 2003, then IMF Managing Director Horst Kohler acknowledged the utility of capital controls on outflows for crisis management purposes, going further than his erstwhile colleague, then Deputy Managing Director Stanley Fischer's endorsement of controls only on capital inflows à la Chile and Colombia.

There is also no systematic empirical evidence to suggest that the East Asian crises were either triggered by or principally due to microeconomic factors related to productivity declines, over-invest-ments, Asian values, developmental states, industrial policy, corporate governance or cronyism, though such problems were undoubtedly present (Rasiah 2001). Nonetheless, such factors continue to be invoked by the international business media, and by casual, but influential observers whose pronouncements have distracted atten-tion from the major systemic cause of the crisis, namely financial liberalisation. With the patent failure of currency crises theories, the mainstream explanation for the crises has instead pointed to nebulous claims about corporate governance failures in the region.

As suggested in Chapter 2, the socio-economic impact of the crises on Malaysia was comparatively less severe with little political disruption and instability — unlike the political upheavals and social unrest experienced in Indonesia and even Korea. This may have been due to the different nature and economic consequences of the crisis in Malaysia. By not having to resort to IMF financial assistance, Malaysia had greater policy autonomy and flexibility. However, the Malaysian macroeconomic policy responses from December 1997 mirrored the conventional policies and orthodox analyses of the IMF, itself greatly influenced by the powerful US Wall Street-Treasury Department nexus. After failing to ensure quick recovery by refla-tionary fiscal policies and debt restructuring measures from mid-1998, Malaysia resorted to capital control measures to stem further capital outflows and to restore monetary and financial stability.

Coming 14 months after the crisis began, some observers insist that the measures were only intended to contain the likely adverse market consequences of then Prime Minister Mahathir's early

September 1998 purge of his popular Deputy and Finance Minister Anwar. While this may well have been one motive, the controls may also be understood as a desperate attempt to reverse the situation — with no apparent end to the crisis in sight — as perceived in August 1998. Although some Malaysian recovery plan measures clearly helped some cronies or politically influential business interests much more than others, the evidence currently offered to support the claims that the capital controls were intended for this purpose (Johnson and Mitton 2003) — and therefore had adverse microeconomic consequences (Forbes 2003) — does not conclusively support these claims.

Despite the common perception that all four crisis-hit countries were similarly vulnerable to crisis and experienced similar crises, Malaysia's financial vulnerability was significantly different from its three East Asian counterparts that sought IMF emergency credit facilities. Despite a more open economy, Malaysia's external debt was relatively lower, thanks in part to greater prudential regulation after its late 1980s' banking crisis. However, Malaysia was vulnerable to contagion as it had successfully sought portfolio investments to boost its stock market. Such differences have had some bearing on the nature of post-crisis banking and corporate restructuring in Malaysia.

This study has evaluated bank and corporate restructuring, focusing on government bail outs of corporations, supposedly in the national interest. It has argued that government bail outs may be necessary and desirable, especially during systemic crises. Such interventions can be further justified if bank or corporate collapses are likely to have far-reaching adverse consequences if simply left to more time-consuming and unpredictable market-based solutions. In any case, private sector-led solutions are less likely to work in developing countries or so-called emerging markets for well-known reasons. Therefore, government bail out programmes should be regarded as one possible option when dealing with systemic financial crises, or even to expedite needed bank or corporate restructuring and other institutional reforms.

Bail outs have been generally stigmatised as necessarily involving misallocation of resources, cronyism, moral hazards, rents, and so forth. However, such objections are often a matter of perspective — "cronyism" may provide "social capital", while "rents" can accelerate economic development (Khan and Jomo 2000). Bail outs may also be counterproductive in the absence of appropriate incentives and disciplinary measures to ensure positive outcomes. Hence, a bail out programme must be conducted in a transparent manner to ensure public accountability and to minimise abuse. Public resources must be deployed to improve social welfare as well as economic capabilities and capacities for long-term economic growth. Performance standards and monitoring mechanisms should also be in place to minimise moral hazard and abuse, as well as to ensure desirable outcomes. Last, but certainly not least, periodic monitoring and evaluation of the viability and performance of bailed out corporations should be conducted.

Malaysia's earlier privatization policy exacerbated its crisis-related problems, requiring bank and corporate restructuring as well as bail outs of several large privatised entities. While the case for privatisation is problematic to begin with, in Malaysia, this was exacerbated by poor information, regulatory capacity, incompetence and gross abuse by politically influential business interests. The lack of clear guidelines and rigorous assessment of the optimum mode of privatisation, poor or ignored criteria for determining suitability for privatisation and for the selection of awardees, and lack of transparency and accountability in decision making exacerbated inefficiencies and abuses in the implementation of its privatisation programme. Political considerations and the vested interests of key decision makers meant that privatisation was characterised by arbitrary and *ad hoc* administrative actions that undermined the efficiency and other gains from privatisation (Jomo [ed.] 1995).

Thus far, Malaysia's banking and corporate restructuring programmes have received generally positive feedback from the financial and corporate community despite some clear abuses adversely affecting the public, but not corporate interests. Malaysia's special purpose vehicles (SPVs) — Danaharta, Danamodal and the CDRC — have, on the whole, achieved their broad objectives of reducing NPLs, helping some giant corporate groups through debt (and, in some cases, operational) restructuring to improve their balance sheets as well as strengthen the financial and corporate sectors. In most instances, corporate bail outs seem to have been abused, though this seems less true of financial sector debt restructuring. Government-led restructuring to bail out MAS, the UEM-Renong group and the two light rail transport (LRT) operators (STAR and PUTRA) have raised more than eyebrows, mainly benefiting the major shareholders of these largely indebted corporations at public expense.

Bail out programmes, often involving "re-nationalisation", have been conducted at the expense of taxpayers. Nonetheless, if these corporations can be effectively turned around, then bail outs can: (i) minimise the negative "externalities" of corporate distress, which have accounted for much of total non-performing loans (NPLs) in the banking system, (ii) save financially distressed, but economically viable business entities, related jobs and economic capacities and capabilities, and (iii) require the financial restructuring of large corporate groups, which could reduce the net costs to the public of these bail outs.

So far, MAS's operational restructuring, for example, has had some positive results, returning it to profitability during the financial year ending 31 March 2003, although the subsequent SARS outbreak may have tipped the airline back into the red. The UEM-Renong group and LRT operators have also been implementing various programmes to improve performance, "profitability" and "shareholder value". Bail outs — in the form of debt restructuring — have given these corporations the necessary financing to continue and even expand operations. Of course, failure by these companies to repay could impose further costs on the government and taxpayers. Strict, impartial and effective monitoring, performance requirements and regulation are therefore imperative to enhance viability and profitability, and to avoid abuses and failure.

Thus, while bail outs may be necessary and even desirable to mitigate the adverse consequences of systemic crises on the financial system, corporate viability, growth and employment, they must be planned and implemented to minimise the likelihood of abuse. The failure to do so in the Malaysian case has undermined public acceptance of and support for such interventions that have basically deployed limited public resources ostensibly to "save" the national economy, by propping up and bailing out the financial system and some larger — usually politically connected — enterprises. Clear bias in favour of such politically influential business interests has discredited the programme. However, such abuses of Malaysia's bail outs should not obscure their desirability, especially when such problems can be avoided or overcome. In other words, one should not throw out the baby of such state interventions with the bath water of abuses which have undoubtedly tainted the Malaysian experience.

Malaysia's Capital Controls: Policy Lessons

What lessons can be drawn from Malaysia's 1998 capital controls? Most importantly, Chapter 2's examination of the circumstances preceding the introduction of the controls as well as the specific nature of the controls and their apparent consequences require caution in making gross generalisations. Instead, the Malaysian experience urges greater attention to context and detail.

Capital controls did not cause the recovery in Malaysia to be slower than in the other crisis countries. The 1998 collapse was less deep in Malaysia than in Thailand and Indonesia, while the recovery in Malaysia was faster after early 1999. Malaysia's pre-crisis problems were less serious to begin with owing to strengthened prudential regulations after the late 1980s' banking crisis (when non-performing loans went up to 30 per cent of total loans). There were strict controls on Malaysian private borrowing from abroad, with borrowers generally required to demonstrate likely foreign exchange earnings from investments to be financed with foreign credit. Hence, although Malaysia seemingly has the most open economy in the East Asian region after Hong Kong and Singapore, with the total value of its international trade around double national income, its foreign borrowings and share of short-term loans in total credit were far less than the more closed economies of South Korea, Indonesia and Thailand before the regional crisis.

The coincidentally simultaneous timing of Paul Krugman's *Fortune* article advocating capital controls reinforced the impression that the Malaysian measures were primarily intended to provide monetary policy independence to reflate the economy. However, international developments from August 1998 also created new monetary conditions that facilitated the adoption of reflationary policies in the rest of the region. Though Malaysia missed out on most of the renewed capital flows to the region from the last quarter of 1998, such easily reversible capital inflows may not have been all that desirable.

The more serious problem has been the subsequent credibility of government policies, which many critics claim has adversely affected foreign direct investment into the country as well as risk premiums for Malaysian bonds. Subsequent policy reforms, especially after Mahathir's retirement in October 2003, have sought to regain market confidence, with increasing signs of success. But it is also clear that green-field FDI has declined world wide since the late 1990s, with China accounting for an even greater share of FDI in East Asia.

While the Malaysian authorities had long claimed full capital account liberalisation, there were in fact quite a number of important constraints preceding the 1994 and 1998 controls. This suggests that while a country may claim to have an open capital account, it is possible to have enabling legislation and administrative regulations that will qualify this openness in important ways that may well serve macroeconomic management and developmental governance. Such options may well be the most relevant options for most developing economies today when there is a great deal of pressure to maintain open capital accounts (Epstein, Grabel and Jomo 2003).

Only a few large countries enjoying greater degrees of policy autonomy for various historical and political reasons — such as China and India — are able to effectively withstand such pressures. In any case, many of the old measures for managing closed capital accounts may no longer be effective, appropriate or desirable in contemporary circumstances. This does not mean that countries should surrender whatever remaining sovereignty they may enjoy and instead open their capital accounts, but rather that far more attention should be given to substance over form, to actual regulations and constraints, rather than formal claims to openness, and so forth.

This seems especially crucial since the IMF Interim Committee has already agreed to amend its Articles of Agreement to extend its jurisdiction from the current account to the capital account.[1] Many modern capital account management tools qualify capital account openness, rather than close capital accounts altogether. This is especially true of so-called "managed market" "market-friendly" — as distinct from — instruments. Counter-cyclical instruments are often needed for macroeconomic policy capacity, e.g. to smooth business cycles.

Considerations of macroeconomic prudence suggest that the Malaysian authorities were right to limit exposure to foreign bank borrowings, while their neighbours in East Asia allowed, facilitated and even encouraged such capital inflows from the late 1980s. It is important to stress that the vulnerability of other East Asian economies to such borrowings was not merely due to the greed of financial interests for arbitrage and other related opportunities, or of corporate interests seeking cheaper credit on easier terms. BIS regulations greatly encouraged short-term lending while European and Japanese banks generally preferred dollar-denominated lending over other alternatives. In other words, criticism of "bad lending" to East Asia before the crisis should not only focus on the borrowers and national regulations, but also on the lenders and the rules regulating international lending.

The Malaysian experience also rejects the claim that the East Asian crisis was only due to foreign bank borrowings, which could have been avoided by greater reliance on the capital market, especially stock markets. While capital flows to stock markets undoubtedly have different implications from foreign bank lending, such portfolio capital flows are even more easily reversible than short-term foreign loans. Malaysian bank vulnerability during the crisis was not so much due to foreign borrowings, but rather, to their extensive lending for stock market investments and property purchases, as well as their reliance on shares and real assets as loan collateral.

While there is no evidence that portfolio capital inflows significantly contributed to productive investments or economic growth, the reversal of such flows proved to be highly disruptive, greatly exacerbating volatility. Their impact has been largely due to the "wealth effect" and its consequences for consumption and investment. When these reversals were large and sustained, they contributed to significant disruption, if not disaster. The disruptive effect has been exacerbated by the fact that portfolio capital inflows tend to build up slowly, while outflows tend to be massive and sudden.

Such outflows from late 1993 resulted in a collapse of the Malaysian capital market and the introduction of controls on inflows to discourage yet another build-up of such potentially disruptive inflows. However, these were withdrawn after half a year due to successful lobbying by those interests desiring yet another foreign portfolio capital-induced stock market bubble. It is likely that if the early 1994 controls had not been withdrawn, the massive build-up

in 1995–96 would not have occurred, and Malaysia would consequently have been far less vulnerable to the sudden and massive
capital flight from July 1997.

Kaplan and Rodrik (2001) argue that Malaysia's September
1998 controls sought to avert yet another crisis in the making.
They suggest that the Singapore-centred overseas ringgit market was
putting increasingly unbearable pressure on the Malaysian monetary
authorities, reflected in the very high overnight interest rate for ringgit
in Singapore. The September 1998 currency control measures succeeded in defusing this pressure. While this analysis has been disputed
by those who claim the market was too thin to be as significant as
suggested by Kaplan and Rodrik, the debate is unlikely to be settled
without reference to details of the actual situation. However, their
analysis points to the desirability of not allowing national currency
reserves to build up abroad. In East Asia, Japan and Singapore have
long resisted attempts to internationalise their currencies.

After over a year of considerable international monetary instability, the East Asian crisis was believed to be spreading with the
outbreak of the Russian crisis in August 1998. This, in turn, contributed to the collapse of Long-Term Capital Management (LTCM),
a previously very successful hedge fund. Considering the global
and regional situation at the end of August 1998, it is understandable
that the Malaysian authorities tried to stem further haemorrhage by
adopting capital and currency controls. It was not possible for them
to predict that US Fed would finally respond to the spreading crisis
— after over a year of blaming its main victims as well as poor corporate governance in the region, supposedly rooted in Asian values and
manifested in cronyism and other "bad" business practices violating
Anglo-American corporate governance norms.

However, in September 1998, it became clear that the US
Federal Reserve had coordinated a private sector bail out for LTCM.
Soon, it also reduced US interest rates, which stemmed, and even
reversed capital outflows from East Asia, allowing East Asian currencies
to rise and stabilise significantly in the last quarter of 1998. In some
important regards, the sudden improved regional fortunes rendered
the Malaysian controls unnecessary, if not irrelevant, but this, of
course, could not have been foreseen when the decision to adopt the
measures was being made late in the previous month.

Thailand, Indonesia and South Korea had received IMF emergency credit and had been subject initially to contractionary policy conditionalities, which exacerbated the regional recessions. While insisting on strict monetary policies despite their earlier deflationary impact, the Fund was more willing to abandon its early insistence on "fiscal discipline", perhaps after belatedly recognising that most of the East Asian crisis economies (except Indonesia) had been running budgetary surpluses for years. Thus, by late 1998, the IMF had been forced to permit counter-cyclical (reflationary) fiscal policies by allowing budgetary deficits.

Malaysia's recession continued over the next two quarters, through the last quarter of 1998 and the first quarter of 1999, in effect lagging behind the hesitant recoveries of the three economies under IMF tutelage, including Indonesia, from the first quarter of 1999. However, by the end of 1999, it was clear that the Malaysian recovery was stronger than those of its Southeast Asian neighbours, lagging only behind Korea's. But so many things were going on that it is impossible to attribute the Malaysian difference, for better or worse, to the September 1998 measures alone, although this has not prevented proponents and opponents from doing so, as it suits them.

The IMF revised its policy advice and allowed fiscal reflationary efforts with budgetary deficits in the East Asian economies under its tutelage from mid-1998. Ironically, of the four crisis-hit economies, only Malaysia had maintained a (small) budget surplus in 1997 although it was not under any IMF programme and only cut its spending from December 1997. It is quite possible that the V-shaped economic recoveries achieved by the major crisis-hit economies of East Asia were due to these fiscal reflationary efforts despite the IMF's own predictions of protracted slowdowns and gradual U-shaped recoveries. It is difficult to assess and compare the effects of such fiscal measures. Besides the sise of the fiscal deficits, it is also important to consider other relevant factors such as the nature of the fiscal packages and the strength of domestic economic linkages and multiplier effects.

As is clear from the second part of this book, the control measures were only part of a package of measures to revive the Malaysian economy. Focusing solely on the control measures ignores the significance of the other measures. It is possible for the effects of successful controls to have been wiped out by the failure of accompanying programmes, or vice versa. The IMF imposed different policy packages on the other East Asian economies that sought emergency credit facilities from the Fund. To varying extents, the different national authorities were able to differentially implement the packages as well as other policies not specified in the packages. It is important for other developing country governments to recognise that the packages and their implementation were often the outcomes of hard-fought policy battles, in which different fiscal capacities, negotiating and implementation capabilities as well as national experiences all had bearing on the outcomes.

Very importantly, the conceptualisation, financing, governance and actual operations of national asset management companies involved in bank and corporate debt restructuring were especially crucial in shaping the nature, speed and strength of national economic recovery as well as subsequent corporate capacities and capabilities. Also, it is likely that climatic and other environmental factors — such as El Nino, La Nina as well as large and protracted forest fires — had greater effects on agricultural output than the financial crisis itself.

The forced bank mergers in the wake of the crisis were poorly conceived, if not downright biased to suit certain political interests, and hence less likely to achieve their ostensible ends. The authorities' push for the rapid merger of banks and financial companies were not well designed to enhance synergies, efficiency and competitiveness beyond achieving certain economies of scale and reducing some wasteful duplication and redundancy. While the consolidation of the financial sector may be desirable to achieve economies of scale and other advantages in anticipation of further financial liberalisation, the acceleration of its pace in response to the crisis seemed less well conceived except to take advantage of the financial institutions' weakness and vulnerability during the crisis.

The efficacy of the Malaysian controls was also due to their effective design. Many market-based sceptics did not consider the Malaysian authorities capable of designing and implementing such effective controls, but now concede that they were proven wrong. They seemed to address the problem identified by Kaplan and Rodrik (2001), while aspects were subsequently revised from early 1999 as the authorities revised their assessment of the situation and sought to demonstrate their commitment to market and investor friendliness. Most importantly, they emphasised from the outset that the measures were directed to check currency speculation, not FDI. Although FDI to Malaysia has declined since 1996, this has been true globally since the last 1990s, and of the Southeast Asian region as a whole (including Singapore), with China and a few others being the only exceptions as noted earlier.

Johnson and Mitton (2001; 2003) have argued that the Malaysian capital controls provided a "screen behind which favoured firms could be supported". If this claim is true, the analysis of how such firms were supported would have to shift to the other measures introduced in order to provide such support since the controls only provided a protective screen in this view. However, the Johnson and Mitton evidence points to a significantly greater appreciation of stock prices associated with Mahathir in the month right after the introduction of controls, i.e. before such support could have been provided except in a small minority of cases. Hence, an alternative interpretation more consistent with their evidence is that investors expected the September 1998 measures to principally benefit crony companies associated with Mahathir, causing their share prices to appreciate much more than others.

There are ongoing debates as to whether the continued retention of some of the September 1998 controls, albeit in modified forms, is in Malaysia's best interest. The capital controls *per se* ended with a whimper in September 1999, while the surviving currency controls have a different rationale, explained by Mahathir in terms of the desirability of a fixed exchange rate. In fact, for some time now, the Malaysian authorities have been trying to revive the very same portfolio investment inflows which ended in capital flight from late 1993 and again, from mid-1997. There have not been any efforts to re-introduce the controls on inflows introduced in early 1994 and withdrawn half a year later, or any similar measures. Rather, the government has pointed gleefully to the Kuala Lumpur Stock Exchange (KLSE) Composite Index (KLCI) recovery after September 1998. Key economic policies and other initiatives seem to be primarily concerned with bolstering the stock market, which many blame for the EPF's loss of over RM10 billion in 1998 in addition to the government spending on similar stock market recovery efforts.

For many critics, the undervalued pegged ringgit has also had negative implications for a broad recovery, which depends upon imported inputs. It is also not clear that the peg has really given a major boost to exports. There are costs to maintaining an undervalued ringgit, especially in the context of a very open economy. An undervalued ringgit may help some exports in the short term, but it also makes imports of capital and intermediate goods more expensive, thus impeding recovery and capacity expansion in the medium term. Malaysia's trade surplus has declined with the import compression due to the undervalued ringgit. Together with an apparently stubborn negative services balance, this has meant a reduced current account surplus despite the economic upturn.

While there is a need to continue to press ahead for international financial reform as well as for new regional monetary arrangements in the absence of adequate global reform, little is gained by retaining the present regime of currency controls. It may even be argued that their retention provides a false sense of security as they were designed to deal with problems which are no longer around and are unlikely to recur in their previous form. Instead, if the regime succeeds in attracting short-term portfolio capital, as various subsequent amendments to the original regime have sought to do, the controls would be largely ineffective in the event of another currency crisis and financial panic. The remaining 1998 controls on outflows can be dismantled while introducing a more suitable and effective regulatory framework to reduce financial vulnerability and to moderate capital flow surges into and out of the country. While Malaysia can afford to return to ringgit convertibility, this should be phased in with effective measures to avoid the internationalisation of the ringgit in order to reduce vulnerability to external currency speculation. This can include measures such as not permitting offshore ringgit accounts as well as non-resident borrowing of ringgit.

Clearly, the Malaysian controls did not lead to the unmitigated disaster promised by its most strident critics. On the contrary, there is little evidence of any serious harm to the Malaysian economy that can be attributed to the introduction of the controls. However, this is different from asserting that the controls have had no adverse impacts whatsoever. It is difficult to prove that the continued existence of the controls have had absolutely no negative effects on desired long-term foreign direct investments, though of course, reduced FDI since 1996 cannot be attributed to the September 1998 measures. The Malaysian authorities have attributed the FDI decline since 1996 to misunderstandings and misperceptions, and have spent considerable energy and resources trying to correct these "misimpressions".

Undoubtedly, however, investor confidence — in the Malaysian government's policy consistency and credibility after years of successful investment promotion efforts — was undermined by the apparent reversal of policy. The controls regime may thus have become counter-productive in terms of the overall consistency of government policy and may have had some adverse medium-term, indeed long-term, consequences in terms of the government's desire to reform the status quo ante. The problem was probably exacerbated by the Prime Minister's declared intention to retain the regime until the international financial system was reformed. The problem has not been helped by unnecessarily hostile and sometimes ill-informed official rhetoric, though the Mahathir and Abdullah administrations have since sought to "improve" its international image, especially since the events of September 11, 2001. Hence, the government has gradually phased out much of the September 1998 and subsequent capital and currency control measures in light of their ambiguous contributions to economic recovery and the seemingly adverse consequences of retaining such measures.

Since the desired reforms to the international financial architecture are unlikely to materialise in the foreseeable future, the Malaysian government should institute a permanent, but flexible, market-based regime of prudential controls to moderate capital inflows and deter speculative surges, both domestic and foreign, in order to avert future crises. This could include a managed float of the currency with convertibility, but no internationalisation, which would minimally require a ban on offshore ringgit holdings and accounts as well as limits on off-shore foreign exchange accounts and on foreign borrowings. There is clearly also an urgent need for greater monetary cooperation in the region. It is now clear that currency and financial crises have a primarily regional character. Hence, regional cooperation is a necessary first step towards the establishment of an East Asian monetary facility. Only responsible, constructive and proactive Malaysian relations with its neighbours will contribute to realising such regional cooperation.

The window of opportunity offered by the government initiatives was undoubtedly abused by certain powerfully-connected business interests, not only to secure government funded bailouts at public expense, but also to consolidate and extend their corporate domination, especially in the crucial financial sector. Capital controls were part of a package used to save friends of the regime, at public expense whether directly or indirectly. For example, while ostensibly not involving public funds, the government-sponsored restructuring of the ruling party-linked Renong conglomerate will cost the government, and hence the public, billions of ringgit in foregone toll and tax revenue. Also, non-performing loans (NPLs) of the thrice-bankrupted Bank Bumiputera — taken over by politically well-connected banking interests with its huge debt cleared — were not heavily discounted like other banks' NPLs, although it had long abandoned its ostensible "social agenda" of helping the politically dominant Bumiputera community for all practical purposes.

Other elements in the Malaysian government's economic strategy since then reinforce the impression that the mid-1998 recovery measures were probably motivated by political considerations as well as the desire to protect politically well-connected businesses. For example, the Malaysian ringgit's exchange rate was pegged against the US dollar in the afternoon of 2 September 1998, hours before Deputy Prime Minister and Finance Minister Anwar Ibrahim was sacked from the government, probably to pre-empt currency volatility and speculation after the firing. Malaysia's 1998 experiment with capital controls has thus been seen as compromised by political bias, vested interests and inappropriate policy instruments. However, it would be a serious mistake to reject the desirability of capital controls as well as other economic recovery initiatives on account of the flawed Malaysian experience.

Capital controls on outflows and other such efforts to defend a currency already under attack may be ineffective and may actually unwittingly subsidise further speculative actions. Instead, measures to insulate the domestic banking system from short-term volatility through regulatory measures, including capital controls on easily reversible short-term inflows as well as stricter prudential regulation and supervision, may be far more effective and sustainable. International cooperation and coordination have often not only provided the best responses during crisis episodes, but have also been important for effective prudential and regulatory initiatives as well as reducing "policy arbitrage".

Priorities for International Financial System Reform

The experiences of the 1997–98 East Asian crises offer six major lessons for international financial reform. First, existing mechanisms and institutions for preventing financial crises are grossly inadequate. As recent experiences suggest, current trends in financial liberalisation are likely to increase — rather than decrease — the likelihood, frequency and severity of currency and financial crises. Too little was done by the national authorities and their foreign advisers to discourage short-term capital flows, and too much emphasis has been placed on the expected protection provided by international adherence to codes and standards (Rodrik 1999a).

Financial liberalisation has also reduced the macroeconomic instruments available to governments for crisis aversion, and has instead left governments with little choice but to react pro-cyclically, which tends to exacerbate economic downturns. Governments need to be assured of their autonomy in relation to national macroeconomic policy in order to enable them to intervene counter-cyclically to avoid crises, which have had much more devastating consequences in developing countries than elsewhere. Recognition of the exaggerated effects of currency movements at the international level should also lead to greater surveillance and coordination among the three major international currency issuers: Japan, the United States, and Europe.

Second, existing mechanisms and institutions for financial crisis management are also grossly inadequate. The greater likelihood, frequency and severity of currency and financial crises in middle-income developing countries in recent times — with devastating consequences for the real economy and for innocent "bystanders in the neighbourhood" through "contagion", as in the East Asian crises — makes speedy crisis resolution imperative. There is an urgent need to increase emergency financing during crises and to establish adequate new procedures for timely and orderly debt standstills and workouts. International financial institutions, including regional institutions, should be able to provide adequate counter-cyclical financing, for instance, for social safety nets during crises (Ocampo 2000). Instead of current arrangements, which tend to benefit foreign creditors, new procedures and mechanisms are needed to ensure that they too share responsibility for the consequences of their lending practices.

Third, the agenda for international financial reform needs to go beyond the recent preoccupation with crisis prevention and resolution to address the declining availability and provision of development finance, especially to small and poor countries (Ocampo 2000) that have limited and expensive access to capital markets. The IMF, in particular, is facing growing pressure to return to its supposedly core function of providing emergency credit and core competencies of crisis prevention and mitigation. Meanwhile, the World Bank and other multilateral development banks have either abandoned or sharply reduced industrial financing, further limiting the likelihood that developing countries will be able to secure funding to develop new manufacturing capacities and capabilities. The United Nations Conference on Financing for Development, held in Monterrey in March 2002, clearly did not address this challenge adequately despite the build-up to the Monterrey consensus.

Fourth, inertia and vested interests stand in the way of urgently needed international institutional reforms. The international financial institutions need to reform their governance to ensure greater and more equitable participation and decision-making — and hence ownership — by developing countries at all levels and in various tasks that the new international financial system must begin to address more adequately. There is also a need to reduce the concentration of power in and the power of some apex institutions, such as the IMF, by delegating authority to other agencies — e.g. the proposed World Financial Organisation or World Financial Authority — as well as by encouraging decentralisation, devolution, complementarity and competition with other international financial institutions, including regional ones. The Group of Seven must engage in more serious consultations with developing countries in relation to international economic issues in order to avoid insensitive and potentially disastrous oversights and further loss of policy legitimacy (Rodrik 1999a).

Fifth, the reforms should restore and ensure national economic authority and autonomy, which have been greatly undermined by international deregulation and recent regulation, but remain essential for more effective macroeconomic management and development initiatives. Policy conditionalities accompanying IMF financing must be minimised, if not eliminated altogether. One size clearly does not fit all, and imposed policies have not contributed much, either to economic recovery or growth (Weisbrot *et al.* 2000), let alone sustainable development. Such ownership will ensure greater legitimacy for public policies and must include regulation of the capital account and choice of exchange rate regime. Because international financial reforms in the foreseeable future are unlikely to adequately provide the global public goods and international financial services most developing countries need, it is imperative that reforms of the international system assure national policy independence so that governments are better able to address regulatory and interventionist functions beyond a global and regional purview.

Finally, appreciation is growing of the desirability of regional monetary cooperation in the face of growing capital mobility and the increasing frequency of currency and related financial crises, often with devastating consequences for the real economy. Some observers argue, for instance, that growing European monetary integration in recent decades arose out of governments' recognition of their declining sovereignty in the face of growing capital mobility, especially as their capital accounts were liberalised (Baines 2002). Instead of trying to assert greater national control with probably limited efficacy, cooperation among governments in a region is more likely to be effective in the face of the greater magnitude and velocity of capital flows. However, no single formula or trajectory for fostering such cooperation is available, and it probably cannot be promoted successfully, independently of economic cooperation on other fronts.

The existence of such regional arrangements also offers an intermediate alternative between national and global levels of action and intervention, and reduces the existing monopolistic powers of global authorities. To be successful and effective, such regional arrangements must be flexible, but credible, and capable of effective counter-cyclical initiatives for both crisis prevention and management. In East Asia, the Japanese proposal for an Asian monetary facility soon after the outbreak of the Asian crises could have made a major difference in checking and managing the crises, but Western opposition blocked the proposal. With the growing reluctance in the West —

especially the US — to allow the IMF to serve as a lender of last resort, there should be more tolerance to cooperative regional monetary arrangements as alternatives.

Concluding Remarks

In early September 2003, then IMF Managing Director Horst Kohler acknowledged that Malaysia's September 1998 controls seemed to have worked, and went on to recognise the right of countries to impose temporary controls on capital outflows to cope with crisis situations. This endorsement of controls on outflows went much further than IMF Senior Deputy Managing Director Stanley Fischer's 1998 grudging endorsement of controls on inflows, as in Chile and Colombia.

Meanwhile, the promised gains from international financial liberalisation have not materialised. While there have been brief episodes to the contrary, the overwhelming evidence suggests that net capital flows following capital account convertibility have been from the capital poor to the capital rich, rather than in the opposite direction. This has been true of the so-called "transition economies", Africa, Latin America and most of Asia for most of the last two decades. While there have undoubtedly been temporary net flows into East Asia during the early and mid-1990s, and into Latin America at other times, the overall record clearly undermines the promises of its proponents.

In mid-2003, IMF research — by Economic Counsellor and Research Department Director Kenneth Rogoff and his colleagues — acknowledged that financial liberalisation did not seem to have contributed to economic growth. More heterodox research has found more adverse consequences, including deflationary macroeconomic policy pressures, slower growth and greater vulnerability to crisis. In East Asia and Latin America, inflow surges have contributed to asset (especially stock) price bubbles, consumption binges, misallocation of financial resources, including "mal-investments", as well as greater vulnerability to currency, banking and other financial crises.

Similarly, there is little evidence of a significant and sustained decline in the costs of capital for various reasons, perhaps including the increased share of financial rents in the OECD economies since the 1970s and the mixed consequences of financial deepening (Epstein, Grabel and Jomo 2003). There is also little evidence that financial deepening has reduced financial volatility and vulnerability to crisis. While some old sources of volatility and vulnerability have undoubtedly been reduced by the new financial instruments and derivatives, there has clearly been a significant increase in the frequency of currency, banking and other financial crises in the recent period. While the origins, nature and consequences of recent crises have undoubtedly changed over time, and there have been some advances in crisis aversion and management, this has not significantly reduced the occurrence and frequency of financial crises. Economic liberalisation and international financial integration have also resulted in the greater likelihood of cross-border transmission of financial crises, acknowledged by more frequent references to the dangers of contagion.

Financial liberalisation has followed the ascendance of international finance, reflected in institutional reform and public policy, e.g. advocacy of greater central bank independence from government executives. This has inevitably greatly influenced macroeconomic, especially monetary, policy in favour of financial including foreign interests which has been reflected in greater policy sensitivity to market expectations as well as policy advice from the international financial institutions. International financial liberalisation has also undermined financial policy instruments and institutions that have been so important for industrial or investment policy initiatives associated with developmental states over the last two centuries.

Importantly, the earlier Washington Consensus advocacy of financial liberalisation was not based on the theoretical analysis advocating financial liberalisation, or at least one of its early proponents, Ronald McKinnon. His original critique with Shaw was based on the singular case of Korea during the 1960s, when savings rates continued to rise despite alleged financial repression. Later, however, McKinnon was apparently so alarmed by the advocacy of wrongly sequenced financial liberalisation that he felt compelled to write *The Order of Financial Liberalization,* where he reiterated that capital account liberalisation should be the last — and certainly not the first — step in financial liberalisation. However, this has not discouraged advocates of financial liberalisation from pushing strongly for universal capital account liberalisation.

Note

1.   In 1997, the Interim Committee of the IMF agreed that the Fund's Articles of Agreement be amended to include currency convertibility for capital transactions. First mooted in its April meeting, the decision was confirmed in Hong Kong in September after the East Asian currency and financial crises had begun in Thailand in July, spreading immediately to the rest of Southeast Asia. Since then, Fund officials have reiterated that capital account liberalisation should become one of its basic objectives (Fischer 1998e). Ironically, this decision was made as the world's first serious "capital account crisis" was building up and later confirmed after it had started in July 1997. Since then, there has been no explicit *mea culpa* from the protagonists involved, although it is now grudgingly acknowledged that financial liberalisation has not contributed to growth in emerging markets (Prasad *et al.* 2003).

Bibliography

Abdelal, Rawi and Laura Alfaro (2002). "Malaysia: Capital and Control". Harvard Business School Case 702-040, revised 4 June.

——— (2003). "Capital and Control: Lessons from Malaysia". *Challenge* 46 (4) (July–August): 36–53.

Abdul Rahman Embong and Jurgen Rudolph (2000). *Southeast Asia into the Twenty First Century, Crisis and Beyond.* Penerbit Universiti Kebangsaan Malaysia, Bangi, Malaysia.

Abdul Rahman Othman (2001). "Daim Lied in Parliament". 22 Mar. Available from <http://www.malaysia.net/lists/sangkancil/2001-03/msg01029.html>.

Adam, Christopher and Will Cavendish (1995). "Background". In Jomo K.S. (ed.). *Privatizing Malaysia: Rents, Rhetoric, Realities.* Boulder: Westview Press.

ADB (1999). *Asian Development Outlook.* New York: Oxford University Press for Asian Development Bank, Manila.

Aganin, A. and P.F. Volpin (2003). "History of Corporate Ownership in Italy". European Corporate Governance Institute (ECGI) Finance Working Paper No. 17/2003. Available from <http://ssrn.com/>.

Agenor, P., M. Miller, D. Vines, and A. Weber (1999). *The Asian Financial Crisis: Causes, Contagion and Consequences.* Cambridge: Cambridge University Press.

Aghion, P., O. Hart, and J. Moore (1992). "The Economics of Bankruptcy Reform". *Journal of Law, Economics and Organization* 8: 523–46 <http://papers.nber.org/papers/w4097.pdf>.

——— (1994). "Improving Bankruptcy Procedure". Discussion Paper No. 142, Harvard Law School, Cambridge, MA.

Alchian, Armen A. (1950). "Uncertainty, Evolution and Economic Theory". *Journal of Political Economy,* 58 (June): 211–21.

Alchian, Armen A. and Reuben Kessel (1962). "Competition, Monopoly, and the Pursuit of Money". In National Bureau of Economic Research. *Aspects of Labor Economics.* Princeton: Princeton University Press, pp. 157–83.

Alesina, Alberto, Vittorio Grilli, and Gian M. Milesi-Ferretti (1993). *The Political Economy of Capital Controls.* NBER Working Paper Series,

No. 4353, National Bureau of Economic Research, Cambridge, MA, May.

Ali Abdul Kadir (2000). "Beyond the Asian Financial Crisis — Challenges and Perspectives for the Malaysian Capital Market". Speech at the MACPA 42nd Anniversary Commemorative Lectures & Luncheon, Renaissance Hotel, Kuala Lumpur, Securities Commission, 24 Oct.

AMCHAM (2002). American Malaysian Chamber of Commerce, Kuala Lumpur <http://www.amcham.com.my/bizresource/Advisor2002.pdf>.

Amsden, Alice (1989). *Asia's Next Giant*. New York: Oxford University Press.

———— (2000). *The Rise of "the Rest": Challenges to the West from Late-Industrializing Economies*. New York: Oxford University Press.

Amsden, Alice and Hikino Takashi (1994). "Project Execution Capability, Organizational Know-how and Conglomerate Corporate Growth in Late Industrialization". *Industrial and Corporate Change* 3 (1): 111–47.

Anwar Ibrahim (1996). "Malaysia's Middle Way: Growth with Equity". *New Perspectives Quarterly* 13 (4): 34–42.

Ariff, Mohamed (1998). "Options for the Ringgit". In Mohamed Ariff, *et al. Currency Turmoil and the Malaysian Economy: Genesis, Prognosis and Response*. Malaysian Institute of Economic Research, Kuala Lumpur.

Ariff, Mohamed and Yasmin Abu Bakar (1999). "The Malaysian Financial Crisis: Economic Impact and Recovery Prospects". *The Developing Economies*, Dec.

Ariff, Mohamed and Ahmed M. Khalid (2000). *Liberalization, Growth and the Asian Financial Crisis*. Cheltenham, UK: Edward Elgar.

Ariyoshi, Akira, Karl Habermeier, Bernard Laurens, Inci Otker-Robe, Jorge Ivan Canales-Kriljenko, and Andre Kirilenko (2000). "Capital Controls: Country Experiences with Their Use and Liberalization". IMF Occasional Paper 190, International Monetary Fund, Washington DC.

Armijo, L. Elliot (1999). "Mixed Blessing: Expectations about Foreign Capital Flows and Democracy in Emerging Markets". In Leslie Elliot Armijo (ed.). *Financial Globalization and Democracy in Emerging Markets*. London: Macmillan.

Armour, J. (2001). "The Law and Economics of Corporate Insolvency: A Review". Working Paper No. 197, ESRC Centre for Business Research, University of Cambridge, Cambridge.

Arnoot, Richard and Joseph E. Stiglitz (1988). *The Basic Analytics of Moral Hazard*. NBER Working Paper 2484, National Bureau of Economic Research, Cambridge, MA, Jan.

Arthur, N., G. Garvey, P. Swan, and S. Taylor (1993). "Agency Theory and 'Management Research': A Comment". *Australian Journal of Management* 18 (1), June.

ASEAN Economic Bulletin (2000) 17 (2), August. "The Asian Financial Crisis: Hindsight and Foresight". Institute of Southeast Asian Studies, Singapore.

Asiafeatures (2000). "Getting Back on Track". May 15. Available from <http://www.asiafeatures.com/current_affairs/0004,0130,03a.html>.

ADB (2000a). *Asian Recovery Report 2000.* Asian Development Bank, Manila. Available from <http://aric.adb.org>.

_____ (2000b). "Recent Corporate Governance Reforms in the Five Affected Countries". Asian Development Bank, Manila. Available from <http://www.adb.org/Documetns/Books/Corporate_Governance/Vol1/chapter4.pdf>.

_____ (2003). "Key Indicators 2003". Asian Development Bank, Manila. Available from <www.adb.org/statistics>.

Asiaweek, various issues.

Associated Press (2000). "Renewed war of words may delay CLOB resolution". Kuala Lumpur, 2 Feb. Available from <http://www.singapore-window.org/sw00/000202ap.htm>.

Athukorala, Prema-Chandra (1998a). "Malaysia". In Ross H. McLeod and Ross Garnaut (eds.). *East Asia in Crisis: From Being a Miracle to Needing One.* London: Routledge, pp. 85–101.

_____ (1998b). "Swimming against the tide: Crisis management in Malaysia". *ASEAN Economic Bulletin* 15 (3) (Dec.): 281–9.

_____ (2000a). "The Malaysian Experiment". In Peter Drysdale (ed.). *Reforms and Recovery in East Asia: The Role of State and Economic Enterprise.* London: Routledge, pp. 170–90.

_____ (2000b). "Capital Account Regimes, Crisis, and Adjustment in Malaysia". *Asian Development Review* 18 (1): 17–48.

_____ (2001). *Crisis and Recovery in Malaysia: The Role of Capital Controls.* Cheltenham: Edward Elgar.

Aybar, Sedat and Costas Lapavitsas (2003). "Financial System Design and The Post-Washington Consensus". In Ben Fine, Costas Lapavitsas, and Jonathan Pincus (eds.). *Development Policy in the Twenty-First Century: Beyond the Post-Washington Consensus.* London: Routledge, pp. 28–51.

Bacha, Obiyathula (1998). "Malaysia: From Currency to Banking Crisis". *Malaysian Journal of Economic Studies* 35 (1 & 2) (June–Dec.): 73–94.

Baig, T. and I. Goldfajn (1998). "Financial Market Contagion in the Asian Crisis". IMF Working Paper No. 155, International Monetary Fund, Washington DC.

Baines, Adam (2002). "Capital Mobility and European Financial and Monetary Integration: A Structural Analysis". *Review of International Studies* 28: 337–57.

Baird, D. G. (1986). "The Uneasy Case for Corporate Reorganisations". *Journal of Legal Studies* 15: 127–47.

—— (1993). "Revisiting Auctions in Chapter 11". *Journal of Law and Economics* 36: 633–53.

Baker, Gerard. (1998). "US looks to G7 backing on Asia crisis". *Financial Times,* Feb. 19.

Baliño, Tomás J. T., C. Enoch, A-M. Gulde, C-J. Lindgren, M. Quintyn, and L. Teo (1999). "Financial Sector Crisis and Restructuring: Lessons from East Asia". September, International Monetary Fund, Washington DC.

Bank Negara Malaysia (BNM). *Annual Report.* Various years. Bank Negara Malaysia, Kuala Lumpur.

——. *Interbank Interest Rates.* Bank Negara Malaysia, Kuala Lumpur. Available from <http://www.bnm.gov.my/>.

——. *Monthly Statistical Bulletin.* Various months. Bank Negara Malaysia, Kuala Lumpur.

——. Press Release. Various releases. Bank Negara Malaysia, Kuala Lumpur. Available from <http://www.bnm.gov.my/pa>.

——. *Quarterly Economic Bulletin.* Various quarters. Bank Negara Malaysia, Kuala Lumpur.

——. *Stock Market Indices Daily Update.* Bank Negara Malaysia, Kuala Lumpur. Available from <http://www.bnm.gov.my/>.

—— (1999). *The Central Bank and the Financial System in Malaysia: A Decade of Change, 1989–1999.* Bank Negara Malaysia, Kuala Lumpur.

—— (2001). *The Masterplan: Building a Secure Future,.* Bank Negara Malaysia, Kuala Lumpur.

Bank of International Settlements (BIS) (1992). "Recent Developments in International Interbank Relations". Bank of International Settlements, Basel.

—— (1998). *Report on the Maturity and Nationality of International Bank Lending.* Bank of International Settlements, Basel, Jan.

Bansfield, E-C. (1995). "Business-Government Collusion". *The Freeman* 48 (2), Feb. Available from <http://www.libertyhaven.com/theoretical orphilosophicalissues/protectionismpopulismandinterventionism/ business.html>.

Barrock, L. (2002). "Taking over the wheel of Park May: Kumpulan Kenderaan to acquire 63.7 per cent stake in bus operator via share swap". *The Edge*, 25 Feb.

Bebchuk, L. A. (1988). "A New Approach to Corporate Reorganization". *Harvard Law Review* 101: 775–804.

———— (1997). "Chapter 11". Discussion Paper No. 227, Harvard Law School, Cambridge, MA.

———— (1998). "Chapter 11". In Peter Newman (ed.). *The New Palgrave Dictionary of Economics and the Law*. Macmillan: Basingstoke.

Beeson, Mark (2000). "Mahathir and the Markets: Globalization and the Pursuit of Economic Autonomy in Malaysia". *Pacific Affairs* 73 (3): 335–52.

———— (2003). "East Asia, the International Financial Institutions and Regional Regulatory Reform: A Review of the Issues". *Journal of the Asia Pacific Economy* 8 (3): 305–26.

Belcher, A. (1997). *Corporate Rescue*. London: Sweet & Maxwell.

Belka, M. (1994). "Financial Restructuring of Banks and Enterprises in Poland". *Moct-Most* 4 (3): 71–84.

Bello, Walden, Kamal Malhotra, Nicola Bullard, and Marco Mezzera (2000). "Notes on the Ascendancy of Regulation on Speculative Capital". In Walden Bello, Nicola Bullard, and Kamal Malhotra (eds.). *Global Finance: New Thinking on Regulating Speculative Capital Markets*. London: Zed Books, pp. 1–26.

Bello, Walden, Nicola Bullard, and Kamal Malhotra (eds.) (2000). *Global Finance: New Thinking on Regulating Speculative Capital Markets*. London: Zed Books.

Berglof, Erik and E. L. von Thadden (1999). "The Changing Corporate Governance Paradigm: Implications for Transition and Developing Countries". William Davidson Institute Working Papers Series 263, William Davidson Institute, University of Michigan Business School, Ann Arbor, Michigan.

Berle, Adolph A. and Gardiner C. Means (1933). *The Modern Corporation and Private Property*. New York: Macmillan.

Bernama, 21 May 2004, "UEM World to raise bonds worth RM1bn for expressway expansion". Available from <http://www.bernama.com.my/bernama/v3/news_business.php?id=68352>.

Bhagwati, Jagdish (1998a). "The Capital Myth: The difference between trade in widgets and dollars". *Foreign Affairs* 77 (3) (May–June): 7–12.

———— (1998b). "Free thinker: Free trader explains why he likes capital controls". *Far Eastern Economic Review*, 15 Oct.: 14.

_____ (1998c). "Yes to free trade and maybe to capital control". *Wall Street Journal,* 16 Nov.: A–38.

Bhalla, A.S. (2001). *Market or Government Failures? An Asian Perspective.* Palgrave: Basingstoke.

Bhattacharya, Anindya K. (2001). "The Asian Financial Crisis and Malaysian Capital Controls". *Asia Pacific Business Review* 7 (3) (Spring): 181–93.

Biers, Dan (ed.) (1998). *Crash of '97: How the Financial Crisis is Reshaping Asia.* Hong Kong: Far Eastern Economic Review.

Biersteker, Thomas (1990). "Reducing the Role of the State in the Economy: A Conceptual Exploration of IMF and World Bank Prescriptions". *International Studies Quarterly* 34 (4) (Dec.).

Binamira, J. A. and W. C. Haworth (2000). "Debt Restructuring in East Asia: Government and the Corporate Sector". *Managing Financial and Corporate Distress: Lessons from Asia.* Brookings Institution, Washington DC.

Bird, Graham (1999). "Crisis Averter, Crisis Lender, Crisis Manager: the IMF in search of systematic role". *The World Economy* 22 (7) (Sep.).

Blair, M. (1995). *Ownership and Control: Rethinking Corporate Governance for the Twenty-first Century.* Brookings Institution, Washington DC.

Blaustein, M. (2001). "Globally Competitive Organization Behavior and Industrial Organization in Asian Economies". Harvard Project for Asian and International Relations, Cambridge MA. Available from <http://hcs.harvard.edu/~hpair/hpair2001/workshop6briefing.htm>.

Blinder, Alan (1999). "Eight Steps to a New Financial Order". *Foreign Affairs* 78 (5) (Sep./Oct.): 50–63.

Block, Thorsten H. (1998). "Financial Market Liberalization and the Changing Character of Corporate Governance". Working Paper No. 3, Center for Economic Policy Analysis, New School for Social Research, New York, May.

Boadway, Robin W., Dale Chua, and Frank Flatters (1995a). "Indirect Taxes and Investment Incentives in Malaysia". In Anwar Shah (ed.). *Fiscal Incentives for Investment and Innovation.* Oxford: Oxford University Press, pp. 375–97.

_____ (1995b). "Investment Incentives and the Corporate Tax System in Malaysia". In Anwar Shah (ed.). *Fiscal Incentives for Investment and Innovation.* Oxford: Oxford University Press, pp. 341–73.

Bonin, John P. and Bozena Leven (2000). "Can Banks Promote Enterprise Restructuring?: Evidence From a Polish Bank's Experience". William Davidson Institute Working Paper No. 294, Mar., William Davidson Institute at the University of Michigan Business School, Michigan.

Boorman, Jack, Timothy Lane, Mariane Schulze-Ghattas, Ales Bulir, Atish Ghosh, Javier Hamann, Alexander Mourmouras, and Steven Phillips (2000). "Managing Financial Crises: The Experience in East Asia". IMF Working Paper No. 107, International Monetary Fund, Washington DC.

Booth, Anne (1999). "The Causes of South East Asia's Economic Crisis: A Sceptical Review of the Debate". Paper presented at ASEASUK Seminar on the South East Asian Crisis, University of North, London, June.

Borgini, P., S. Claessens, and G. Ferri (2000). "Political Economy of Distress in East Asian Financial Institutions". World Bank Policy Research Paper WP 2265, World Bank, Washington DC.

Bosworth, Barry and Susan M. Collins (2000). *From Boom to Crisis and Back Again: What Have We Learned?*. ADB Institute Working Paper 7, Asian Development Bank Institute, Tokyo, Feb.

Boughton, James M. (2000). "From Suez to Tequila: the IMF as crisis manager". *Economic Journal* 110 (Jan.): 273–91.

Bowie, Alisdair (1988). "Redistribution with Growth? The Dilemmas of State-sponsored Economic Development in Malaysia". *Journal of Developing Societies* 4: 52–69.

Bradley, M. and M. Rosenzweig (1992). "The Untenable Case for Chapter 11". *The Yale Law Journal* 101: 1043–95.

Brett, E.A. (1985). *The World Economy Since The War: The Politics of Uneven Development.* London: Macmillan.

Brouwer, Gordon de (2001). *Hedge Funds* in *Emerging Markets.* Cambridge: Cambridge University Press.

Brown, Stephen J., William N. Goetzmann, and James Park, G. (1998). "Hedge Funds and the Asian Currency Crisis of 1997". NBER Working Paper 6427, National Bureau of Economic Research, Cambridge, MA.

Caballero, R. J. and Mohamad L. Hammour (1994). "On the Timing and Efficiency of Creative Destruction". NBER Working Paper No. 4768, National Bureau of Economic Research, Cambridge, MA, June.

Calvo, G.A. and Enrique Mendoza (1998). *Rational Herd Behavior and the Globalization of Securities Markets.* University of Maryland, College Park.

_____ (2000). "Rational Contagion and the Globalization of Securities Markets". *Journal of International Economics* 51 (1): 79–113.

Cambridge Journal of Economics, Nov.1998.

Camdessus, Michel (1998a). "The IMF and its Programs in Asia". Speech at the Council on Foreign Relations, New York, 6 Feb.

———— (1998b). "Reflections on the Crisis in Asia". Speech at the Extraordinary Ministerial Meeting of the Group of 24. Caracas, Venezuela, 7 Feb.

Campbell, A. (1994). "Company Rescue: The Legal Response to the Potential Rescue of Insolvent Companies". The International Centre for Criminal Law Reform and Criminal Justice Policy (ICCLR): 1.

Caprio, Gerard and Laurence Summers (1993). "Finance and Its Reform: Beyond Laissez-Faire". Policy Research Working Paper No. 1171, World Bank, Washington DC.

———— (1995). "Finance and Its Reform: Beyond Laissez-Faire". In *Financing Prosperity into the 21ˢᵗ Century*. New York: Macmillan.

Carleton, P. D., B. P. Rosario, and W. T. Woo (2000). "The Unorthodox Origins of the Asian Financial Crisis: Evidence from Logit Estimations". *ASEAN Economic Bulletin* 17 (1) (Apr.).

Case, William (1995). "Malaysia: Aspects and Audiences of Legitimacy". In Muthiah Alagappa (ed.). *Political Legitimacy in Southeast Asia*. Stanford: Stanford University Press, pp. 67–107.

CDRC (Corporate Debt Restructuring Committee) website: <http://www.bnm.gov.my/CDRC/>.

———— (1999). "The Renong Group Debt Restructuring Plan". Press release, Corporate Debt Restructuring Committee, Kuala Lumpur, 8 Mar. Available from <http://www.bnm.gov.my/CDRC/news.asp?sid=19990308>.

———— (2001). "Debt Restructuring of STAR-LRT and PUTRA-LRT". Press release, Corporate Debt Restructuring Committee. Kuala Lumpur, 30 Nov. Available from <http://www.bnm.gov.my/CDRC/news.asp?sid=20011130>.

———— (2002a). "Status Report as at 31 December 2001". Press release, Corporate Debt Restructuring Committee, Kuala Lumpur, 30 Jan.

———— (2002b). "Closure of the CDRC: Status at 15 August 2002". Press release, Corporate Debt Restructuring Committee, Kuala Lumpur, 21 Aug.

Chang, Ha-Joon (1993). "The Political Economy of Industrial Policy in Korea". *Cambridge Journal of Economics* 17 (2).

———— (1998). "Korea: The Misunderstood Crisis". *World Development* 26 (8): 1555–61.

———— (2000). "The Hazard of Moral Hazard — Untangling the Asian Crisis". *World Development* 28 (4): 775–88.

Chang, Ha-Joon and Hong-Jae Park (1999). "An Alternative Perspective on Post-1997 Corporate Reform in Korea". First draft, December: <http://www.econ.cam.ac.uk/faculty/chang/index.htm>.

Chang, Ha-Joon, Hong-Jae Park, and C. G. Yoo (1998). "Interpreting the Korean Crisis: Financial Liberalization, Industrial Policy and Corporate Governance". *Cambridge Journal of Economics* 22: 735–46.

Chang, Ha-Joon and Robert Rowthorn (1995). "Role of the State in Economic Change: Entrepreneurship and Conflict Management". In Ha-Joon Chang and Robert Rowthorn (eds.). *The Role of the State in Economic Change*. Oxford: Oxford University Press.

Chang, Li Lin and Ramkishen S. Rajan (2001). "The economies and politics of monetary regionalism in Asia". *ASEAN Economic Bulletin* 18 (1): 103–18.

Chang, Roberto and Andres Velasco (1998). "The Asian Liquidity Crisis". Working Paper No. 98–11, Federal Reserve Bank of Atlanta, July.

———— (1999). "Liquidity Crises in Emerging Markets: Theory and Policy". Working Paper No. 99–15, Federal Reserve Bank of Atlanta, Oct.

Channelnewsasia (2001). "Malaysia to suspend LRT bond issue indefinitely: Daim". 29 May. Available from <http://www.channelnewsasia.com/articles/2001/05/29/business61360.htm>.

Cheung, Anthony B. L. (2000). "Globalization versus Asian Values: Alternative Paradigms in Understanding Governance and Administration". *Asian Journal of Political Science* 8 (2): 1–15.

Chin, Kok Fay and Jomo K. S. (2003). "From Financial Liberalization to Crisis in Malaysia". In Chung H. Lee (ed.). *Financial Liberalization and the Economic Crisis in Asia*. London: Routledge.

Chin, Kok Fay and Kristen Nordhaug (2002). "Why Were There Differences in the Resilience of Malaysia and Taiwan to Financial Crisis?". *European Journal of Development Research* 14 (1) (June): 77–100.

Chin, Joseph (2001). "Daim approved RHB-Utama merger talks". *The Edge*. Available from <http://www.theedge.com.my/>.

Chinn, M.D. (1998). "Before the Fall: Were East Asian Currencies Overvalued?" NBER Working Paper No. 6491, National Bureau of Economic Research, Cambridge, MA.

Cho, Won-Dong and Michael Pomerleano (2001). "Corporate Debt Restructuring: The Missing Link in Financial Stabilization". Paper presented at a conference on "Policy Challenges for the Financial Sector in the Context of Globalization", Washington DC, 12–15 June.

Cho, Yoon Je (1997). "Government Intervention, Rent Distribution, and Economic Development in Korea". In M. Aoki, H. Y. Kim, and M. Okuno-Fujiwara (eds.). *The Role of Government in East Asian Economic Development: Comparative Institutional Analysis*. Oxford: Clarendon Press.

Chung, Un-Chan (1999). "East Asian Economic Crisis — What is and What Ought to be Done: The Case of Korea". Working Paper, Seoul National University, Korea.

Claessens, Stijn (1998). "Systemic Banks and Corporate Restructuring: Experiences and Lessons from East Asia". Discussion Paper, World Bank, Washington DC.

Claessens, Stijn, Simeon Djankov, and Daniela Klingebiel (1999a). "Bank and Corporate Restructuring in East Asia: Opportunities for Further Reform". Background Paper for IMF Annual Meetings Seminar, Sep.

———— (1999b). "Financial Restructuring in East Asia: Halfway There?". Financial Sector Discussion Paper No. 3, World Bank, Washington DC, Sep.

Claessens, Stijn, Simeon Djankov, and Larry Lang (2000). "The Separation of Ownership and Control in East Asian Corporations". *Journal of Financial Economics* 58: 81–112.

Claessens, Stijn, Daniela Klingebiel, and L. Laeven (2001). "Financial Restructuring in Systemic Crises: What Policies to Pursue?". Paper prepared for NBER Conference on "Management of Currency Crises", World Bank, Washington DC.

Cohen, Benjamin (2002). "Capital Controls: The Neglected Option". In Geoffrey R.D. Underhill and Xiaoke Zhang (eds.). *What Is To Be Done? Global Economic Disorder and Policies for a New International Financial Architecture*. Cambridge: Cambridge University Press.

Cooper, Richard (1998). "Should Capital Account Convertibility be a World Objective?". In P. Kenen (ed.). *Should the IMF Pursue Capital Account Convertibility?* Princeton Essays in International Finance 207 (May): 11–9.

Corbett, Jenny and David Vines (1999a). "East Asian Currency and Financial Crises: Lessons from Vulnerability, Crisis and Collapse". Asia Pacific School of Economics and Management Working Papers 99–3, Asia Pacific Press, Australia.

———— (1999b). "The Asian Currency and Financial Crisis: Lessons from Vulnerability, Crisis and Collapse". *World Economy* 22 (2) (Mar.): 155–77.

Corden, W.M. (1999). *The Asian Crisis: Is There a Way Out?* Singapore: Institute of Southeast Asian Studies.

Cornford, Andrew (1999). "Some Remarks on Banking Regulation and Supervision and Their Limitations in Relation to a New Financial Architecture". Paper presented at a Conference on "Structure, Instability and the World Economy: Reflections on the Economics of Hyman P. Minsky", Apr.

Corsetti, Giancarlo, Paolo Pesenti, and Nouriel Roubini (1998a). "What

Caused the Asian Currency and Financial Crisis?". Working Paper, New York University, New York.

_____ (1998b). "Paper Tigers, A Model of the Asian crisis". NBER Working Paper 6783, National Bureau of Economic Research, Cambridge, MA, 5 Nov.

_____ (1999). "Fundamental Determinants of the Asian Crisis: The Role of Financial Fragility and External Imbalances". Prepared for the NBER Tenth Annual East Asia Seminar, National Bureau of Economic Research, Cambridge, MA, May.

Coy, Peter, Manjeet Kripalani, and Mark Clifford (1998). "Capital Controls: Lifeline or Noose?". *Business Week*, 28 Sep.

Credit Suisse First Boston (1998). "Malaysia: Last in (to recession), First Out". *Asia Economic Perspective*, Hong Kong, Sep.

Cui, Zhiyuan (1999). "Incomplete Markets, Second Best, and Soft Budget Constraint: Exploring the Dilemmas Within the 'Invisible Hand' Paradigm". Processed, Political Science Department, Massachusetts Institute of Technology, Cambridge, MA.

Daily Express, 21 Dec. 2000. Available from <http://www.infosabah. com.my/ Daily_Express/dec/21–12–2000.htm#news12>.

Damis, A. and S. Poosparajah (2002). "Crux of public transport woes". 31 Mar. Available from <http://kliaekspres.emedia.com.my/Special/ ERL/Articles/Current/20020401114028/fullnews/>.

Damodaran, Sumangala (2000). "Capital Account Convertibility: Theoretical Issues and Policy Options". In Walden Bello, *et al.* (eds.). *Global Finance: New Thinking on Regulating Speculative Capital Markets*. London: Zed Books, pp. 159–76.

Danaharta website: <http://www.danaharta.com.my/>.

Danaharta (1999a). *Operations Report for the Six Months Ended 31 December 1998*. Pengurusan Danaharta Nasional Bhd, Kuala Lumpur.

_____ (1999b). *Operations Report for the Six Months Ended 30 June 1999*. Pengurusan Danaharta Nasional Bhd, Kuala Lumpur.

_____ (1999c). "Appendix 1" of the *Operations Report Half-Year Ended 30 June 1999*. Pengurusan Danaharta Nasional Bhd, Kuala Lumpur.

_____ (2000). *Operations Report for the Six Months Ended 31 December 1999*. Pengurusan Danaharta Nasional Bhd, Kuala Lumpur.

_____ (2001a). *Operations Report for the Six Months Ended 31 December 2000*. Pengurusan Danaharta Nasional Bhd, Kuala Lumpur.

_____ (2001b). "Appendix 1" of the *Operations Report Six Months Ended 31 December 2000*. Pengurusan Danaharta Nasional Bhd, Kuala Lumpur.

_____ (2001c). *Quarterly Update as at 31 March 2001*. Press release, Pengurusan Danaharta Nasional Bhd, Kuala Lumpur, 8 May.

—— (2001d). *Quarterly Update as at 30 September 2001*, Press release, Pengurusan Danaharta Nasional Bhd, Kuala Lumpur, 9 Nov.

—— (2002a). *Operations Report for the Six Months Ended 31 December 2001.* Press release, Pengurusan Danaharta Nasional Bhd, Kuala Lumpur, 12 Mar.

—— (2002b). *Annual Report 2001.* Pengurusan Danaharta Nasional Bhd, Kuala Lumpur.

—— (2003a). *Operations Report for the Six Months Ended 31 December 2002.* Pengurusan Danaharta Nasional Bhd, Kuala Lumpur.

—— (2003b). *Annual Report 2002.* Pengurusan Danaharta Nasional Bhd, Kuala Lumpur.

—— (2003c). *Quarterly Update as at 31 March 2003.* Press release, Pengurusan Danaharta Nasional Bhd, Kuala Lumpur, 12 Mar.

—— (2003d). "Danaharta Board Appointment". Press release, Pengurusan Danaharta Nasional Bhd, Kuala Lumpur, 30 July.

—— (2003e). *Operations Report for the Six Months Ended 30 June 2003.* Pengurusan Danaharta Nasional Bhd, Kuala Lumpur.

—— (2004a). *Quarterly Update as at 31 March 2004.* Press release, Pengurusan Danaharta Nasional Bhd, Kuala Lumpur, 17 May.

—— (2004b). *Operations Report for the Six Months Ended 30 June 2004.* Pengurusan Danaharta Nasional Bhd, Kuala Lumpur.

Danamodal website: <http://www.bnm.gov.my/danamodal/ff_vital.htm>.

Danamodal (2001). Press Release, 22 Dec. Danamodal, Kuala Lumpur. Available from <http://www.bnm.gov.my/index.php?ch=32& tpl_id=36>.

Das, Dilip K. (2000). "Asian Crisis: Distilling Critical Lessons". Discussion Paper No. 152, UNCTAD, Geneva, Dec.

Das, T. (1999). "East Asian Economic Crisis and Lessons for Debt Management". In A. Vasudevan (ed.). *External Debt Management: Issues, Lessons and Preventive Measure.* Mumbai: Reserve Bank of India, pp. 77–95.

Delhaise, P.F. (1998). *Asia in Crisis: The Implosion of the Banking and Finance Systems.* Singapore: John Wiley & Sons.

Demirguc-Kunt, Asli and Enrica Detragiache (1998). "The Determinants of Banking Crises in Developing and Developed Countries". *IMF Staff Papers* 45 (1): 81–109.

Diaz-Alejandro, Carlos (1985). "Goodbye Financial Repression, Hello Financial Crash". *Journal of Development Economics* 19: 1–24.

Dieter, Heribert (1998). "Crisis in Asia or Crisis of Globalisation?". CSGR Working Paper 15/98, University of Warwick, UK.

Disini Network website (2003). "40 per cent growth in mobile data sector". Vol. 13, May. Available from <http://www.disini.com.my/>.

Dobrinsky, R., N. Dochev, and B. Nikolov (1997). "Debt Workout and Enterprise Performance in Bulgaria: Lessons from Transition Experience and Crisis". Center for Economic and Strategic Research, Department of Economics, School of Management, Heriot-Watt University, Edinburgh.

Donaldson, Lex and James H. Davis (1991). "Stewardship Theory or Agency Theory: CEO Governance and Shareholder Returns". *Australian Journal of Management* 16 (1) (June).

Dooley, Michael P. (1996). "A Survey of Literature on Controls over International Capital Transactions". *IMF Staff Papers* 43 (4): 639–87.

_____ (1999). "Are Capital Inflows to Developing Countries a Vote for or against Economic Policy Reform?" In P. Agenor, M. Miller, D. Vines, and A. Weber (eds.). *The Asian Financial Crisis: Causes, Contagion and Consequences*. Cambridge: Cambridge University Press.

_____ (2000). "A Model of Crises in Emerging Markets". *Economic Journal* 110: 256–72.

Dore, Ronald (2000). *Stock Market Capitalism: Welfare Capitalism. Japan and Germany versus the Anglo-Saxons*. Oxford: Oxford University Press.

Dornbusch, Rudiger (1998). "Capital Controls: An Idea Whose Time is Past". In Peter B. Kenen (ed.). *Should the IMF Pursue Capital-Account Convertibility?*. Essays in International Finance No. 207, International Financial Section, Department of Economics, Princeton University, May.

_____ (2001). "Malaysia: Was It Different?". NBER Working Paper No. 8325, Oct., National Bureau on Economic Research, Cambridge, MA.

Dornbusch, Rudiger, Yung Chul Park, and Stijn Claessens (2000). "Contagion: Understanding How It Spreads". *The World Bank Research Observer* 15 (2) (Aug.): 177–97.

Dziobek, Claudia (1998). "Market-Based Policy Instruments for Systemic Bank Restructuring". IMF Working Paper 98/113, International Monetary Fund, Washington DC.

Dziobek, Claudia and Ceyla Pazarbasioglu (1997). "Lessons from Systemic Bank Restructuring: A Survey of 24 Countries". IMF Working Paper 97/161, International Monetary Fund, Washington DC.

Eatwell, John (1997). "International Financial Liberalization: The Impact on World Development". Discussion Paper Series, Office of Development Studies, United Nations Development Programme, New York.

Economic Planning Unit (1999). *White Paper: Status of the Malaysian Economy.* Prime Minister's Department, Malaysia, Kuala Lumpur, Apr.

Economist (1998). "No Room for Rivals in Mahathir's Malaysia". 26 Sep.

Eddy, Lee (1998). *The Asian Financial Crisis.* International Labour Office, Geneva.

Edison, Hali J., Pongsak Luangaram, and Marcus Miller (1998). "Asset Bubbles, Leverage and 'Lifeboats': Elements of the East Asian Crisis". *Economic Journal* 110 (Jan.): 309–34.

Edwards, Sebastian (1998). "Asia Should Beware of Chilean-style Capital Controls". *Asian Wall Street Journal,* 8 Sep.

_____ (1999a). "How Effective Are Capital Controls?". *Journal of Economic Perspectives* 13 (4) (Fall): 65–84.

_____ (1999b). "A Capital Idea? Reconsidering a Financial Quick Fix". *Foreign Affairs* 78 (3): 18–22.

Eichengreen, Barry (1999). "Toward A New International Financial Architecture: A Practical Post-Asia Agenda". Institute for International Economics, Washington DC.

_____ (2000). "Taming Capital Flows". *World Development* 28 (6): 1105–16.

_____ (2002). *Financial Crises, and What to Do About Them.* New York: Oxford University Press.

Eichengreen, Barry and Charles Wyplosz (1996). "Taxing International Financial Transactions to Enhance the Operation of the International Monetary System". In Mahbub Ul-Haq, Inge Kaul, and Irene Grunberg (eds.). *The Tobin Tax: Coping with Financial Volatility.* New York: Oxford University Press, pp. 73–90.

Enoch, Charles, Gillian Garcia, and V. Sundararajan (1999). "Recapitalizing Banks with Public Funds: Selected Issues". IMF Working Paper 99/139, International Monetary Fund, Washington DC.

Epstein, Gerald, Ilene Grabel and Jomo K. S. (2003). "Capital Management Techniques in Developing Countries: An Assessment of Experiences from the 1990's and Lessons for the Future". G-24 Technical Paper. Working Paper No. 56, Political Economy Research Institute, University of Massachusetts, Amherst. Available from <http://www.umass.edu/peri/pdfs/WP56.pdf.>.

Evans, Peter (1995). *Embedded Autonomy — States and Industrial Transformation.* Princeton: Princeton University Press.

FAC News (2001). "MAS' NTA — Daim lied in Parliament". 28 Mar. Available from <http://www.freeanwar.com/facnews/facnews280301.htm>.

Fane, George (2000). *Capital Mobility, Exchange Rates and Economic Crises.* Cheltenham, UK: Edward Elgar.

Far Eastern Economic Review (1996). 31 Oct.: 54.

———— (2001). "Day of the shareholder". 13 Sep.: 53, 54.

———— (2002). "We are about in the middle", 23 May. Available from <http://www.feer.com>.

Feldstein, Martin (1998). "Refocussing the IMF". *Foreign Affairs* 77 (2) (Mar.–Apr.): 20–33.

———— (ed.)(1991). *The Risk of Economic Crisis.* Chicago: University of Chicago Press.

Financial Supervisory Commission (1999). "Corporate Restructuring: Performance and Future Plan". Financial Supervisory Commission, Seoul, Korea, 14 Jan.

Financial Times (1997). "Mahathir tries to reassure foreigners". 8 Sep.

Fischer, Bernhard and Helmut Reisen (1992). "Towards Capital Account Convertibility". Policy Brief No. 4, OECD Development Centre, Organization for Economic Co-Operation and Development, Paris.

Fischer, Stanley (1998a). "The Asian Crisis: A View from the IMF". Address at the Midwinter Conference of the Bankers Association for Foreign Trade, Washington DC, 22 Jan.

———— (1998b). "The IMF and the Asian Crisis". Speech, 20 Mar., Los Angeles. Available from <http://www.imf.org/external/np/speeches/1998/030298.HTM>.

———— (1998c). "The Asian Crisis and the changing role of the IMF". *Finance and Development* 35 (2) (June): 2–5.

———— (1998d). "Lessons from a Crisis". *The Economist,* 3 Oct.: 19–23.

———— (1998e). "Reforming World Finance: Lessons from a Crisis". *IMF Survey,* 19 Oct. (special supplement): iii–iv, International Monetary Fund, Washington DC.

———— (1999a). "The Road to a Sustainable Recovery in Asia". IMF Speech at the World Economic Forum, Singapore, 18 Oct.

———— (1999b). "On the Need for an International Lender of Last Resort" <http://www.imf.org/external.no/speeches/1999/010399.htm>.

———— (2001). "Exchange Rate Regimes: Is the Bipolar View Correct?". *Finance and Development* 38 (2) (June): 18–21.

Flood, Robert and Nancy Marion (1999). "Perspectives on the Recent Financial Crisis Literature". *International Journal of Finance and Economics* 4: 1–26.

Flood Robert and Peter Garber (1984). "Gold Monetization and Gold Discipline". *Journal of Political Economy* 92 (1): 90–107.

Forbes, Eric C. (1992). *Dictionary of Malaysian Business*. Petaling Jaya: Pelanduk.

Forbes, Kristin J. (2003). "Capital Controls: Mud in the Wheels of Market Discipline". Processed, Council of Economic Advisers, Washington DC, and MIT-Sloan School of Management, Cambridge, MA, 21 Nov.

Frankel, Jeffrey A. (1998). "The Asian Model, the Miracle, the Crisis and the Fund". Paper delivered at the U. S. International Trade Commission, 16 Apr.

freeanwar (2000). "Malaysia Defends MAS, LRT Acquisitions". 24 Dec. Available from <http://www.freeanwar.com/news/reuters261200.html>.

freeMalaysia (1999a). "Renong: Dead Man Walking". 13 Mar. Available from <http://www.freemalaysia.com/political/renong_dead.htm>.

―――― (1999b). "Banking Daim-inance: Malaysia's Great Bank Robbery". 3 Sep. Available from <http://www.freemalaysia.com/economic/bank_daiminance.htm>.

――――. "Bank Bailouts? More Like Buddy Bailouts". Available from <http://www.freemalaysia.com/economic/bank_bailout.htm> [accessed 2001].

―――― (2001). "Renong Redux". Available from <http://www.freemalaysia.com/>.

Friedman, Milton (1953). "The Methodology of Positive Economics". In *Essays in Positive Economics*. Chicago: University of Chicago Press.

Fries, Steven M. and Timothy D. Lane (1994). "Financial and Enterprise Restructuring in Emerging Market Economies". IMF Working Paper 94/34, International Monetary Fund, Washington DC.

Fuller, Thomas (2000). "Bailout in Malaysia Signals Policy Failure". *International Herald Tribune*, 26 Dec. Available from <http://komentar.tripod.com/abailout281200.htm>.

Furman, Jason and Joseph E. Stiglitz (1998). "Economic Crises: Evidence and Insights from East Asia". *Brookings Papers on Economic Activity*, 2. Brookings Institute, Washington DC: 1–36.

Gabriel, Anita (2001). "Hitting them where it hurts". *The Edge*, 13 Aug. Available from <http://www.theedge.com.my/>.

―――― (2002). "A new lease of life — Proposal to split Malaysia Airlines into two may just be the medicine it needs". *The Edge*, 4 Feb.

Gan Wee Beng (2000). "The Perils of the Fixed Exchange Rate Systems (even in the presence capital controls)". *Ekonomika* 12 (3) (Jul.): 6–8.

Gan Wee Beng and Soon Lee Ying (2001). "Credit crunch during a currency crisis, the Malaysian experience". *ASEAN Economic Bulletin* 18 (2) (Aug.): 176–92.

Garnaut, Ross (1998). "The Financial Crisis: A Watershed in Economic Thought About East Asia". *Asian Pacific Economic Literature* 12 (1) (May): 1–11.

Gertner, Robert and Randal C. Picker (1992). "Bankruptcy and the Allocation of Control". Processed, University of Chicago, Chicago.

Ghani, Ejaz and Vivek Suri (1999). "Productivity Growth, Capital Accumulation and the Banking Sector: Some Lessons from Malaysia". World Bank Policy Research WP 2252, World Bank, Washington DC.

Gill, Ranjit (1998). *Black September*. Epic Management Services, Singapore.

Gilson, Stuart C., John Kose, and Larry H. P. Lang (1990). "Troubled Debt Restructurings: An Empirical Study of Private Reorganization of Firms in Default". *Journal of Financial Economics* 27: 315–53.

Glen, J., K. Lee and Ajit Singh (2000). "Competition, Corporate Governance and Financing of Corporate Growth in Emerging Markets". Discussion Paper in Accounting and Finance. No. AF46, Department of Applied Economics, University of Cambridge, Cambridge.

Glick, Reuven and Andrew K. Rose (1998). *Contagion and Trade: Why Are Currency Crises Regional?* Berkeley: University of California Press.

Godement, Francois (1999). *The Downsizing of Asia*. London: Routledge.

Goldstein, Morris (1998). *The Asian Financial Crisis: Causes, Cures, and Systemic Implications*. Institute for International Economics, Washington DC.

Goldstein, Morris, Graciela L. Kaminsky, and Carmen M. Reinhart (2000). *Assessing Financial Vulnerability: Developing an Early Warning System for Emerging Markets*. Institute for International Economies, Washington DC.

Gomez, E.T. (1990). *Politics in Business: UMNO's Corporate Investments*. Forum, Kuala Lumpur.

_____ (1991). *Money Politics in the Barisan National*. Forum, Kuala Lumpur.

_____ (1994). *Political Business: Corporate Involvement of Malaysia Political Parties*. Centre for Southeast Asian Studies, James Cook University, Townsville, Queensland.

_____ (ed.) (2002). *Political Business in East Asia*. London: Routledge.

Gomez, E.T. and Jomo K.S. (1999). *Malaysia's Political Economy: Politics, Patronage and Profits*. New York: Cambridge University Press

Gourevitch, P. A. (1993). "Democracy and Economic Policy: Elective Affinities and Circumstantial Conjectures". *World Development* 21 (8): 1271–80.

Government of Malaysia (1999). *White Paper: Status of the Malaysian Economy*. Percetakan Nasional Malaysia Berhad, Kuala Lumpur.

Grabel, Ilene (1996). "Marketing the Third World: The Contradictions of Portfolio Investment in the Global Economy". *World Development* 24 (11): 1761–76.

———— (1999). "Mexico Redux? Making Sense of the Financial Crisis of 1997–98". *Journal of Economic Issues* 33 (2): 375–81.

———— (2003). "Averting Crisis? Assessing Measures to Manage Financial Integration in Emerging Economies". *Cambridge Journal of Economics* 27 (3): 317–36.

Gray, C.W. and A. Holle (1996). "Bank-led Restructuring in Poland: The Reconciliation Process in Action". *Economics of Transition* 4 (2): 349–70.

Green, D.J. and J.E. Campos (2000). "Fiscal Lessons from the East Asian Financial Crisis". *Journal of Asian Economics* 12 (3): 309–31.

Greenspan, Alan (1999). "Maintaining Economic Vitality". Millennium Lecture Series sponsored by the Gerald R. Ford Foundation and Grand Valley State University, 8 Sep.

Gregorio, J.D., S. Edwards, and R.O. Valdes (2000). "Controls on Capital Inflows: Do They Work?" NBER Working Paper No. 7645, National Bureau of Economic Research, Cambridge, MA.

Griffith-Jones, Stephany, Jacques Cailloux, and Stephan Pfaffenzeller (1998). "The East Asian Financial Crisis: A Reflection on its Causes, Consequences and Policy implications". Institute of Development Studies, Brighton, UK, Sep.

Grilli, Vittorio, and G.M. Milesi-Ferretti (1995). "Economic Effects and Structural Determinants of Capital Controls". *IMF Staff Papers* 42 (Sep.): 517–51.

Grossman, Sanford J. and Oliver D. Hart (1980). "Takeover Bids, the Free Rider Problem and the Theory of the Corporation". *Bell Journal of Economics* 11: 42–64.

Guitián, Manuel (1997). "Reality and the Logic of Capital Flow Liberalization". In Christine P. Ries and Richard J. Sweeney (eds.). *Capital Controls in Emerging Economies*. Boulder, CO: Westview Press, pp. 234–43.

Gunasegaram, P. (2001a). "Should Halim take Renong and UEM private?". *The Edge*, 9 Jul.

———— (2001b). "What went wrong with privatization?". *The Edge*, 22 Oct.

———— (2002a). "Are minorities getting too good a deal?". *The Edge*, 4 Feb.

———— (2002b). "Letting the public benefit from PLUS listing". *The Edge*, 25 Mar.

Haan, Marco and Yohanes Riyanto (2000). "The Effects of Takeover Threats on Shareholders and Firm Value". Working Paper, University of Groningen, Netherlands.

Haggard, Stephan (1998a). "Why We Need the IMF". Available from <http://www-igcc.ucsd.edu/IGCC2/newsletter98s/html/feature. html>.

_____ (1998b). "The Asian Currency Crisis: the Stakes for US Policy" <http://www-igcc.uscd.edu/IGCC2/ucdc/UCDCTESTIMONY. html>.

_____ (2000). *The Political Economy of the Asian Financial Crisis.* Institute for International Economics, Washington DC.

Haggard, Stephan and Linda Low (2000). "The Politics of Malaysia's Capital Controls". University of California, San Diego. Available from <http://www-irps.ucsd.edu/faculty/shaggard/Malaysia.13a.doc.html>.

Hakim, S., Seidenstat, P. and Bowman, G. (1996). "Review and Analysis of Privatization Efforts in Transportation". In S. Hakim, P. Seidenstat and G. Bowman (eds.). *Privatized Transportation Systems.* London: Praeger.

Halcrow Consultants (1999). "Kuala Lumpur public transport restructuring final report". Corporate Debt Restructuring Committee, Kuala Lumpur.

Hale, David (1998). "The case for financial peacekeeping". *Foreign Affairs* 77 (6) (Nov./Dec.).

Haley, Mary Ann (1999). "Emerging Market Makers: The Power of Institutional Investors". In Leslie Armijo Elliot (ed.). *Financial Globalization and Democracy in Emerging Markets.* London: Macmillan.

Hart, Oliver (1999). "Different Approaches to Bankruptcy". Preliminary draft prepared for the roundtable on "New Comparative Economic Systems", 21 June, World Bank-CAE conference on Governance, Equity and Global Markets, Paris. Available from <http://www. worldbank.org/research/abcde/eu_99/eu/hart.pdf>.

Hawkins, J. and Turner, P. (1999). *Bank Restructuring in Practice: An Overview,* BIS Policy Papers No. 6, Bank for International Settlements, Basle, Sep.

Hayek, Friedrich A. (1982). *Law, Legislation and Liberty. A new statement of the liberal principles of justice and political economy.* London: Routledge and Kegan Paul.

Healy, Tim (1998). "Capital controls, interventions and what they mean to free markets". *Asiaweek,* 18 Sep. Available from <http://www.asiaweek. com/asiaweek/98/0918/cs4.html>.

Hellman, Thomas, Kevin Murdock, and Joseph E. Stiglitz (1996). "Deposit Mobilisation Through Financial Restraint". In N. Hermes and

R. Lensink (eds.). *Financial Development and Economic Growth*. London: Routledge.

―――― (1997). "Financial restraint and the Market Enhancing View". Paper presented at the International Economic Association Conference on the "Institutional Foundations of Economic Development in East Asia".

Henderson, Callum (1998). *Asia Falling? Making Sense of the Asian Currency Crisis and its Aftermath*. New York: McGraw-Hill.

Heong, Y. S. (2001). "Govt buys into MAS to help overcome problems: Daim". In *Bernama*, 18 Jan. Available from <http://ww8.malaysia directory.com/news/12/011806.html>.

Higgott, Richard (1998). "The Politics of Economic Crisis in East Asia: Some Longer term Implications". CSGR Working Paper No. 02/98, Centre for the Study of Globalisation and Regionalisation, University of Warwick, United Kingdom, Mar.

Hill, Hal (1998). "Malaysia's risky gamble". *Asian Wall Street Journal*, 9–10 Oct.

Ho, Andrew (2001). "Stop the bleeding at MAS". *AsiaWise*, 25 Apr. Available from <http://www.asiawise.com/mainpage.asp?mainaction=50& articleid=1526>.

Ho, Jacqueline (2002). "Time Engineering smoke screen". *The Edge*, 4 Feb.

Holloway, John (1995). "Global Capital and the National State". In W. Bonefeld and John Holloway (eds.). *Global Capital, National State and the Politics of Money*. London: St. Martin's Press, pp. 116–40.

Honohan, P. and D. Klingebiel (2000). "Controlling the Fiscal Costs of Banking Crises". Policy Research Working Paper 2441, World Bank, Washington DC.

Hook, G. D. *et al.* (2001). *Japan's International Relations: Politics, Economics and Security*. London: Routledge.

Horowitz, Shale and Uk Heo (eds.) (2001). *The Political Economy of International Financial Crisis: Interest Groups, Ideologies, and Institutions*. Singapore: Institute of Southeast Asian Studies.

Hotchkiss, Edith S. (1995). "Post-bankruptcy Performance and Management Turnover". *Journal of Finance* 50: 3–21.

Hotchkiss, Edith S. and Robert M. Mooradian (1997). "Vulture Investors and the Market for Control of Distressed Firms". *Journal of Financial Economics* 43: 401–32. Available from <http://pages.stern.nyu.edu/ ~nroubini/asia/AsiaChronology1.html>.

―――― (1998). "Acquisitions as a Means of Restructuring Firms in Chapter 11". *Journal of Financial Intermediation* 7: 240–62. Available from <http://www.img.org/external/np/exr/ib/2001/030901.htm>.

Hughes, Alan (1989). "The Impact of Mergers: A Survey of Empirical Evidence for the UK, 1950–1990". In J. Fairburn and J.A. Kay (eds.). *Mergers and Merger Policy*. 2nd edn., Oxford: Oxford University Press.

Hutchison, Michael (2001). "A Cure Worse than the Disease? Currency Crises and the Output Costs of IMF-supported Stabilization Programs". NBER Working Paper No. 8305, National Bureau of Economic Research, Cambridge, MA.

IMF. *International Financial Statistics*, various years. International Monetary Fund, Washington DC.

———. *World Economic Outlook*, various issues. International Monetary Fund, Washington DC.

———. *Annual Report*, various years. International Monetary Fund, Washington DC <http://www.imf.org>.

——— (1997a). *World Economic Outlook and International Financial Markets: Interim Assessment*. International Monetary Fund, Washington DC.

——— (1997b). "Thailand". Press Release No. 97/37, International Monetary Fund, Washington DC.

——— (1997c). "Indonesia". Press Release No. 97/50, International Monetary Fund, Washington DC.

——— (1997d). "South Korea". Press Release No. 97/55, International Monetary Fund, Washington DC.

——— (1998a). *World Economic Outlook, Financial Crises, Causes and Indicators*. May. International Monetary Fund, Washington DC.

——— (1998b). "Reforming World Finance: Lessons from a Crisis". *IMF Survey*, Special Supplement (19 Oct.), International Monetary Fund, Washington DC.

——— (1998c). *World Economic Outlook and International Financial Markets: Interim Assessment*, International Monetary Fund, Washington DC, Dec.

——— (1999). *World Economic Outlook 1999*. International Monetary Fund, Washington DC.

——— (2000). *IMF Survey*, 29 (2), International Monetary Fund, Washington DC, 24 Jan.

——— (2001a). "Malaysia: from Crisis to Recovery". Occasional Paper 207, International Monetary Fund, Washington DC.

——— (2001b). "Reforming the International Financial Architecture: Progress Through 2000". *IMF Issues Brief*, International Monetary Fund, Washington DC, 9 Mar.

——— (2002a). "IMF-Supported Programs in Capital Account Crises". Occasional Paper 210, International Monetary Fund, Washington DC.

_____ (2002b). "Moral Hazard, Does IMF Financing Encourage Imprudence by Borrowers and Lenders?" *Economic Issues* 28, International Monetary Fund, Washington DC.

Ito, Takatoshi (1999). "Capital Flows in Asia". NBER Working Paper 7134, National Bureau of Economic Research, Cambridge, MA, May.

Ishak Shari, *et al.* (1999). "Social Impact of Financial Crisis: Malaysia". Report submitted to the United Nations Development Program, Kuala Lumpur.

Iskander, M.R. and N. Chamlou (2000). *Corporate Governance: A Framework for Implementation.* World Bank, Washington DC.

Jackson, K.D. (ed.) (1999). *Asian Contagion: The Causes and Consequences of a Financial Crisis.* Boulder: Westview Press.

Jalil Hamid (2000). "Update 1 — Investors give Malaysia's UEM Deal the Thumbs Down". 13 Dec. Available from <http://asia.news.yahoo.com/reuters/nklr251308.html>.

James, Harold (1999). "Is Liberalization Reversible?" *Finance and Development* 36 (Dec.): 4.

James, William E. and Anwar Nasution (2003). "The Debt Trap and Monetary-Fiscal Policy in Indonesia: The Gathering Storm". *East Asian Economic Perspectives* 14 (2): 68–87.

Jayasankaran, S. (1999a). "Merger by decree". *Far Eastern Economic Review*, 9 Sep. Available from <http://www.feer.com>.

_____ (1999b). "Changing fortunes". *Far Eastern Economic Review*, 23 Dec. Available from <http://www.feer.com>.

_____ (2000). "Merger muddle". *Far Eastern Economic Review*, 10 Aug. Available from <http://www.feer.com>.

_____ (2001). "Bank restructuring: A political conundrum". *Far Eastern Economic Review*, 22 Feb. Available from <http://www.feer.com>.

_____ (2003). "Danaharta in the dock". *Far Eastern Economic Review*, 23 Jan. Available from <http://www.feer.com>.

Jesudason, James V. (1989). *Ethnicity and the Economy: The State, Chinese Business, And Multinationals in Malaysia.* Singapore: Oxford University Press.

Johnson, Simon and Todd Mitton (2001). "Cronyism and Capital Controls: Evidence from Malaysia". National Bureau of Economic Research meeting on "The Malaysian Currency Crisis", National Bureau of Economic Research, Washington DC, Feb. Revised 20 Aug.

_____ (2003). "Cronyism and Capital Controls: Evidence from Malaysia". *Journal of Financial Economics* 67 (2) (Feb.): 351–82.

Johnston, R.B. and N.T. Tamirisa (1998). *Why Do Countries Use Capital Controls?* IMF Working Paper 181, International Monetary Fund, Washington DC, Dec.

Jomo, K.S. (2001). "Growth After the Asian Crisis: What Remains of the East Asian Model?" Group of 24 Discussion Paper No. 10, United Nations Conference on Trade and Development, Geneva, and Harvard University, Kennedy School of Government, Cambridge, MA.

――― (2002). "Lessons From The East Asian Crisis of 1997–98". Paper presented to the European Annual World Bank Conference on Development Economics, Oslo, June.

――― (2003). "Malaysia's September 1998 Controls: Background, Context, Impacts, Comparisons, Implications, Lessons". Paper presented to the G-24 meeting, UNCTAD, Geneva, 15 Sep.

――― (ed.)(1995). *Privatizing Malaysia: Rents, Rhetoric, Realities*. Boulder: Westview Press.

――― (ed.) (1998). *Tigers in Trouble: Financial Governance, Liberalization and Crises in East Asia*. London: Zed Books.

――― (ed.) (2001). *Malaysian Eclipse, Economic Crisis and Recovery*. London: Zed Books.

――― (ed.) (2002). *Paper Tigers in Southeast Asia? Behind Miracle and Debacle*. London: Routledge.

Jomo, K.S., H.L. Khong, and Shamsulbahriah K.A. (1987). *Crisis and Response in the Malaysian Economy*. Kuala Lumpur: Malaysian Economic Association.

Jomo, K.S., Chen Yun Chung, Brian C. Folk, Irfan ul-Haque, Pasuk Phongpaichit, Batara Simatupang, and Mayuri Tateishi (1997). *Southeast Asia's Misunderstood Miracle: Industrial Policy and Economic Development in Thailand, Malaysia, and Indonesia*. Boulder, CO: Westview.

Jomo, K.S. and Michael T. Rock (1998). "Economic Diversification and primary Commodity Processing in Second-tier South-East Asian Newly Industrializing Countries". UNCTAD Discussion Paper No. 136, United Nations Conference on Trade and Development, Geneva.

Jomo, K.S. and Tan Kock Wah (eds.) (1999). *Industrial Policy in East Asia: Lessons for Malaysia*. Kuala Lumpur: University of Malaya Press.

Kaminsky, Gabriela and C. M. Reinhart (1996). "The Twin Crises: The Causes of Banking and Balance-of-Payments Problems". Working Paper no. 17, University of Maryland, Centre for International Economics, Baltimore, MD.

Kaminsky, Gabriela and Sergio Schmukler (2000). "Short and Long Run Integration, Do Capital Controls Matter?" *Brookings Trade Forum*: 125–78.

Kaminsky, Gabriela and C.M. Reinhart (2001). "Bank Lending and Contagion: Evidence from the Asian Crisis". In T. Ito and Anne

Krueger (eds.). *Regional and Global Capital Flows: Macroeconomic Causes and Consequences.* Chicago University Press, Chicago, for National Bureau of Economic Research.

Kaminsky, Gabriela and Sergio Schmukler (2002). "Emerging Market Instability: Do Sovereign Ratings Affect Country Risk and Stock Returns?" *The World Bank Economic Review* 16 (2): 171–95.

Kaminsky, Gabriela and Carmen Reinhart (2002). "The Center and the Periphery: The Globalization of Financial Turmoil". IMF Global Linkages Conference, Washington DC, 30 Nov.

Kanda, Hideki (1992). "Systemic Risk and International Financial Markets". In Franklin R. Edwards and Hugh T. Patrick (eds.). *Regulating International Financial Markets: Issues and Policies.* Dordrecht: Kluwer Academic Publishers.

Kaplan, Ethan and Dani Rodrik (2001). "Did the Malaysian Capital Controls Work?" NBER Working Paper No. 8142, National Bureau of Economic Research, Cambridge, MA, Feb.

Kapur, Devesh (1998). "The IMF: A Cure or a Curse?" *Foreign Policy* 111 (Summer): 114–29.

Kaufman, George (1996). "Bank Failures, Systemic Risk, and Bank Regulation". *Cato Journal* 16 (1) (Spring/Summer).

Kawai, M. (2000). "The Resolution of the East Asian Crisis: Financial and Corporate Sector Restructuring". *Journal of East Asian Economics* 11 (2): 133–67.

Keasey, K., Steve Thompson, and Mike Wright (1999). "Introduction". In K. Keasey, Steve Thompson, and Mike Wright (eds.). *Corporate Governance, Volume I: Aspects of Corporate Governance.* Cheltenham: Edward Elgar.

Keen Phillips, Guide to Administrative Receivership. Available from <http://www.keen-phillips.co.uk/insoladrec.htm>.

Keynes, J.M. (1936). *The General Theory of Employment, Interest and Money.* Harcourt Brace Jovanovich, New York. 1973 reprint of 3rd edn. London: Macmillan.

Khan, Mushtaq and Jomo K. S. (eds.) (2000). *Rents, Rent-Seeking, and Economic Development: Theory and Evidence in Asia.* Cambridge: Cambridge University Press.

Khazanah Nasional Bhd website. "Group of Companies". Available from <http://www.khazanah.com.my/>.

Khoo Boo Teik (1995). *Paradoxes of Mahathirism: An Intellectual Biography of Mahathir Mohamad.* Kuala Lumpur: Oxford University Press.

Khor, Martin (2000). "Why Capital Controls and International Debt Restructuring Mechanisms are Necessary to Prevent and Manage Crises". In

Walden Bello, *et al.* (eds.). *Global Finance: New Thinking on Regulation Speculative Capital Markets.* London: Zed Books, pp. 140–58.

Kim, S. and B. Cho (1999). "Korean Economic Crisis: New Interpretation and Alternative Economic Reform". Paper presented to the Annual Conference of Studies in Political Economy, Ottawa, Canada, 29 Jan.

Kim, S-H (1999). "Asian Crisis". Available from <http://www.nd.edu/~skim/academic/asiancrisis.doc>.

Kindleberger, Charles (1989). *Maniacs, Panics and Crashes. A History of Financial Crisis.* New York: Basic Books.

Kitley, P. (1998). "The Asian Crisis". *The Toowoomba Chronicle,* 11 Apr., and *The Sunshine Coast Daily,* 14 Apr.

Klingebiel, D. (2000). "The Use of Asset Management Companies in the Resolution of Banking Crises: Cross-Country Experiences". Working Paper No. 2284, Feb., World Bank, Washington DC.

KLSE (1998). "KLSE Announces Transfer of CLOB Accounts". Kuala Lumpur Stock Exchange, Kuala Lumpur. Available from <http://www.klse.com.my/website/news/pr/1998/980917.htm>.

—————— (2001). "Articles entitled UEM to sell assets and Halim's put option on Renong stake terminated". General announcement, Kuala Lumpur Stock Exchange, Kuala Lumpur. Available from <http://announcements.klse.com.my/EDMS%5Cannweb.nsf/0/482568AD00295D0748256B2200329ECA? OpenDocument>.

—————— (2003). "Proposed Disposal by Renong Berhad (Renong or Company) of its Entire Equity Interest of 29,222,203 Ordinary Shares of RM1.00 Each in Crest Petroleum Bhd (Crest) Representing Approximately 38.56 per cent Equity Interest Therein to Sapura Telecommunications Berhad (Sapura) for a Total Cash Consideration of RM105,199,930.80". General announcement, Kuala Lumpur Stock Exchange, Kuala Lumpur, 21 Apr.

Knowles, J.C., E.M. Pernia, and Mary Racelis (1999). "Social Consequences of the Financial Crisis in Asia". ADB Economic Staff Paper No. 60, Asian Development Bank, Manila.

Kose, M. Ayhan, Eswar S. Prasad, and Marco E. Terrones (2003). "Volatility and Comovement in a Globalized World Economy: An Empirical Exploration". IMF Working Paper 03/246, International Monetary Fund, Washington DC, Dec.

Kregel, Jan A. (1998a). "East Asia is Not Mexico: The Differences between Balance of Payments Crises and Debt Deflation". In Jomo K. S. (ed.). *Tigers in Trouble: Financial Governance, Liberalisation, and Crises in East Asia.* London: Zed Books.

_____ (1998b). "Yes, 'It Did Happen Again' — A Minsky Crisis Happened in Asia". Working Paper No. 234, Jerome Levy Economics Institute of Bard College, New York, Apr.

Krueger, Anne (2002). "Sovereign Debt Restructuring Mechanism". International Monetary Fund, Washington DC.

Krugman, Paul (1979). "A Model of Balance of Payments Crises". *Journal of Money, Credit and Banking* 11: 311–25.

Krugman, Paul (1994). "The Myth of Asia's Miracle". *Foreign Affairs* 73 (6): 62–78.

_____ (1998a). "Bubble, Boom, Crash: Theoretical Notes on Asia's Crisis". Jan. Available from <http://www.mit.edu/Krugman>.

_____ (1998b). "What Happened in Asia?". Processed, Jan. Available from <http://www.mit.edu/Krugman>.

_____ (1998c). "Fire-sale FDI". Paper prepared for NBER conference on "Capital Flows to Emerging Markets". 20–21 Feb. Available from <http://web.mit.edu/krugman/www/FIRESALE.htm>.

_____ (1998d). "Will Asia Bounce Back?" Speech for Credit Suisse First Boston, Hong Kong, Mar.

_____ (1998e). "An Open Letter to Prime Minister Mahathir". September 1. Reprinted in *Fortune* 138 (6) (28 Sep.): 35–6.

_____ (1998f). "Saving Asia: It's time to get radical". *Fortune,* 7 Sep.: 74–80.

_____ (1998g). "Malaysia's Opportunity?". *Far Eastern Economic Review* 161 (38) (17 Sep.): 32–3.

_____ (1998h). "The confidence game: How Washington worsened Asia's Crash". *The New Republic,* 5 Oct.: 23–5.

_____ (1999a). "The return of depression economics". *Foreign Affairs* 78 (1) (Jan./Feb.): 56–74.

_____ (1999b). "The Indispensable IMF". In Lawrence J. Mcquillan and Peter C. Montgomery (eds.). *The International Monetary Fund: Financial Medic to the World.* Stanford: Hoover Institution Press.

_____ (1999c). "Recovery? Don't bet on it." *Time,* 21 June <http://cnn.com/ASIANOW//time/asia/magazine/1999/990621/cover4.html>.

_____ (1999d). "Capital Control Freaks: How Malaysia Got Away with Economic Heresy". *Slate – The Dismal Science,* 27 Sep. Available from <http://slate.msn.com/Dismal/99_09_27/Dismal.asp>.

Kynge, James (1997). "Malaysian PM sets up GBP 12bn fund to support market". *Financial Times,* 4 Sep.

Lane, Timothy (1999). "The Asian Financial Crisis: What Have We Learned?" *Finance & Development* 36 (3) (Sep.): 44–7.

Lane, Timothy, Atish Ghrosh, Javier Hamann, Steven Phillips, Marianne Schulze-Ghattas and Tsidi Tsikata (1999). "IMF-Supported Programs in Indonesia, Korea and Thailand: A Preliminary Assessment". IMF Occasional Paper 178, International Monetary Fund, Washington DC, 30 June.

Lanyi, A. and Y. Lee (1999). "Governance Aspects of the East Asian Financial Crisis". IRIS Working Paper No. 226, Institutional Reform and the Informal Sector (IRIS) Center, University of Maryland, College Park.

Latifah Merican Cheong (2000). "Capital Flows and Capital Controls: the Malaysian Experience". Paper presented at the conference on "Globalization in the New Millennium", Seoul, Korea, 14–16 June.

Laurens, Bernard and Jaime Cardoso (1999). "Managing Capital Flows: Lessons From the Experience of Chile". IMF Working Paper 168, International Monetary Fund, Washington DC.

Lauridsen, L. S. (1998). "Thailand: Causes, Conduct, Consequences". In Jomo K. S. (ed.). *Tigers in Trouble: Financial Governance, Liberalization and Crises in East Asia*. London: Zed Books.

Lee Min Keong (2000). "Malaysia's privatization at crossroads". 15 May. Available from <http://www.asiafeatures.com/current_affairs/004,0130,01.html>.

Lee Tsun-Siou (2001). "Economic Development and Financial System Reform in Taiwan". In Masayoshi Tsurumi (ed.). *Financial Big Bang in Asia*. Aldershot: Ashgate.

Lee, C. H. (1992). "The Visible Hand and Economic Development: The Case of South Korea". In J. A. Roumasset and Susan Barr (eds.). *The Economics of Cooperation: East Asian Development and the Case for Pro-Market Intervention*. Boulder: Westview Press.

Lee, Eddy (1999). "The Debate on the Causes of the Asian Crisis: Crony Capitalism Versus International System Failure". *International Politics and Society* 2: 162–7.

Leff, Nathaniel (1978). "Industrial Organization and Entrepreneurship in Developing Countries: The Economic Groups". *Economic Development and Cultural Change* 4 (26): 661–75.

_____ (1979). "Entrepreneurship and Economic Development: The Problem Revisited". *Journal of Economic Literature* 17: 46–64.

Levine, R. (2000). "Bank-Based or Market-Based Financial System: Which is Better?" Paper prepared for the conference on "Financial Structure and Economic Development". World Bank, Washington DC, 10–11 Feb.

Lim Chong-Yah (2000). "From Recession to Recovery in East Asia: A Non-IMF and Non-World Bank Explanation". Special Lecture given at the

7th Pacific Basin Symposium, University of Malaya, Kuala Lumpur, 30 Aug.

Lim Kit Siang (1998). *Economic* and *Financial Crisis*. DAP Economic Committee, Kuala Lumpur.

―――― (2002). "Bailouts in Our Country". Media Conference Statement, 15 Jan. Available from <http://www.malaysia.net/sarawak/messages/8711.html>.

Lim Kok Wing (1998). *Hidden Agenda*. Kuala Lumpur: Limkokwing.

Lim Lin Lean and Chee Peng Lim (1984). *The Malaysian Economy at the Crossroads: Policy Adjustment or Structural Transformation*. Kuala Lumpur: Malaysian Economic Association.

Lim Say Boon (1999). "Premature smugness". *Far Eastern Economic Review*, 27 May. Available from <http://www.feer.com>.

Lim, Joseph (1999). "The Macroeconomics of the East Asian Crisis and the Implications of the Crisis for Macroeconomic Theory". *The Manchester School* 67 (5): 428–59.

Lin See-Yan (1993). "The institutional perspective of financial market reforms: the Malaysian experience". In Shaki Faruqui (ed.). *Financial Sector Reforms in Asian and Latin American Countries: Lessons of Comparative Experience*. World Bank, Washington DC.

―――― (1998). "Rebuilding ASEAN in the Wake of the Current Economic Crisis-Causes, Impact, Response and Lessons: A Malaysian Perspective". Paper presented at the Roundtable Discussion on the "Current Economic Crisis in ASEAN", Kuala Lumpur, 9–10 Apr.

Lin, Diaan-Yi (2001). "Distribution and Development: Malaysia's New Economic Policy and After, 1971–2001". Individual Student Research Report, Harvard Business School, Autumn.

Lopez, Leslie (1999). "Cleaning up the mess". *The Asian Wall Street Journal*, 15 Jan.

Low Chee Keong (ed.) (2000). *Financial Markets in Malaysia*. Kuala Lumpur: Malayan Law Journal Sdn Bhd.

Loweinstein, R. (2000). *When Genius Failed: The Rise and Fall of Long-Term Capital Management*. New York: Random House.

MacIntyre, Andrew (2001). "Institutions and Investors: The Politics of the Economic Crisis in Southeast Asia". *International Organization* 55 (1) (Winter): 81–122.

Maddison, Angus (1991). *Dynamic forces in capital development: A long-run perspective*. Oxford: Oxford University Press.

Mahani Zainal Abidin (2000a). "Implications of the Malaysian Experience on Future International Financial Arrangements". *ASEAN Economic Bulletin* 17 (2) (Aug.).

———— (2000b). "Malaysia's Alternative Approach to Crisis Management". In D. Singh and A. L. Smith (eds.). *Southeast Asian Affairs 2000.* Singapore: Institute of Southeast Asian Studies, pp. 184–202.

———— (2002). *Rewriting the Rules, The Malaysian Crisis Management Model.* Petaling Jaya: Prentice Hall.

Mahathir Mohamad (1998a). *The Way Forward.* London: Weidenfeld & Nicolson.

———— (1998b). *The Challenges of Turmoil.* Petaling Jaya: Pelanduk.

———— (1998c). *In the Face of Attack: Currency Turmoil, Selected Speeches.* Prime Minister's Department, Malaysia, Kuala Lumpur.

———— (1998d). "Revitalization of Japanese and East Asian economies". Speech at the Fifth Symposium of the Institute for International Monetary Affairs, Tokyo, 2 June.

———— (1998e). "Speech at the 6th ASEAN Summit", Hanoi, Vietnam, 15 Dec.

———— (1999a). *A New Deal for Asia.* Petaling Jaya: Pelanduk.

———— (1999b). "We had to decide things for ourselves". *Executive Intelligence Review,* 19 Feb.

———— (1999c). "Why Malaysia's Selective Currency Controls are Necessary and Why They Have Worked". Speech given at the Symposium of the First Anniversary of Currency Controls, Kuala Lumpur, 2 Sep.

———— (1999d). "Asia's Road to Recovery: The Challenge of Pragmatism". Speech at the East Asia Economic Summit organized by the World Economic Forum, Singapore, 18 Oct.

———— (2000). *The Malaysian Currency Crisis: How and Why it Happened.* Petaling Jaya: Pelanduk.

———— (2002). *Reflections on Asia.* Petaling Jaya: Pelanduk.

Maher, M. and Andersson, T. (2000). "Corporate Governance: Effects on Firm Performance and Economic Growth". OECD Working Paper, Feb., Organization for Economic Co-operation and Development, Paris.

Maisara Ismail (2002). "PLUS to wrap up debt revamp by end-May". *Business Times,* 3 May.

Mako, W.P. (2001a). "Corporate Restructuring Strategies: Recent Lessons". Paper presented at the "Asian Regional Seminar on Financial Reform and Stability". Hyderabad, India, 29 Mar.

———— (2001b). "Corporate Restructuring and Reform: Lessons From East Asia". Paper presented at the 26th Senior Policy Forum on "Economic Crisis and Structural Adjustment in Korea", Korean Development Institute (KDI), 5–9 Nov.

Mako, W.P. and Zhang, Chunlin (2002). "Reforming State Asset Management: Lessons from International Experience". World Bank Note, World Bank, Washington DC, 23 Dec.

Malaysia (1996). *The Seventh Malaysian Plan, 1996–2000.* Kuala Lumpur: Government Printers.

———— (1998). *National Economic Recovery Plan: Agenda for Action.* Economic Planning Unit, Kuala Lumpur.

———— (1999). *Mid-Term Review of the Seventh Malaysian Plan, 1996–2000.* Kuala Lumpur: Government Printers.

———— (2001). *The Eighth Malaysian Plan, 2001–2005.* Kuala Lumpur: Government Printers.

———— (2003). *Mid-Term Review of the Eighth Malaysian Plan, 2001–2005.* Kuala Lumpur: Government Printers.

Malaysia Institute of Economic Research (1998). *Currency Turmoil and the Malaysian Economy: Genesis, Prognosis and Response.* Malaysian Institute of Economic Research, Kuala Lumpur.

Manne, Henry G. (1965). "Mergers and the Market for Corporate Control". *Journal of Political Economy* 73: 110–20.

Marshall, D. (1998). "Understanding the Asian Crisis: Systemic Risk as Coordination Failure". Federal Reserve Bank of Chicago. Available from <http://198.252.9.108/govper/EconoPersp/www.frbchi.org/pubs-Speech/publications/ep/1998/ep3Q98_2.pdf>.

Malaysian Airline System Bhd (MAS). "Announcement of Quarterly Report of Unaudited Consolidated Balance Sheet to the KLSE". Various announcements. Malaysian Airline System Bhd, Kuala Lumpur. Available from <http://www.mas.com.my/>.

———— (2001). "MAS's Announcement of Proposed Reorganization to the KLSE". Malaysian Airline System Bhd, Kuala Lumpur. Available from <http://www.mas.com.my/pdf/2001/announcement.pdf>.

———— (2002). *Annual Report, 2001/2002.* Malaysian Airline System Bhd, Kuala Lumpur.

———— (2003a). "Malaysia Airlines to Operate Airbus A380 from 2007". Media Release, Malaysian Airline System Bhd, Kuala Lumpur, 10 Jan. Available from <http://www.malaysiaairlines.com/>.

———— (2003b). "PMB-Malaysia Airlines to Acquire A380". Media Release, Malaysian Airline System Bhd, Kuala Lumpur, 10 Jan. Available from <http://www.malaysiaairlines.com/>.

———— (2003c). "Malaysia Airlines Announces Expansion Plan". Media Release, Malaysian Airline System Bhd, Kuala Lumpur, 30 Jan. Available from <http://www.malaysiaairlines.com/>.

———— (2003d). "Malaysia Airlines Prepares to Establish Secondary Hubs". Media Release, Malaysian Airline System Bhd, Kuala Lumpur, 1 Mar. Available from <http://www.malaysiaairlines.com/>.

_____ (2003e). "Malaysia Airlines Voted into the 'Top Five' League of Skytrax's 'Airline of the Year 2003' Award". Media Release, Malaysian Airline System Bhd, Kuala Lumpur, 19 Mar. Available from <http://www.malaysiaairlines.com/>.

_____ (2003f). "MASkargo's Home Base at KLIA Recognised as Asia's Best Cargo Airport". Media Release, Malaysian Airline System Bhd, Kuala Lumpur, 21 Mar. Available from <http://www.malaysiaairlines.com/>.

_____ (2003g). *Quarterly Report on Unaudited Consolidated Results for Period Ended 31 March 2003*. Announcement in Latest Financial Results Section. Malaysian Airline System Bhd, Kuala Lumpur. Available from <http://www.malaysiaairlines.com/>.

_____ (2003h). "Malaysia Airlines Launches Golden Holidays Great Getaways to Revitalise Domestic Travel". Media Release, Malaysian Airline System Bhd, Kuala Lumpur, 28 May. Available from <http://www.malaysiaairlines.com/>.

_____ (2003i). *Quarterly Report on Unaudited Consolidated Results for Period Ended 30 June 2003*. Announcement in Latest Financial Results Section. Malaysian Airline System Bhd, Kuala Lumpur. Available from <http://www.malaysiaairlines.com/>.

_____ (2003j). "ESPN Appoints Malaysia Airlines as Official Airline for FAPL". Media Release, Malaysian Airline System Bhd, Kuala Lumpur, 17 July. Available from <http://www.malaysiaairlines.com/>.

_____ (2003k). "Malaysia Airlines to Implement Abacus' Single Access Reservation System". Media Release, Malaysian Airline System Bhd, Kuala Lumpur, 22 Jul. Available from <http://www.malaysiaairlines.com/>.

_____ (2003l). "Malaysia Airlines Appointed Official Airline for Real Madrid Asia Tour 2003". Media Release, Malaysian Airline System Bhd, Kuala Lumpur, 23 Jul. Available from <http://www.malaysiaairlines. com/>.

_____ (2003m). "Malaysia Airlines' Scheduled Charter Services for Ipoh/Medan/Ipoh". Media Release, Malaysian Airline System Bhd, Kuala Lumpur, 30 Jul. Available from <http://www.malaysiaairlines.com/>.

_____ (2003n). "Major Upgrade for Malaysia Airlines Aircraft". Media Release, Malaysian Airline System Bhd, Kuala Lumpur, 8 Aug. Available from <http://www.malaysiaairlines.com/>.

_____ (2003o). "Malaysia Airlines Announces First Quarter Results". Media Release, Malaysian Airline System Bhd, Kuala Lumpur, 11 Aug. Available from <http://www.malaysiaairlines.com/>.

_____ (2003p). "Garuda Indonesia and Malaysia Airlines Sign Master Agreement". Media Release, Malaysian Airline System Bhd, Kuala Lumpur, 2 Sep. Available from <http://www.malaysiaairlines.com/>.

—— (2003q). "Malaysia Airlines Finalises Sale of 70% Share of its Catering Subsidiary". Media Release, Malaysian Airline System Bhd, Kuala Lumpur, 25 Sep. Available from <http://www.malaysiaairlines.com/>.

—— (2003r). "Malaysia Airlines Concludes Service Agreements at LIMA 2003". Media Release, Malaysian Airline System Bhd, Kuala Lumpur, 2 Oct. Available from <http://www.malaysiaairlines.com/>.

—— (2003s). "Malaysia Airlines Introduces Direct Services from London to Langkawi & Penang". Media Release, Malaysian Airline System Bhd, Kuala Lumpur, 10 Oct. Available from <http://www.malaysiaairlines.com/>.

—— (2003t). "Malaysia Airlines Announces Profit of RM101.1 million for Second Quarter". Media Release, Malaysian Airline System Bhd, Kuala Lumpur, 2 Nov. Available from <http://www.malaysiaairlines.com/>.

—— (2003u). *Quarterly Report on Unaudited Consolidated Results for Period Ended 30 September 2003*. Announcement in Latest Financial Results Section. Malaysian Airline System Bhd, Kuala Lumpur. Available from <http://www.malaysiaairlines.com/>.

—— (2003v). "Malaysia Airlines Launches Kuching-Kota Kinabalu-Guangzhou Service". Media Release, Malaysian Airline System Bhd, Kuala Lumpur, 10 Nov. Available from <http://www.malaysiaairlines.com/>.

—— (2003w). "Malaysia Airlines Secures Charter Deal to Bring in Italian Tourists". Media Release, Malaysian Airline System Bhd, Kuala Lumpur, 13 Nov. Available from <http://www.malaysiaairlines.com/>.

—— (2003x). *Quarterly Report on Unaudited Consolidated Results for Period Ended 30 December 2003*. Announcement in Latest Financial Results Section. Malaysian Airline System Bhd, Kuala Lumpur. Available from <http://www.malaysiaairlines.com/>.

—— (2004a). *Annual Report, 2003/2004*. Malaysian Airline System Bhd, Kuala Lumpur.

—— (2004b). *Quarterly Report on Unaudited Consolidated Results for Period Ended 30 June 2004*. Announcement in Latest Financial Results Section. Malaysian Airline System Bhd, Kuala Lumpur. Available from <http://www.malaysiaairlines.com/>.

Masina, Pietro (ed.) (2002). *Rethinking Development in East Asia: From Illusory Miracle to Economic Crisis*. Surrey: Curzon Press.

Matthias, J. (2000). "Malaysia's privatization mess". 31 Dec. Available from <http://www.asiafeatures.com/current_affairs/0012,2431,01.html>.

Maull, Hanns W. (1999). "Crisis in Asia: Origins and Implications". *International Politics and Society* 1: 56–66.

Maxfield, Sylvia (1998). "Effects of International Portfolio Flows on Government Policy Choice". In Miles Kahler (ed.). *Capital Flows and Financial Crises*. Ithaca: Cornell University Press, pp. 69–92.

Mayer, C. (1996). "Corporate Governance, Competition and Performance". *Journal of Financial Economics* 38: 163–84.

Mayer, Martin (1998). "The Asian Disease: Plausible Diagnoses, Possible Remedies". Working Paper no. 232. Jerome Levy Economics Institute, Bard College, New York.

McDermott, Darren and Leslie Lopez (1998). "Malaysia Imposes Sweeping Currency Controls". *Wall Street Journal*, 2 Sep.

McDermott, Darren, Raphael Pura, and David Wessel (1998). "Malaysian currency controls roil Asia markets — Billions of dollars at risk in financial contracts; Finance Minister fired". *Wall Street Journal*, 3 Sep.

McKibbin, Warwick (1998). "Modelling the crisis in Asia". *ASEAN Economic Bulletin* 15 (3) (Dec.)

McKinnon, Ronald (1999). "Exchange Rate regimes for Emerging Markets: Moral Hazard and International Overborrowing". *Oxford Review of Economic Policy* 15 (3) (Autumn): 19–38.

McLeod, Ross (ed.) (1998). *East Asia in Crisis*. London: Routledge.

McNulty, Sheila (1998). "Financial crisis reignited old tensions with Singapore: KL's curbs on the markets hit at the heart of the city-state". *Financial Times*, 10 Sep.

McNulty, Sheila and Edward Luce (1998). "Kuala Lumpur orders increase in lending". *Financial Times*, 10 Sep.

Meesook, Kanitta, *et al.* (2001). "Malaysia: From Crisis to Recovery". Occasional Paper 207, International Monetary Fund, Washington DC.

Meltzer, A.H. (1998). "Asian Problems and the IMF". *Cato Journal* 17 (3) (Winter).

Menon, Jayant (2000). "How Open is Malaysia? An Analysis of Trade, Capital and Labour Flows". *The World Economy* 23 (2) (Feb).

Meyerman, G. E. (2000). "The London Approach and Corporate Debt Restructuring in East Asia". In C. Adams, Robert E. Litan, and Michael Pomerleano (eds.). *Managing Financial and Corporate Distress: Lessons from Asia*. Brookings Institution, Washington DC.

MIER (1999). *The Impact of Currency Control Measures on Business Operations*. Malaysian Institute for Economic Research, Kuala Lumpur.

Miliband, Ralph (1973). *The State in Capitalist Society*. London: Quartet Books.

Milne, R.S. and Diane K. Mauzy (1999). *Malaysian Politics Under Mahathir*. London: Routledge.

Ministry of Finance. *Economic Report*, various issues. Kuala Lumpur: Government Printers.

Minsky, Hyman P. (1964). "Longer Waves in Financial Relations: Financial Factors in the More Severe Depressions". *American Economic Review* 54 (May): 324–32.

———— (1972). *Financial Instability Revisited: The Economics of Disaster. Reappraisal of the Federal Reserve Discount Mechanism.* Board of Governors of the Federal Reserve System, Washington DC.

———— (1986). "A Theory of Systemic Fragility". In Edward Altman, and Arnold Sametz (eds.). *Financial Crises in a Fragile Environment.* London: John Wiley.

———— (1993). "The Financial Instability Hypothesis". In Philip Arestis and Malcolm Sawyer (eds.). *Handbook of Radical Political Economy.* Aldershot, UK: Edward Elgar.

Mitton, Todd (1999). "A Cross-Firm Analysis of the Impact of Corporate Governance on the East Asian Financial Crisis". Massachusetts Institute of Technology, Cambridge, MA.

Mishkin, F. S. (1994). *Preventing Financial Crises: an International Perspective.* NBER Working Paper 4636, National Bureau of Economic Research, Cambridge, MA.

Mohammad Sadli (2003). "Indonesian Economic Crisis, Recovery, and Future Prospects in an East Asian Context". *East Asian Economic Perspectives* 14 (2): 52–67.

Monetary Authority of Singapore (2000). "Exchange Rate Policy in East Asia After the Fall: How Much Have Things Changed?" Occasional Paper No. 19, Monetary Authority of Singapore, Singapore.

Montes, M. F. (1998). *The Currency Crisis in Southeast Asia.* Singapore: Institute of Southeast Asian Studies.

Mullins, L. J. (1996). *Management and Organizational Behaviour,* 4th edition. London: Pitman Publishing.

Mussa, Michael, Paul Masson, Alexander Swoboda, Esteban Jadresic, Paolo Mauro, and Andrew Berg (2000). *Exchange Rate Regimes in an Increasingly Integrated World Economy.* International Monetary Fund, Washington DC.

Myers, Stewart and Nicholas Majluf (1984). "Corporate Financing and Investment Decisions When Firms Have Information That Investors do not have". *Journal of Financial Economics* 13 (2): 187–221.

Nakamura, Akihiro (2000). "Capital Flows in Malaysia: the Impact and Policy Implications". ISIS Malaysia, Kuala Lumpur.

Nasution, Anwar (2000). "The Meltdown of the Indonesian Economy: Causes, Responses and Lessons". *ASEAN Economic Bulletin* 17 (2) (Aug.): 148–62.

NEAC (1998). *National Economic Recovery Plan: Agenda for Action.* National

Economic Action Council, Prime Minister's Department, Kuala Lumpur, Aug.

———— (1999). *White Paper: Status of the Malaysian Economy.* National Economic Action Council, Kuala Lumpur, 6 Apr.

———— (2001). "Response to the Recent Assessment on Malaysia by Standard & Poors". National Economic Action Council, 9 Apr. Available from <http://www.neac.gov.my/neac_materials/090401-responsetotherecent.html>.

Navaratnam, Ramon (2001). *Malaysia's Economic Recovery, Policy Reforms for Economic Recovery.* Petaling Jaya: Pelanduk.

Neely, Christopher J. (1999). "An Introduction to Capital Controls". *Federal Reserve Bank of St. Louis Review* 81 (6) (Nov./Dec.): 21–2.

Neiss, Hubert (1999). "The Asian Crisis in Perspective". IMF Media Seminar, Singapore, 2 Apr.

Nembhard, Jessica G. (1996). *Capital Control, Financial Regulation, and Industrial Policy in South Korea and Brazil.* Westport, CT: Praeger Publishers.

Nesadurai, Helen E. S. (1998). "Accommodating Global Markets: Malaysia's Response to Economic Crisis". Available from <http://www.warwick.ac.uk/fac/soc.CSGR/>.

———— (2000). "In Defiance Of National Economic Autonomy? Malaysia's response to the financial crisis". *The Pacific Review* 13 (1): 73–113.

Ng Boon Hooi (2001). "Crony Companies' Bailouts Costly: Economists". *MalaysiaKini.* 10 Apr. Available from <http://www.malaysiakini.com/News/2001/04/2001041011.php3>.

Nixson, Frederick and Bernard Walters (1999). "The Asian Crisis: Causes and Consequences". *The Manchester School* 67 (5).

Noble, Gregory W. and John Ravenhill (2000). *The Asian Financial Crisis, and the Architecture of Global Finance.* Cambridge: Cambridge University Press.

Nor Azimah Hj. Abdul Aziz (1997). "Corporate Rescue — Malaysian Scenario". Presented at the Academic Meetings of the INSOL International 5th World Congress, New Orleans, 23 Mar.

Nordhaug, Kristen (2000). "The US-Japanese Alliance and East Asian Booms and Busts". International Development Studies, Denmark, 21–25 Aug.

Nuryushida Laily Yusof (2002). "PLUS Listing May Only Take Place After June". *Business Times,* 18 Jan. Available from <http://www.renong.com.my/announcements/news_jan02/180102.htm>.

Obiyathullah, I.B. (1997). "The Asian Currency Crisis — A Fait Accompli?" *Malaysian Journal of Economic Studies* 34 (1 & 2) (June & Dec.): 67–91.

Obstfeld, Maurice (1986). "Rational and Self-fulfilling Balance of Payments Crises". *American Economic Review* 76 (Mar.): 72–81.

———— (1994). "The Logic of Currency Crisis". NBER Working Paper 4640, National Bureau of Economic Research, Cambridge, MA.

———— (1995). "Models of Currency Crises with Self-fulfilling Features". NBER Working Paper 5285, National Bureau of Economic Research, Cambridge, MA.

Ocampo, J. A. (2000). "A Broad Agenda for International Financial Reform". In *Financial globalization and the emerging economies*. United Nations Economic Commission for Latin America and the Caribbean, Santiago.

———— (2001). "A Broad Agenda for International Financial Reform". American Economic Association Annual Meeting, New Orleans, 5–7 Jan.

OECD (1999). "The Origins of the Crisis". In *Asia and the Global Crisis: The Industrial Dimension.* Organization for Economic Co-operation and Development, Paris. Available from <http://www.wto.org/english/tratop_e/devel_e/sem03_e/asia_crisis_chap2.pdf>.

Ohanga, M. (1999). "Insolvency Law Review". Ministry of Economic Development, New Zealand. Available from <http://www.med.govt.nz/ri/insolvency/tiertwo/rescue/rescue.html>.

Okposin, Samuel B. and M. Y. Cheng (2000). *Economic Crisis in Malaysia, Causes, Implications and Policy Prescriptions.* Petaling Jaya: Pelanduk.

Oman, C. P. (2001). "Corporate Governance and National Development". Technical Paper No. 180, Sep., OECD Development Centre, Paris.

Ong Hong Cheong (1998). "Coping with Capital Flows and the Role of Monetary Policy: The Malaysian Experience, 1990–95". In C. H. Kwan, Donna Vandenbrink, and Chia Siow Yue (eds.). *Coping with Capital Flows in East Asia.* Singapore: Institute of Southeast Asian Studies, pp. 220–43.

Ong, C. H. and Lee S. H. (2000). "Board Functions and Firm Performance: A Review and Directions for Future Research". *Journal of Comparative International Management* 3 (1) (June).

Ong, Lynette (2001a). "B is for Bumiputera — and Bailout". *AsiaWise,* 29 Mar. Available from <http://www.asiawise.com/mainpage. asp?mainaction=50&articleid=1377>.

———— (2001b). "Corporate Malaysia, falling from grace". *Asia Times Online,* 22 Dec. Available from <http://www.atimes.com/se-asia/CL22Ae01.html>.

Overstone, Lord, S. J. L. (1858). "The Evidence Given by Lord Overstone Before the Select Committee of the House of Commons of 1857 on Bank Acts, London".

Pang, Eul-Soo (2000). "The Financial Crisis of 1997–98 and the end of the Asian Developmental State". *Contemporary Southeast Asia* 22 (3) (Dec.): 570–93.

Park, Y. C. (1996). "East Asian Liberalization, Bubbles, and the Challenge from China". *Brookings Papers on Economic Activity* 2. Brookings Institution, Washington DC.

———— (2000). "East Asian Dilemma: Restructuring Out or Growing Out?". Revised draft, Nov., for *Princeton Essays in International Economics.*

Parker, Steve and H.L. Sung (2000). "Assessing East Asian Export Performance and Technology Upgrading from 1980–1996: Did East Asian Developing Economies Lose Export Competitiveness in the Pre-crisis 1990s?" Asian Development Bank Institute, Tokyo.

Pasuk, Phongpaichit and Chris Baker (2000). *Thailand's Crisis.* Chiang Mai, Thailand: Silkworm Books.

Peacock, A. and G. Bannock (1991). *Corporate Takeovers and the Public Interest.* Edinburgh: David Hume Institute.

Pempel, T. J. (ed.) (1999). *Politics of the Asian Economic Crisis.* Ithaca: Cornell University Press.

Pereira da Silva, Luiz and Masaru Yoshimoto (2001). "Can 'Moral Hazard' Explain the Asian Crisis?". ADB Research Paper 29, Asian Development Bank Institute, Tokyo, Dec.

Perkins, D.H. and Wing T.W. (2000). "Malaysia: Adjusting to Deep Integration with the World Economy". In W.T. Woo, J.D. Sachs, and Klaus Schwab (eds.). *The Asian Financial Crisis: Lessons for a Resilient Asia.* Cambridge, MA: MIT Press.

Pill, Huw R. and Donald H. Mathis (1998). *Bahtulism, Collapse, or Resurrection? Financial Crisis in Asia, 1997–98.* Harvard Business School Case 798-089, Boston.

Pillay, M.S. (1994). "Privatization of sewerage services in Malaysia". Paper presented at the 20th Water, Engineering and Development Centre (WEDC) Conference, Colombo, Sri Lanka. Available from <http://www.lboro.ac.uk/departments/cv/wedc/papers/20/plenary/pillay.pdf>.

Pistor, Katarina (2000). "The Standardization of Law and Its Effect on Developing Economies". Group of 24 Discussion Paper no. 4, United Nations Conference on Trade and Development, Geneva, and Harvard University, Center for International Development, Cambridge, MA.

PLUS (2003). *Annual Report 2002.* PLUS Expressway Bhd, Kuala Lumpur.

Pomerleano, Michael (2000). "Managing Corporate Distress: Lessons from Asia". Paper presented at a seminar for Senior Bank Supervisors from Emerging Economies, World Bank/Federal Reserve System.

Available from <http://www1.worldbank.org/finance/assets/images/wbf_pomer1.pdf>.

Poon, S. (1999). "Malaysia and the Asian Financial Crisis". Lancaster University Management School Working Paper, Lancaster, LUMSWP1999/021.

Prasad, Eswar, Kenneth Rogoff, Shang-jin Wei, and M. Ayhan Kose (2003). "The Effects of Financial Globalization on Developing Countries: Some Empirical Evidence". IMF Working Paper, International Monetary Fund, Washington DC, 17 Mar. Available from <www.imf.org/research>.

Pura, Raphael (1997). "Malaysia's Finance Chief Gains in Stature: Anwar Emerges from Economic as Voice of Reason". *Wall Street Journal*, 22 Sep.

Putra website. Available from <http://www.subways.net/malaysia/kualalampur.htm>.

Quek, Kim (2000). "Halim Saad Loan Scandal: Cronyism Runs Unabated". In *freeAnwar*, 23 Sep. Available from <http://www.freeanwar.com/news/quek220900.html>.

Rabindra Nathan Shearn Delamore & Co. "Insolvency Law Reform: Case study from Malaysia". Regional Technical Assistance No. 5795-REG, Asian Development Bank. Available from <http://www.insolvencyasia.com/>.

Radelet, Steve (1999). "Indonesia: Long Road to Recovery". Processed, Mar., Harvard Institute for International Development, Cambridge, MA.

Radelet, Steve and Jeffrey D. Sachs (1998a). "The Onset of the East Asian Financial Crisis". NBER Working Paper No. 6680, August, National Bureau of Economic Research, Cambridge, MA.

———— (1998b). "The East Asian Financial Crisis: Diagnosis, Remedies, Prospects". *Brookings Papers on Economic Activity* 1: 1–90.

———— (1999). "What Have We Learned So Far From the Asian Financial Crisis?". Processed, Center for International Development, Harvard University, Jan.

Raghavan, Chakravarthi (1998). "BIS Banks Kept Shovelling Funds to Asia Despite Warnings". *Third World Economics*, 16–31 Jan.

Rahim, Lily (2000). "Economic Crisis and the Prospects for Democratisation in Southeast Asia". *Journal of Contemporary Asia* 30 (1).

Rajan, R.G. and Larry Zingales (1998). "Which Capitalism? Lessons from the East Asian Crisis". Working Paper, University of Chicago, Chicago.

Rajaraman, Indira (2003). "Management of the Capital Account: A Study of India and Malaysia". In UNCTAD (ed.). *Management of Capital Flows: Comparative Experiences and Implications for Africa*. Geneva: United Nations, pp. 109–83.

RAM (2003). "Prasarana's Bonds Rated AAA(s) by RAM". Announcement, Rating Agency Malaysia Bhd, Kuala Lumpur, 30 June. Available from <http://www.ram.com.my/custom.cfm?name=press.cfm&id=514>.

Ranawana, Arjuna (2001a). "AI at last — Malaysia focuses on debt restructuring". *Asiaweek,* 10 Aug.

_____ (2001b). "Failure is not an option". *Asiaweek,* 7 Sep. Available from <http://www.asiaweek.com/asiaweek/magazine/Enterprise/0,8782,173042,00.html>.

Ranhill (2002). "Proposed Acquisition of the Following from Time Engineering Berhad for a Total Cash Consideration of RM54,300,000: (i) 4,000,000 Ordinary Shares of RM1.00 Each in Powertron Resources Sdn Bhd (PRSB) Representing 40 Per Cent Equity Interest in PRSB (PRSB Shares); (ii) 11,600,000 Nominal Value of the Outstanding Convertible Unsecured Loan Stocks (CULS) in PRSB, Representing 40 Per Cent of the Outstanding Nominal Value of CULS in PRSB (PRSB CULS); and (iii) 2,940,000 Ordinary Shares of RM1.00 Each in Penjanaan EPE-Time Sdn Bhd (PET) Representing 60 Per Cent Shareholding in PET (PET Shares)". Press announcement, Ranhill Bhd, Kuala Lumpur, 27 Dec.

_____ (2003). "RANHILL BERHAD (Ranhill or the Company) — Proposed Acquisitions of the Following from TIME Engineering Berhad for a Total Cash Consideration of RM54,350,000: (i) 4,000,000 Ordinary Shares of RM1.00 Each in Powertron Resources Sdn Bhd (PRSB) Representing 40% Equity Interest in PRSB (PRSB Shares); (ii) RM11,600,000 Nominal Value of the Outstanding Convertible Unsecured Loan Stocks (CULS) in PRSB, Representing 40% of the Outstanding Nominal Value of CULS in PRSB (PRSB CULS); and (iii) 2,940,000 Ordinary Shares of RM1.00 Each in Penjanaan EPE-TIME Sdn Bhd (PET) Representing 60% Shareholding in PET ("PET Shares"). — Proposed Disposals of the PRSB Shares, PRSB CULS and PET Shares to EPE Power Corporation Berhad ("EPE") to be Satisfied by the Issuance of 54,350,000 New Ordinary Shares of RM1.00 Each In EPE At an Issue Price of RM1.00 Per Share (to be collectively referred to as 'the Proposals')". Press announcement, Ranhill Bhd, Kuala Lumpur, 25 Aug.

Rao, Bhanoji (1998). "East Asian Economies: The Crisis of 1997–98". *Economic and Political Weekly* 33 (23) (June): 1397–1416.

_____ (2001). *East Asian Economies: The Miracle, a Crisis and the Future.* Singapore: McGraw Hill.

Rashid Hussain Research Institute (2002). *Economic Outlook Report for Malaysia.* 22 Mar. Rashid Hussain Research Institute, Kuala Lumpur.

Rasiah, Rajah (1998). "The Malaysian Financial Crisis: Capital Expansion, Cronyism and Contraction". *Journal of Asia Pacific Economy* 3 (3): 358–78.

———— (2001). "Pre-Crisis Economic Weaknesses and Vulnerabilities". In Jomo K. S. (ed.). *Malaysian Eclipse: Economic Crisis and Recovery.* London: Zed Books, pp. 47–66.

Reinhart, Carmen (2002). "Default, Currency Crises, and Sovereign Credit Ratings". *The World Bank Economic Review* 16 (2): 151–70.

Reisen, Helmut (1999). "After The Great Asian Slump: Towards Coherent Approach to Global Capital Flows". Policy Brief No. 16, OECD Development Centre, Organization for Economic Co-Operation and Development, Paris.

Renong (1998). "Calendar of events". Renong Bhd, Kuala Lumpur. Available from <http://www.renong.com.my/diary/caleve98.htm>.

———— (2000). "Renong and UEM to Reduce Debt Through Asset Disposal". Announcement, Renong Bhd, Kuala Lumpur, 13 Mar. Available from: <http://www.renong. com.my/announcements/press/13mac00.htm>.

———— (2001a). *Annual Report 2001.* Renong Bhd, Kuala Lumpur. Available from: <http://www.renong.com.my>.

———— (2001b). "Calendar of events". Renong Bhd, Kuala Lumpur. Available from <http://www.renong.com.my/diary/caleve01.htm>.

———— (2002). "Appointment of Liquidators for Projek Usahasama Transit Ringan Automatik Sdn Bhd ('Putra'), a Wholly-owned Subsidiary of Renong Berhad ('Renong')". Announcement, Renong Bhd, Kuala Lumpur, 26 Apr. Available from <http://www.renong.com.my>.

———— (2003a). "Renong to Complete Crest Divestment by End April 2003". Press announcement, Renong Bhd, Kuala Lumpur, 14 Mar. Available from <http://www.renong.com.my>.

———— (2003b). "The Remaking of UEM Group Through Corporate and Debt Restructuring Scheme". Press release, Renong Bhd, Kuala Lumpur, 27 Mar. Available from <http://www.renong.com.my>.

———— (2003c). *Annual Report 2003.* Renong Bhd, Kuala Lumpur. Available from <http://www.renong.com.my/>.

————. *Annual Report,* various years. Renong Bhd, Kuala Lumpur.

Reynolds, Stephen E., Somchai Ratanakomut, and James Gander (2000). "Bank Financial Structure in Pre-crisis East and Southeast Asia". *Journal of Asian Economics* 11: 319–31.

Ries, P. (1998). *The Asian Storm: Asia's Economic Crisis Examined.* Boston: Tuttle.

Robinson, Richard, Kevin Hewison, and Richard Higgott (1987). *Southeast Asia in the 1980s: The Politics of Economic Crisis.* Sydney: Allen & Unwin.

Robison, Richard, Mark Beeson, Kanishka Jayasuriya, and H-R Kim (eds.) (2000). *Politics and Markets in the Wake of the Asian Crisis.* London: Routledge.

Rodrik, Dani (1998). "The Global Fix". *The New Republic.* 2 Nov.: 10–5.

―――― (1999a). "Governing the Global Economy: Does One Architectural Style Fit All?" Paper prepared for the Brookings Institution Trade Policy Forum Conference on Governing in a Global Economy, 14–16 Apr.

―――― (1999b). *The New Global Economy And Developing Countries: Making Openness Work.* Baltimore: Johns Hopkins University Press.

―――― (2000). "Institutions for High-Quality Growth: What They Are and How to Acquire Them". NBER Working Paper No. 7450, National Bureau of Economic Research, Cambridge, MA, Feb.

Roe, M. (1983). "Bankruptcy and Debt: A New Model for Corporate Reorganization". *Columbia Law Review* 83: 527–602.

Rubin, Robert (1998). "Strengthening the Architecture of the International Financial System". Public statement delivered at the Brookings Institution, Washington DC, 14 Apr.

Russell Jr., George F. (1998). "East Asia's Present and Future". Opening address to the 'East Asia in Crisis' conference, cosponsored by The National Bureau of Asian Research and the Strategic Studies Institute of the U.S. Army War College, Seattle, 9–10 June. Available from <http://www.nbr.org/publications/briefing/russell98/>.

Ruzita Mohd Amin and Rokiah Alavi (1997). "The Contagion and Policy Effects on Financial Markets Behaviour in Malaysia". *Malaysian Journal of Economic Studies* 34: 123–41.

S. Hakim, P. Seidenstat and G. Bowman (eds.) (1996). *Privatized Transportation Systems.* London: Praeger.

Sakakibara, Eisuke (2000). "Thai Crisis Played Part in IMF Idea". *Yomiuri Shimbun,* 25 Nov.

Saxena, Sweta C. and Kar-yiu Wong (1999). "Currency Crises and Capital Controls: A Selective Survey". Unpublished Working Paper, University of Washington, 2 Jan.

Schneider, Benu (ed.) (2003). *The Road to International Financial Stability: Are Key Financial Standards the Answer?* Basingstoke: Palgrave Macmillan.

Schultz, J. (2001). "Day of the Shareholder". *Far Eastern Economic Review,* 13 Sep.

Schumpeter, Joseph A. (1942). *Capitalism, Socialism, and Democracy.* New York: Harper and Brothers.

Securities Commission (2001). *Capital Market Masterplan Malaysia.* Kuala Lumpur, Malaysia.

Sen, Sunanda (1998). "Asia: Myth of a Miracle". *Economic and Political Weekly,* 17 Jan.: 111–4.

Seneviratne, Kalinga (1999). "Malaysia: Mahathir Not Yet Through With Speculators". Available from <http://www.oneworld.org/ips2/august99/04_03_003.html>.

Shamsher Mohd Annuar Md Nassir (2000). *The East Asian Crisis: Myths, Lessons, Recovery.* Serdang, Malaysia: Universiti Putra Malaysia Press.

Shari, Michael (1999). "Malaysia: Look, folks, no capital curbs! Mahathir bets big that investors will stay when controls end". *Business Week.* Available from <http://www.businessweek.com/1999/99_36/b3645085.htm>.

Sharma, Shalendra D. (2003). "The Malaysian Capital Controls and the Debates on the New International Financial Architecture". *Review of Asian and Pacific Studies* 25 (2): 1–25.

Shin, Jang-Sup and Chang, Ha-Joon. (2003). *Restructuring Korea Inc.: Financial Crisis, Corporate Reform, and Institutional Transition.* London: Routledge.

Shirai, Sayuri (2000). "APF Brainstorming Workshop on How to Prevent Another Crisis". Document No. 5, Asian Development Bank Institute, Tokyo, 3 Mar.

―――― (2001). "Overview of Financial Market Structures in Asia: Cases of the Republic of Korea, Malaysia, Thailand and Indonesia". ADB Institute Research Paper 25, Tokyo, Sep.

Shleifer, Andre and Robert W. Vishny (1992). "Liquidation Values and Debt Capacity: A Market Equilibrium Approach". *Journal of Finance* 47: 1343–66.

―――― (1997). "A Survey of Corporate Governance". *Journal of Finance* 52: 737–83.

Shleifer, Andre and L.H. Summers (1988). "Breach of Trust in Hostile Takeovers". In A. Auerbach (ed.). *Corporate Takeovers: Causes and Consequences.* Chicago: University of Chicago Press.

Shostak, Frank (2000). "Bursting Malaysia's Bubble". *Asian Wall Street Journal,* 28 Jan.

Sibexnews (2001). "Malaysia: Government has yet to decide on acquisition of Putra and Star LRT", 29 May. Available from <http://www.unido-aaitpc.com/freenews/sibexnews/nsb29051.shtml>.

Singh, Ajit (1992). "Corporate Takeovers". In John Eatwell, Murray Milgate, and Peter Newman (eds.). *The New Palgrave Dictionary of Money and Finance.* London: Macmillan, pp. 480–6.

―――― (1995a). "Corporate Financial Patterns in Industrializing Economies: A Comparative International Study". IFC Technical Paper 2, International Finance Corporation, Washington DC.

―――― (1995b). "The Causes of Fast Economic Growth in East Asia". *UNCTAD Review* (1995): 91–127.

_____ (1997). "Financial Liberalisation, Stock Mmarkets and Economic Development". *Economic Journal* 107 (442) (May): 771–82.

_____ (1998). "Liberalisation, the Stock Market and the Market for Corporate Control: A Bridge Too Far for the Indian Economy?" In I.J. Ahluwalia and I.M.D. Little (eds.). *India's Economic Reforms and Development: Essays for Manmohan Singh*. Oxford: Oxford University Press, pp. 169–96.

_____ (1999). "'Asian Capitalism' and the Financial Crisis". In Jonathan Michie and John Grieve Smith (eds.). *Global Instability: The Political Economy of World Economic Governance*. London: Routledge, pp. 9–36.

_____ (2000). "The Anglo-Saxon Market for Corporate Control: The Financial System and International Competitiveness". In Candice Howes and Ajit Singh (eds.). *Competitiveness Matters: Industry and Economic Performance in the US*. Ann Arbor: University of Michigan Press, pp. 89–105.

_____ (2002). "Competition, Corporate Governance and Selection in Emerging Markets". *Economic Journal* 113 (491) (Nov. 2003): F443–F464.

Singh, Ajit and Bruce Weisse (1998). "Emerging Stock Markets, Portfolio Capital Flows and Long Term Economic Growth, Micro and Macroeconomic Perspectives". *World Development* 26 (4): 607–22.

Singh, Ajit, Alaka Singh, and Bruce Weisse (2002). "Corporate Governance, Competition, the New International Financial Architecture and Large Corporations in Emerging Markets". Processed, Faculty of Economics & Politics, University of Cambridge, Cambridge, UK.

Singh, Ajit and J. Hamid (1992). "Corporate Financial Structures in Developing Countries". IFC Technical Paper No. 1, International Finance Corporation, Washington DC.

Singh, Kavaljit (2000). *Taming Global Financial Flows: A Citizen's Guide*. Delhi: Madhyam Books.

Singh, Supriya (1984). *Bank Negara Malaysia: The First 25 Years, 1959–1984*. Bank Negara Malaysia, Kuala Lumpur.

Sloman, John (1997). *Economics*. 3rd edn. London: Prentice Hall.

Soederberg, Susanne (2002). "The New International Financial Architecture: Imposed Leadership and Emerging Markets". In Leo Panitch and Colin Leys (eds.). *Socialist Register*. London: Merlin Press, pp. 175–92.

_____ (2002). "Beyond the Efficacy Debates: Towards an Historical Materialist Account of the Malaysian Capital Controls". Processed, Department of Political Science, University of Alberta, Canada.

Soros, George (1995). *Soros on Soros*. New York: John Wiley & Sons.

_____ (1998). *The Crisis of Global Capitalism: Open Society Endangered*. Public Affairs, New York.

———— (1999). "Capitalism Last Chance?". *Foreign Policy* 113 (Winter): 55–66.

Steenbeek, Onno W. (1998). "Financial Regulation and Systemic Risk: The Case of Japan". *The Euro-Asia Management Studies Association (EAMSA) 15 Paper Proceedings*: 41–69.

Stein, J.C. (1988). "Takeover Threats and Managerial Myopia". *Journal of Political Economy* 96 (1): 61–80.

———— (1989). Efficient Stock Market, Inefficient Firms: A Model of Myopic Corporate Behaviour. *Quarterly Journal of Economics*, Nov.

Stiglitz, Joseph E. (1994). "The Role of the State in Financial Markets". In Michael Bruno and Boris Pleskovic (eds.). *Proceedings of the World Bank Annual Conference on Development Economics 1996*. World Bank, Washington DC, pp. 19–52.

———— (1998a). "Restoring the Asian Miracle". *The Wall Street Journal*, 3 Feb.

———— (1998b). "Sound Finance and Sustainable Development in Asia". Keynote address presented at the Asia Development Forum, "East Asia: the Unfinished Agenda", 9–13 Mar., Manila, Philippines.

———— (2000a). "IMF: Smart People, Stupid Policies". *The Sunday Times*, 16 Apr.

———— (2000b). "The Insider: What I learned at the world economic crises". *The New Republic*, 17 Apr.

———— (2000c). "Capital Market Liberalization, Economic Growth and Instability". *World Development* 28 (6): 1075–86.

———— (2002). *Globalization and its Discontents*. New York: WW Norton.

Stiglitz, Joseph E. and Amar Bhattacharya (1999). "Underpinnings for a Stable and Equitable Global Financial System: From Old Debates to a New Paradigm". Paper prepared for the Eleventh Annual Bank Conference on Development Economics, 28–30 Apr.

Stiglitz, Joseph E. and Shahid Yusuf (eds.) (2001). *Rethinking the East Asian Miracle*. New York: Oxford University Press.

Stone, M. R. (1998). "Corporate Debt Restructuring in East Asia: Some Lessons From International Experience". IMF Paper on Policy Analysis and Assessment No. 98/13, International Monetary Fund, Washington DC.

———— (2000). "Large-Scale Post-Crisis Corporate Sector Restructuring". Policy Discussion Paper 00–1147, International Monetary Fund, Washington DC.

———— (2002). "Corporate Sector Restructuring: The Role of Government in Times of Crisis". *Economic Issue* No. 31, International Monetary Fund, Washington DC.

Summers, Lawrence H. (1999). "Speech at the London Business School". *Financial Times,* 15 Dec. <http://www.lbs.ac.uk/news-events/scripts/summers>.

_____ (2000). "International financial crises: Causes, prevention and cures". *American Economic Review* 90 (2) (May): 1–16.

Syed Husin Ali (2001). "MAS Bailout? Why Not Rescue Smallholders Too?" 19 Jan. Available from <http://mindarakyat_2tripod.com/2001jan/i2001-0243i.htm>.

Taing, Anna (1998). "Walking a tightrope: Bankers have to lend more but balance sheet still weak". *The Edge.* Available from <http://www.bizedge.com.my/MEM/220/71298focus2.html>.

_____ (1999). "Merger exercise will be tough and complex". *The Edge.* Available from <http://www.bizedge.com.my/MEM/255/160899 corp2.html>.

Tamirisa, Natalia T. (2004). "Do Macroeconomic Effects of Capital Control Vary by Their Type? Evidence from Malaysia". IMF Working Paper 04/3, Jan., International Monetary Fund, Washington DC.

Tan C. S. (1999). "It is efficiency, not just size, that matters". *The Edge.* Available from <http://www.bizedge.com.my/MEM/243/240599 bigmoney.html>.

_____ (2002). "Time is not sovereign". *The Edge,* 4 Feb.

Tan Eu Chye (1997). "The Present Malaysian Economic Crisis with Reference to the Crisis of the Mid-1980s". *Malaysian Journal of Economic Studies* 34 (1–2) (June–Dec.): 113–22.

Taylor, Lance (1997). "Editorial: The Revival of the Liberal Creed — The IMF and the World Bank in a Globalized Economy". *World Development* 25 (2): 145–52.

Taylor, M.P. and Lucio Sarno (1997). "Capital Flows to Developing Countries: Long- and Short-Term Determinants". *The World Bank Economic Review* 11 (Sep.): 451–70.

Tharmaratnam, M. (2000). "Exclusive: How Malaysia's CDRC Really Views the Renong Group". *FinanceAsia.com,* 24 July. Available from <http://www.financeasia.com/articles/F18E7F26-6055-11D4-8C100008C72B383C.cfm>

The Asian Banker (2002). "Malaysia: Banks still lag in operational risk management, says report". 23 Jul. Available from <http://www.theasianbanker.com/>.

_____ (2003). "Malaysia banks not ready for more mergers". 3 Jul. Available from <http://www.theasianbanker.com/>.

The Economist. "Emerging-Market Indicators", various issues.

_____ (1995). "Those damned dominos". 4 Mar.: 92.

_____ (1999). "The bank-merger splurge". 28 Aug.

The Edge (1999). "Two approaches to restructuring". Available from <http://www.bizedge.com.my/MEM/240/030599focus2.html>.

———— (2001). "MAS: Will it be different this time?". 9 Jul.

————, various issues. Available from <http://www.theedge.com.my/ http://www.bizedge.com.my/>.

The Edge Daily, 14 May 2004, "The remaking of M'sia Inc". Available from <http://www.theedgedaily.com/>.

The Insolvency Service. Available from <http://www.insolvency.gov.uk/ information/guidanceleaflets/guide/chapter11.htm>.

The New Straits Times, 30 Jul. 2001. "Guessing game over UEM: Disposal of group's asset may be next on the cards".

————, 9 Aug. 2001. "Government to get tough with corporate debtors".

————, 31 Aug. 2001. "Star LRT moving on right track".

————, 27 Sep. 2001. "RM4.75 insurance surcharge — MAS' levy on domestic and international tickets".

————, 5 Nov. 2002. "Property Times: Commercial buildings".

————, 30 Dec. 2002. "EPE takeover to spur Ranhill's diversification".

————, 9 Jul. 2003. "Renong rakes in RM594m from sale of CAHB".

————, 14 Apr. 2003. "Wahid takes on the immense challenge".

————, 15 May 2004a, "Khazanah set to become giant investment house": 1.

————, 15 May 2004b, "GLC changes only after Khazanah board revamp": 1.

————, 15 May 2004c, "New Khazanah chief takes on biggest job in his career": 1.

————, 27 May 2004, "Azman, Nur Jazlan appointed directors": 1.

The Star, 17 May 2001. "MAS Plans RM800mil preference shares issue".

————, 18 May 2001. "Analysts endorse MAS plan for preference shares".

————, 30 May 2001. "Multi-prong strategy to turn MAS around".

————, 31 May 2001. "Airline analysts welcome MAS restructuring".

————, 2 June 2001. "MAS to restructure into nine divisions".

————, 28 June 2001. "Halim quits as UEM exec vice-chairman".

————, 10 Jul. 2001. "MAS: No plan to split domestic and international ops".

————, 13 Jul. 2001. "Renong clarifies Dow Jones report".

————, 19 Jul. 2001. "Higher air fares will be a great help for MAS, say analysts".

————, 10 Aug. 2001. "CDRC sets deadline to clear debt backlog".

————, 13 Aug. 2001. "Look beyond restructuring. Consider future prospects after revamp, say analysts".

————, 1 Sep. 2001. "LRT firms' takeover plan revived".

————, 5 Sep. 2001. "RM39b NPLs resolved by Danaharta so far".

————, 21 Sep. 2001a. "Tough task ahead in Renong/UEM revamp".

————, 21 Sep. 2001b. "Azman sees his role in UEM as almost over".

_____, 26 Sep. 2001. "Govt to reinstate level of insurance for MAS".

_____, 1 Oct. 2001a. "Insight into re-engineering Malaysia".

_____, 1 Oct. 2001b. "Takeover of LRT firms and debt conversion plan gets nod".

_____, 9 Oct. 2001. "Renong and UEM appoint top executive posts".

_____, 15 Oct. 2001. "Stocks: KLSE Main Board".

_____, 19 Oct. 2001. "A corporate restructuring wish list for Budget 2002".

_____, 31 Oct. 2001. "MAS makes more changes at the top".

_____, 1 Nov. 2001. "More responsibilities for independent directors under new code".

_____, 8 Nov. 2001. "Malaysian culture not conducive to corporate raiding, says adviser".

_____, 9 Nov. 2001. "Resolution of 2 debts cut bank NPLs by 1%: Azman".

_____, 10 Nov. 2001. "RM42bil NPLs resolved by Danaharta as at end-September".

_____, 1 Dec. 2001a. "First phase of Star/Putra debt revamp done".

_____, 1 Dec. 2001b. "LRT debts — banks seen as getting a good deal".

_____, 4 Dec. 2001. "Govt now a Putra creditor, Renong tells the KLSE".

_____, 6 Dec. 2001. "MAS appoints 3 new non-exec directors".

_____, 11 Dec. 2001. "UEM/Renong close to finalizing revamp plan".

_____, 12 Dec. 2001. "Time Engineering in talks with bondholders".

_____, 20 Dec. 2001a. "Debt revamps restore investor confidence".

_____, 20 Dec. 2001b. "Time fails to meet bond repayment deadline".

_____, 21 Dec. 2001. "Rights of Time Engineering bondholders".

_____, 28 Dec. 2001. "Time Engineering bond holders seek solution".

_____, 2 Jan.2002. "PM: Foreign airlines keen to buy stakes in MAS".

_____, 8 Jan.2002. "MAS raising RM6.1bil to retire some debts".

_____, 9 Jan. 2002. "MAS moving in right direction, say analysts".

_____, 17 Jan. 2002. "Renong expects to sell assets to repay RM8b debt".

_____, 29 Jan. 2002. "MAS to be taken private".

_____, 30 Jan.2002a. "MAS revamp will benefit minorities".

_____, 30 Jan. 2002b. "MAS domestic services to be operated by newco".

_____, 30 Jan. 2002c. "Khazanah offers to buy Time bonds".

_____, 31 Jan. 2002. "CDRC resolves 37 cases of debts worth RM34.5b".

_____, 4 Feb. 2002. "Speed of restructure bodes well": 3.

_____, 5 Feb. 2002. "CDRC to stop taking new debts by April".

_____, 6 Feb. 2002. "Survey: Growing awareness of corporate governance among CEOs": 3.

_____, 19 Feb. 2002a. "Report Lodged: MAS lodges report against previous management".

_____, 19 Feb. 2002b. "KKMB to control 63.68% of Park May".

_____, 25 Feb. 2002. "UEM asset divestment on track".

————, 28 Feb. 2002a. "Ex-Im Bank believed given M'sia loan plane purchase".

————, 28 Feb. 2002b. "Snapshot: MAS".

————, 6 Mar. 2002. "Putra wants to increase LRT coaches".

————, 13 Mar. 2002. "RM47.7b NPLs under Danaharta".

————, 21 Mar. 2002. "Progress recorded in debt restructuring".

————, 22 Mar. 2002. "Putra served with 2 winding up petitions".

————, 4 Apr. 2002. "MoF unit to take over light rail operators".

————, 10 Apr. 2002. "Danaharta property tender gets encouraging response".

————, 12 Apr. 2002. "Rating outlook upgrade positive sign for banks".

————, 19 Apr. 2002. "M'sia currency ratings get the Fitch thumbs-up".

————, 29 Apr. 2002. "Stocks: Main Board".

————, 1 May 2002, Stocks: Main Board".

————, 2 May 2002. "Marketing of Plus IPO set to get under way".

————, 8 May 2002. "Renong okays RM8.2b bonds transfer from PLUS to UEM".

————, 30 July 2002. "MAS board approves revamp".

————, 31 July 2002. "MAS charts new flight path".

————, 1 Aug. 2002a. "Analyst hail MAS revamp plan".

————, 1 Aug. 2002b. "Options for domestic air services under study".

————, 5 Aug. 2002. "MAS draws up major strategy to raise yields".

————, 8 Aug. 2002. "MAS plans more flights to more destinations".

————, 28 Mar. 2003. "UEM-Renong finalises revamp".

————, 29 Mar. 2003a. "Renong revamp: The good and bad".

————, 29 Mar. 2003b. "UEM-Renong revamp draws mixed reactions from investors".

————, 1 Apr. 2003. "For the record".

————, 9 Apr. 2003. "Sapura shareholders okay Crest buy".

————, 9 Jul. 2003. "Renong sells 6.17% stake in CAHB for RM594mil cash".

————, 15 Sep. 2003. "Stock: KLSE Main Board".

————, 24 Apr. 2004. "Way clear for foreign partner in Proton".

————, 15 May 2004a. "Govt sets regional goal for Khazanah": 1.

————, 15 May 2004b. "Remake for M'sia Inc": 1.

————, 15 May 2004c. "Expert: KPI doesn't mean firms must be fully private": 3.

————, 18 May 2004a. "Azman Mokhtar the man to watch in coming months": 1.

————, 18 May 2004b. "Most GLC shares close lower": 3.

————, 20 May 2004. " New heads for Telekom and TNB": 1.

————, 25 May 2004. "GLCs' reform still at infancy": 5.

_____, 26 May 2004. "A business-savvy CEO for TNB": 5.

_____, 27 May 2004. "Azman Mokhtar and Nur Jazlan are Telekom's new directors": 3.

_____, 29 May 2004. "Different tack to be adopted for Proton".

_____, 2 June 2004. "Pardas to be new UEM Group MD".

_____, 25 Sep. 2004. "The journey has begun".

_____, 16 Jan. 2004. "Court Rules Danaharta Immune from Injunctions

The Sun, 12 Feb. 2001. "Star and Putra to continue operating LRT — Govt to lease

_____, 17 Jul. 2001. "Govt will not divest shares to foreigners".

_____, 2 Nov. 2001. "Renong revises loss to RM1.37b on provisions".

_____, 3 Nov. 2001. "Danaharta to sell RM500m asset-backed bonds".

_____, 10 Nov. 2001. "Danaharta has dealt with 83% of NPLs, recovery rate at 57%".

_____, 27 Nov. 2001a. "MAS' net loss widens in H1".

_____, 27 Nov. 2001b. "Renong turns around in Q1".

_____, 27 Nov. 2001c. "UEM to keep concessionaires".

_____, 14 Feb. 2002. "Construction sector to grow 26% in 2002. Quicker implementation of deals, revival of old projects".

_____, 15 Feb. 2001. "Petronas chairman takes the helm at MAS".

_____, 19 Feb. 2002. "MAS asks for probe: Alleges management irregularities when Tajudin was in charge".

_____, 3 Apr. 2002. "LRT operator faces closure. Bank seeks petition to wind up STAR over RM1b debt".

_____, 11 May 2002. "Prolink disposes land to Ho Hup".

_____, 1 Mar. 2003. "Renong posts RM537m net profit on sale of UEM stake".

Thillainathan, R. (2000). "Malaysian Financial and Corporate Sector Under Distress — A Mid-term Assessment of Restructuring Efforts". Processed, revised version of paper originally prepared for a World Bank conference, Tokyo, Jan.

Tobin, James (1978). "A Proposal for International Monetary Reform". *Eastern Economic Journal* 4 (Jul.-Oct.): 153–9.

Toyoda, Maria (2001). "Malaysia's Ethnic Cleavages and Controlled Liberalization". In Shale Horowitz, and Uk Heo (eds.). *The Political Economy of International Financial Crises*. Lanham, MD: Rowman and Littlefield.

Transparency International (1997). "Corruption Perception Index". Available from <www.transparency.de/documents/source-book/c/cvA/a6.html>.

UEM World (2004a). *Annual Report 2003*. UEM World Bhd, Kuala Lumpur. Available from <http://www.bursamalaysia. com.my>.

UEM World (2004b). *Quarterly Report on Consolidated Results for the First Quarter Ended 31 March 2004*. UEM World Bhd, Kuala Lumpur. Available from <http://www.bursamalaysia.com/>.

UEM World website. "Corporate Profile". Available from <http://www.uemworld.com/>.

UEM-Renong Group Corporate Newsletter, Inaugural issue, Jan. 2003.

UNCTAD and International Chamber of Commerce (ICC) (1998). "Financial Crisis in Asia and Foreign Direct Investment". Available from <http://www.unctad.org/en/press/bg9802en.htm>.

_____. *Trade and Development Report*, various years. United Nations Conference for Trade and Development, Geneva.

Unger, R. M. (1998). *Democracy Realized: The Progressive Alternative*. London: Verso.

University of Puget Sound (1999). "Bubbles: The Era of Global Finance". Available from <http://www.ups.edu/ipe/asiacrisis/bubbles.htm>.

Utusan Malaysia (1998). "Konspirasi Pihak Atasan Jatuhkan Saya, Anwar" (Anwar: "There is a Conspiracy at the Highest Level to End My Career"), 4 Sep.

Vietor, Richard H.K. (1999). *Asia's Financial Crisis*. Case 798-081, Harvard Business School, Boston.

Volcker, Paul A. (1988). "Emerging Economies in a Sea of Global Finance". Lecture delivered at the Paul H. Nitze School of Advanced International Studies, Johns Hopkins University, Baltimore, Apr. 9.

Wade, Robert (1998a). "From 'Miracle to Cronyism': Explaining the Great Asian Slump". *Cambridge Journal of Economics* 22: 693–706.

_____ (1998b). "The Coming Fight Over Capital Flows". *Foreign Policy* 113 (Winter): 41–53.

_____ (1998c). "The Asian Crisis and the Global Economy: Causes, Consequences and Cure". Available from <http://www.currenthistory.com/archivenov98/wade.html>.

Wade, Robert and Frank Veneroso (1998a). "The Asian Crisis: The High Debt Model Versus the Wall Street-Treasury-IMF Complex". *New Left Review* 228: 3–24.

_____ (1998b). "The Gathering Support for Capital Controls". *Challenge* (Nov./Dec.): 14–26.

Wain, Barry (1999). "Bank Bumi reanimated". *The Asian Wall Street Journal*, 19 Mar.

Wee, V. (2000). "Mechanism and Policies for National Economic Recovery". In Low C.K. (ed.). *Financial Markets in Malaysia*. Kuala Lumpur: Malayan Law Journal Sdn Bhd.

Weisbrot, Mark (eds.) (2000). "The Emperor Has No Growth: Declining Economic Growth Rates in the Era of Globalization". Center for Economic Policy Research, Washington DC.

Wessel, David and Darren McDermott (1997). "Soros and Malaysia's Mahathir cross swords". *Wall Street Journal,* 22 Sep.

White, M. J. (1989). "The Corporate Bankruptcy Decision". *Journal of Economic Perspectives* 3: 129–51.

Wijnbergen, S. V. (1997). "On the Role of Banks in Enterprise Restructuring: The Polish Example". *Journal of Comparative Economics* 24 (1) (Feb.): 44–64.

_____ (1998). "Bank Restructuring and Enterprise Reform". European Bank for Reconstruction and Development Working Paper No. 29. Available from <http://ebrd.com/english/region/workingp/wp29.pdf>.

Williamson, John (1997). "The Washington Consensus Revisited". In Louis Emmerij (ed.). *Economic and Social Development into the XXI Century.* Washington DC: Johns Hopkins University Press, pp. 48–61.

_____ (1999). "Implications of the East Asian Crisis for Debt Management". In A. Vasudevan (ed.). *External Debt Management: Issues, Lessons and Preventive Measures.* Mumbai: Reserve Bank of India, pp. 127–48.

_____ (2000). "What Should The World Bank Think About The Washington Consensus?" *The World Bank Research Observer* 15 (2) (Aug.): 251–64.

Wing, T.W., J.D. Sachs, and K. Schwab (eds.) (2000). *The Asian Financial Crisis: Lessons for a Resilient Asia.* Cambridge, MA: MIT Press.

Winters, Jeffrey (1999). "The Determinants of Financial Crisis in Asia". In T. J. Pempel (ed.). *Politics of the Asian Economics Crisis.* Ithaca: Cornell University Press.

Winters, S. G. Jr (1964). "Economic 'Natural Selection' and the theory of the firm". *Yale Economic Essays* 4 (1) (Spring): 225–72.

Wong Choon Mei (2001). "Malaysian Market Watchdog Says More Reform Needed". 24 Jan. Available from <http://asia.news.yahoo.com/reuters/nsp92241.html>.

Wong Sook Ching (2002). "The Role of Government in Managing Corporate Distress After the 1997 Crisis: Theories and Case Studies of Selected Malaysian Corporations". M. Ec. Research Paper, Faculty of Economics and Administration, University of Malaya, Kuala Lumpur.

Wong, Hwa Kiong and Jomo K. S. (2001). "The Impact of Foreign Capital Inflows on the Malaysian Economy, 1966–1996". Processed, Faculty of Economics and Administration, University of Malaya, Kuala Lumpur.

Woo Wing Thye (2000). "Coping with Accelerated Capital Flows from the Globalization of Financial Markets". *ASEAN Economic Bulletin* 17 (2) (Aug.): 148–204.

Woo Wing Thye, Patrick D. Carleton, and Brian P. Rosario (2000). "The Unorthodox Origins of the Asian Currency Crisis, evidence from Logit Crisis". *ASEAN Economic Bulletin* 17 (2) (Aug.): 120–34.

Woo Wing Thye, Jeffrey Sachs, and Klaus Schwab (eds.) (2001). *The Asian Financial Crisis, Lessons for a Resilient Asia.* Cambridge: MIT Press.

World Bank. *World Development Report*, various issues. World Bank, Washington DC.

_____ (1993). *The East Asian Miracle: Economic Growth and Public Policy.* New York: Oxford University Press.

_____ (1998). *East Asia: The Road to Recovery.* World Bank, Washington DC.

_____ (1999). "Malaysia Structural Policy Review: Path to Recovery". 16 June, World Bank, Washington DC.

_____ (2000a). *East Asia: Recovery and Beyond.* World Bank, Washington DC.

_____ (2000b). "Malaysia: Social and Structural Review Update". World Bank, Washington DC. Available from <http://wbh0018.worldbank. org/eap/eap.nsf/Attachments/Malaysia/$File/malaysia.pdf>.

_____ (2000c). "Malaysia Public Expenditures: Managing the Crisis, Challenging the Future". World Bank, Washington DC, 22 May.

_____ (2000d). "East Asia's Recovery: Gathering Force: An Update". World Bank, Washington DC, 18 Sep.

_____ (2000e). "Special Focus: Poverty During Crisis and Recovery". World Bank, Washington DC, 18 Sep.

_____ (2000f). "Effective Insolvency Systems: Principles and Guidelines". Processed, October, World Bank, Washington DC.

_____ (2000g). "Asian Restructuring: From Cyclical Recovery to Sustainable Growth". *Global Economic Prospectus,* World Bank, Washington DC.

_____ (2001). *Finance for Growth, Policy Choices in a Volatile World.* World Bank Policy Research Report. Oxford: Oxford University Press.

Wruck, K. H. (1990). "Financial Distress, Reorganization, and Organizational Efficiency". *Journal of Financial Economics* 27: 419–44.

Wu Min Aun (1990). *The Malaysian Legal System.* 2nd edition 1999. Kuala Lumpur: Longman.

Yamabe, Taku, Megumi Suto, and Junichi Yamada (1999). "The Effectiveness and Major Issues of Capital Controls Policy in Malaysia". OECF Research Papers No. 33, Research Institute of Development Assistance, Tokyo, Japan.

Yee, Elayne (1999). "MIER Scope: Good Corporate Governance is Vital". *The New Straits Times*, 17 Apr.

Yoshihara Kunio (1988). *The Rise of Ersatz Capitalism in South-East Asia.* Kuala Lumpur: Oxford University Press.

Yoshitomi, Masaru and Sayuri Shirai (2000). "Technical Background Paper Policy Recommendations for Preventing Another Capital Account Crisis". Asian Development Bank Institute, Tokyo, 7 Jul.

YY Property Solutions (2002). "Office Snapshot Kuala Lumpur". Oct.

Zainal Aznam Yusof (1997). "Global Capital Flows and Their Implications for Intra-ASEAN Investment". High Level Roundtable for the "Formulation of Strategic Plans on Cooperation and Promotion of Foreign Direct Investment (FDI) in ASEAN", Kuala Lumpur, 24–25 Feb.

_____ (1999). *Economic Recovery and Capital Controls.* Paper presented at "The Malaysia Business Forecast", Kuala Lumpur, 9 Feb.

_____, *et al.* (1994). "Financial Reform in Malaysia". In Gerard Caprio, *et al.* (eds.). *Financial Reform: Theory and Experience.* Cambridge: Cambridge University Press.

Zainal Aznam Yusof, Denis Hew, and Gomathy Nambiar (1999). "The International Financial Architecture: Scope for Reforms". Institute of Strategic and International Studies, Kuala Lumpur. Processed.

_____ (2000). "Capital Controls: A View from Malaysia". In Brigitte Granville (ed.). *Essays on the World Economy and Its Financial System.* London: Royal Institute of International Affairs, pp. 66–92.

Zakaria Haji Ahmad and Baladas Goshal (1999). "The political future of ASEAN after the Asian Crisis". *International Affairs* 75 (4) (Oct.).

Zeti Akhtar Aziz (1998). *Preparing for the New International Financial Architecture: Malaysia's Programme.* Speech at the International Conference on "Managing the Asian Financial Crisis: Lessons & Challenges". 2–3 Nov. Available from <http://www.bnm.gov.my/spch/1998/1102.htm>.

Zhang, Peter G. (1998). *IMF and the Asian Financial Crisis.* World Scientific Asian Economic Profiles. River Edge, New Jersey: World Scientific Publishing Co.

Zhuang Juzhong, *et al.* (2000). *Corporate Governance and Finance in East Asia: A Study of Indonesia, Republic of Korea, Malaysia, Philippines, and Thailand.* Asian Development Bank, Manila.

Zingales, Luigi (1997). "Corporate Governance". In *The New Palgrave Dictionary Economics and the Law.* Basingstoke: Macmillan.

Useful Websites

Asian Development Bank Institut: <http://www.adbi.org>
Bank Negara Malaysia: <http://www.bnm.gov.my>
Bank for International Settlements: <http://www.bis.org>
Bursa Malaysia Berhad (then Kuala Lumpur Stock Exchange:
    <http://www.bursamalaysia.com/>)
Corporate Debt Restructuring Committee (CDRC):
    <http://www.bnm.gov.my/cdrc>
Danaharta: <http://www.danaharta.com.my>
Danamodal: <http://www.bnm.gov.my/danamodal>
East Asian crisis websites: <http://faculty.washington.edu/karyiu>
    <http://www.stern.nuy.edu/globalmacro>
Economic Planning Unit: <http://www.epu.jpm.my>
Export-Import Bank of Japan OEXTIM-QECF):
    <http://www.japanexim.go.jp>
Institute of Strategic and International Studies, ISIS Malaysia:
    <http://www.isis.org.my>
Khazanah Nasional Bhd: <http://www.khazanah.com.my/>
Malaysian Institute of Corporate Governance – MICG:
    <http://www.micg.net>
Malaysian Civil Service Link, MCSL/MAMPU:
    <http://mcsl.mampu.gov.my>
Malaysia, Department of Statistics: <http://www.statistics.gov.my>
Malaysia, Ministry of Finance/Treasury: <http://www.treasury.gov.my>
Malaysia, New Straits Times e-media: <http://www.emedia.com.my>
Malaysian Products: <http://www.malaysiaproducts.com>
MIDA: <http://mida.gov.my>
Ministry of Human Resources: <http://www1.jaring.my/ksmL>
Moody's rating agency: <http://www.moodys.com>
Morgan Stanley Investments Company: <http://www.morganstanley.com>
National Economic Action Council (NEAC)/MTEN:
    <http://www.neac.gov.my>
NEAC, Globalisation Group: <http://www.myglobal.gov.my>
Paul Krugman: <http://web.mit.edu/krugman>
Petronas: <http://www.petronas.com.my>
Rating Agency Malaysia Bhd (RAM): <http://www.ram.com.my>
Salomon Smith Barney: <http://www.smithbarney.com>
Security Commission: <http://www.sc.com.my>
South East Asian Central Banks-SEACEN: <http://www.seacen.org>
Standard & Poor's rating agency: <http://www.funds-sp.com>
United Engineers (Malaysia) Bhd: <http://www.uemworld.com>.

Newspaper and Magazine Sources

Asahi Evening News, Tokyo
Asian Wall Street Journal, Hong Kong
Asiaweek, Hong Kong (interrupted in 2001)
Business Times, Kuala Lumpur (included in the *New Straits Times* since 2002)
Business Week, Hong Kong
Economic Intelligence Review, Washington DC
Far Eastern Economic Review, Hong Kong
Fortune, New York
International Herald Tribune, Kuala Lumpur
Le Monde, Paris
New Straits Times, Kuala Lumpur
Newsweek, International edition
Straits Times, Singapore
The Asahi Shimbun, Tokyo
The Economist, London
The Edge, Kuala Lumpur
The Financial Times, London
The Japan Times, Tokyo
The Nation, Bangkok
The Nikkei Weekly, Tokyo
The Star, Kuala Lumpur
The Sun, Kuala Lumpur
Time, International edition

Index